Classmates

volume one
d o u k y u s e i

story and art
Asumiko Nakamura

CONTENTS

Introduction

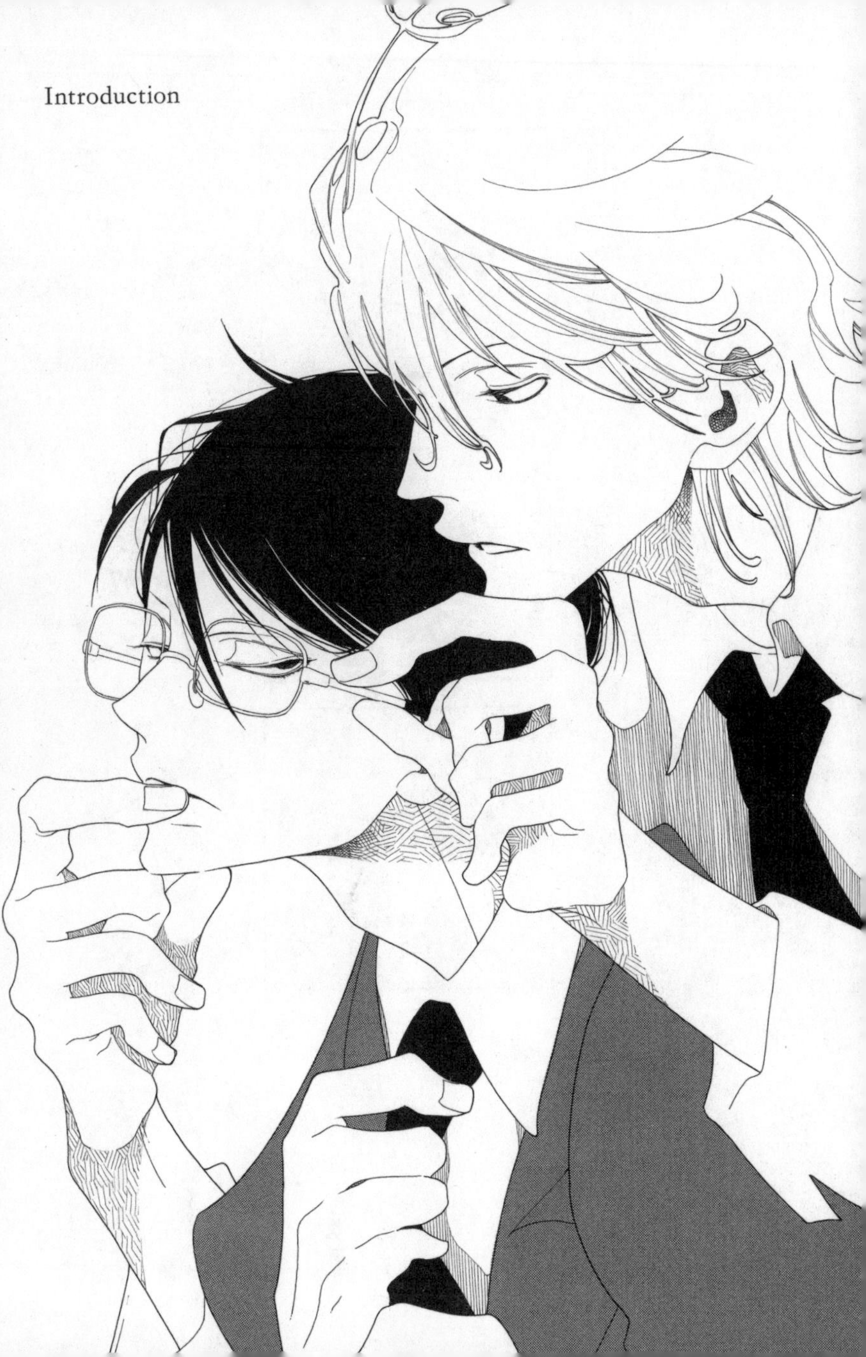

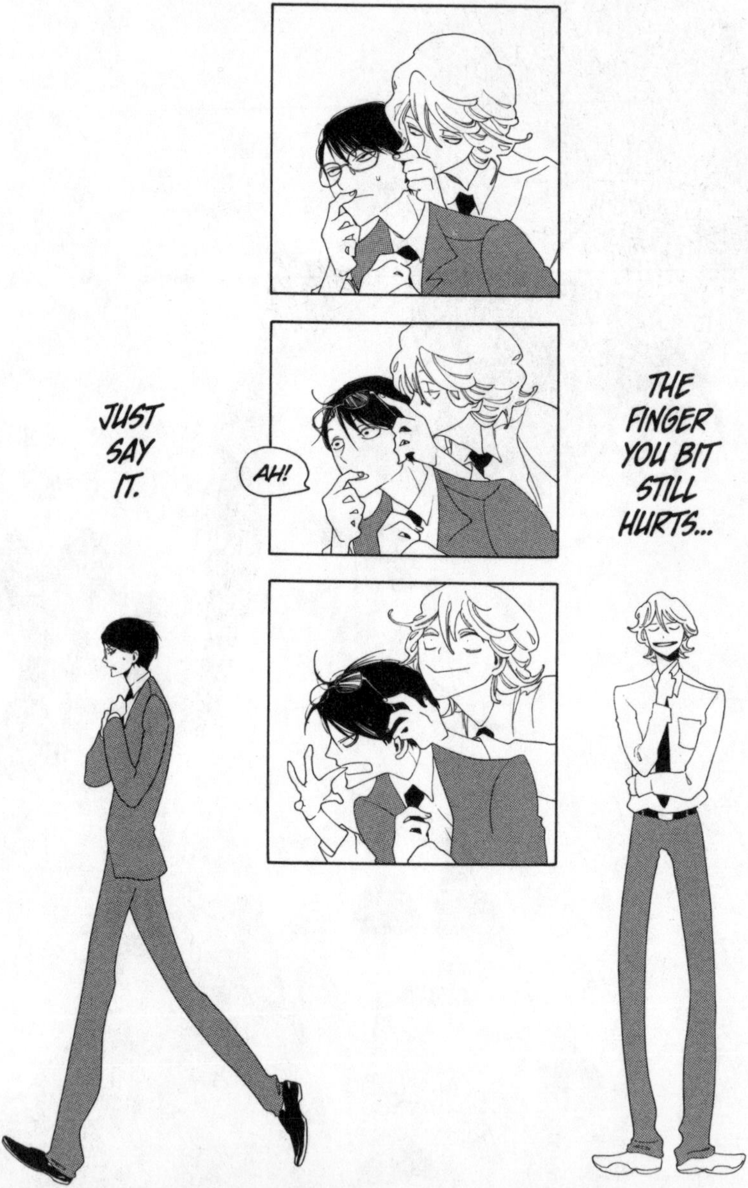
THE FINGER YOU BIT STILL HURTS...
AH!
JUST SAY IT.

[Summer]

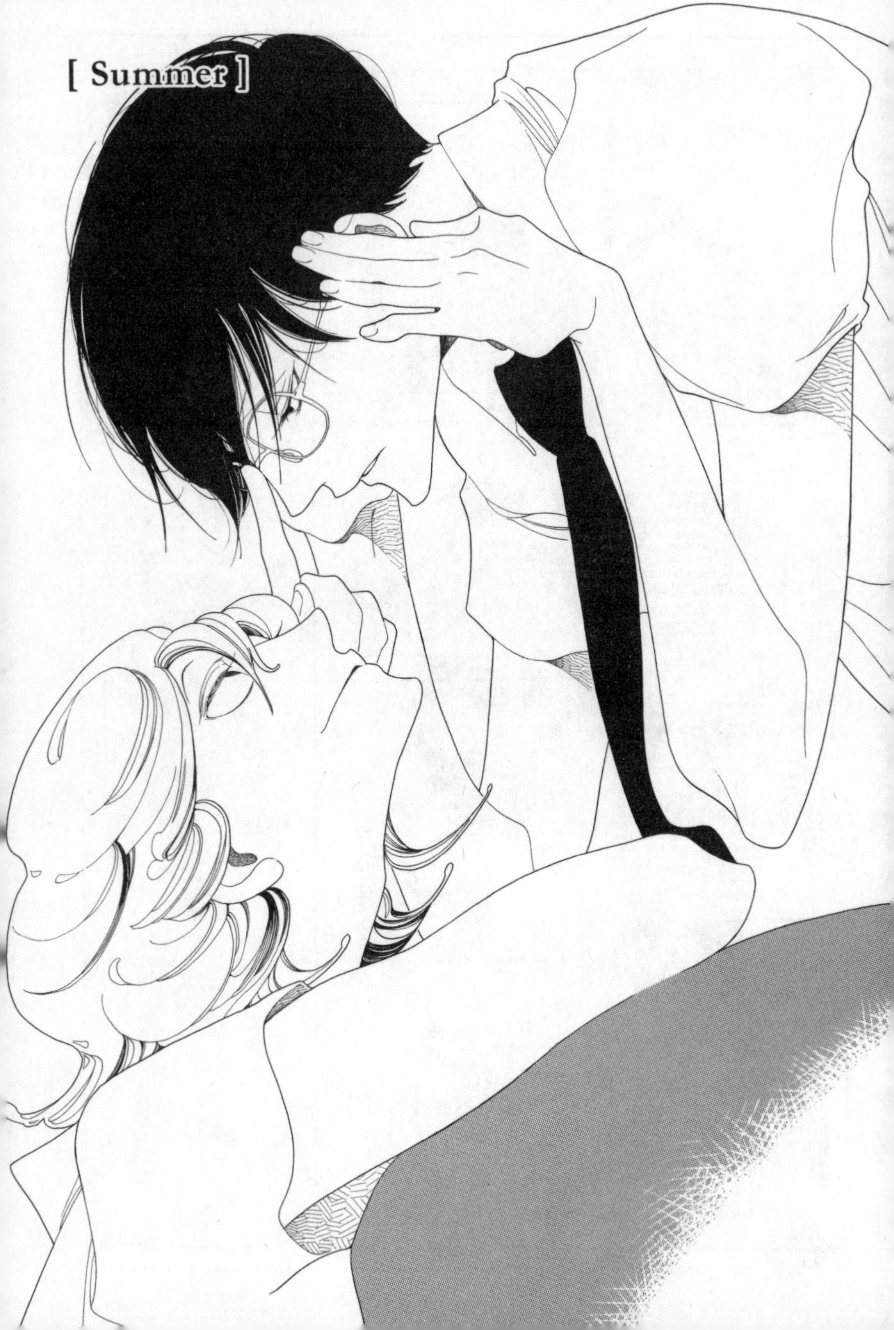

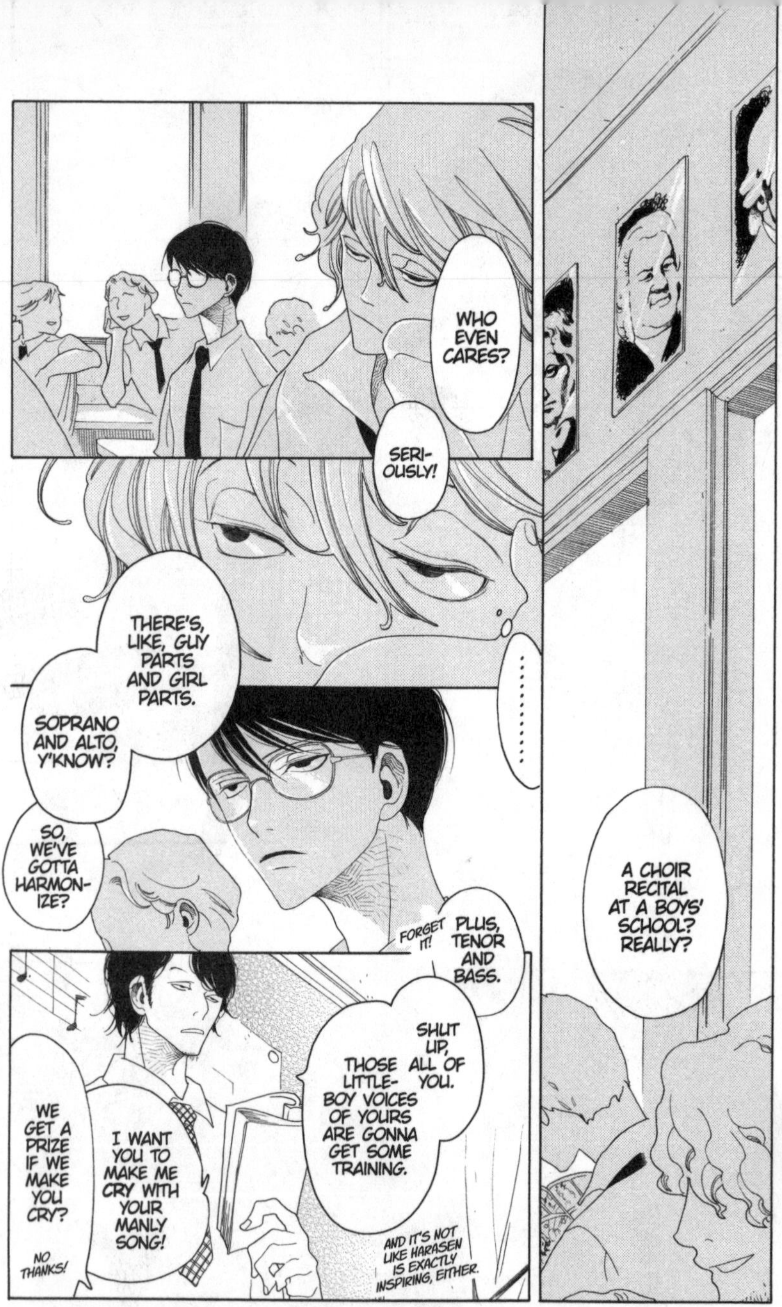
A CHOIR RECITAL AT A BOYS' SCHOOL? REALLY?
WHO EVEN CARES?
SERIOUSLY!
......
THERE'S, LIKE, GUY PARTS AND GIRL PARTS.
SOPRANO AND ALTO, Y'KNOW?
PLUS, TENOR AND BASS.
FORGET IT!
SO, WE'VE GOTTA HARMONIZE?
SHUT UP, ALL OF YOU. THOSE LITTLE-BOY VOICES OF YOURS ARE GONNA GET SOME TRAINING.
I WANT YOU TO MAKE ME CRY WITH YOUR MANLY SONG!
AND IT'S NOT LIKE HARASEN IS EXACTLY INSPIRING, EITHER.
WE GET A PRIZE IF WE MAKE YOU CRY?
NO THANKS!

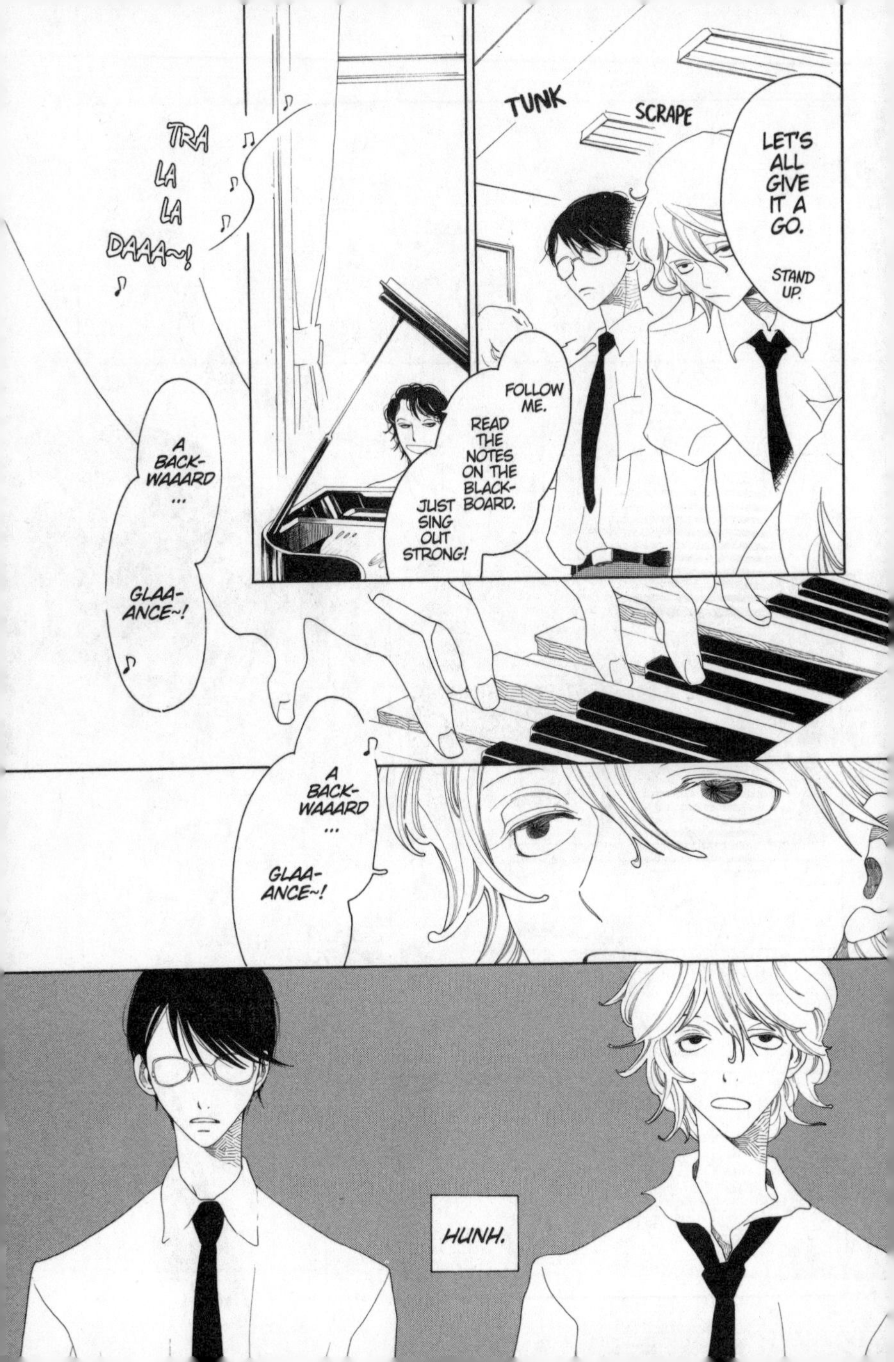

TUNK
SCRAPE
LET'S ALL GIVE IT A GO.
STAND UP.
FOLLOW ME.
READ THE NOTES ON THE BLACKBOARD.
JUST SING OUT STRONG!
TRA LA LA DAAA~!
A BACKWAAARD... GLAA-ANCE~!
A BACKWAAARD... GLAA-ANCE~!
HUNH.

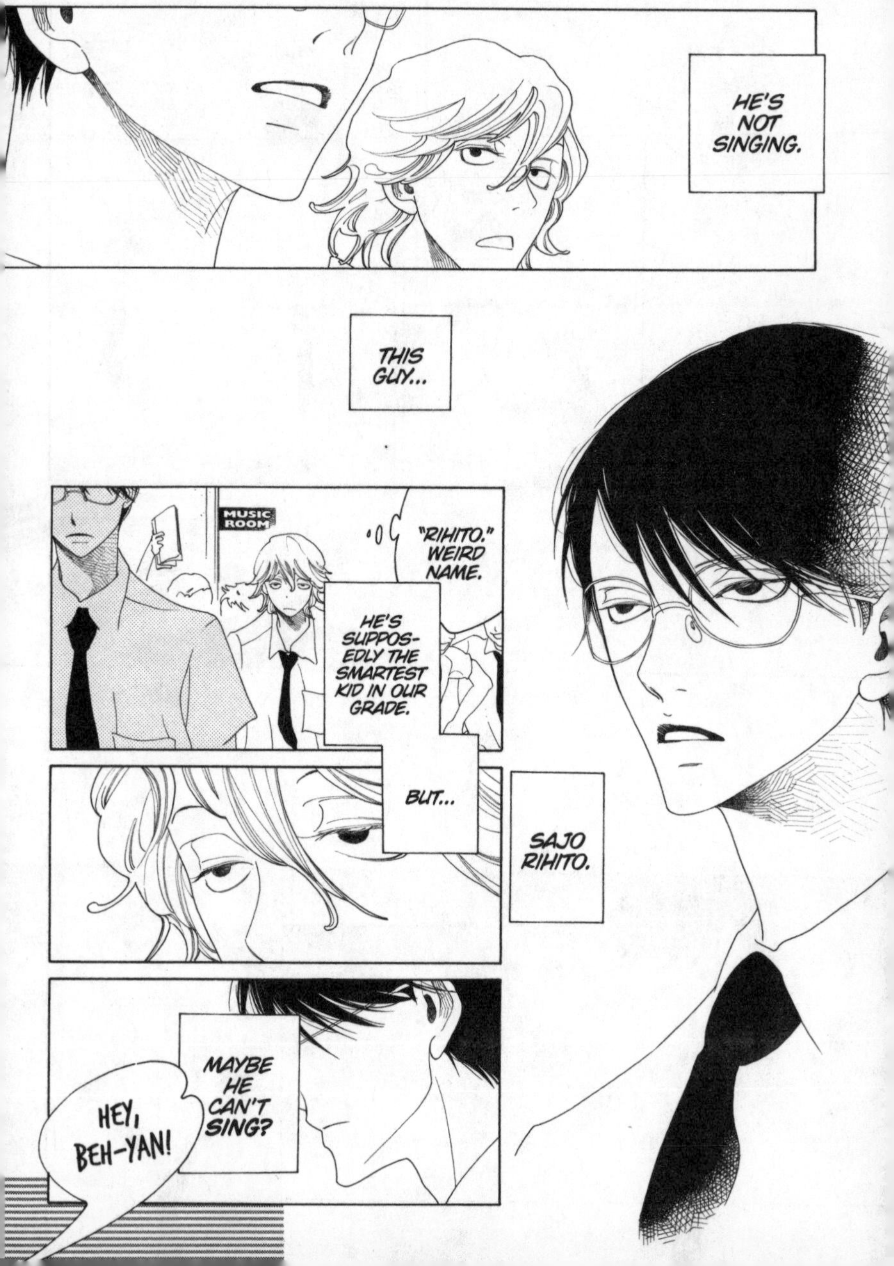
HE'S NOT SINGING.
THIS GUY...
SAJO RIHITO.
"RIHITO." WEIRD NAME.
MUSIC ROOM
HE'S SUPPOSEDLY THE SMARTEST KID IN OUR GRADE.
BUT...
MAYBE HE CAN'T SING?
HEY, BEH-YAN!

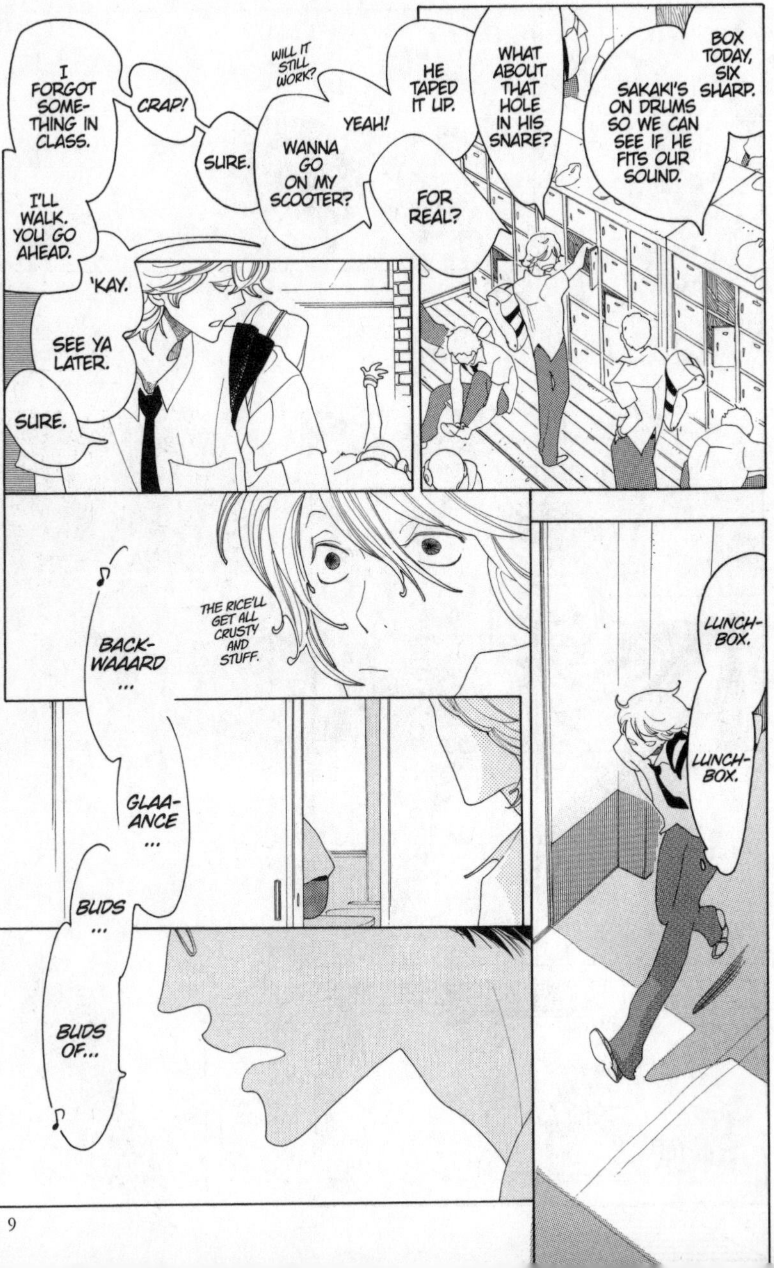
BOX TODAY, SIX SHARP.
SAKAKI'S ON DRUMS SO WE CAN SEE IF HE FITS OUR SOUND.
WHAT ABOUT THAT HOLE IN HIS SNARE?
HE TAPED IT UP.
FOR REAL?
YEAH!
WANNA GO ON MY SCOOTER?
WILL IT STILL WORK?
SURE.
CRAP!
I FORGOT SOME-THING IN CLASS.
I'LL WALK. YOU GO AHEAD.
'KAY.
SEE YA LATER.
SURE.
LUNCH-BOX.
LUNCH-BOX.
THE RICE'LL GET ALL CRUSTY AND STUFF.
BACK-WAAARD ...
GLAA-ANCE ...
BUDS ...
BUDS OF...

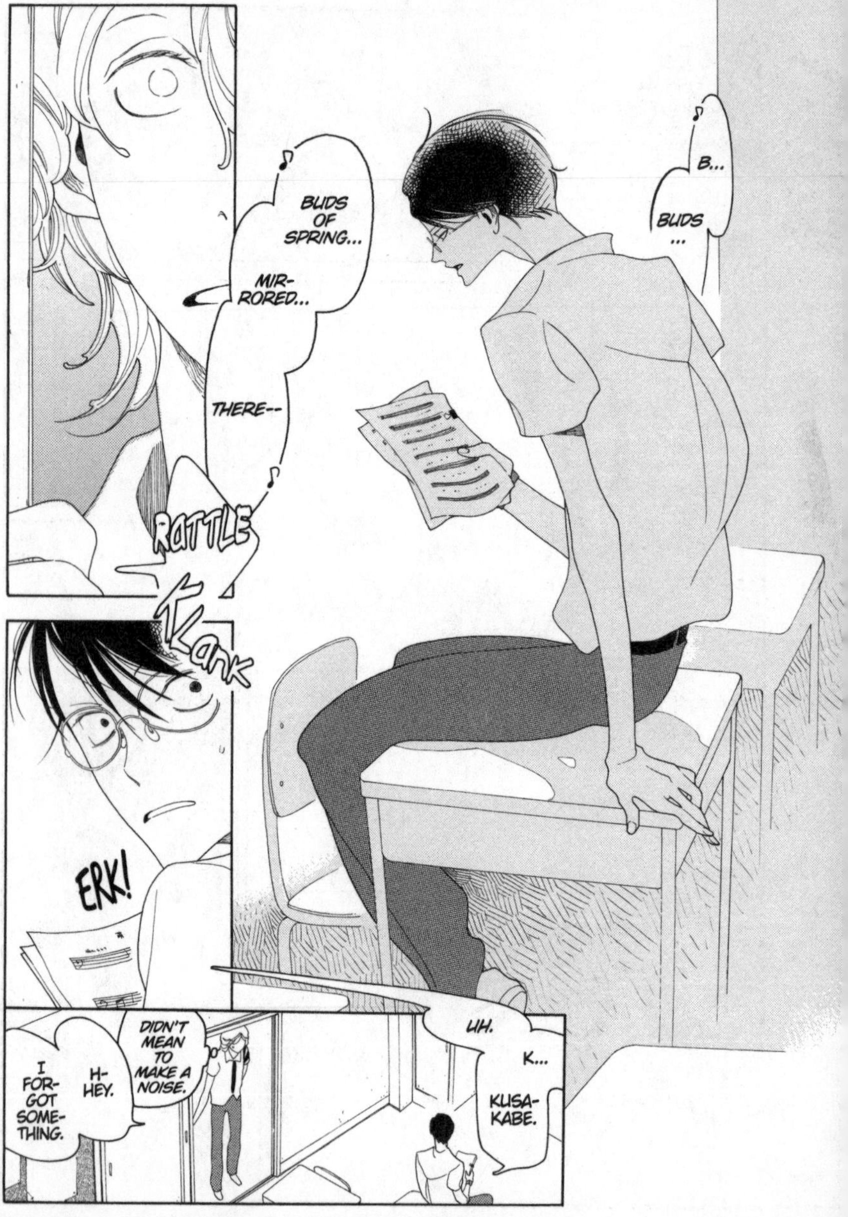
B...
BUDS...
BUDS OF SPRING...
MIRRORED...
THERE--
RATTLE
KLANK
ERK!
UH.
K...
KUSA-KABE.
DIDN'T MEAN TO MAKE A NOISE.
H-HEY.
I FORGOT SOMETHING.

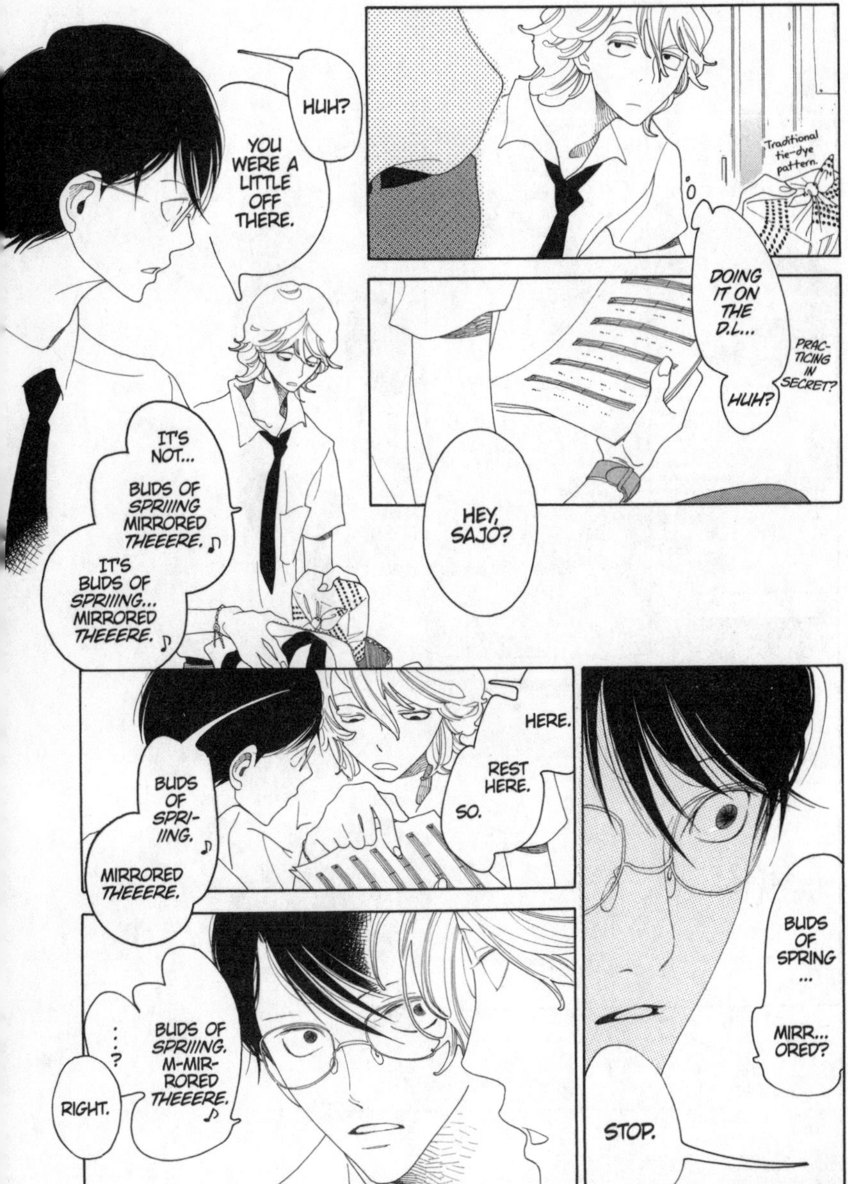

Traditional tie-dye pattern.
DOING IT ON THE D.L...
PRACTICING IN SECRET?
HUH?
HEY, SAJO?
HUH?
YOU WERE A LITTLE OFF THERE.
IT'S NOT...
BUDS OF SPRIIING MIRRORED THEEERE. ♪
IT'S BUDS OF SPRIIING... MIRRORED THEEERE. ♪
BUDS OF SPRING...
MIRR... ORED?
STOP.
HERE.
REST HERE.
SO.
BUDS OF SPRI-IING. ♪
MIRRORED THEEERE.
BUDS OF SPRIIING. M-MIRRORED THEEERE. ♪
...?
RIGHT.

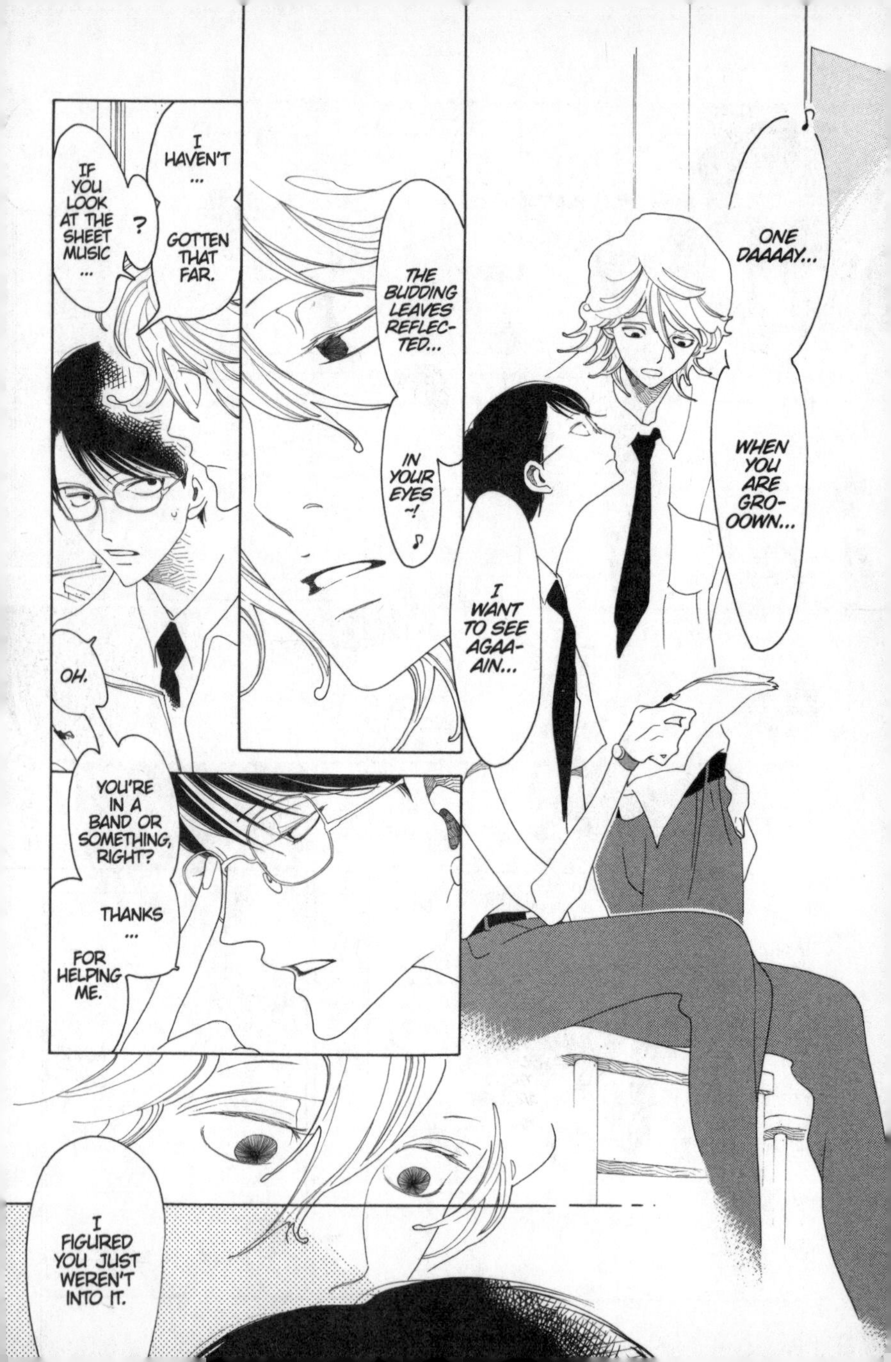
ONE DAAAAY...
WHEN YOU ARE GRO-OOWN...
I WANT TO SEE AGAA-AIN...
THE BUDDING LEAVES REFLECTED...
IN YOUR EYES ~! ♪
IF YOU LOOK AT THE SHEET MUSIC ...
?
I HAVEN'T ... GOTTEN THAT FAR.
OH.
YOU'RE IN A BAND OR SOMETHING, RIGHT?
THANKS ... FOR HELPING ME.
I FIGURED YOU JUST WEREN'T INTO IT.

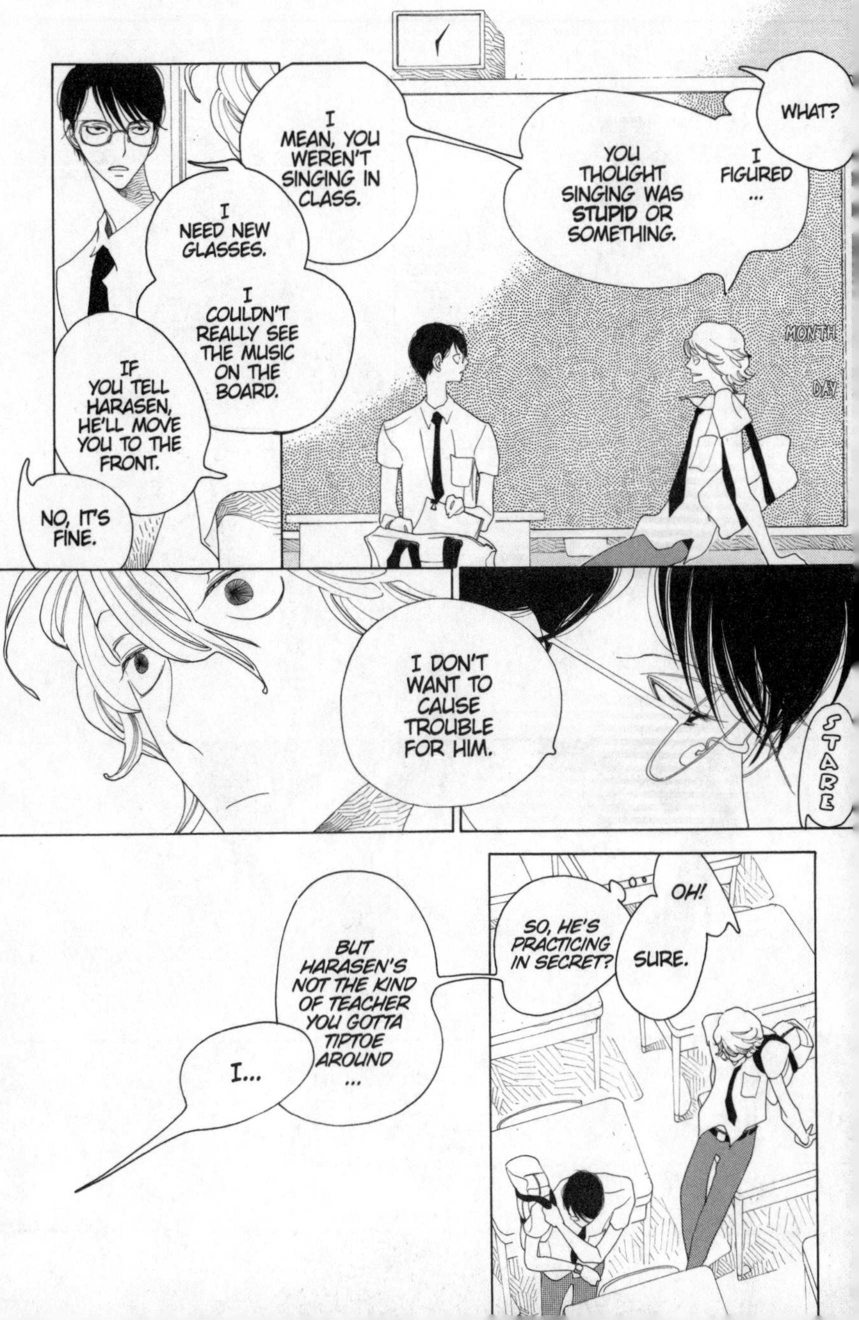
WHAT?
I FIGURED ...
YOU THOUGHT SINGING WAS STUPID OR SOMETHING.
I MEAN, YOU WEREN'T SINGING IN CLASS.
MONTH
DAY
I NEED NEW GLASSES.
I COULDN'T REALLY SEE THE MUSIC ON THE BOARD.
IF YOU TELL HARASEN, HE'LL MOVE YOU TO THE FRONT.
NO, IT'S FINE.
STARE
I DON'T WANT TO CAUSE TROUBLE FOR HIM.
OH!
SURE.
SO, HE'S PRACTICING IN SECRET?
BUT HARASEN'S NOT THE KIND OF TEACHER YOU GOTTA TIPTOE AROUND ...
I...

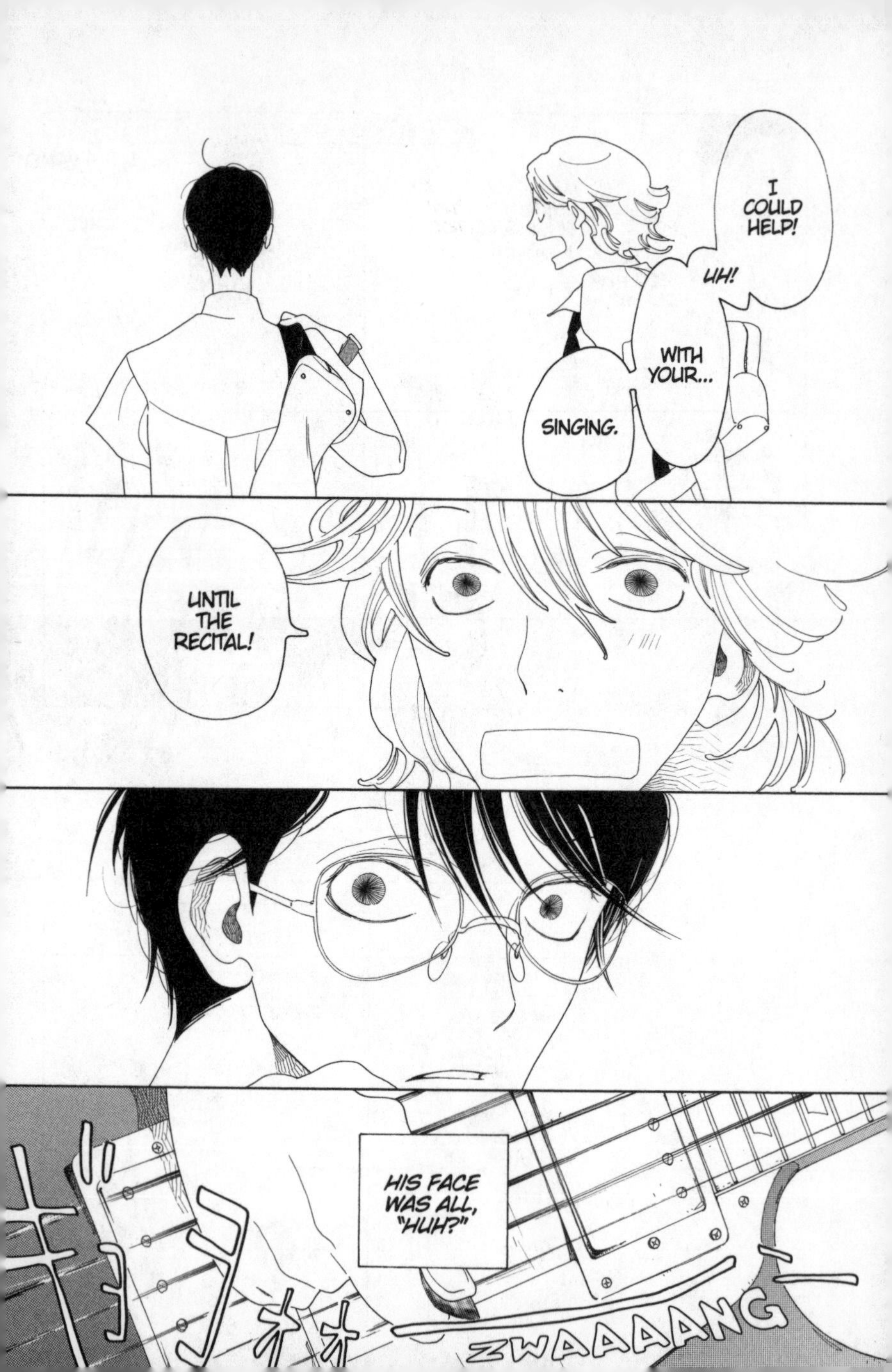
I COULD HELP!
UH!
WITH YOUR...
SINGING.
UNTIL THE RECITAL!
HIS FACE WAS ALL, "HUH?"
ZWAAAANG

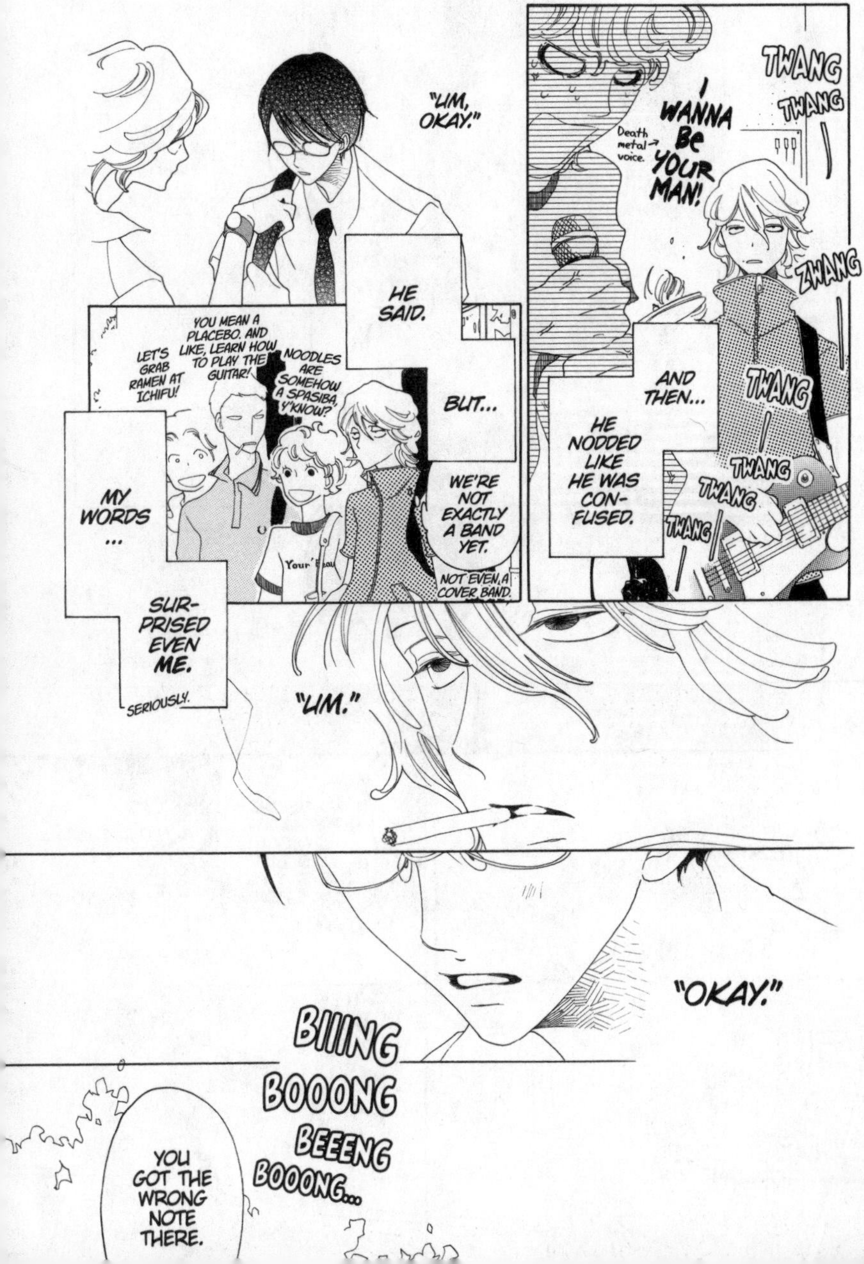
TWANG
TWANG
I WANNA BE YOUR MAN!
Death metal voice.
ZWANG
TWANG
TWANG
TWANG
TWANG
AND THEN...
HE NODDED LIKE HE WAS CON-FUSED.
"UM, OKAY."
HE SAID.
BUT...
WE'RE NOT EXACTLY A BAND YET.
NOT EVEN A COVER BAND.
NOODLES ARE SOMEHOW A SPASIBA, Y'KNOW?
YOU MEAN A PLACEBO. AND LIKE, LEARN HOW TO PLAY THE GUITAR!
LET'S GRAB RAMEN AT ICHIFU!
Your Beau
MY WORDS...
SUR-PRISED EVEN ME.
SERIOUSLY.
"UM."
"OKAY."
BIIING
BOOONG
BEEENG
BOOONG...
YOU GOT THE WRONG NOTE THERE.

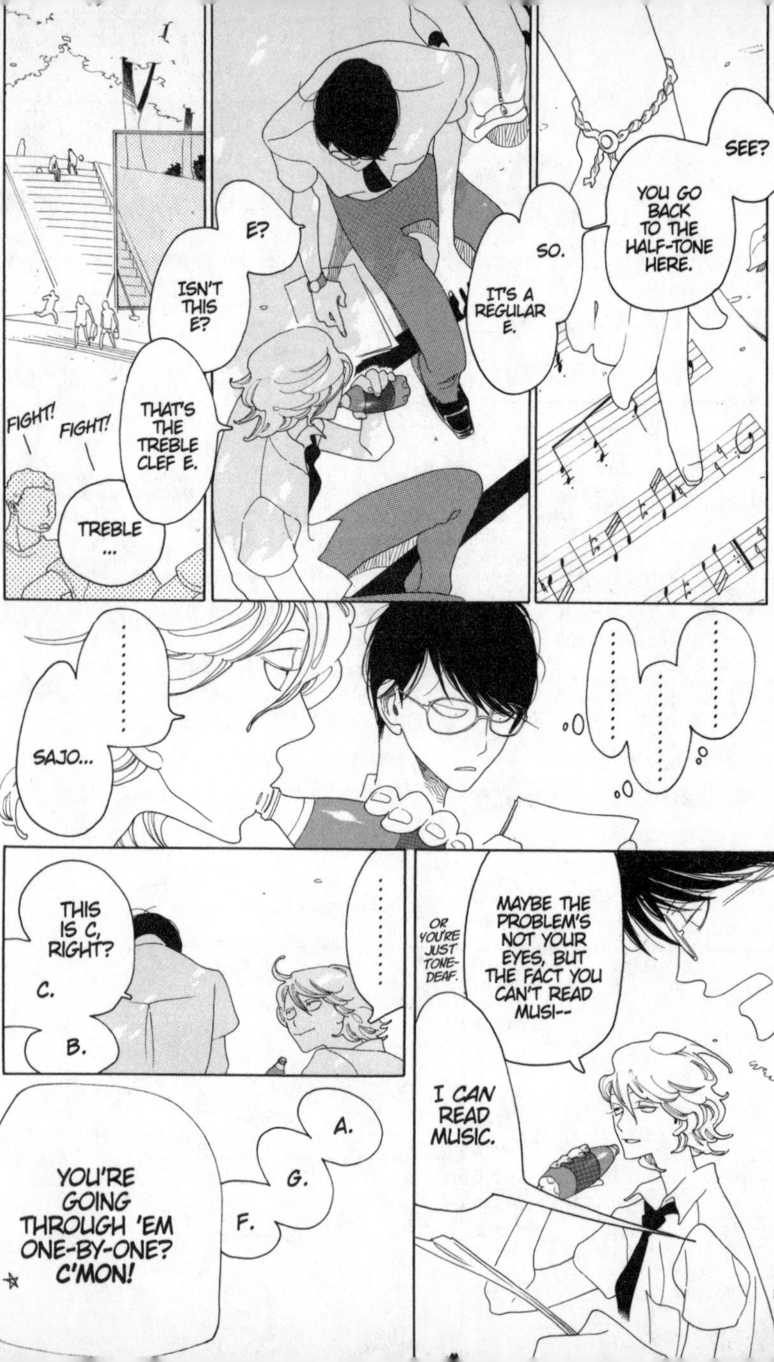
SEE?
YOU GO BACK TO THE HALF-TONE HERE.
SO.
IT'S A REGULAR E.
E?
ISN'T THIS E?
THAT'S THE TREBLE CLEF E.
FIGHT!
FIGHT!
TREBLE...
......
......
......
SAJO...
MAYBE THE PROBLEM'S NOT YOUR EYES, BUT THE FACT YOU CAN'T READ MUSI--
OR YOU'RE JUST TONE-DEAF.
I CAN READ MUSIC.
......
THIS IS C, RIGHT?
C.
B.
A.
G.
F.
YOU'RE GOING THROUGH 'EM ONE-BY-ONE? C'MON!

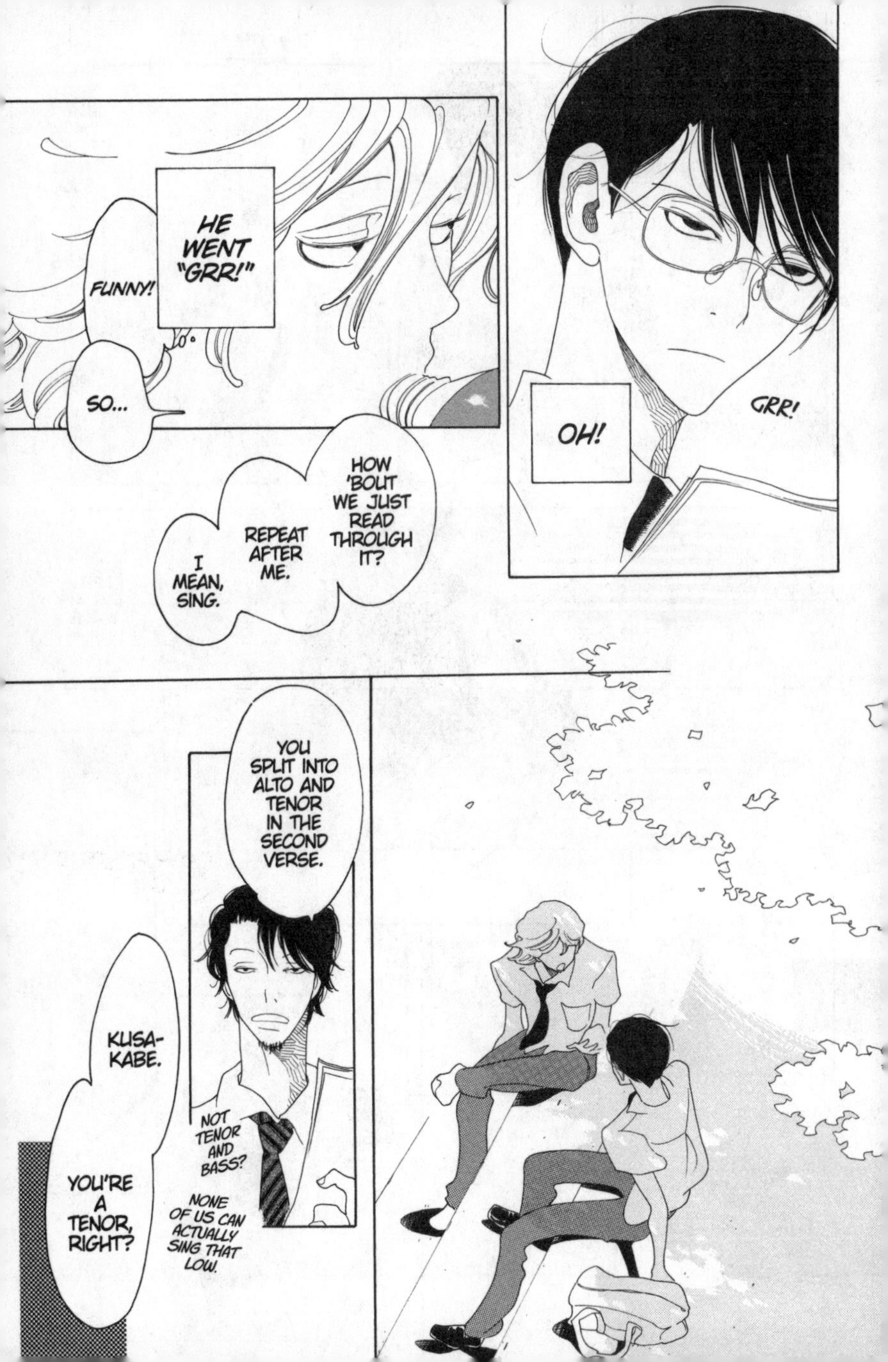
GRR!
OH!
HE WENT "GRR!"
FUNNY!
SO...
HOW 'BOUT WE JUST READ THROUGH IT?
REPEAT AFTER ME.
I MEAN, SING.
YOU SPLIT INTO ALTO AND TENOR IN THE SECOND VERSE.
NOT TENOR AND BASS?
NONE OF US CAN ACTUALLY SING THAT LOW.
KUSA-KABE.
YOU'RE A TENOR, RIGHT?

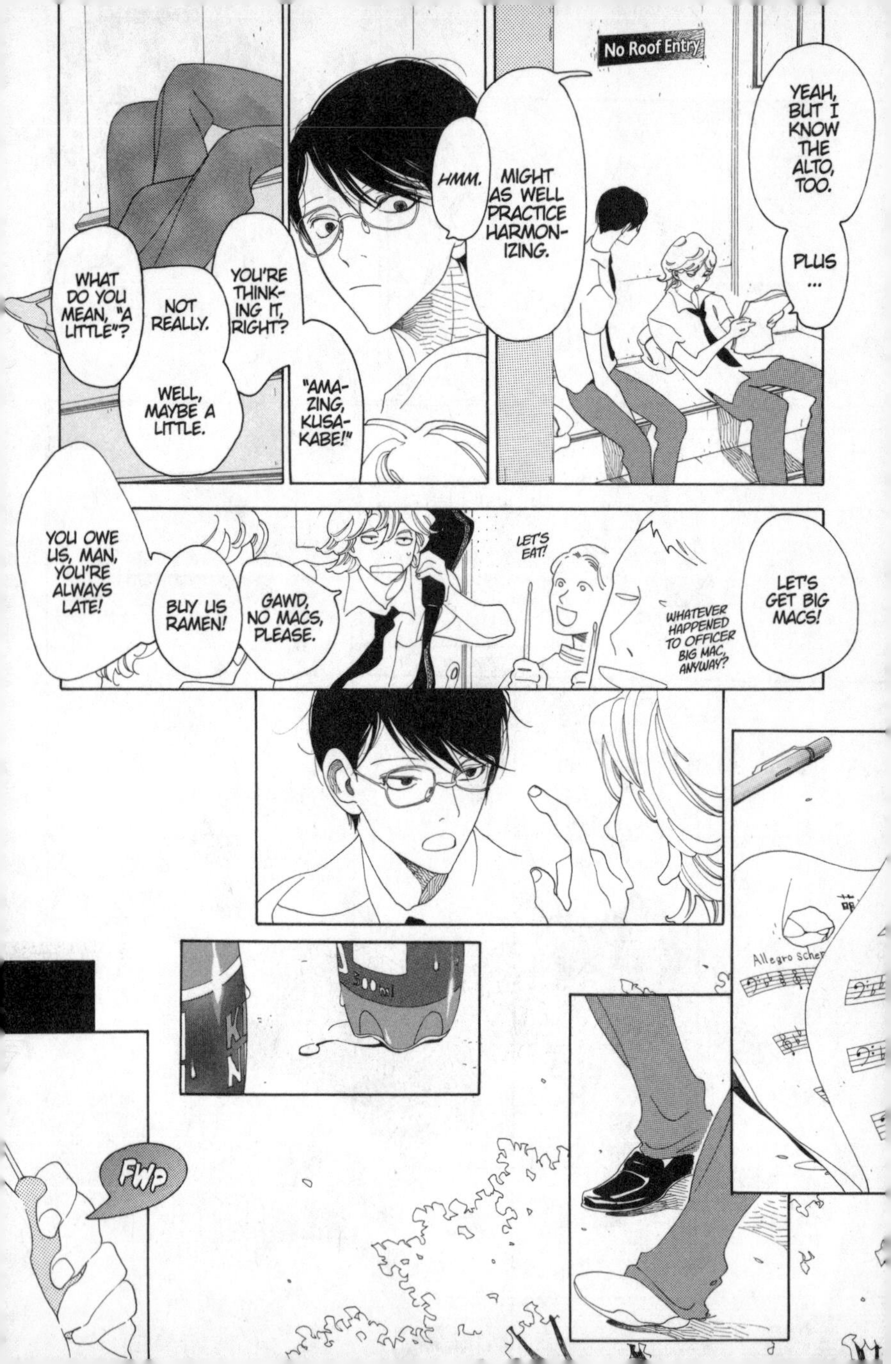
No Roof Entry
YEAH, BUT I KNOW THE ALTO, TOO.
PLUS ...
MIGHT AS WELL PRACTICE HARMONIZING.
HMM.
YOU'RE THINKING IT, RIGHT?
"AMAZING, KUSAKABE!"
NOT REALLY.
WELL, MAYBE A LITTLE.
WHAT DO YOU MEAN, "A LITTLE"?
LET'S GET BIG MACS!
WHATEVER HAPPENED TO OFFICER BIG MAC, ANYWAY?
LET'S EAT!
GAWD, NO MACS, PLEASE.
BUY US RAMEN!
YOU OWE US, MAN, YOU'RE ALWAYS LATE!
300ml
FWP

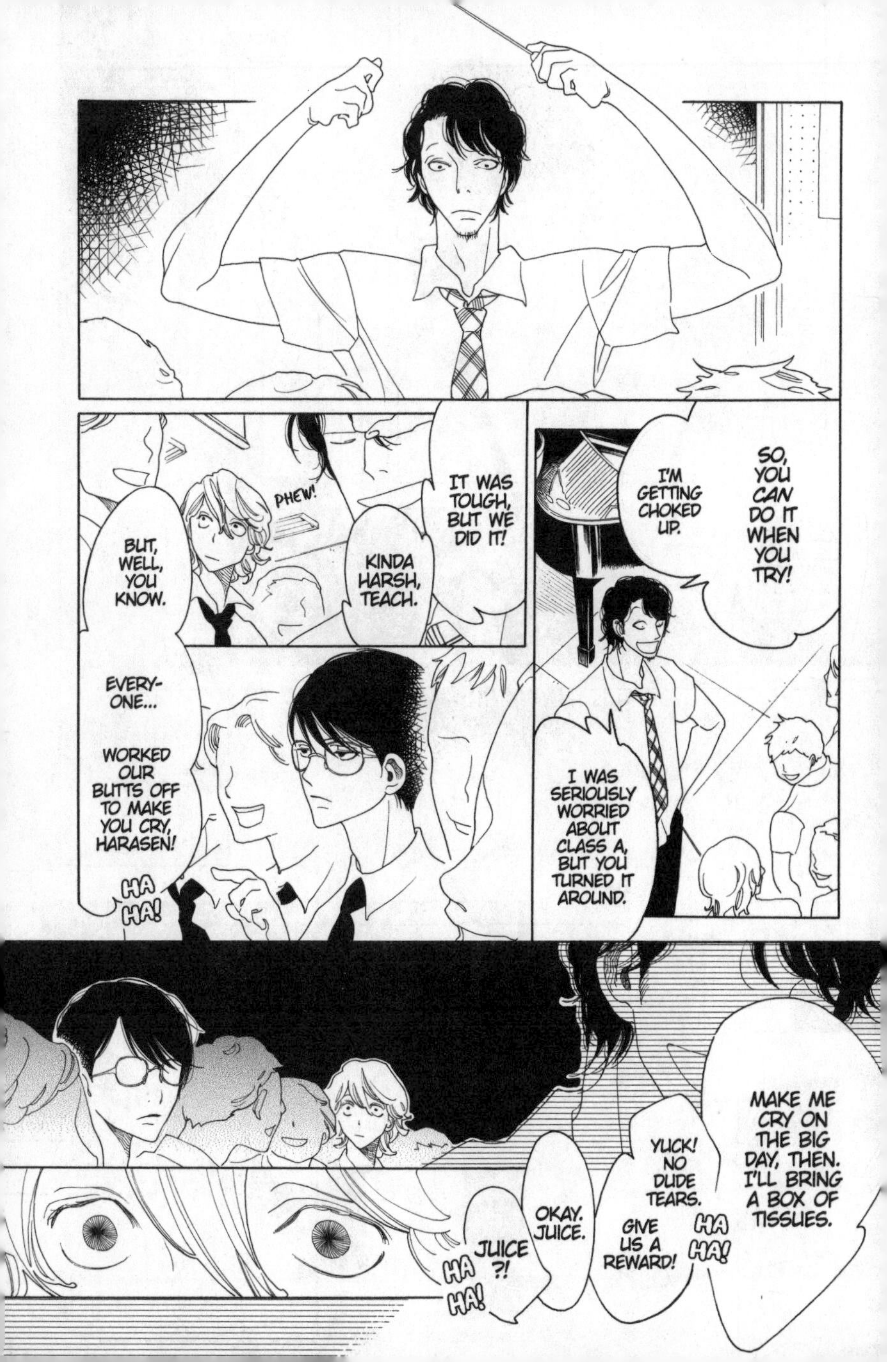
SO, YOU CAN DO IT WHEN YOU TRY!
I'M GETTING CHOKED UP.
I WAS SERIOUSLY WORRIED ABOUT CLASS A, BUT YOU TURNED IT AROUND.
IT WAS TOUGH, BUT WE DID IT!
KINDA HARSH, TEACH.
PHEW!
BUT, WELL, YOU KNOW.
EVERY-ONE...
WORKED OUR BUTTS OFF TO MAKE YOU CRY, HARASEN!
HA HA!
MAKE ME CRY ON THE BIG DAY, THEN. I'LL BRING A BOX OF TISSUES.
HA HA!
YUCK! NO DUDE TEARS.
GIVE US A REWARD!
OKAY. JUICE.
JUICE ?!
HA HA!

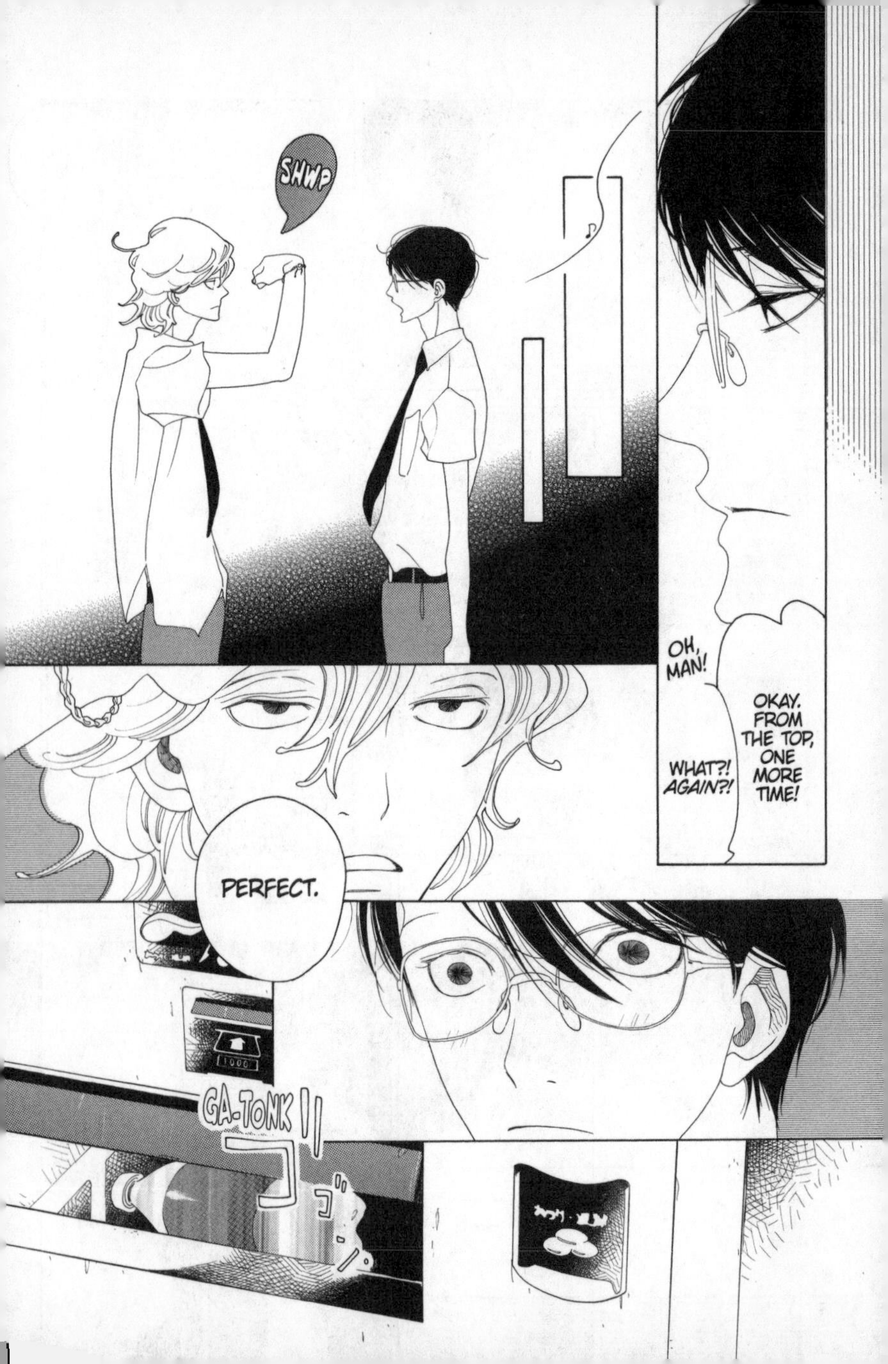
OKAY. FROM THE TOP, ONE MORE TIME!
OH, MAN!
WHAT?! AGAIN?!
SHWP
PERFECT.
GA-TONK

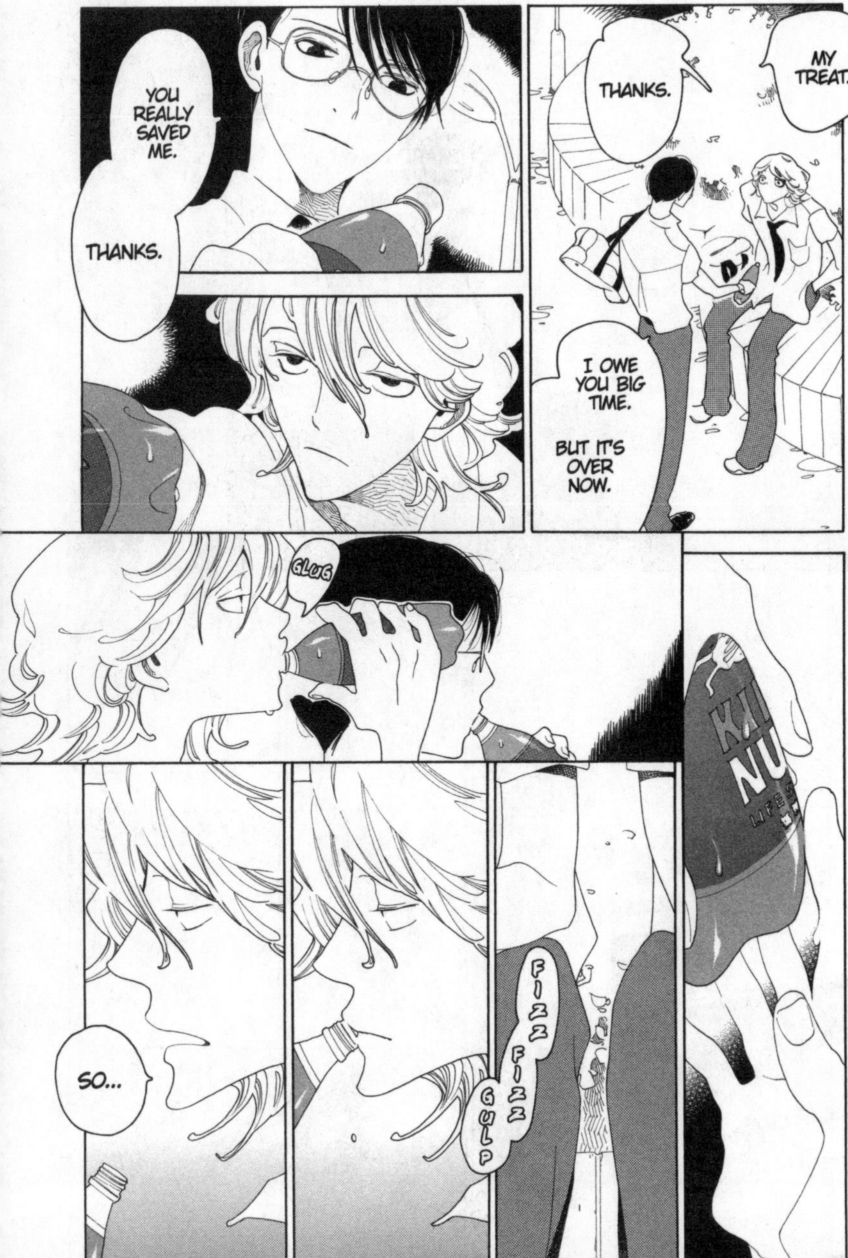
MY TREAT.
THANKS.
I OWE YOU BIG TIME.
BUT IT'S OVER NOW.
YOU REALLY SAVED ME.
THANKS.
GLUG
FIZZ
FIZZ
GULP
SO...

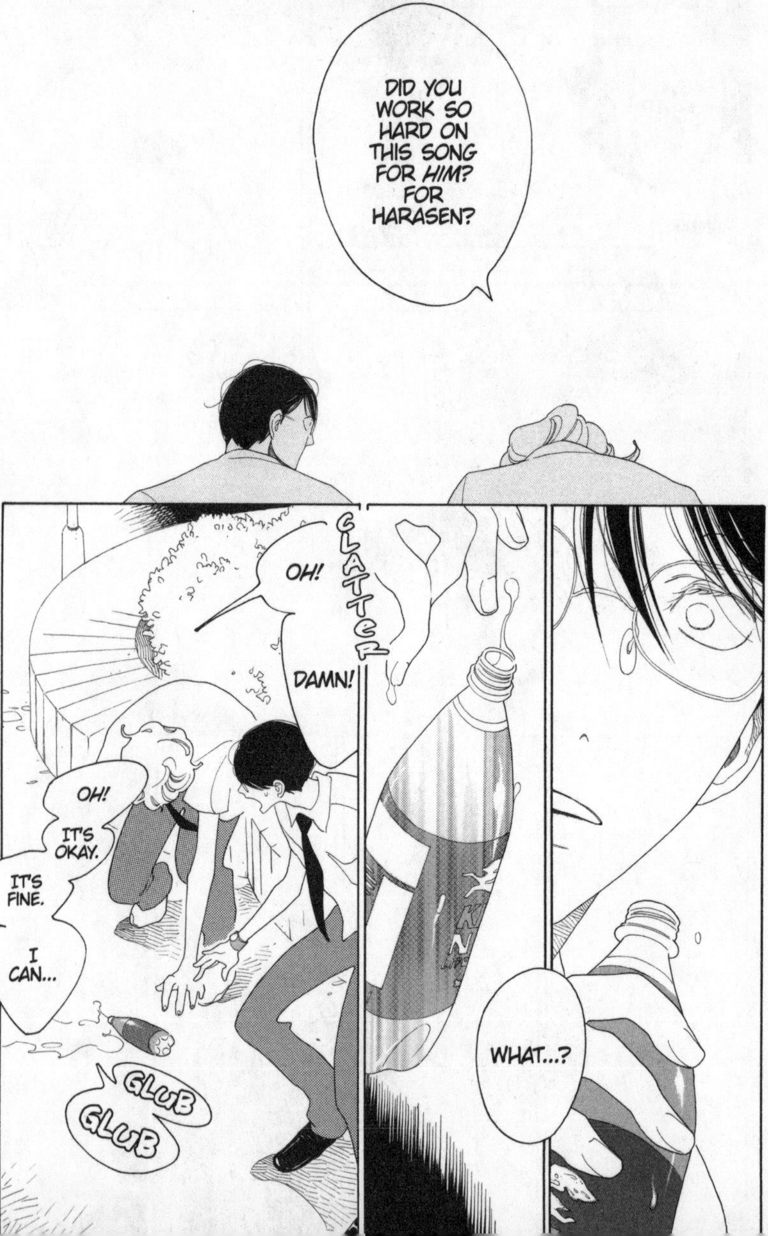
DID YOU WORK SO HARD ON THIS SONG FOR *HIM*? FOR HARASEN?
WHAT...?
CLATTER
OH!
DAMN!
OH!
IT'S OKAY.
IT'S FINE.
I CAN...
GLUB GLUB

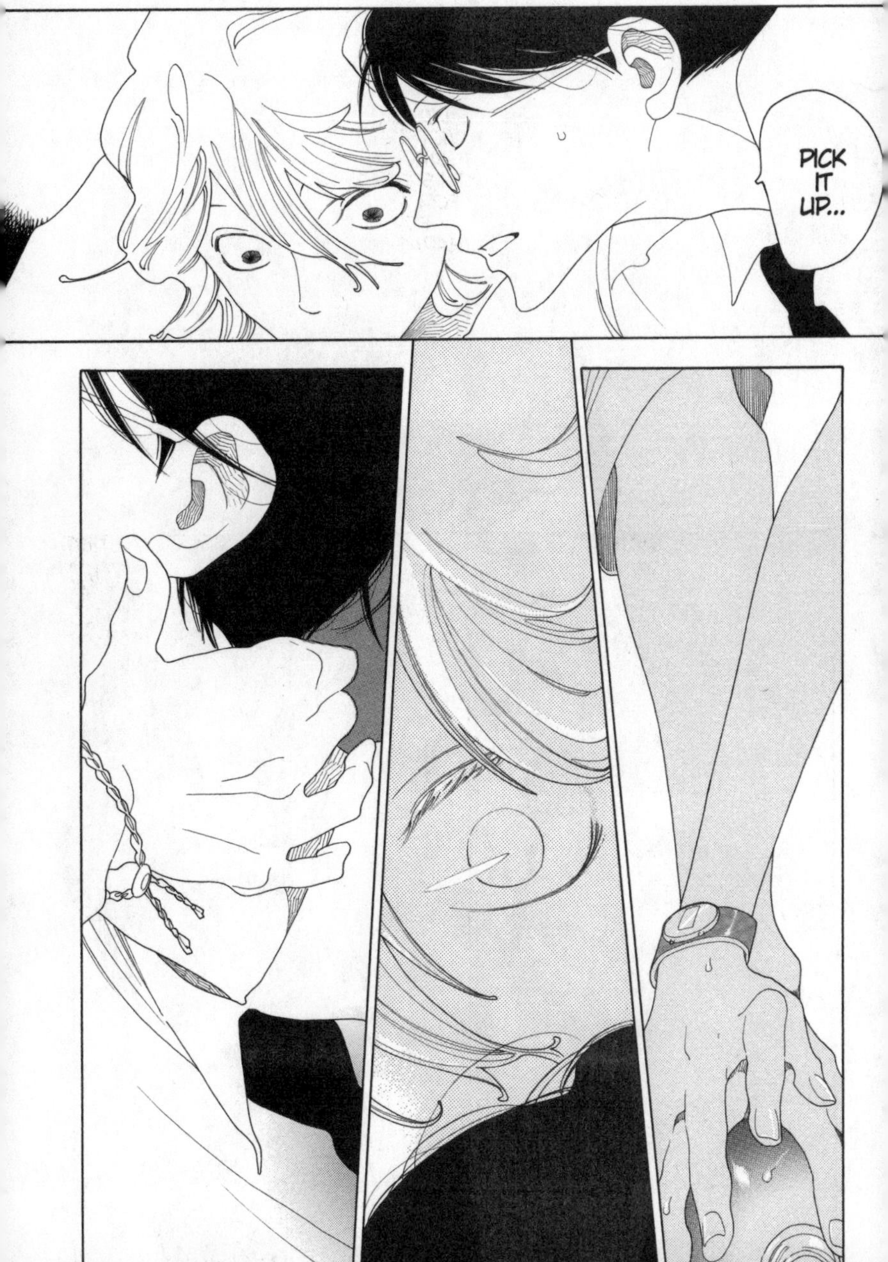
PICK IT UP...

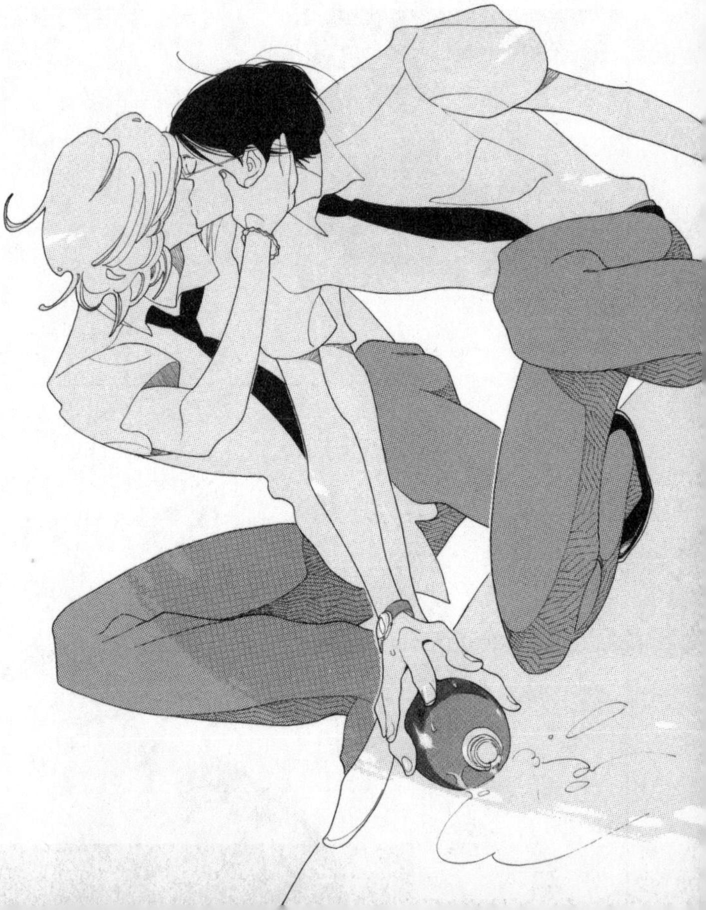

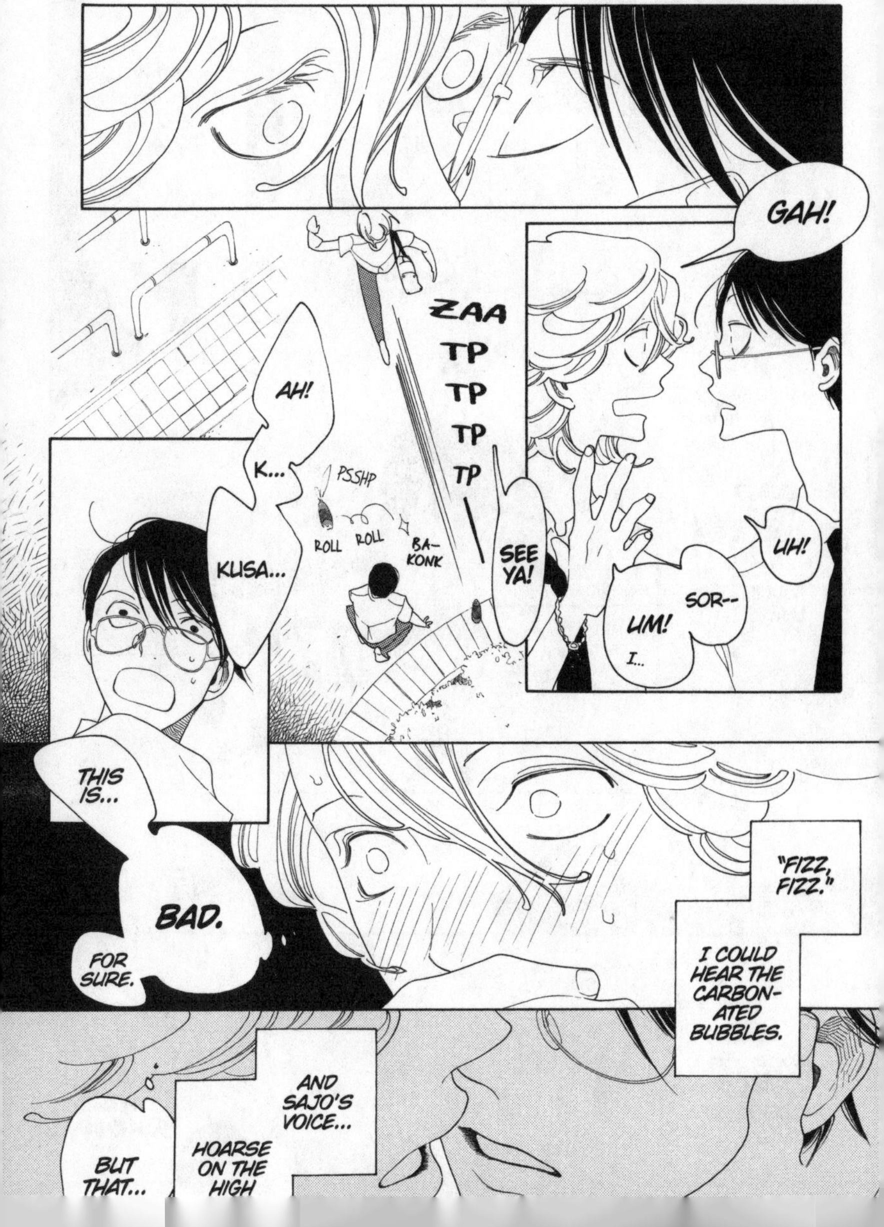
GAH!
UH!
SOR--
UM! I...
ZAA
TP TP TP TP
SEE YA!
PSSHP
ROLL ROLL
BA-KONK
AH! K... KUSA...
THIS IS...
BAD.
FOR SURE.
"FIZZ, FIZZ."
I COULD HEAR THE CARBON-ATED BUBBLES.
AND SAJO'S VOICE...
HOARSE ON THE HIGH
BUT THAT...

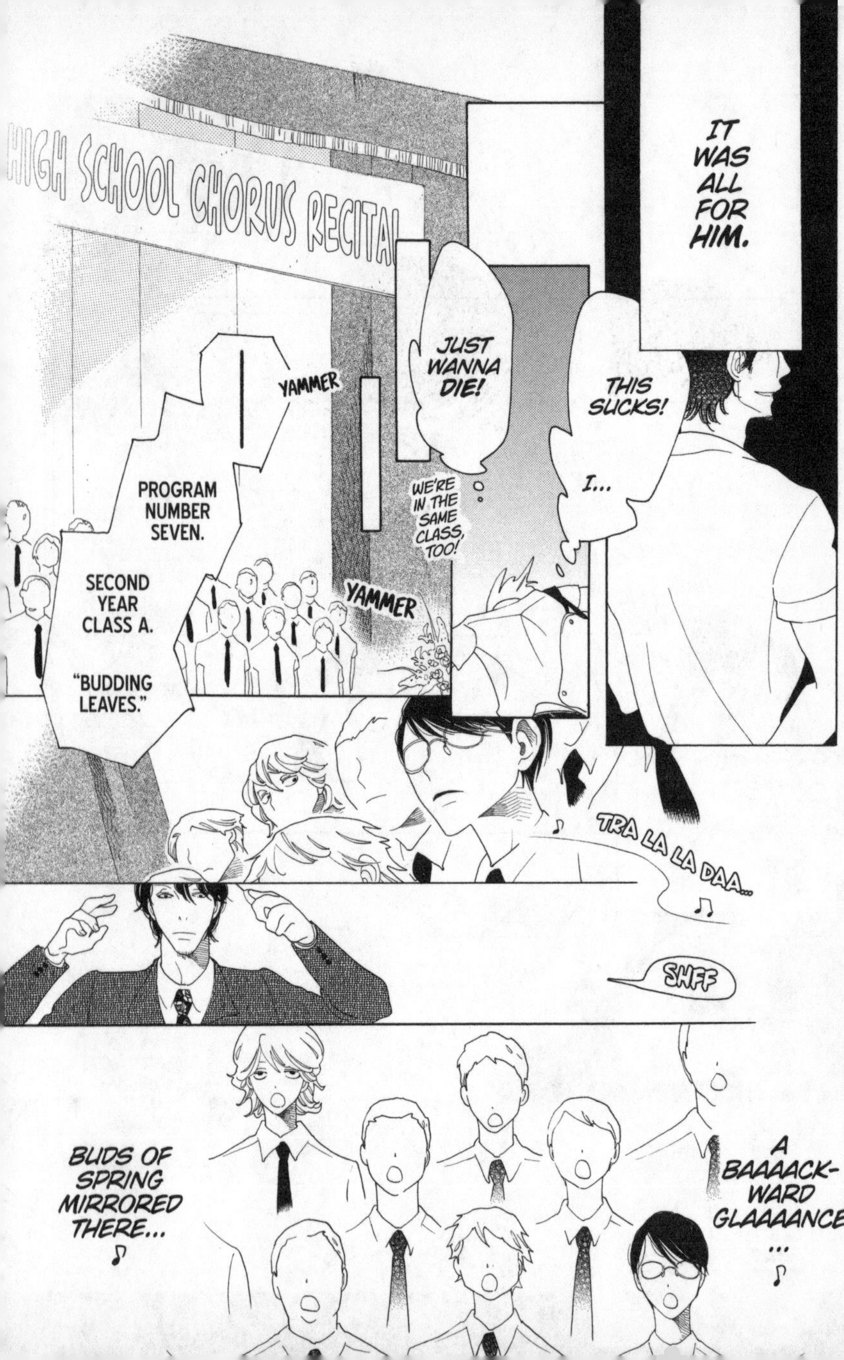
IT WAS ALL FOR HIM.
THIS SUCKS!
I...
JUST WANNA DIE!
WE'RE IN THE SAME CLASS, TOO!
HIGH SCHOOL CHORUS RECITAL
YAMMER
PROGRAM NUMBER SEVEN.
SECOND YEAR CLASS A.
"BUDDING LEAVES."
YAMMER
TRA LA LA DAA...
SHFF
A BAAAACK-WARD GLAAAANCE...
BUDS OF SPRING MIRRORED THERE...

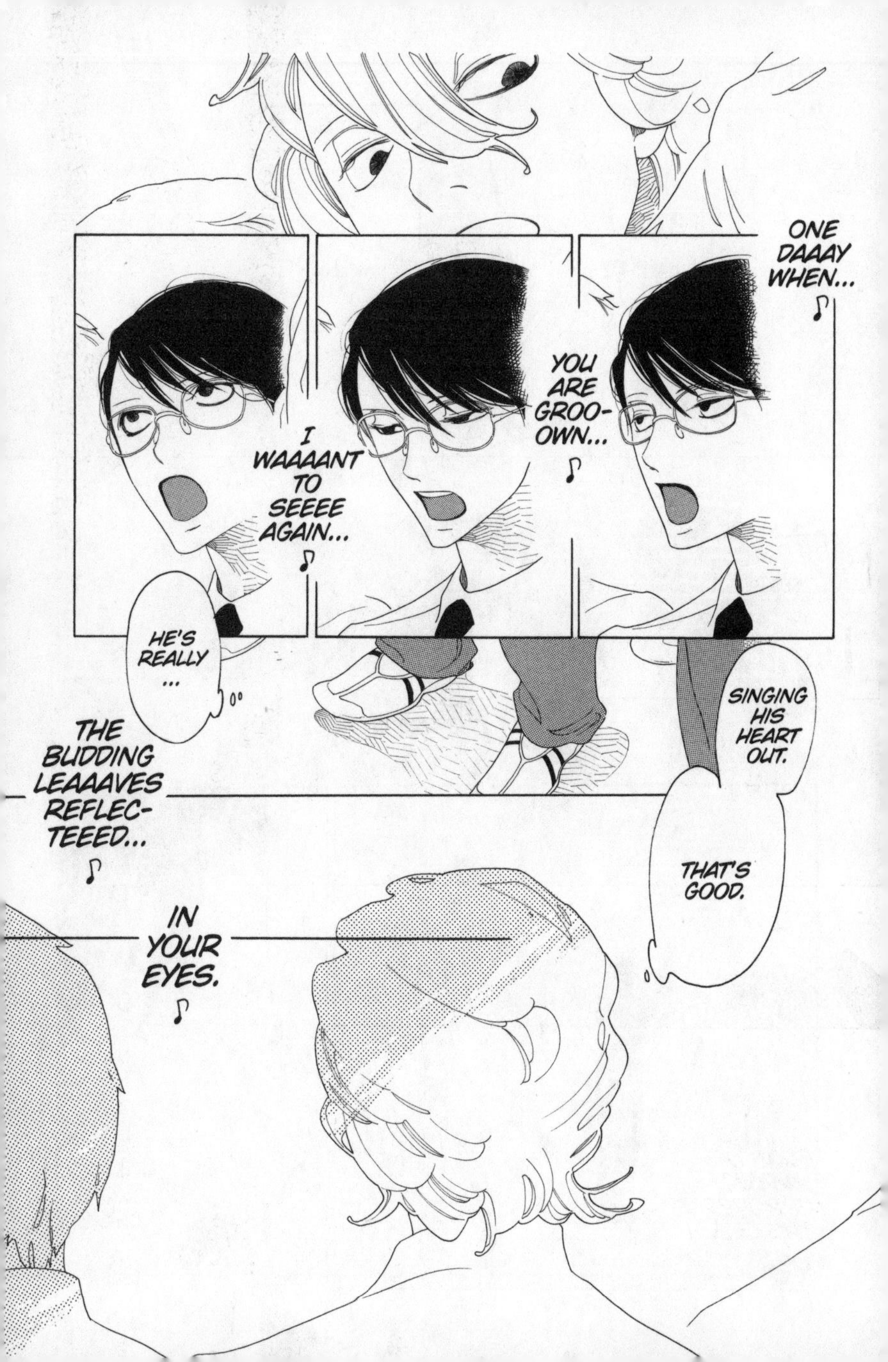
ONE DAAAY WHEN... ♪
YOU ARE GROO-OWN... ♪
I WAAAANT TO SEEEE AGAIN... ♪
HE'S REALLY ...
SINGING HIS HEART OUT.
THAT'S GOOD.
THE BUDDING LEAAAVES REFLEC-TEEED... ♪
IN YOUR EYES. ♪

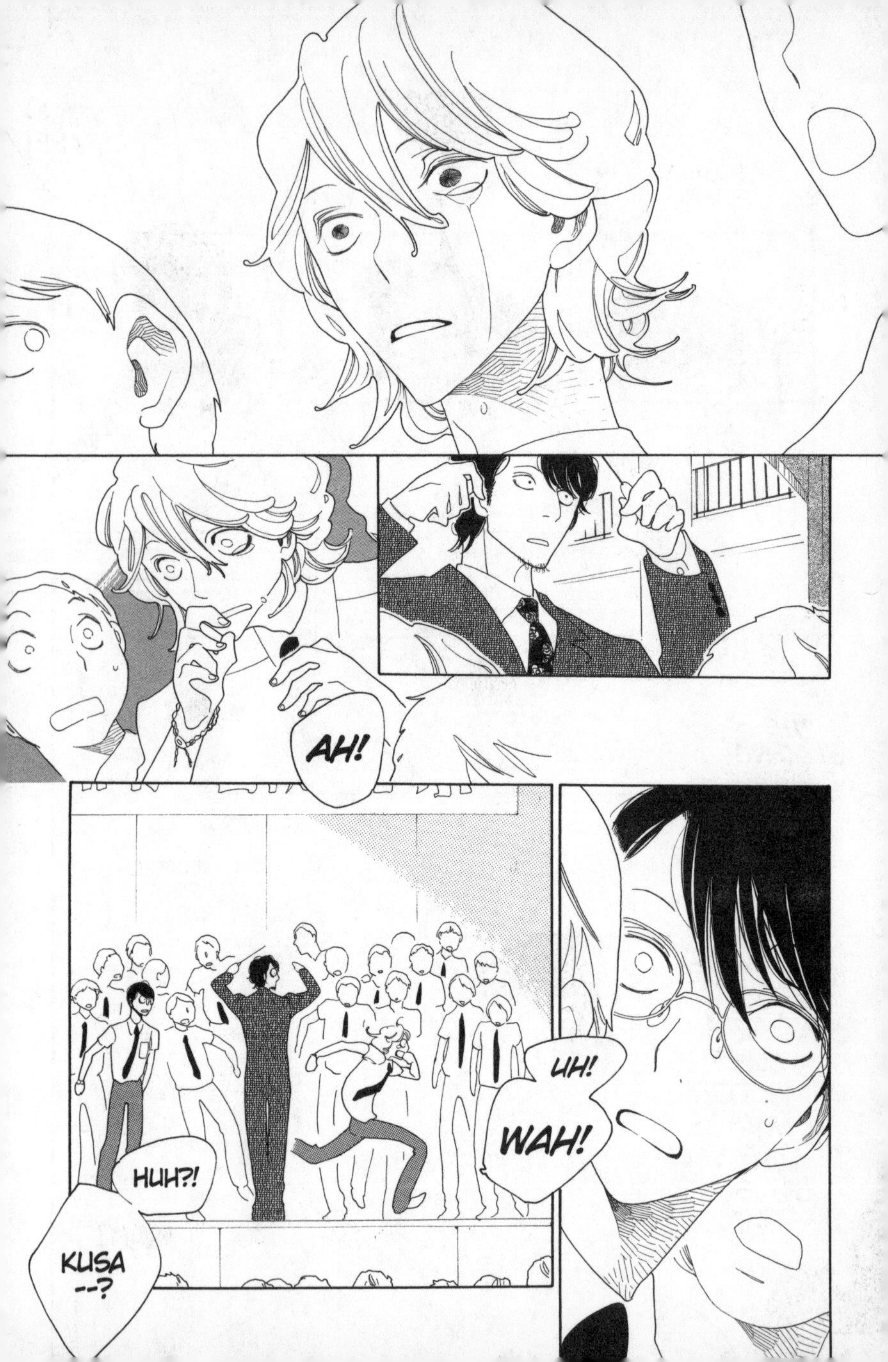
AH!
UH!
WAH!
HUH?!
KUSA --?

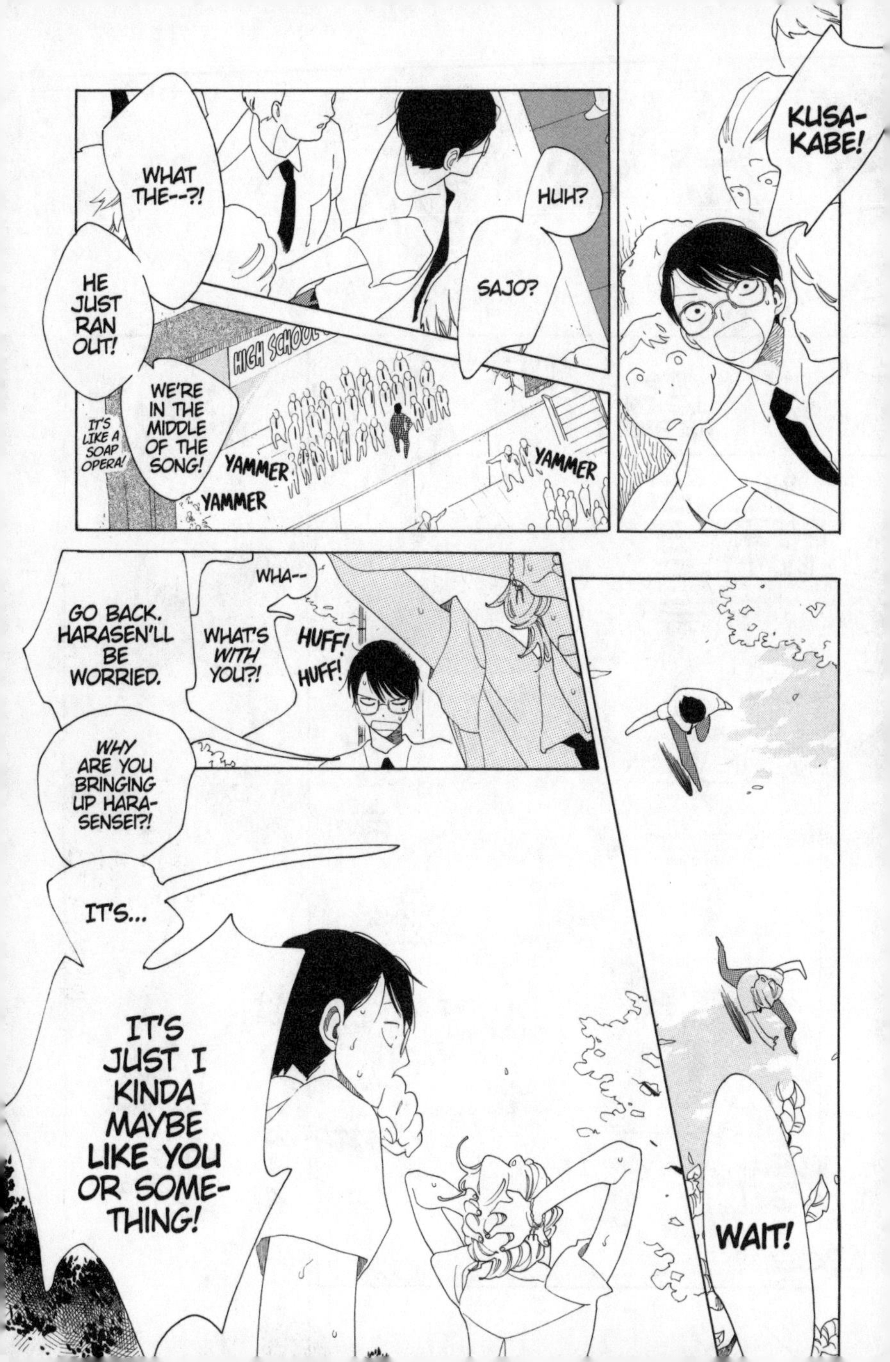
KUSA-KABE!
HUH?
SAJO?
WHAT THE--?!
HE JUST RAN OUT!
HIGH SCHOOL
WE'RE IN THE MIDDLE OF THE SONG!
IT'S LIKE A SOAP OPERA!
YAMMER
YAMMER
YAMMER
WAIT!
WHA--
HUFF! HUFF!
WHAT'S WITH YOU?!
GO BACK. HARASEN'LL BE WORRIED.
WHY ARE YOU BRINGING UP HARA-SENSEI?!
IT'S...
IT'S JUST I KINDA MAYBE LIKE YOU OR SOME-THING!

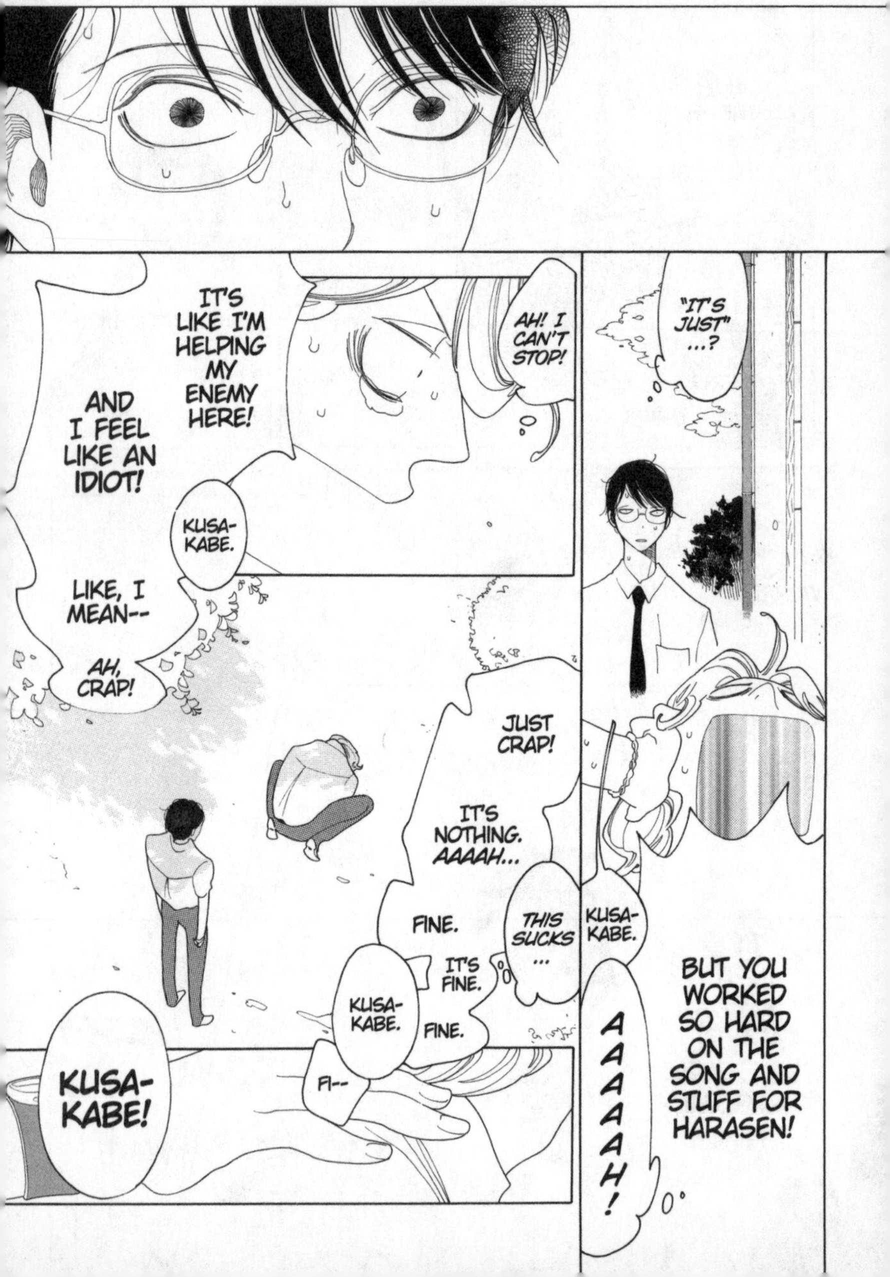

"IT'S JUST"...?
KUSA-KABE.
BUT YOU WORKED SO HARD ON THE SONG AND STUFF FOR HARASEN!
AAAAAAH!
AH! I CAN'T STOP!
IT'S LIKE I'M HELPING MY ENEMY HERE!
AND I FEEL LIKE AN IDIOT!
KUSA-KABE.
LIKE, I MEAN--
AH, CRAP!
JUST CRAP!
IT'S NOTHING. AAAAH...
THIS SUCKS...
FINE.
IT'S FINE.
KUSA-KABE.
FINE.
FI--
KUSA-KABE!

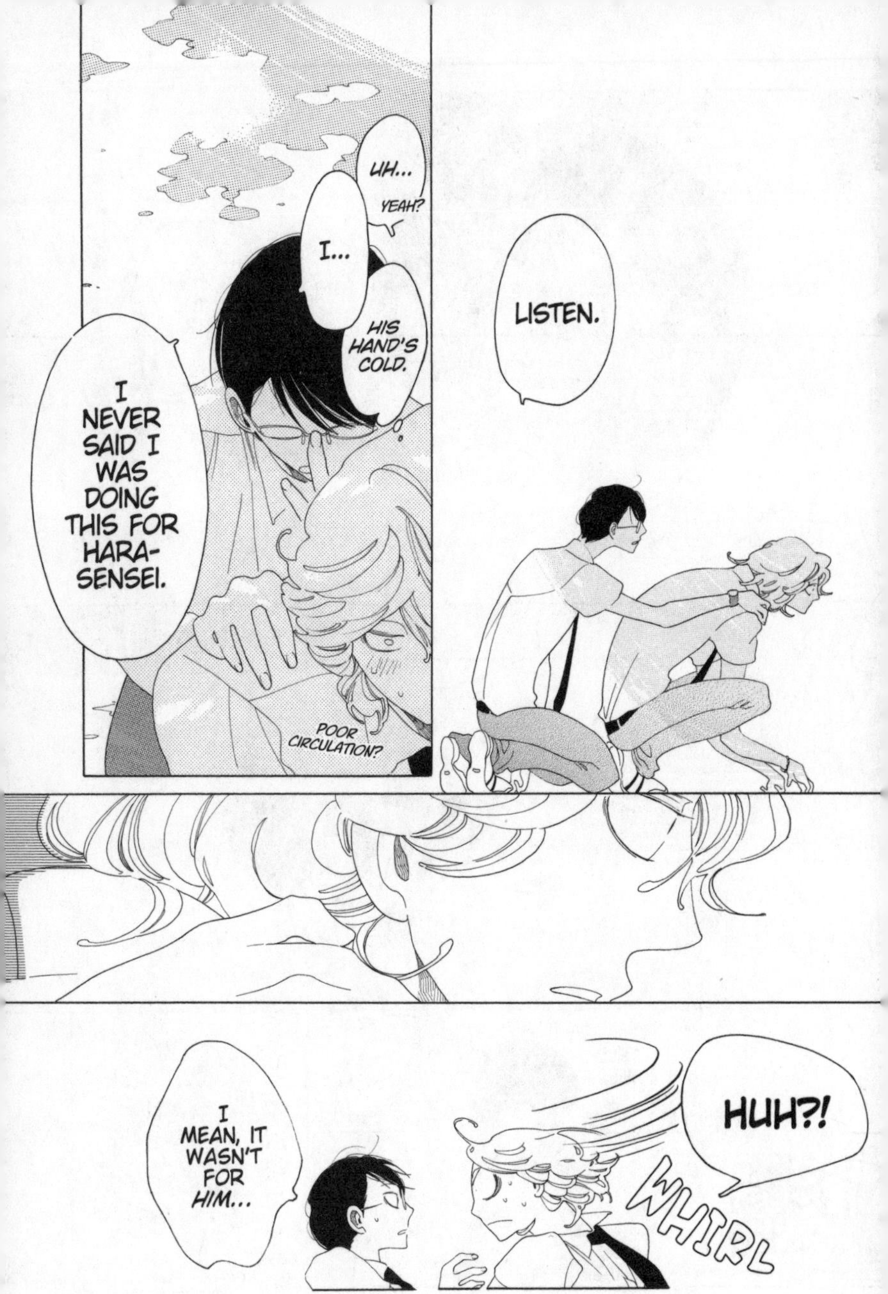
LISTEN.
UH...
YEAH?
I...
HIS HAND'S COLD.
I NEVER SAID I WAS DOING THIS FOR HARA-SENSEI.
POOR CIRCULATION?
HUH?!
WHIRL
I MEAN, IT WASN'T FOR *HIM*...

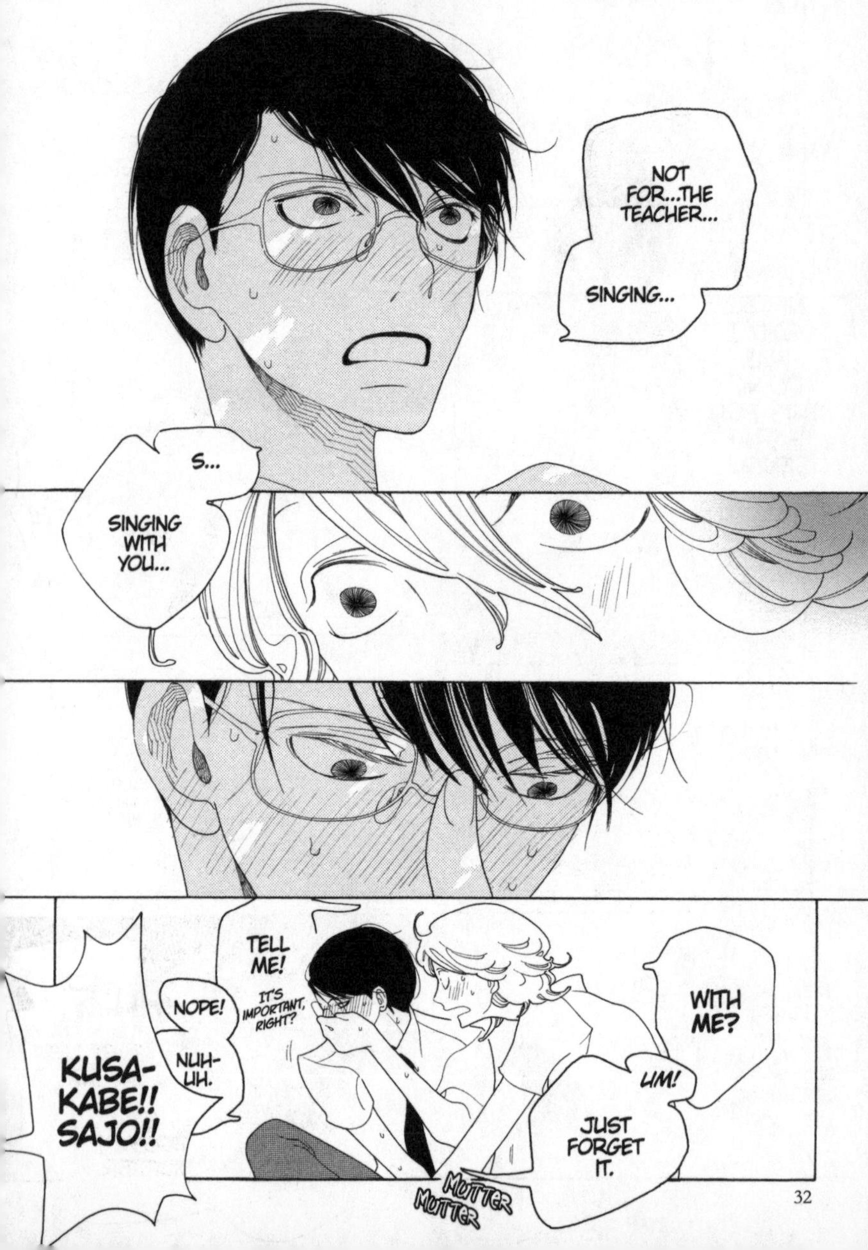
NOT FOR...THE TEACHER...
SINGING...
S...
SINGING WITH YOU...
WITH ME?
UM!
JUST FORGET IT.
MUTTER MUTTER
TELL ME!
IT'S IMPORTANT, RIGHT?
NOPE!
NUH-UH.
KUSA-KABE!! SAJO!!

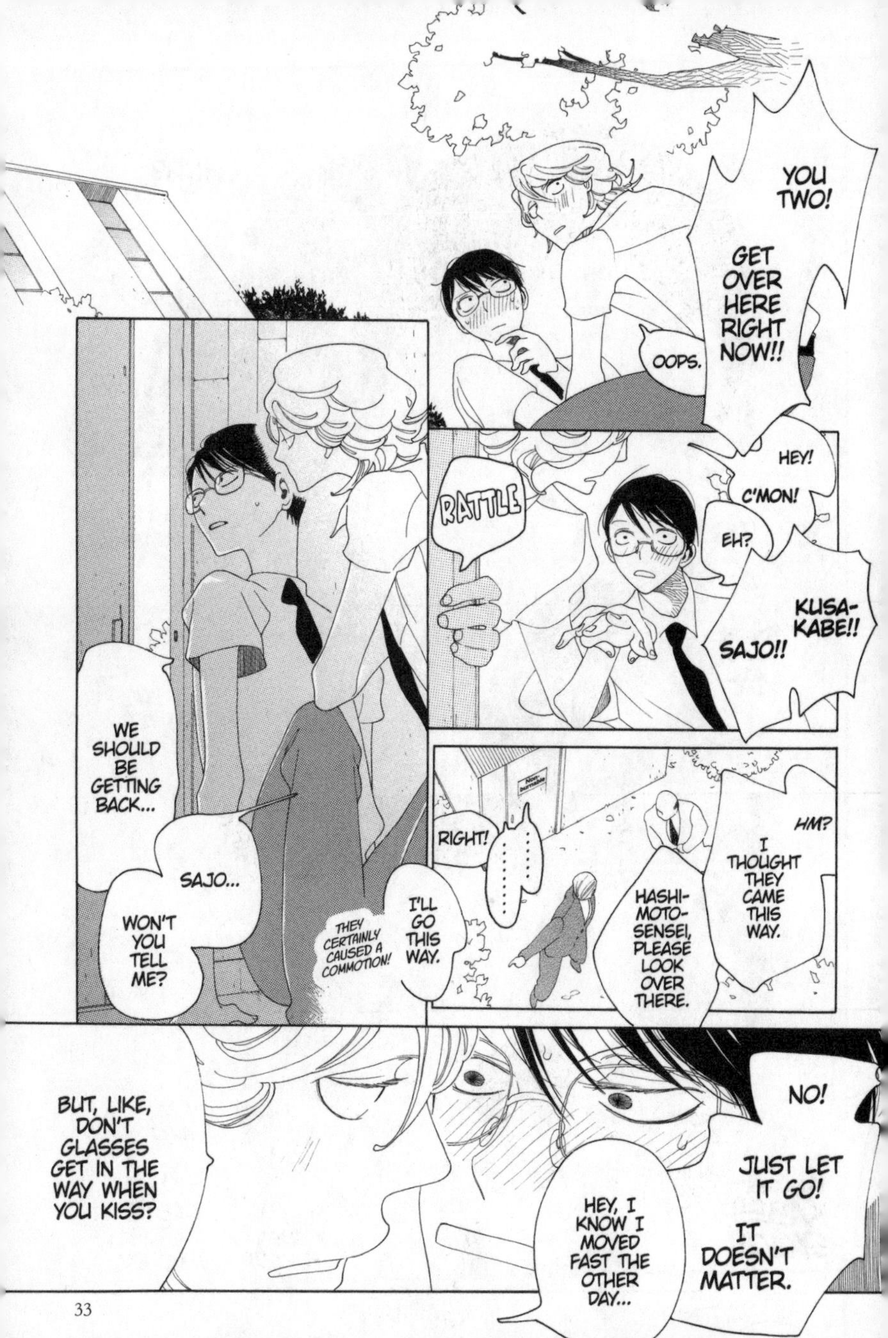
YOU TWO!
GET OVER HERE RIGHT NOW!!
OOPS.
HEY!
C'MON!
EH?
KUSA-KABE!!
SAJO!!
RATTLE
HM?
I THOUGHT THEY CAME THIS WAY.
HASHI-MOTO-SENSEI, PLEASE LOOK OVER THERE.
RIGHT!
......
I'LL GO THIS WAY.
THEY CERTAINLY CAUSED A COMMOTION!
WE SHOULD BE GETTING BACK...
SAJO...
WON'T YOU TELL ME?
NO!
JUST LET IT GO!
IT DOESN'T MATTER.
HEY, I KNOW I MOVED FAST THE OTHER DAY...
BUT, LIKE, DON'T GLASSES GET IN THE WAY WHEN YOU KISS?

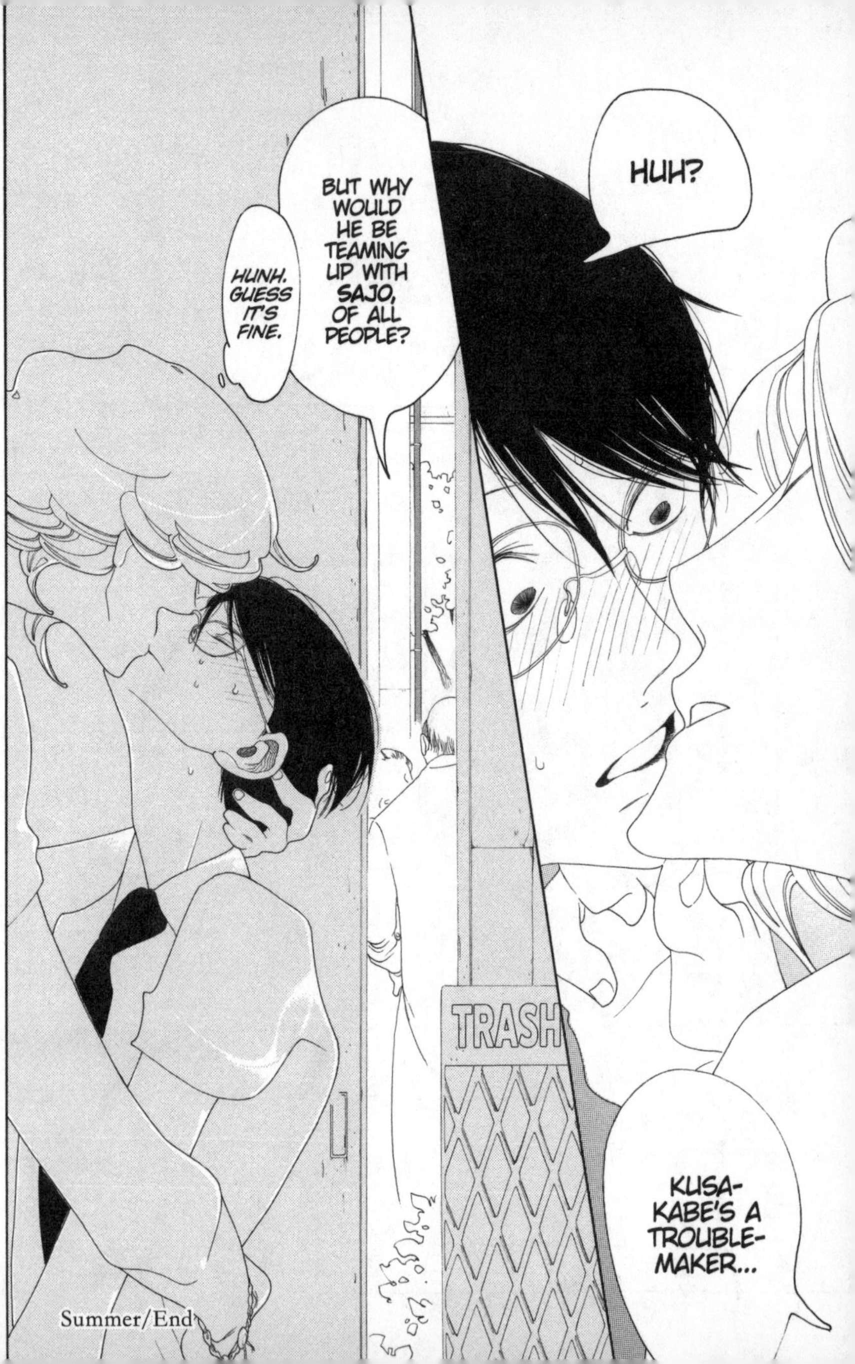
HUH?
KUSA-KABE'S A TROUBLE-MAKER...
BUT WHY WOULD HE BE TEAMING UP WITH SAJO, OF ALL PEOPLE?
HUNH. GUESS IT'S FINE.
TRASH

Summer/End

Classmates

Intermission

GLOMP
HUH? YOU DIDN'T COME OVER FOR A KISS?
THAT...
THAT WAS NOT MY INTENTION.

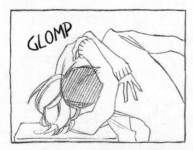

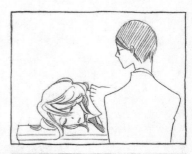

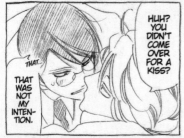

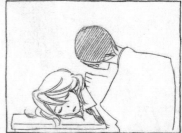

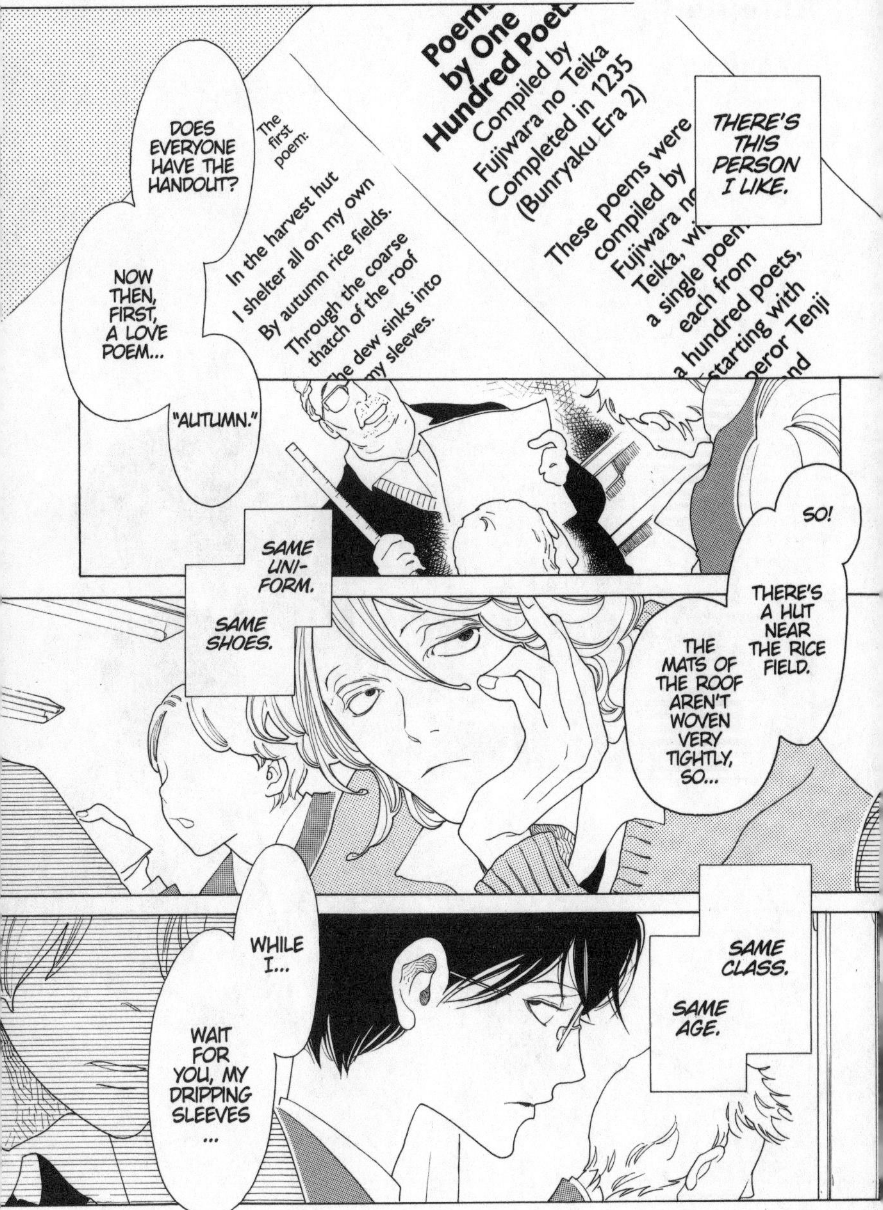

THERE'S THIS PERSON I LIKE.
Poems by One Hundred Poets
Compiled by Fujiwara no Teika
Completed in 1235 (Bunryaku Era 2)
These poems were compiled by Fujiwara no Teika, with a single poem each from a hundred poets, starting with Emperor Tenji and
The first poem:
In the harvest hut
I shelter all on my own
By autumn rice fields.
Through the coarse thatch of the roof
The dew sinks into my sleeves.
DOES EVERYONE HAVE THE HANDOUT?
NOW THEN, FIRST, A LOVE POEM...
"AUTUMN."
SO!
THERE'S A HUT NEAR THE RICE FIELD.
THE MATS OF THE ROOF AREN'T WOVEN VERY TIGHTLY, SO...
SAME UNIFORM.
SAME SHOES.
SAME CLASS.
SAME AGE.
WHILE I...
WAIT FOR YOU, MY DRIPPING SLEEVES ...

[Autumn]

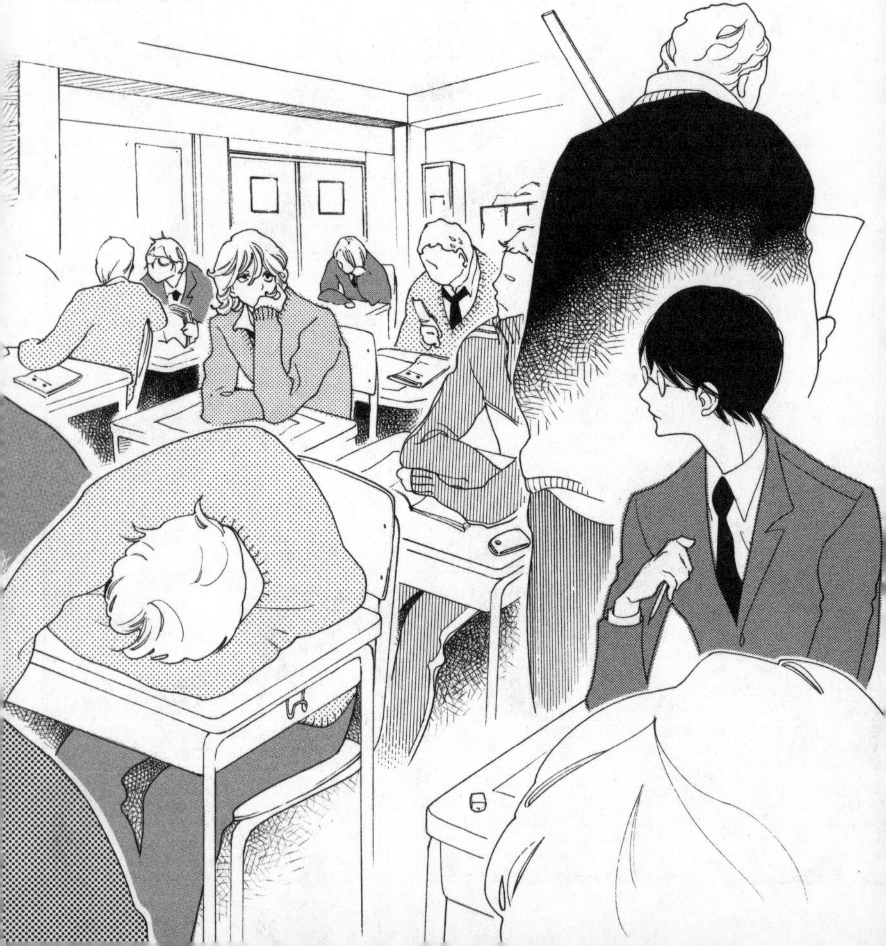

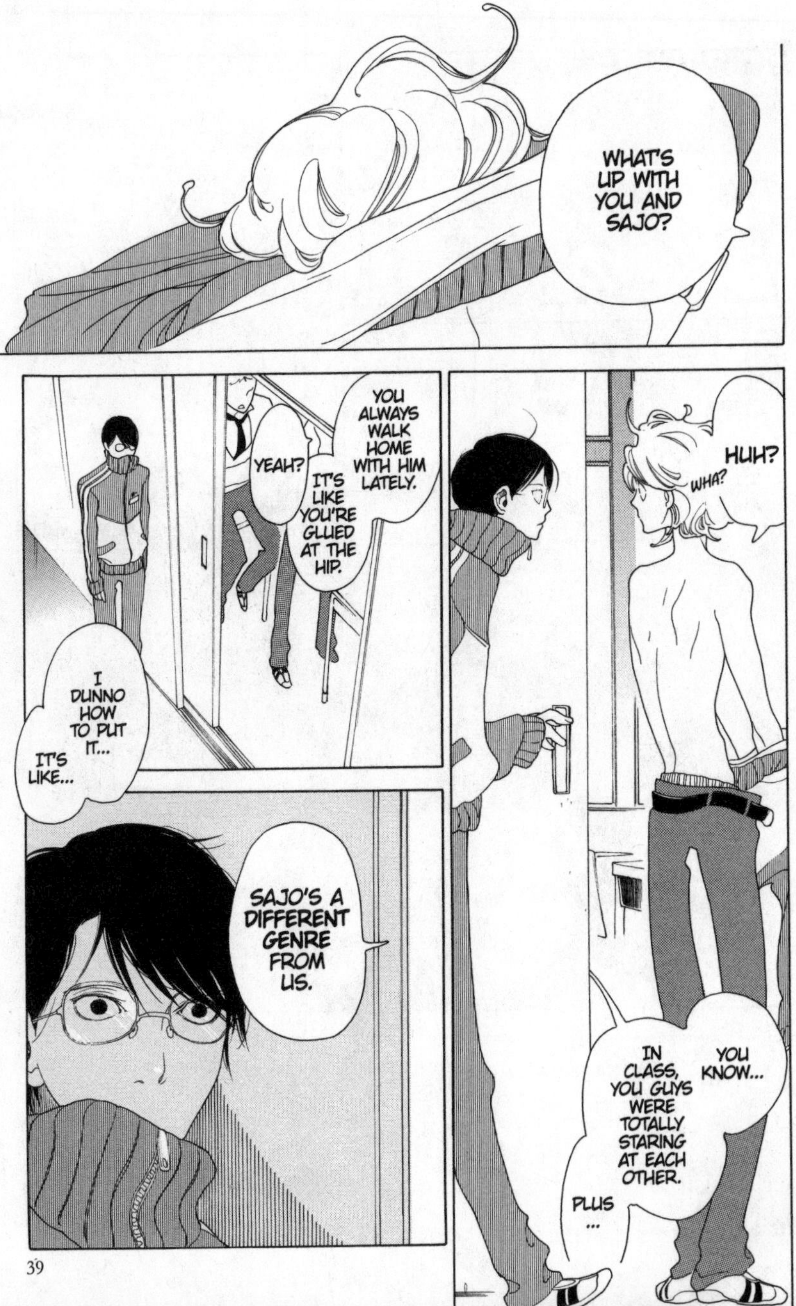
WHAT'S UP WITH YOU AND SAJO?
HUH?
WHA?
YOU KNOW...
IN CLASS, YOU GUYS WERE TOTALLY STARING AT EACH OTHER.
PLUS ...
YOU ALWAYS WALK HOME WITH HIM LATELY.
IT'S LIKE YOU'RE GLUED AT THE HIP.
YEAH?
I DUNNO HOW TO PUT IT...
IT'S LIKE...
SAJO'S A DIFFERENT GENRE FROM US.

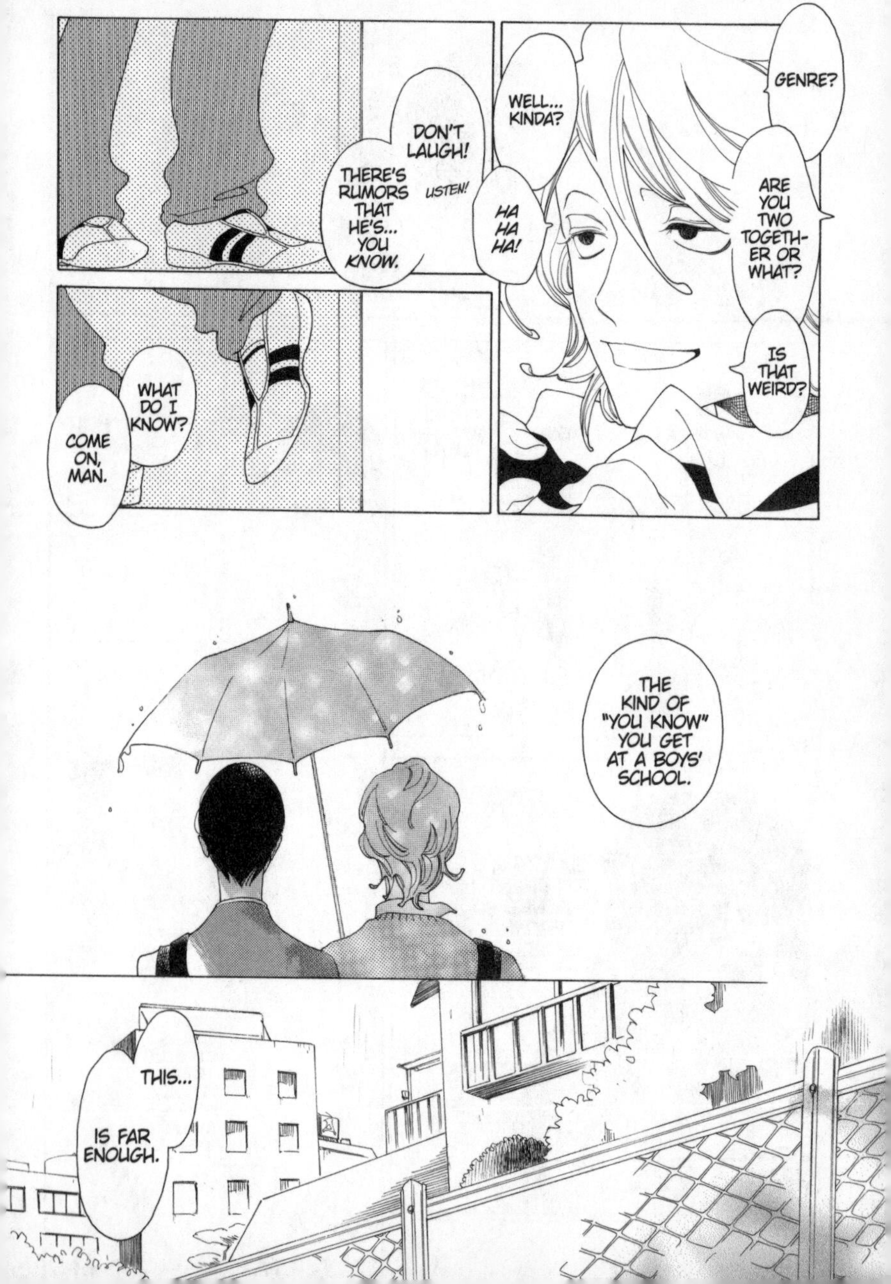
GENRE?
ARE YOU TWO TOGETHER OR WHAT?
IS THAT WEIRD?
WELL... KINDA?
HA HA HA!
DON'T LAUGH!
LISTEN!
THERE'S RUMORS THAT HE'S... YOU KNOW.
WHAT DO I KNOW?
COME ON, MAN.
THE KIND OF "YOU KNOW" YOU GET AT A BOYS' SCHOOL.
THIS...
IS FAR ENOUGH.

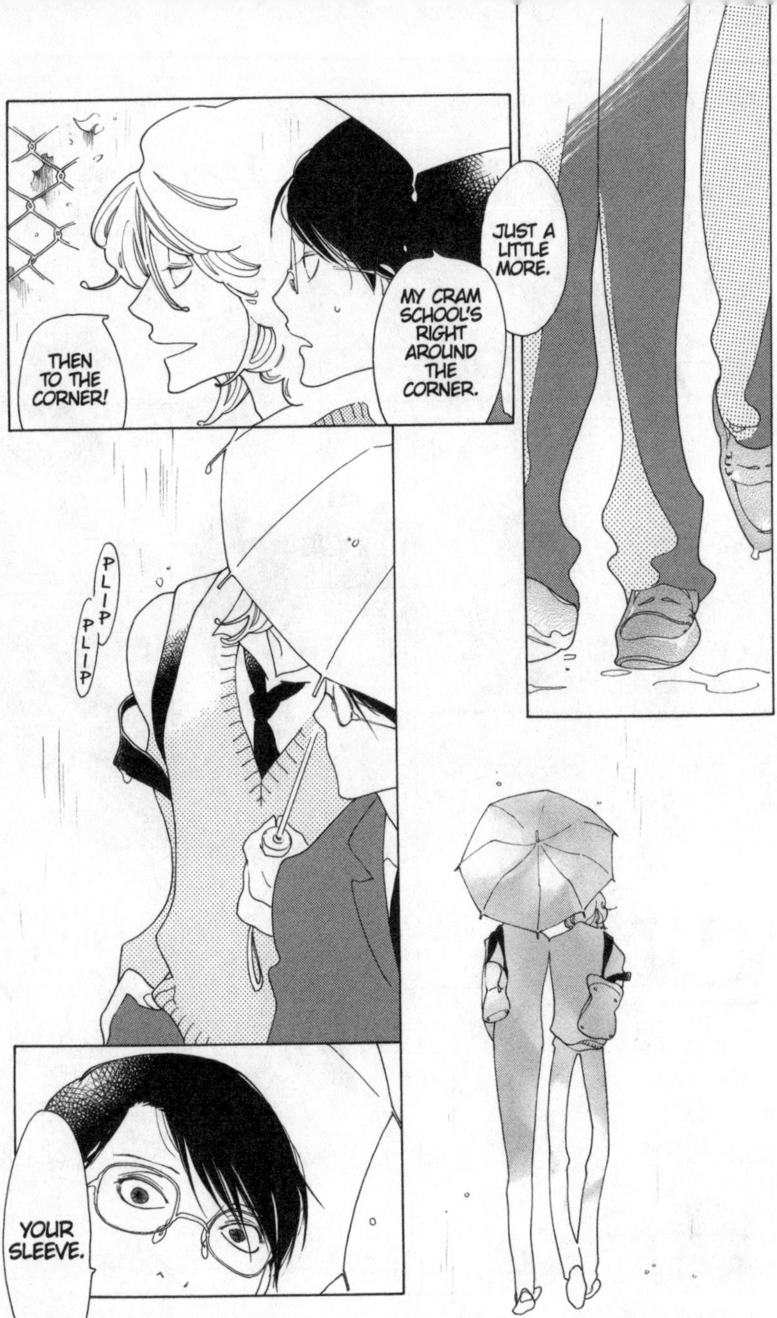
JUST A LITTLE MORE.
MY CRAM SCHOOL'S RIGHT AROUND THE CORNER.
THEN TO THE CORNER!
PLIP PLIP
YOUR SLEEVE.

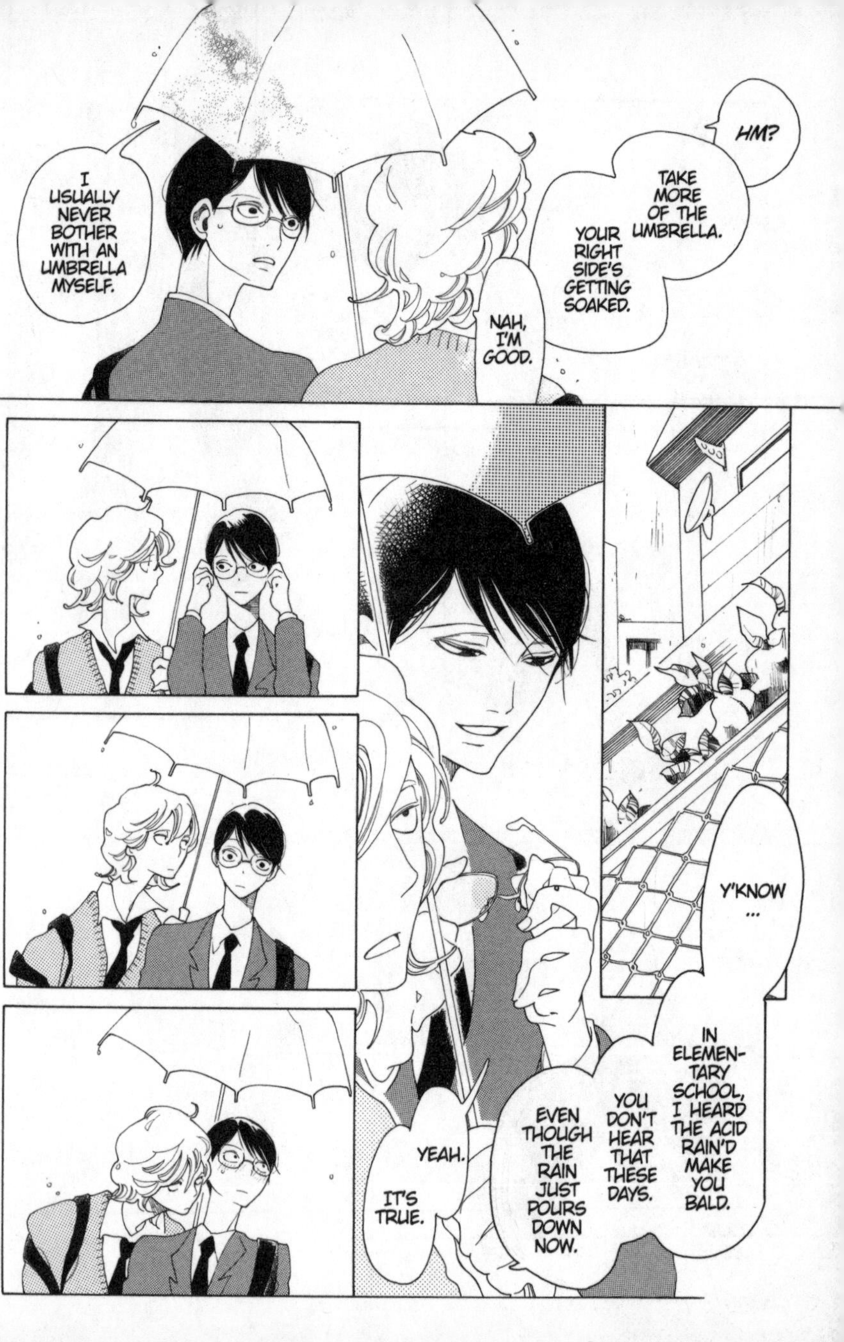
HM?
TAKE MORE OF THE UMBRELLA.
YOUR RIGHT SIDE'S GETTING SOAKED.
NAH, I'M GOOD.
I USUALLY NEVER BOTHER WITH AN UMBRELLA MYSELF.
Y'KNOW ...
IN ELEMENTARY SCHOOL, I HEARD THE ACID RAIN'D MAKE YOU BALD.
YOU DON'T HEAR THAT THESE DAYS.
EVEN THOUGH THE RAIN JUST POURS DOWN NOW.
YEAH.
IT'S TRUE.

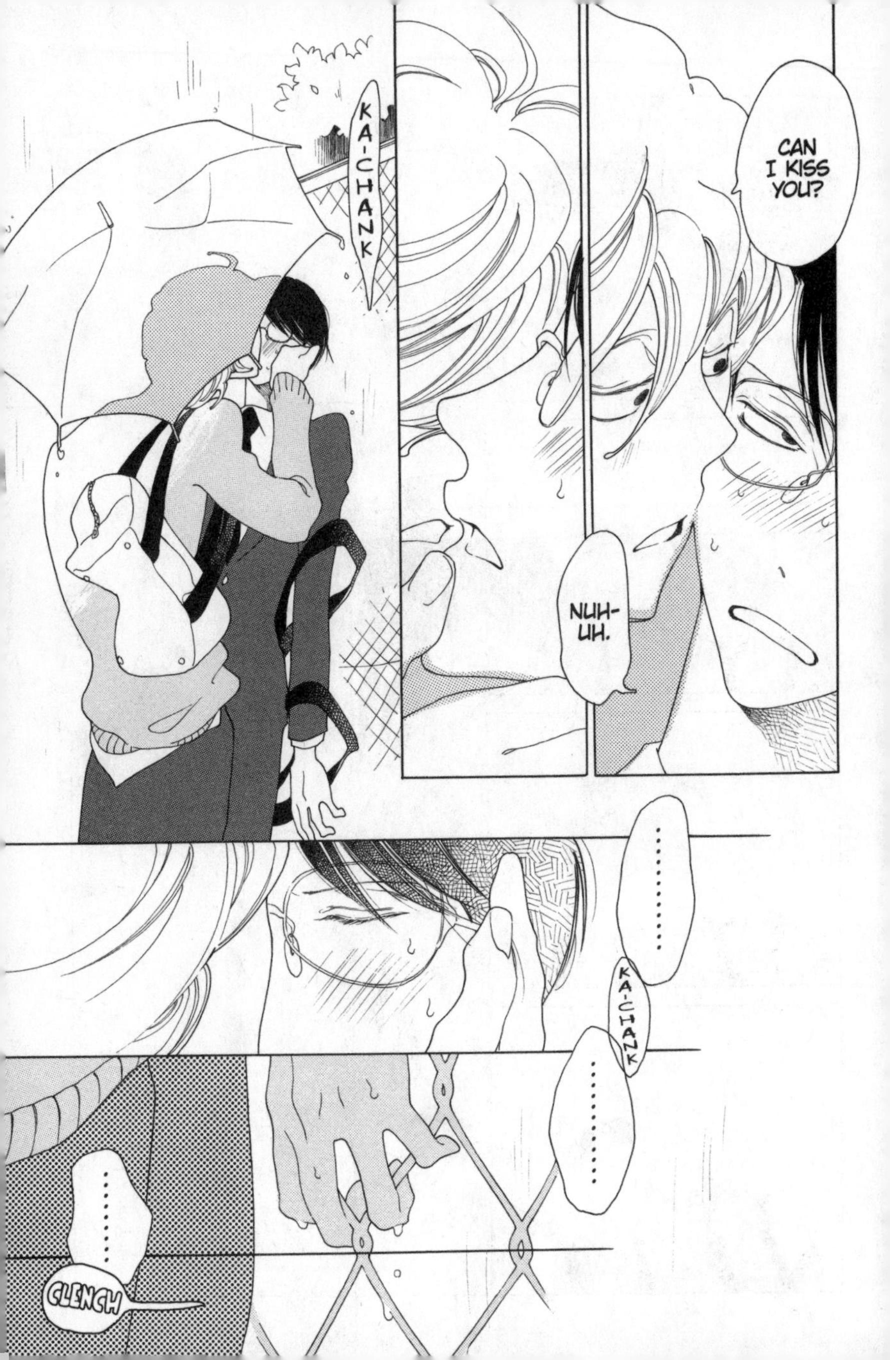

CAN I KISS YOU?
NUH-UH.
KA-CHANK
....
KA-CHANK
....
......
CLENCH

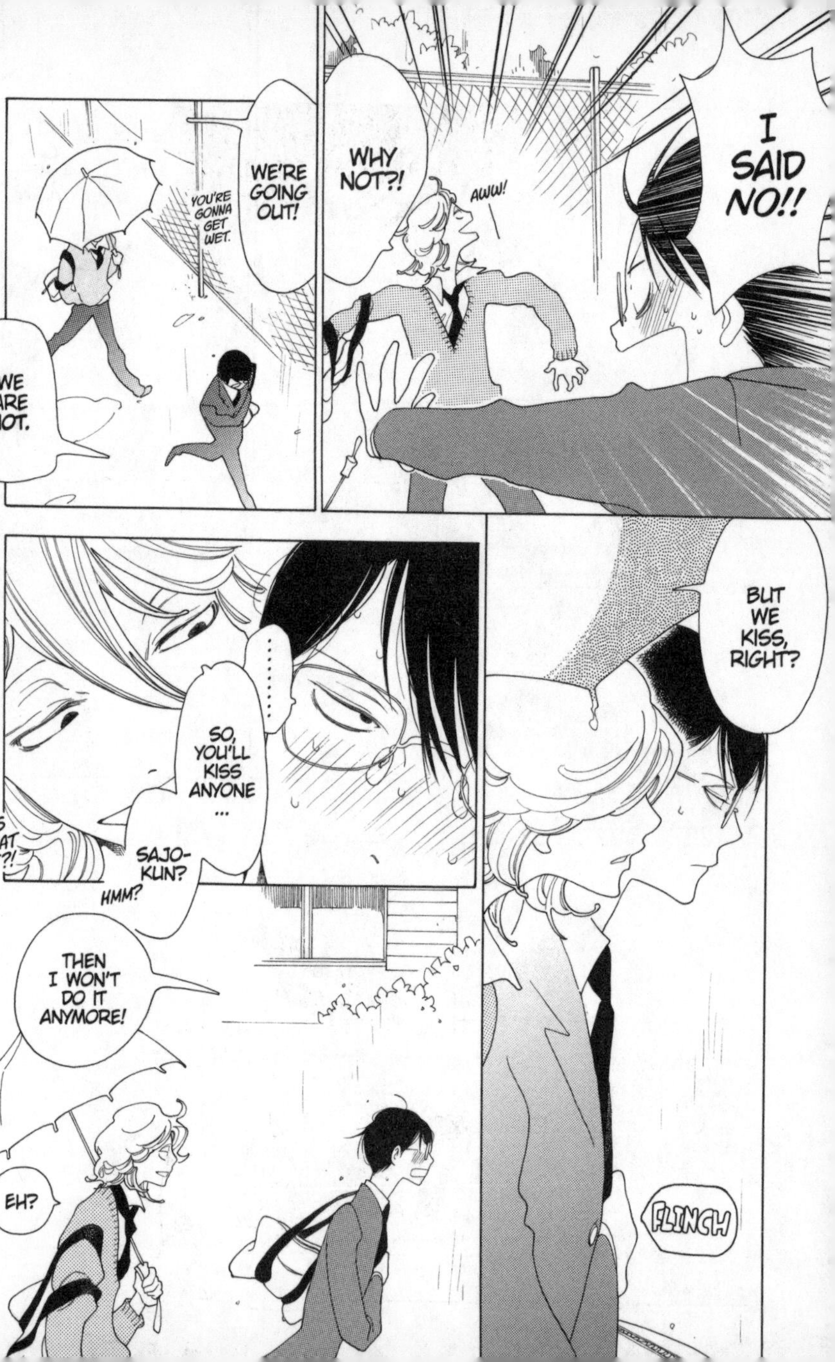
I SAID NO!!
AWW!
WHY NOT?!
WE'RE GOING OUT!
YOU'RE GONNA GET WET.
WE ARE NOT.
BUT WE KISS, RIGHT?
FLINCH
......
SO, YOU'LL KISS ANYONE ...
IS THAT IT?!
SAJO-KUN?
HMM?
THEN I WON'T DO IT ANYMORE!
EH?

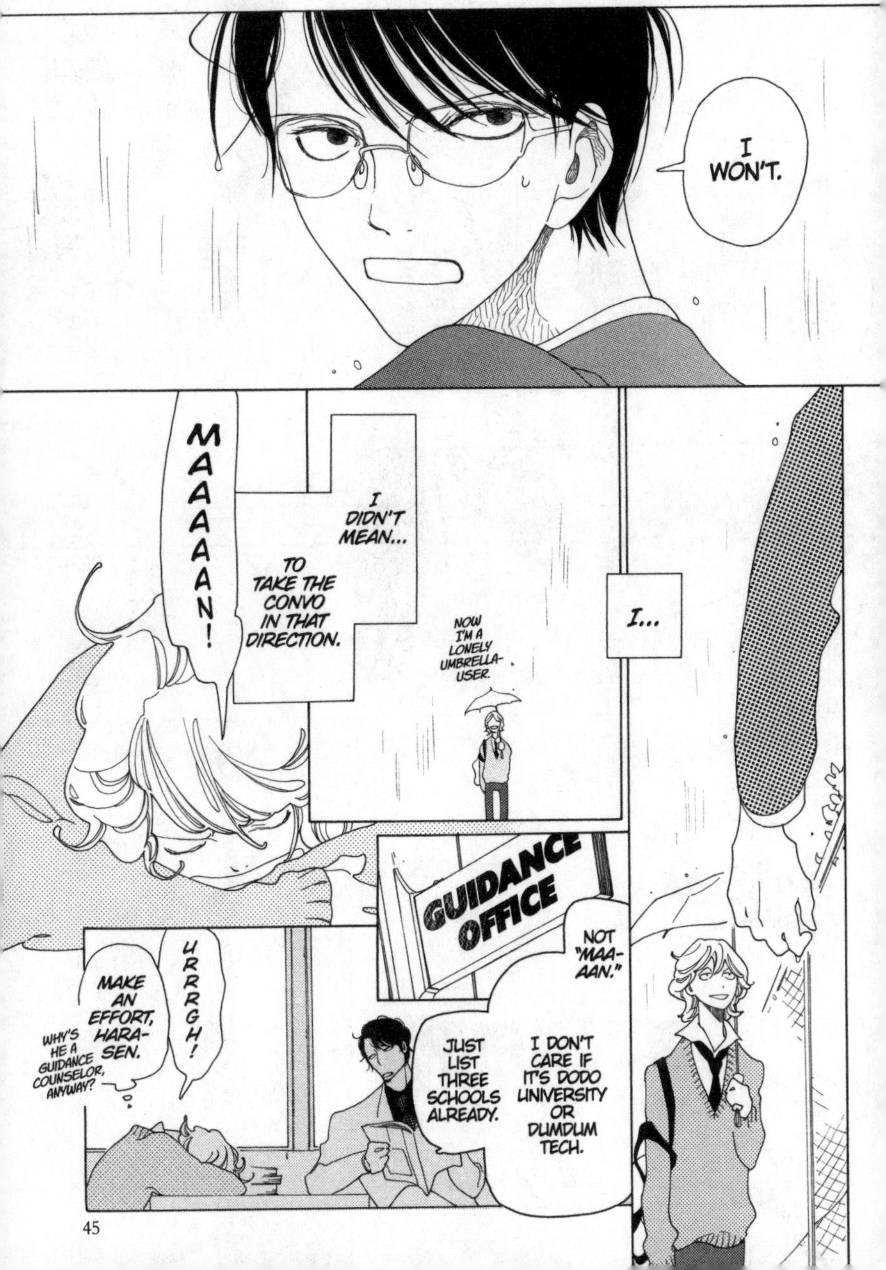
I WON'T.
I...
I DIDN'T MEAN...
TO TAKE THE CONVO IN THAT DIRECTION.
NOW I'M A LONELY UMBRELLA-USER.
MAAAAAAN!
GUIDANCE OFFICE
NOT "MAA-AAN."
I DON'T CARE IF IT'S DODO UNIVERSITY OR DUMDUM TECH.
JUST LIST THREE SCHOOLS ALREADY.
URRRGH!
MAKE AN EFFORT, HARA-SEN.
WHY'S HE A GUIDANCE COUNSELOR, ANYWAY?

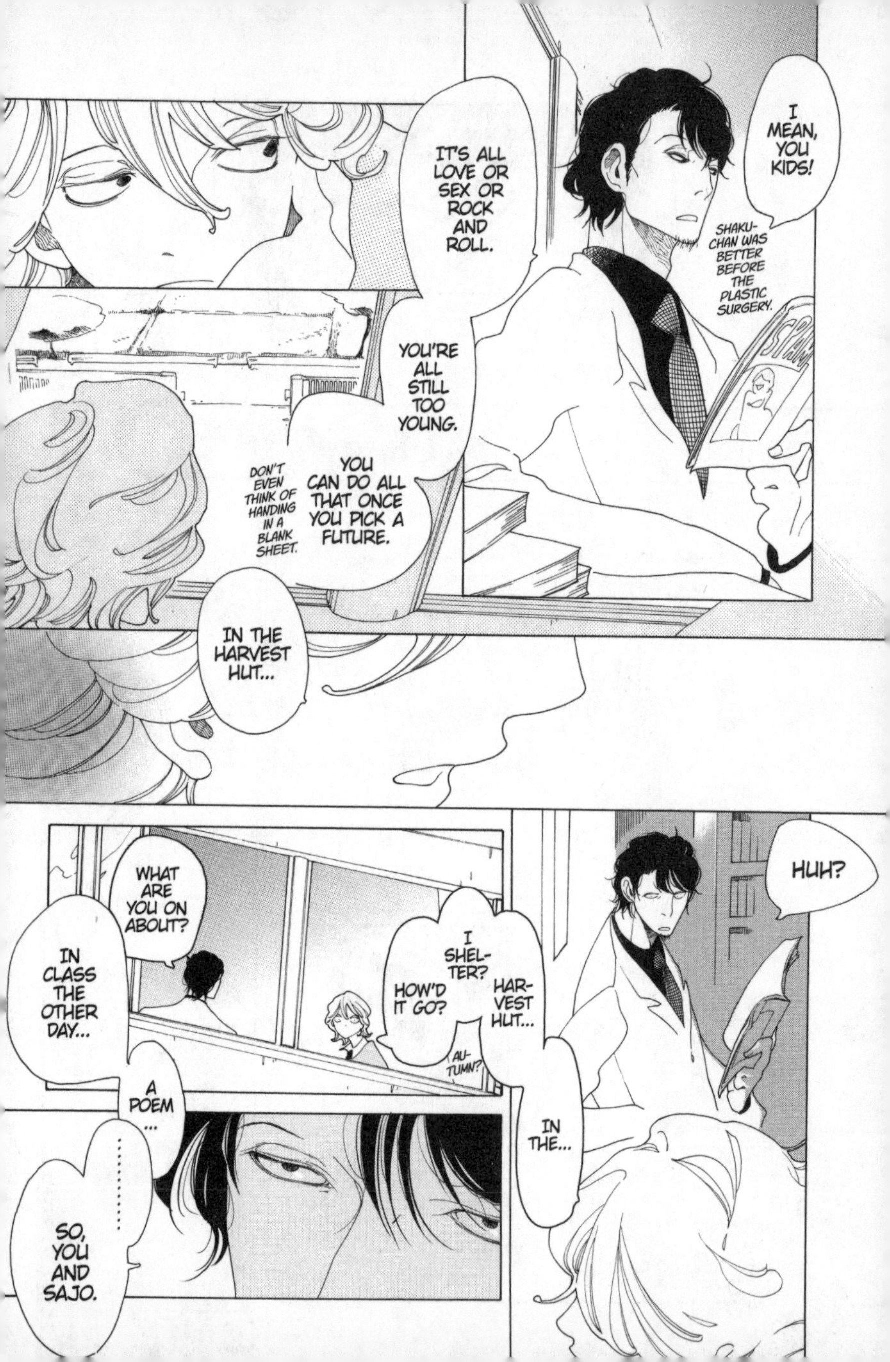
I MEAN, YOU KIDS!
SHAKU-CHAN WAS BETTER BEFORE THE PLASTIC SURGERY.
IT'S ALL LOVE OR SEX OR ROCK AND ROLL.
YOU'RE ALL STILL TOO YOUNG.
YOU CAN DO ALL THAT ONCE YOU PICK A FUTURE.
DON'T EVEN THINK OF HANDING IN A BLANK SHEET.
IN THE HARVEST HUT...
HUH?
HARVEST HUT...
AU-TUMN?
I SHEL-TER?
HOW'D IT GO?
WHAT ARE YOU ON ABOUT?
IN CLASS THE OTHER DAY...
A POEM...
IN THE...
......
SO, YOU AND SAJO.

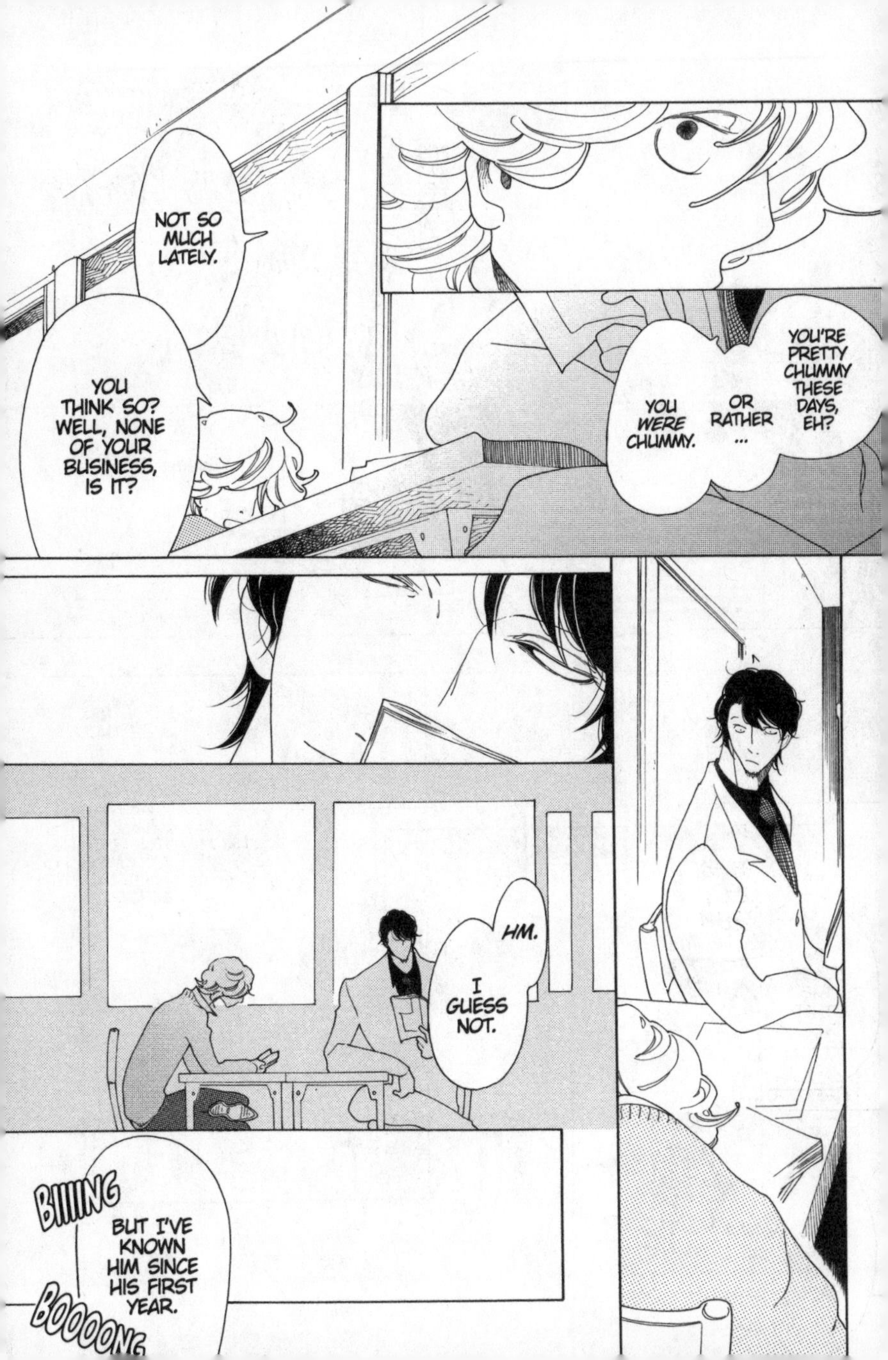
YOU'RE PRETTY CHUMMY THESE DAYS, EH?
OR RATHER ...
YOU *WERE* CHUMMY.
NOT SO MUCH LATELY.
YOU THINK SO? WELL, NONE OF YOUR BUSINESS, IS IT?
HM.
I GUESS NOT.
BIIIING
BUT I'VE KNOWN HIM SINCE HIS FIRST YEAR.
BOOOONG

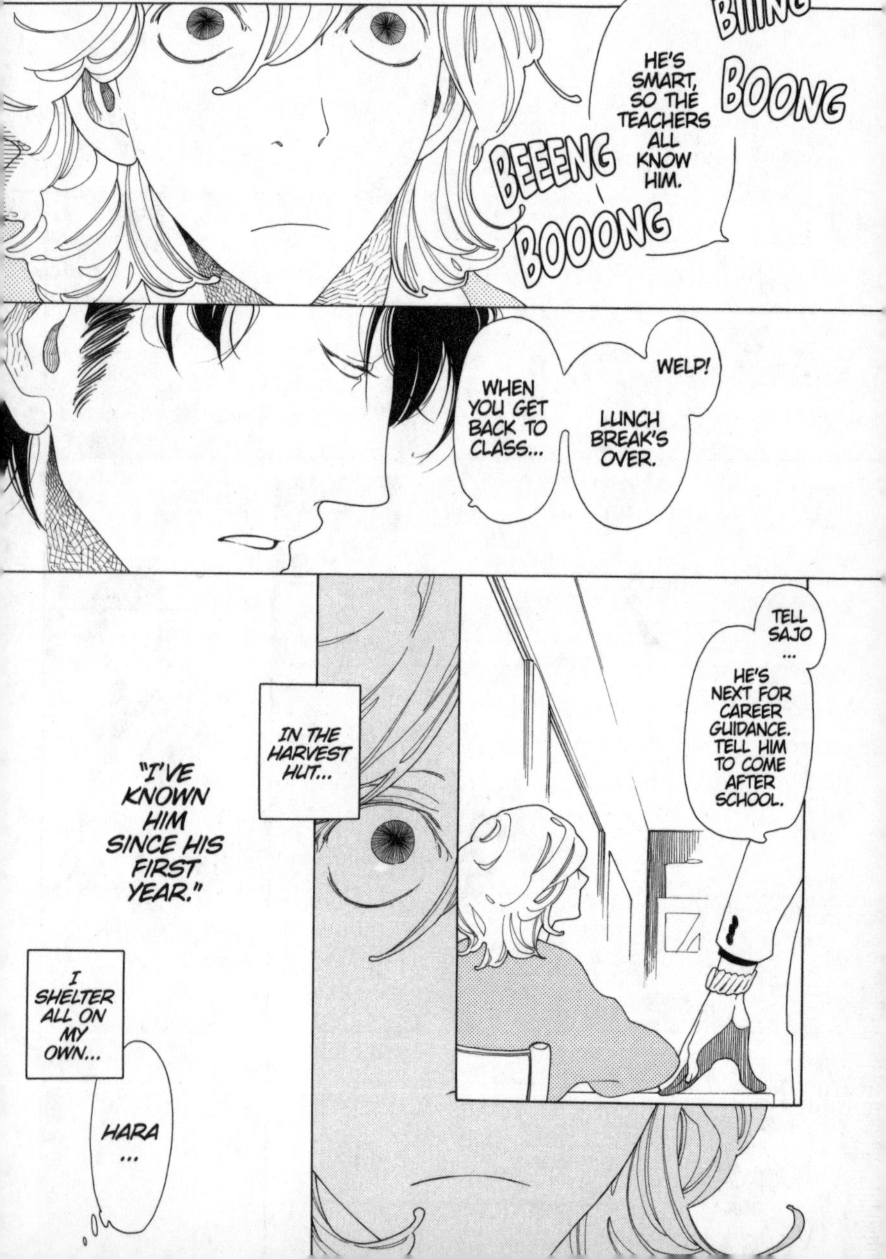
BIIING
BOONG
HE'S SMART, SO THE TEACHERS ALL KNOW HIM.
BEEENG
BOOONG
WELP!
LUNCH BREAK'S OVER.
WHEN YOU GET BACK TO CLASS...
TELL SAJO...
HE'S NEXT FOR CAREER GUIDANCE. TELL HIM TO COME AFTER SCHOOL.
IN THE HARVEST HUT...
"I'VE KNOWN HIM SINCE HIS FIRST YEAR."
I SHELTER ALL ON MY OWN...
HARA...

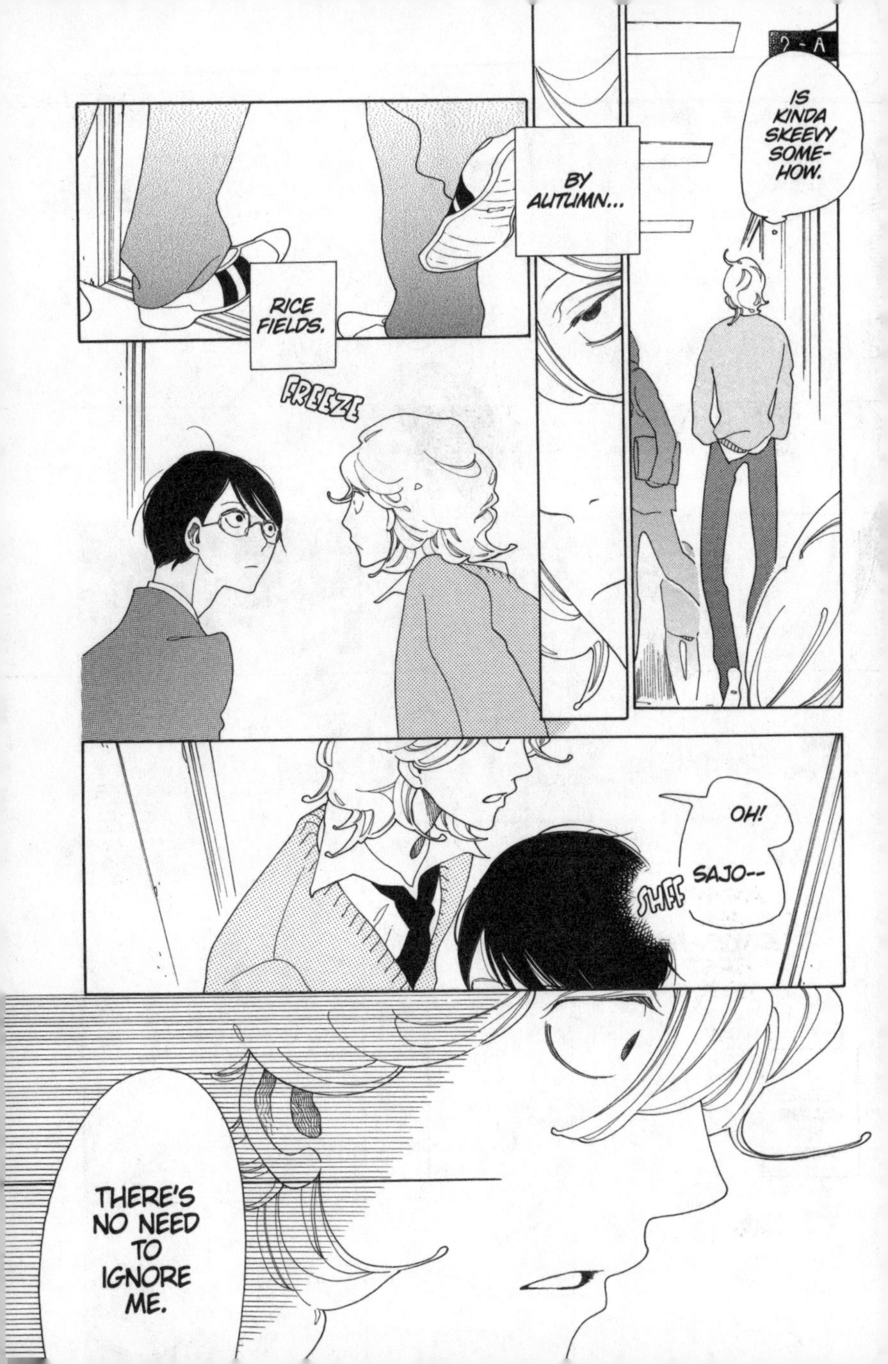
2-A
IS KINDA SKEEVY SOMEHOW.
BY AUTUMN...
RICE FIELDS.
FREEZE
OH!
SAJO--
SHFF
THERE'S NO NEED TO IGNORE ME.

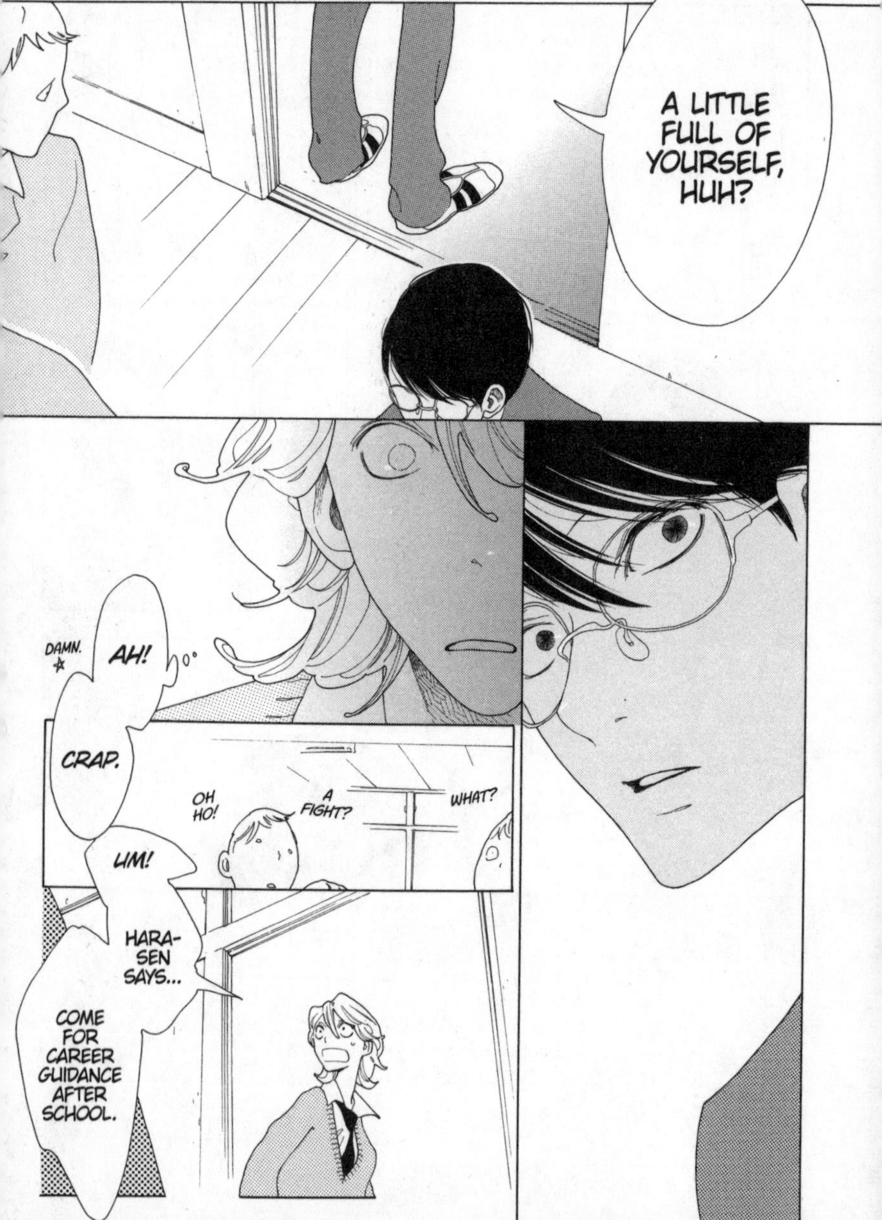
A LITTLE FULL OF YOURSELF, HUH?
AH!
DAMN.
CRAP.
WHAT?
A FIGHT?
OH HO!
UM!
HARA-SEN SAYS...
COME FOR CAREER GUIDANCE AFTER SCHOOL.

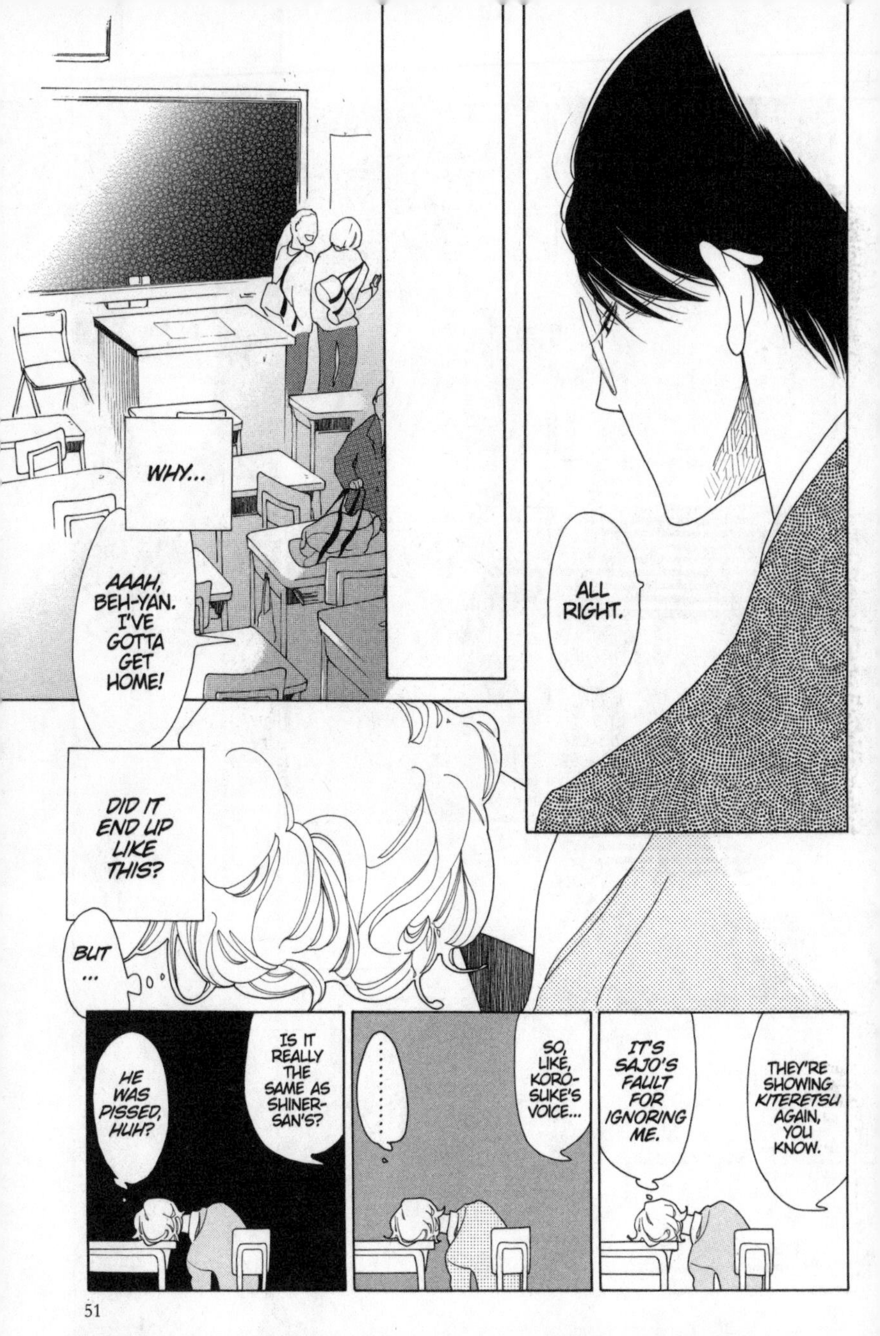
ALL RIGHT.
WHY...
AAAH, BEH-YAN. I'VE GOTTA GET HOME!
DID IT END UP LIKE THIS?
BUT ...
THEY'RE SHOWING KITERETSU AGAIN, YOU KNOW.
IT'S SAJO'S FAULT FOR IGNORING ME.
SO, LIKE, KORO-SUKE'S VOICE...
......
IS IT REALLY THE SAME AS SHINER-SAN'S?
HE WAS PISSED, HUH?

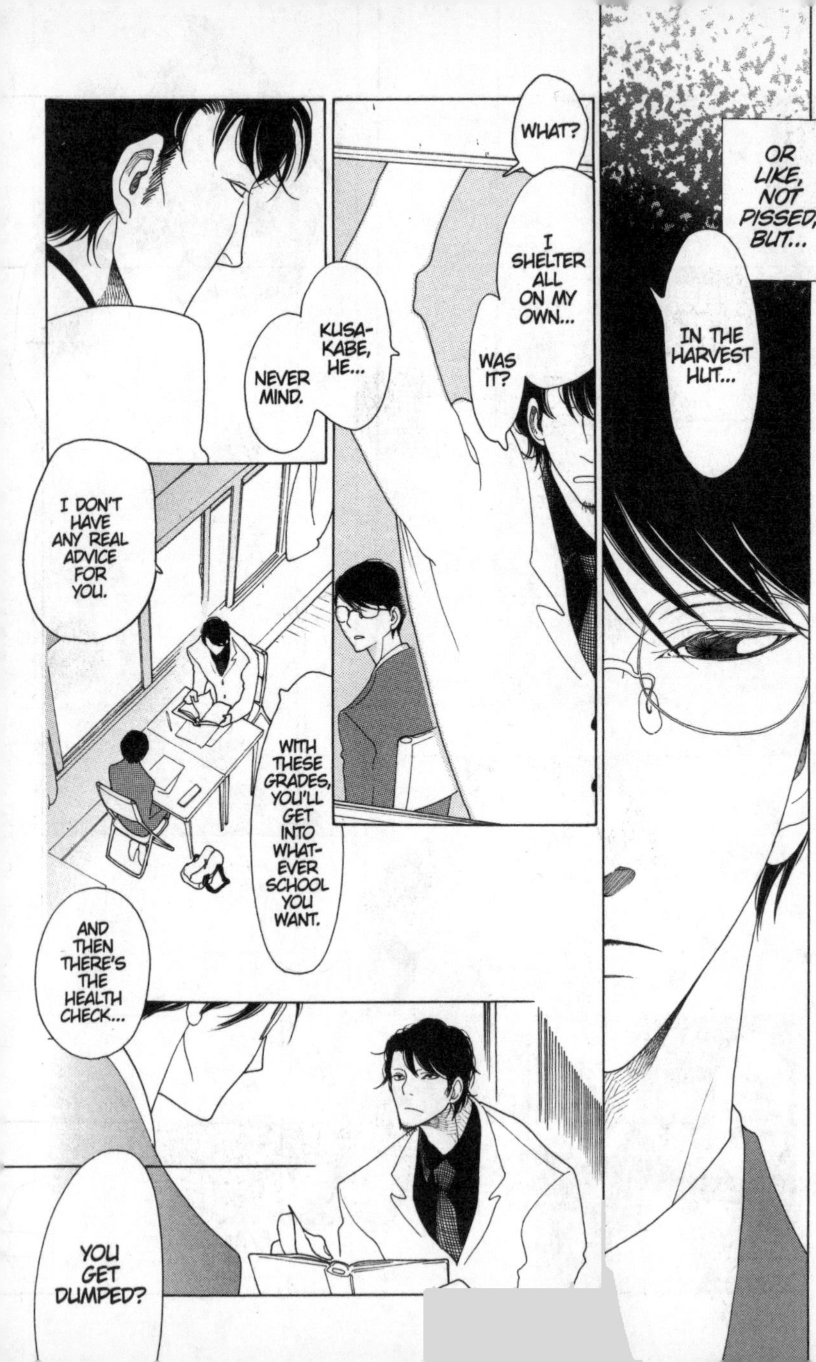
OR LIKE, NOT PISSED, BUT...
IN THE HARVEST HUT...
I SHELTER ALL ON MY OWN...
WAS IT?
WHAT?
KUSA-KABE, HE...
NEVER MIND.
I DON'T HAVE ANY REAL ADVICE FOR YOU.
WITH THESE GRADES, YOU'LL GET INTO WHATEVER SCHOOL YOU WANT.
AND THEN THERE'S THE HEALTH CHECK...
YOU GET DUMPED?

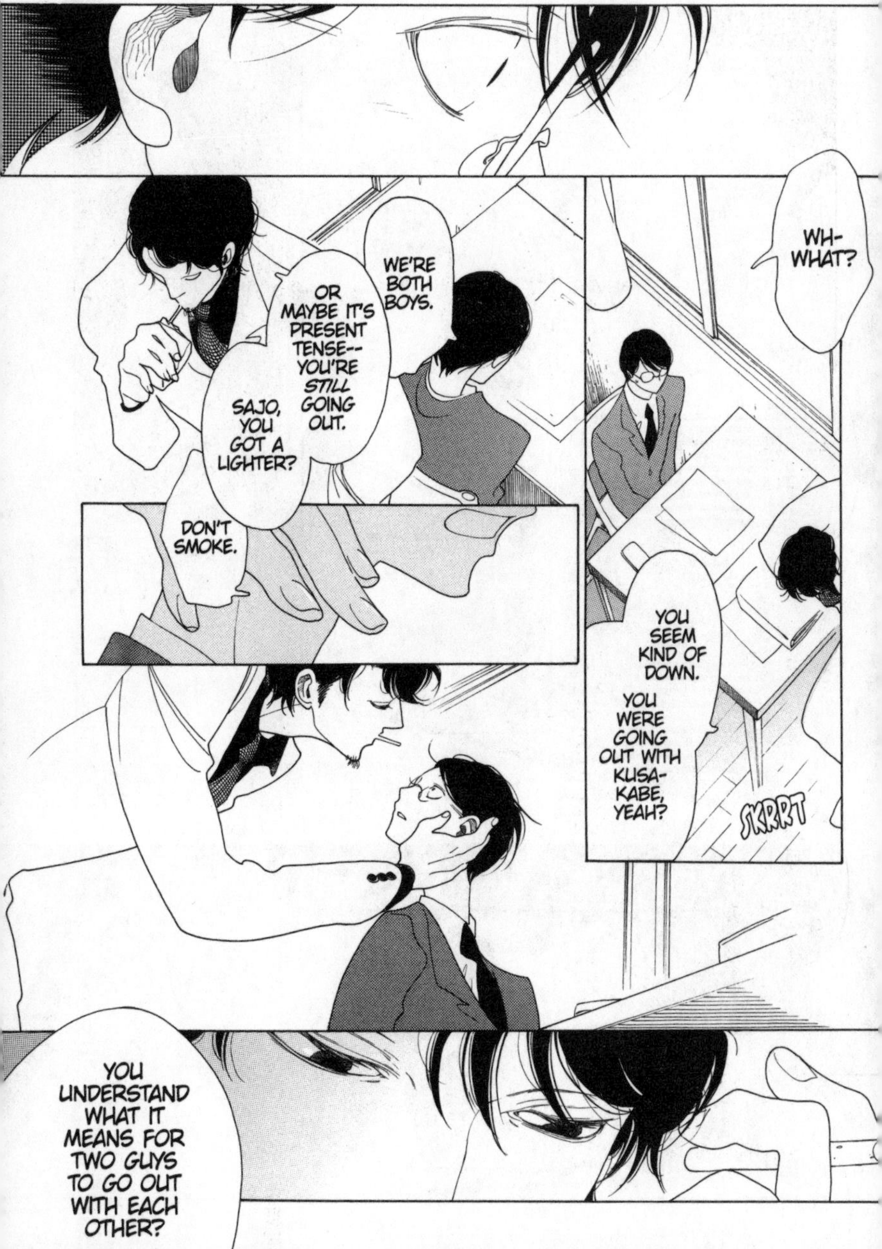
WH-WHAT?
YOU SEEM KIND OF DOWN.
YOU WERE GOING OUT WITH KUSA-KABE, YEAH?
SKRRT
WE'RE BOTH BOYS.
OR MAYBE IT'S PRESENT TENSE--YOU'RE *STILL* GOING OUT.
SAJO, YOU GOT A LIGHTER?
DON'T SMOKE.
YOU UNDERSTAND WHAT IT MEANS FOR TWO GUYS TO GO OUT WITH EACH OTHER?

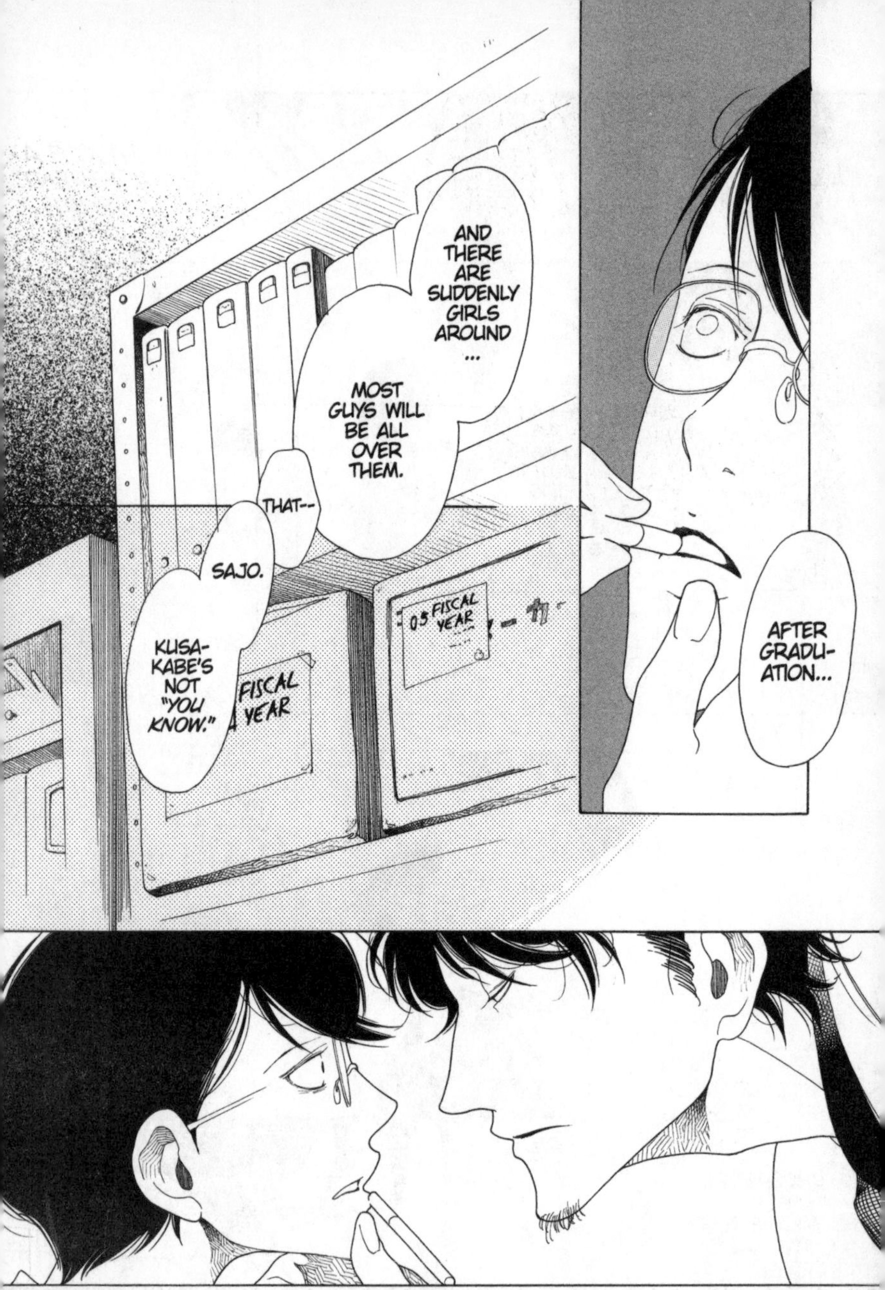
AFTER GRADUATION...
AND THERE ARE SUDDENLY GIRLS AROUND...
MOST GUYS WILL BE ALL OVER THEM.
THAT--
SAJO.
05 FISCAL YEAR
KUSA-KABE'S NOT "YOU KNOW."
FISCAL YEAR

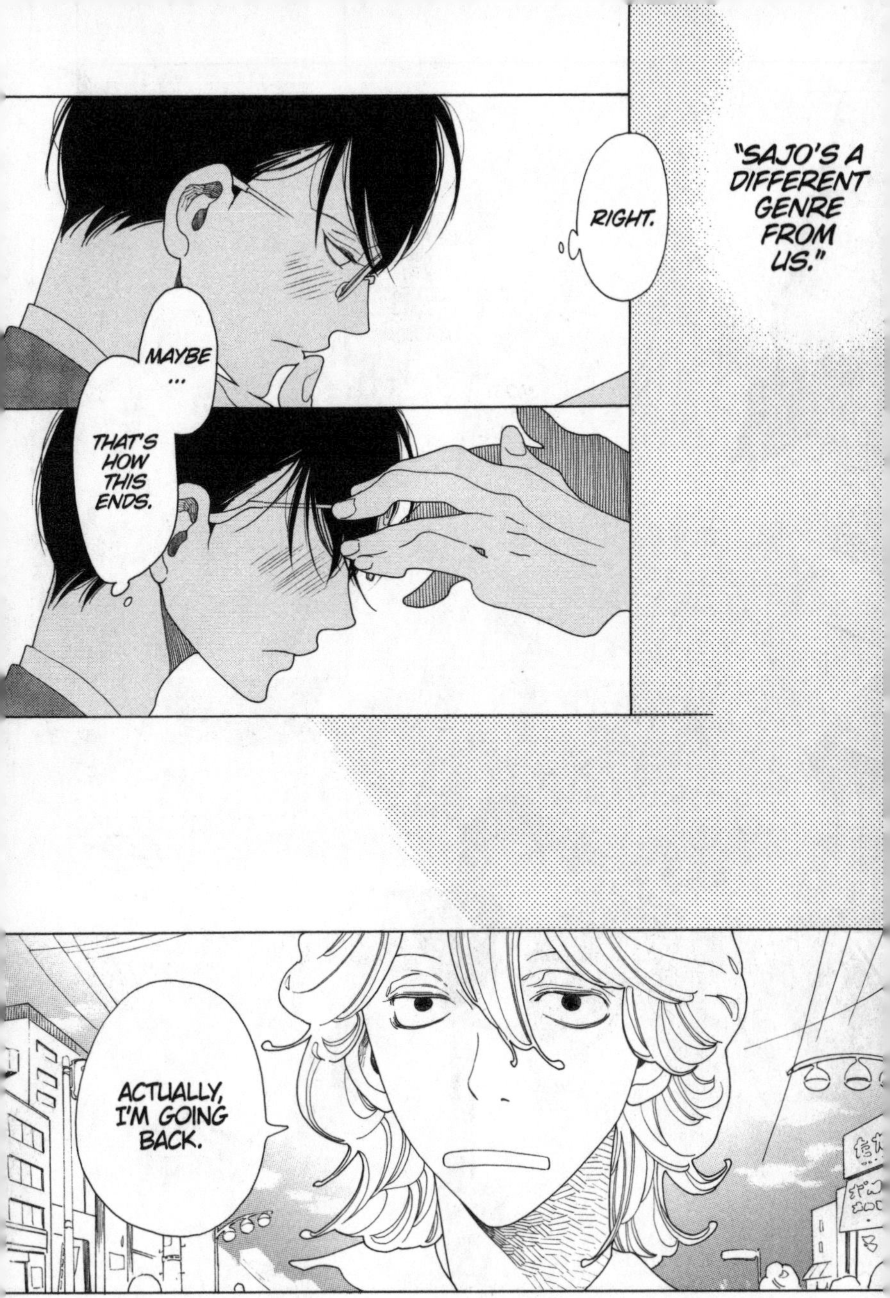
"SAJO'S A DIFFERENT GENRE FROM US."
RIGHT.
MAYBE ...
THAT'S HOW THIS ENDS.
ACTUALLY, I'M GOING BACK.

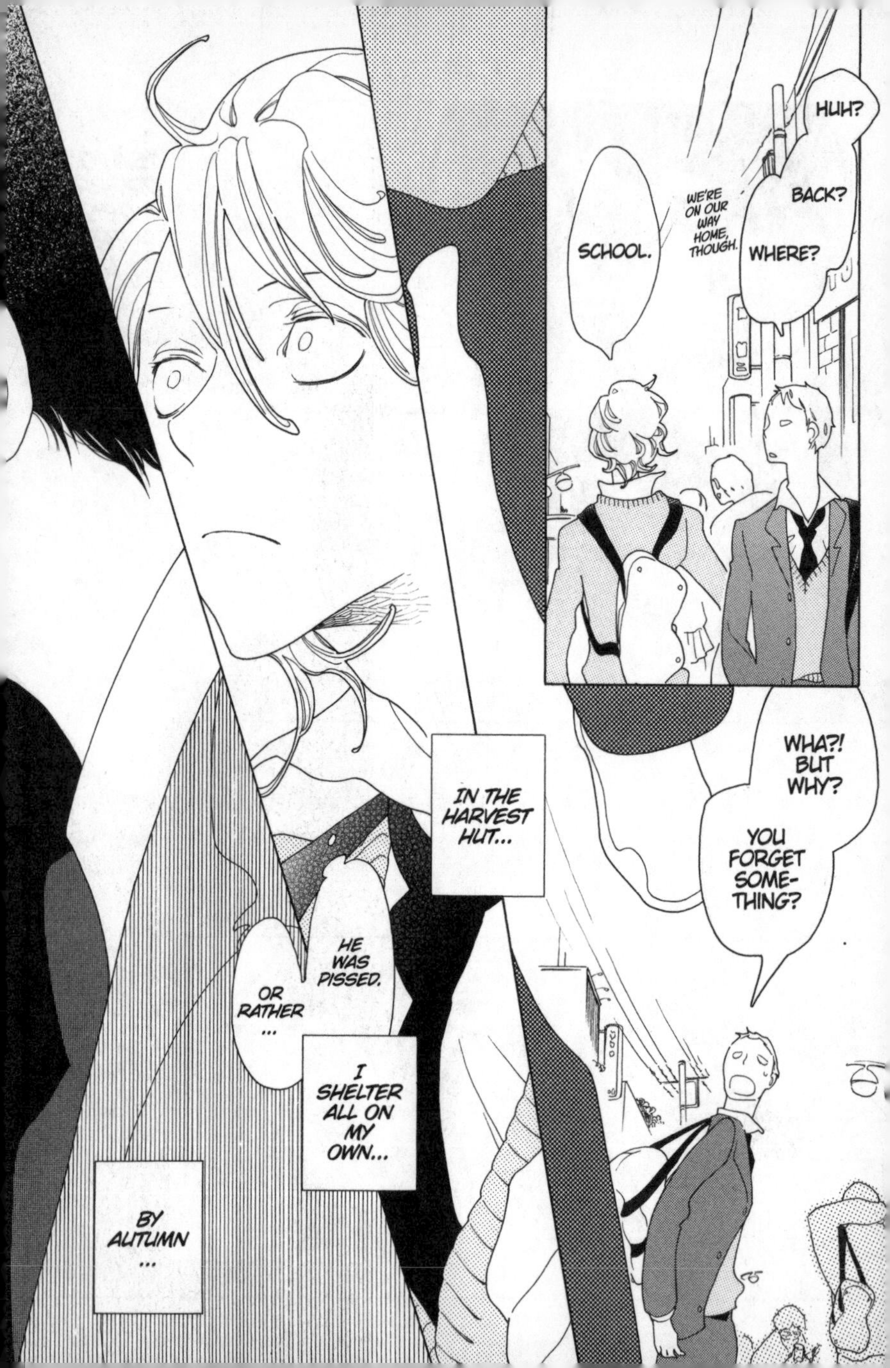
HUH?
BACK?
WHERE?
WE'RE ON OUR WAY HOME, THOUGH.
SCHOOL.
WHA?! BUT WHY?
YOU FORGET SOME-THING?
IN THE HARVEST HUT...
HE WAS PISSED.
OR RATHER ...
I SHELTER ALL ON MY OWN...
BY AUTUMN ...

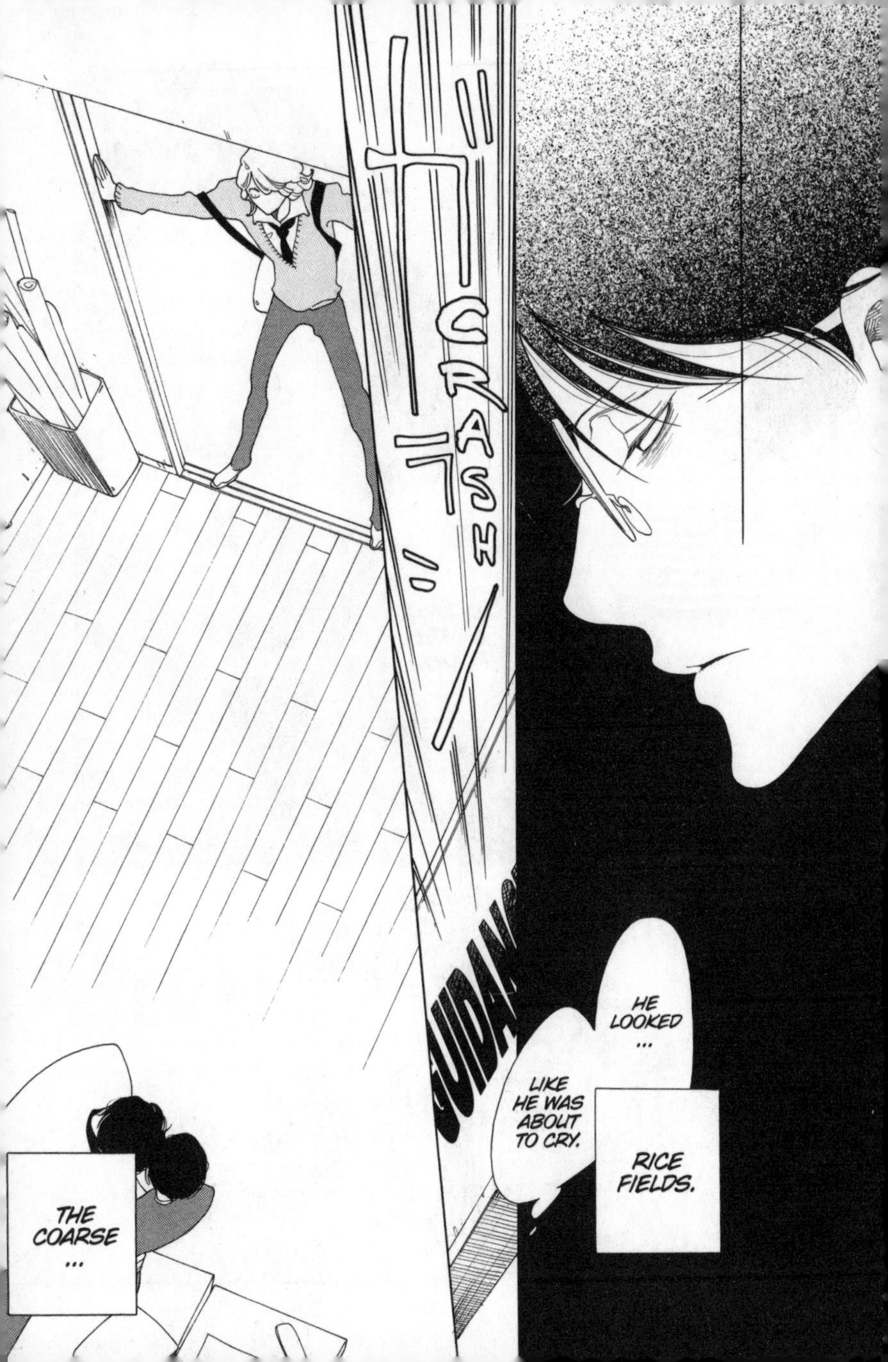
HE LOOKED ...
LIKE HE WAS ABOUT TO CRY.
RICE FIELDS.
CRASH
THE COARSE ...

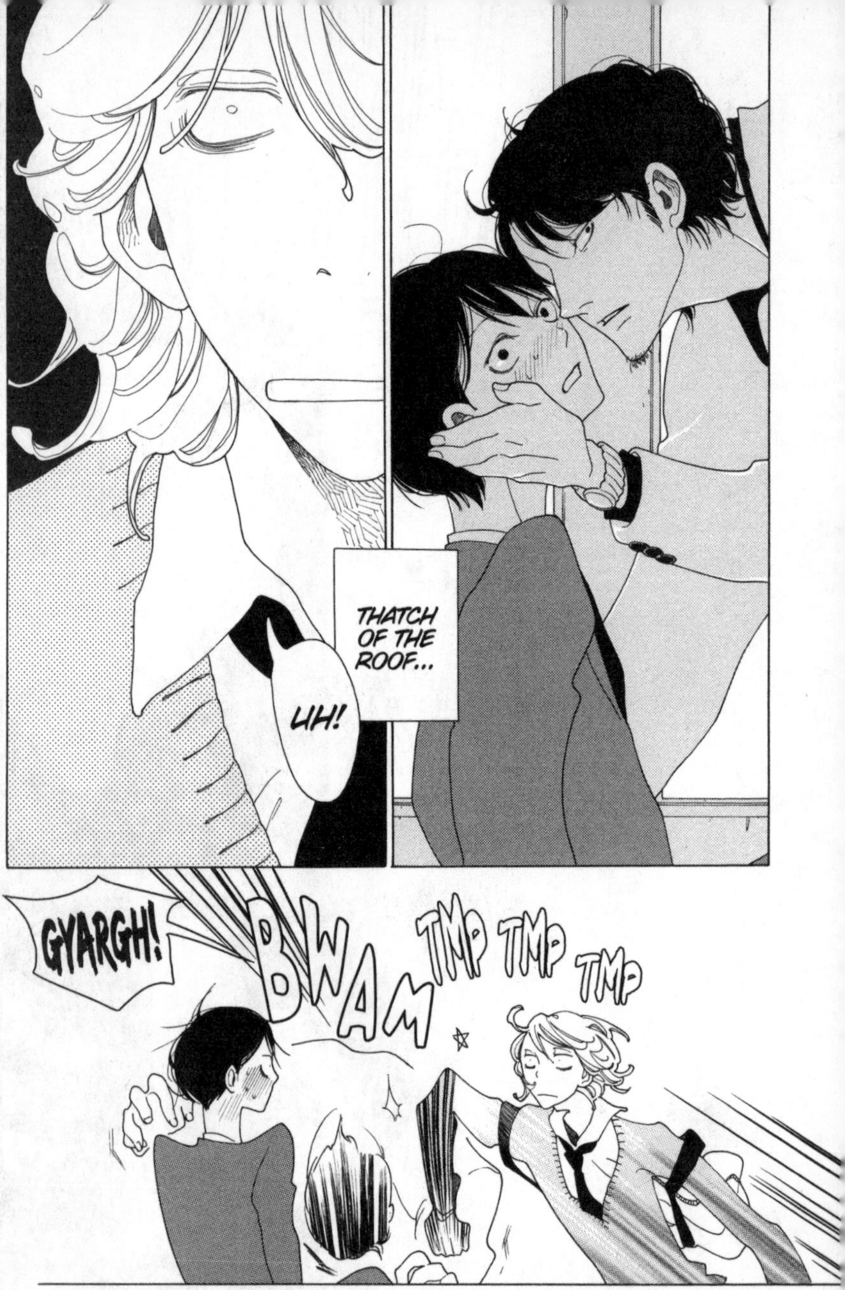
THATCH OF THE ROOF...
UH!
GYARGH!
BWAM
TMP TMP TMP

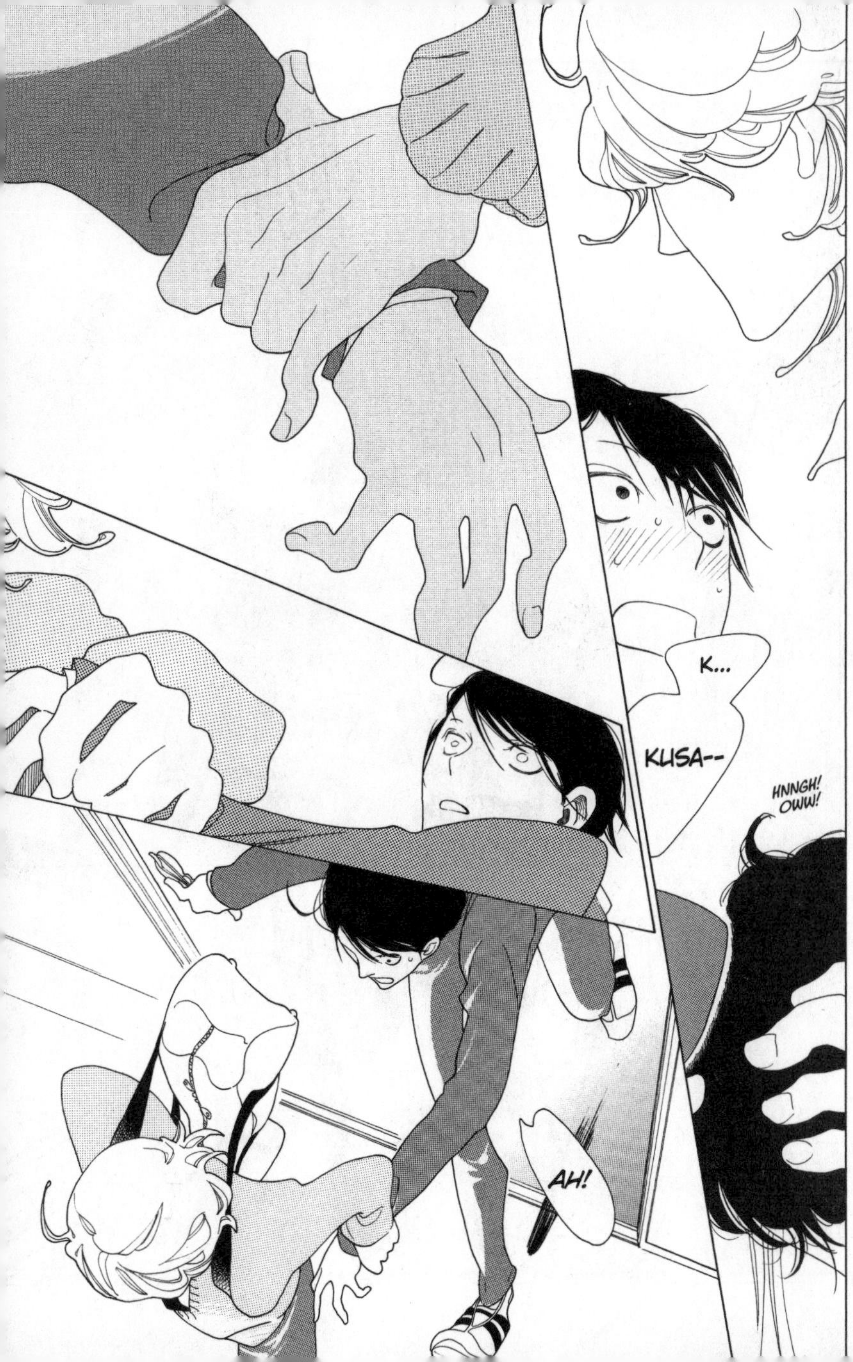
K...
KUSA--
HNNGH! OWW!
AH!

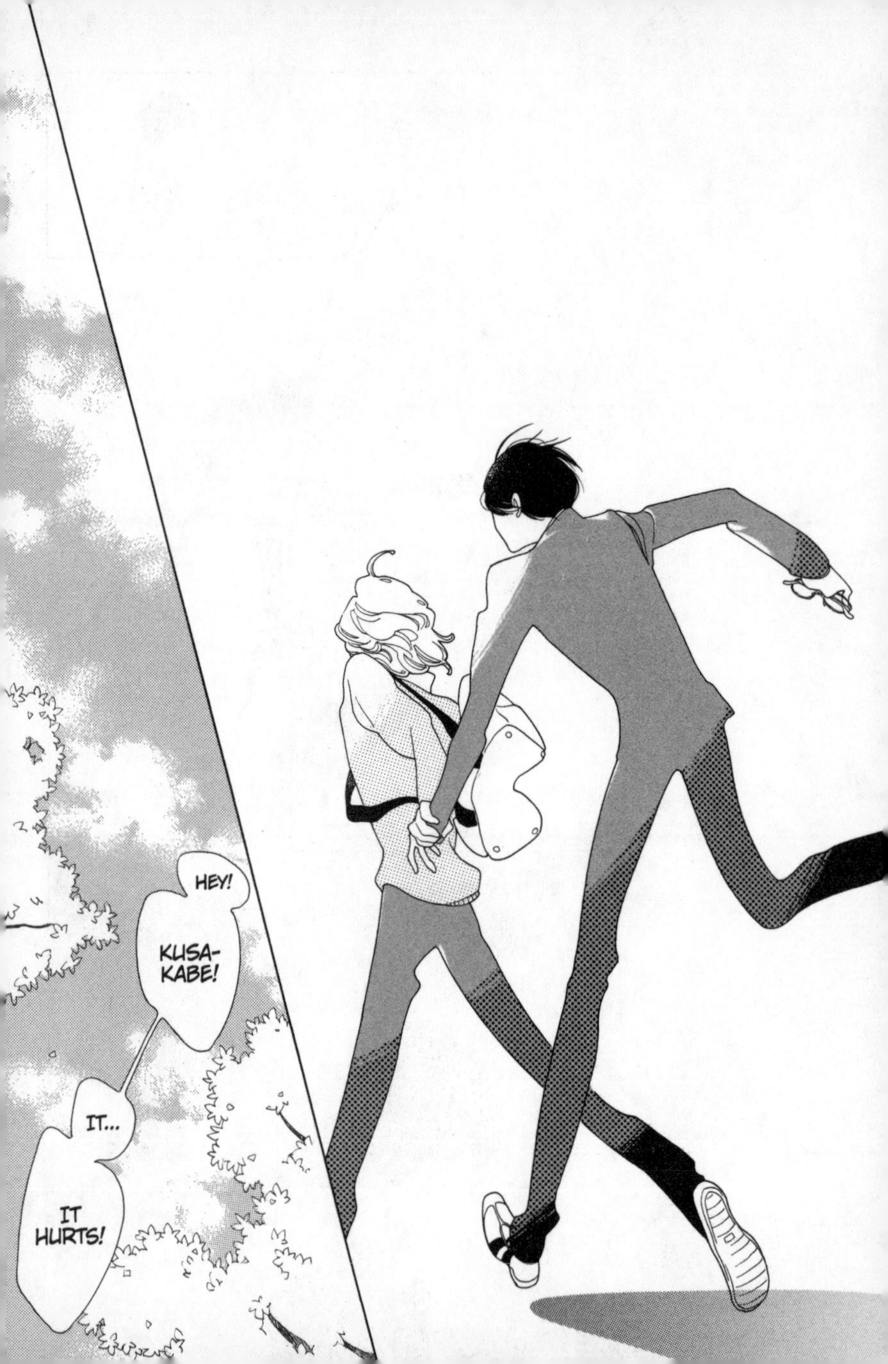
HEY!
KUSA-KABE!
IT...
IT HURTS!

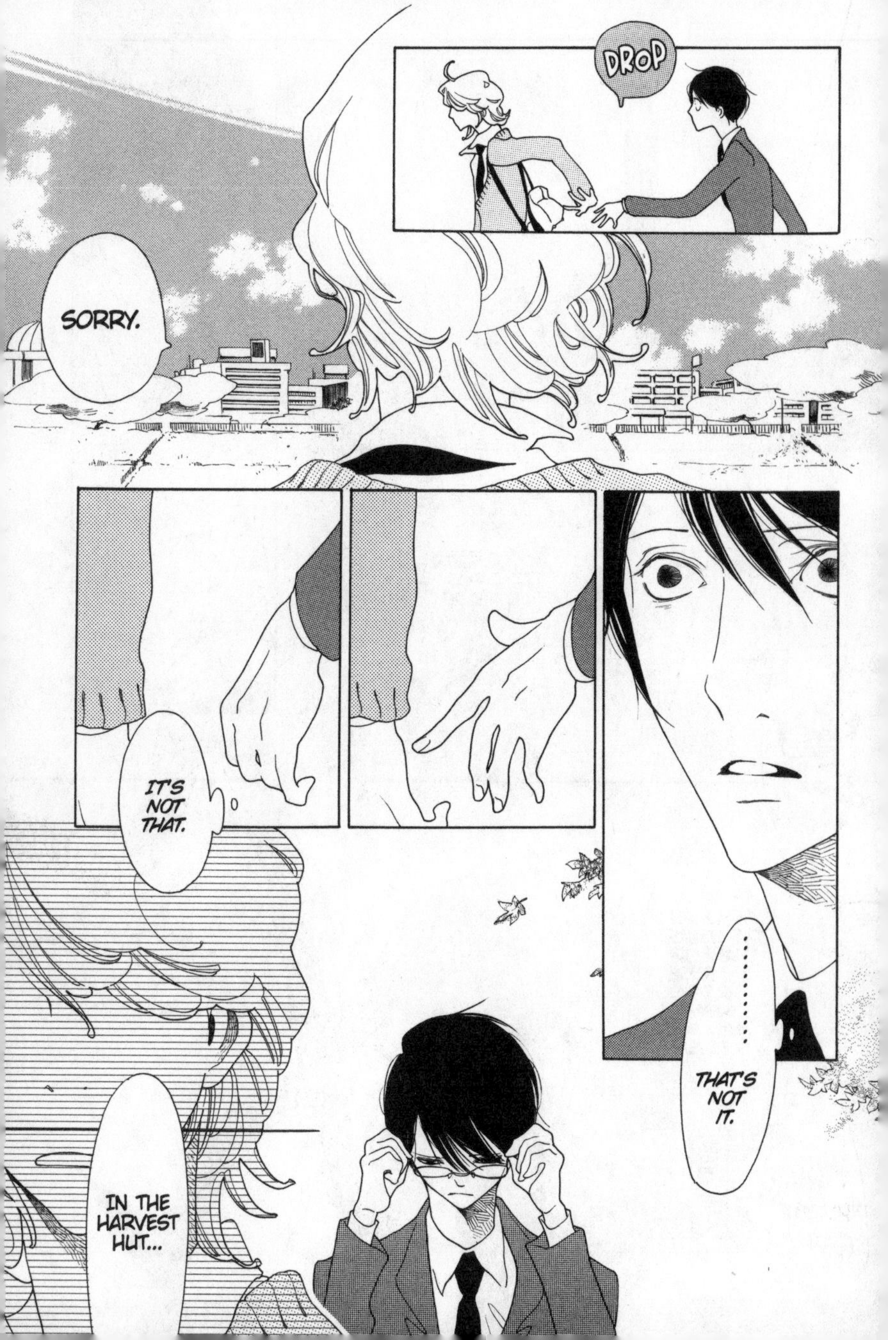
DROP
SORRY.
......
IT'S NOT THAT.
THAT'S NOT IT.
IN THE HARVEST HUT...

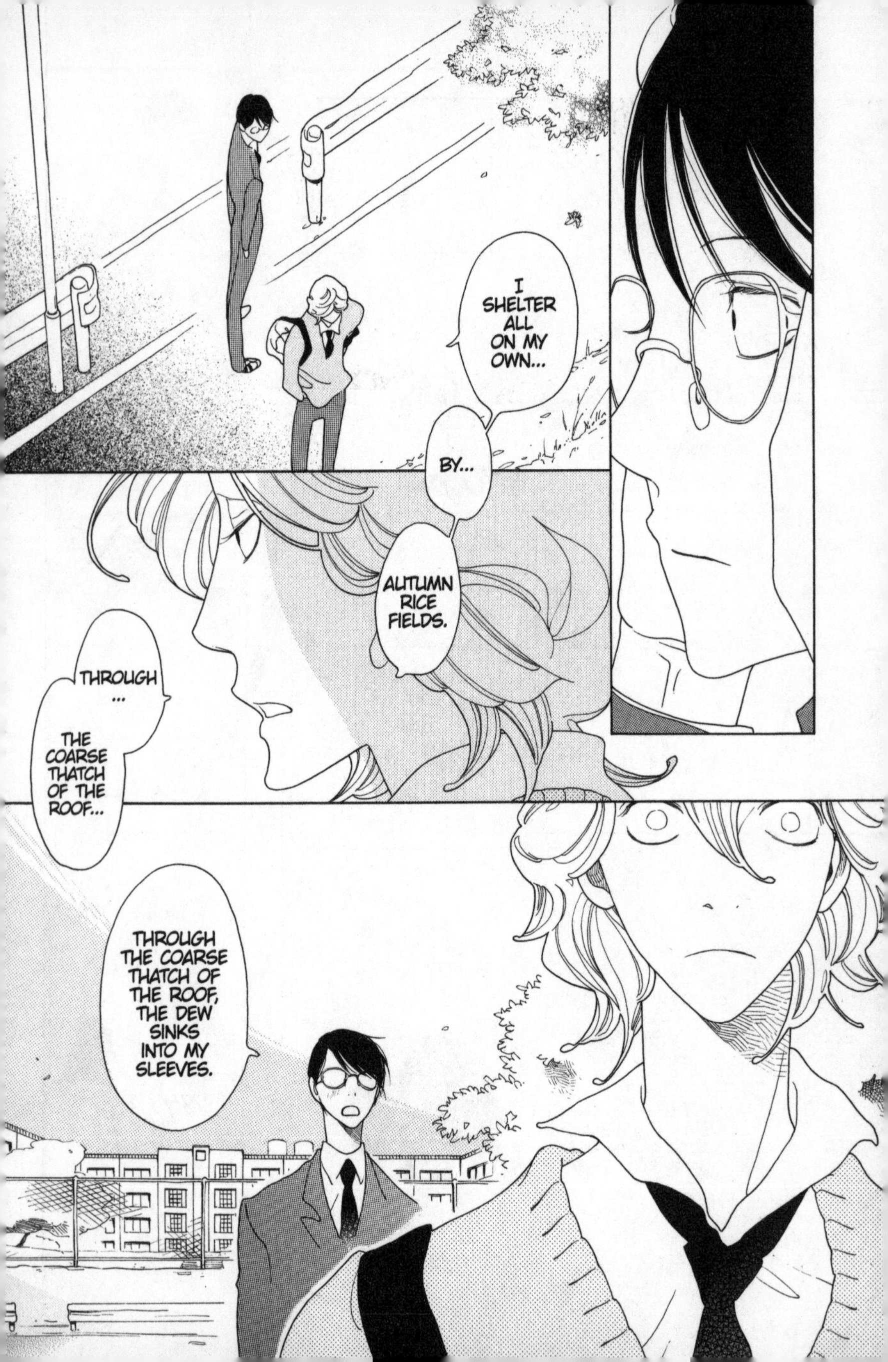
I SHELTER ALL ON MY OWN...
BY...
AUTUMN RICE FIELDS.
THROUGH ...
THE COARSE THATCH OF THE ROOF...
THROUGH THE COARSE THATCH OF THE ROOF, THE DEW SINKS INTO MY SLEEVES.

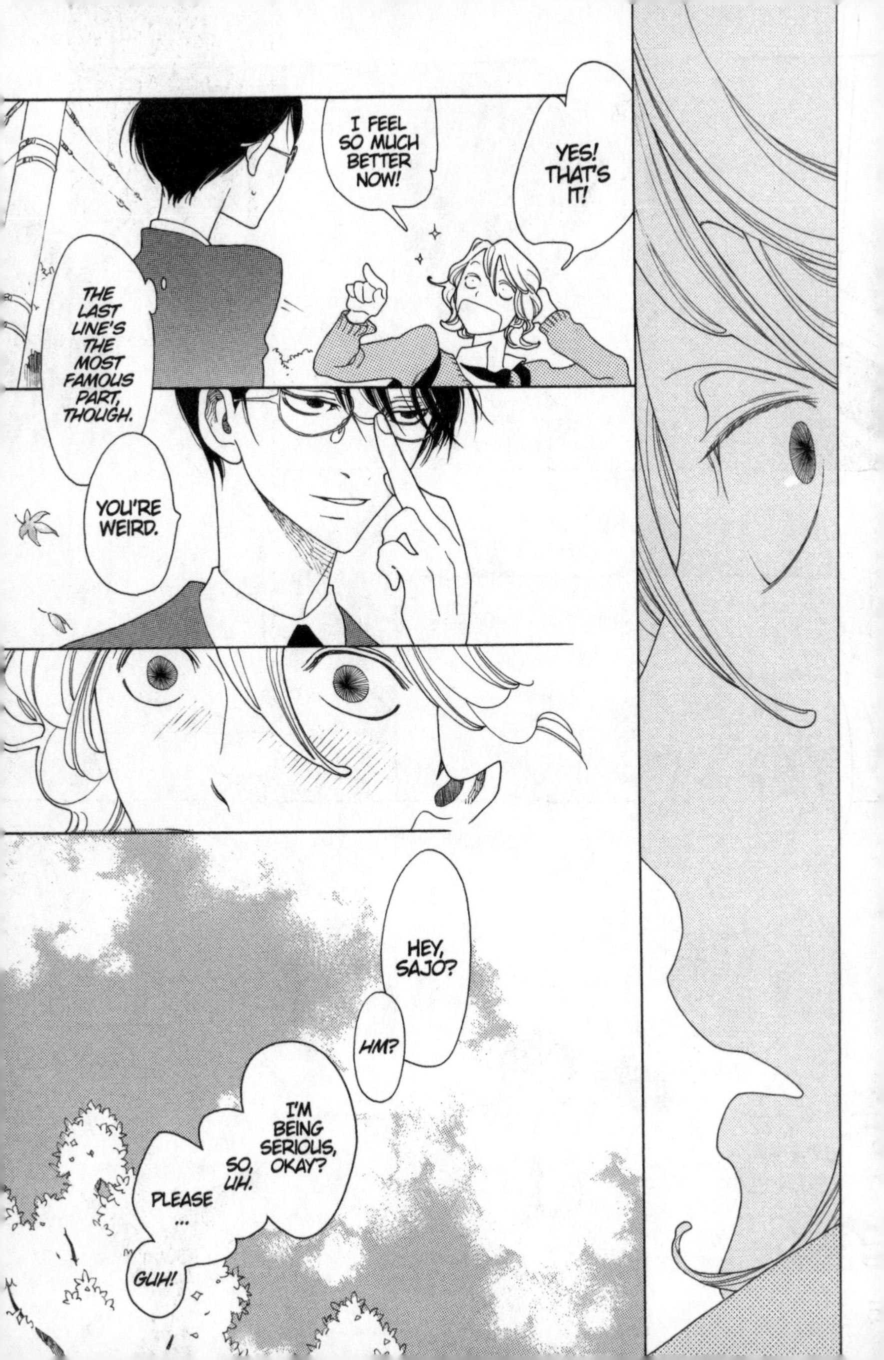
YES! THAT'S IT!
I FEEL SO MUCH BETTER NOW!
THE LAST LINE'S THE MOST FAMOUS PART, THOUGH.
YOU'RE WEIRD.
HEY, SAJO?
HM?
I'M BEING SERIOUS, OKAY?
SO, UH.
PLEASE ...
GUH!

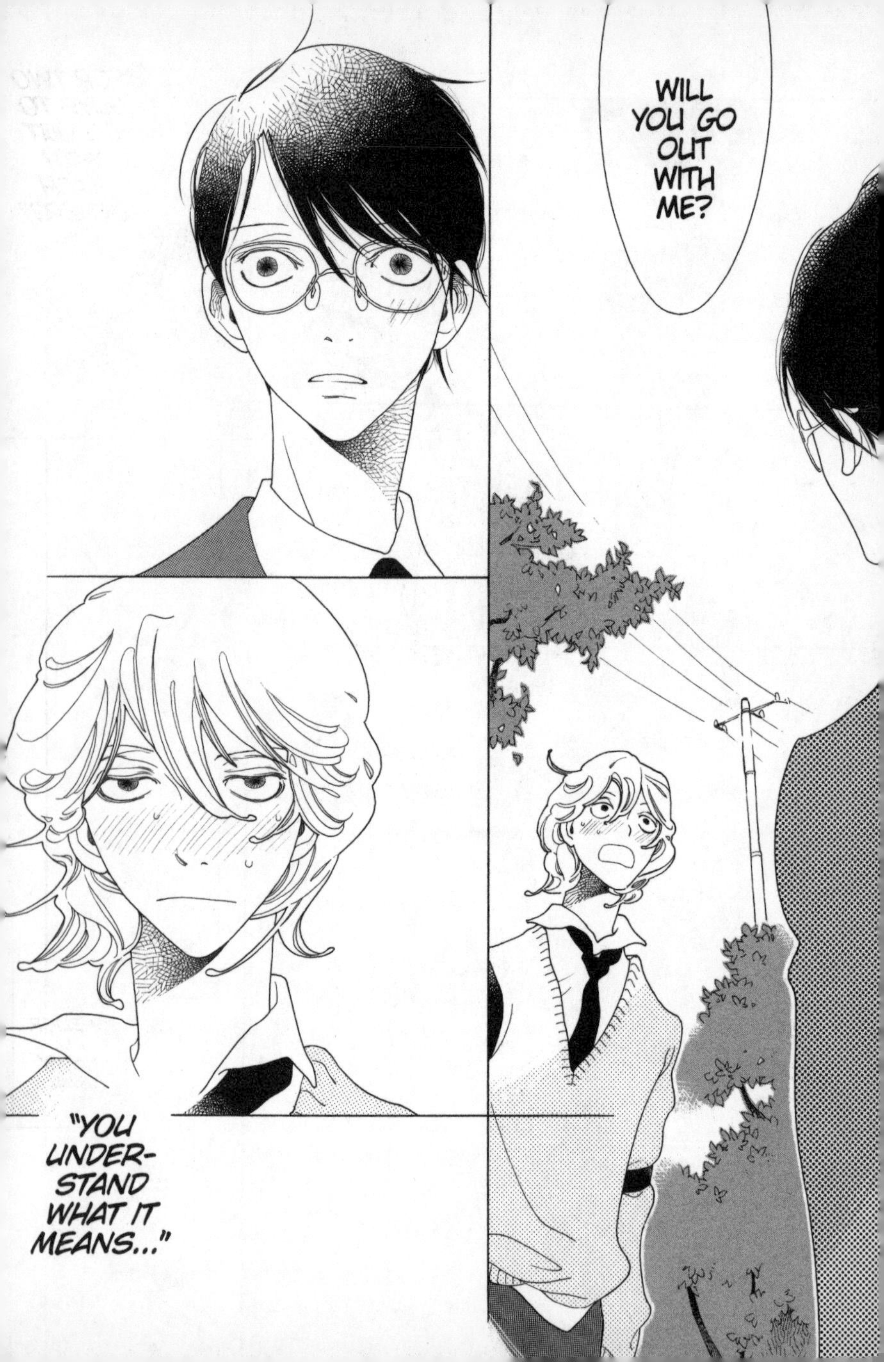
WILL YOU GO OUT WITH ME?
"YOU UNDER-STAND WHAT IT MEANS..."

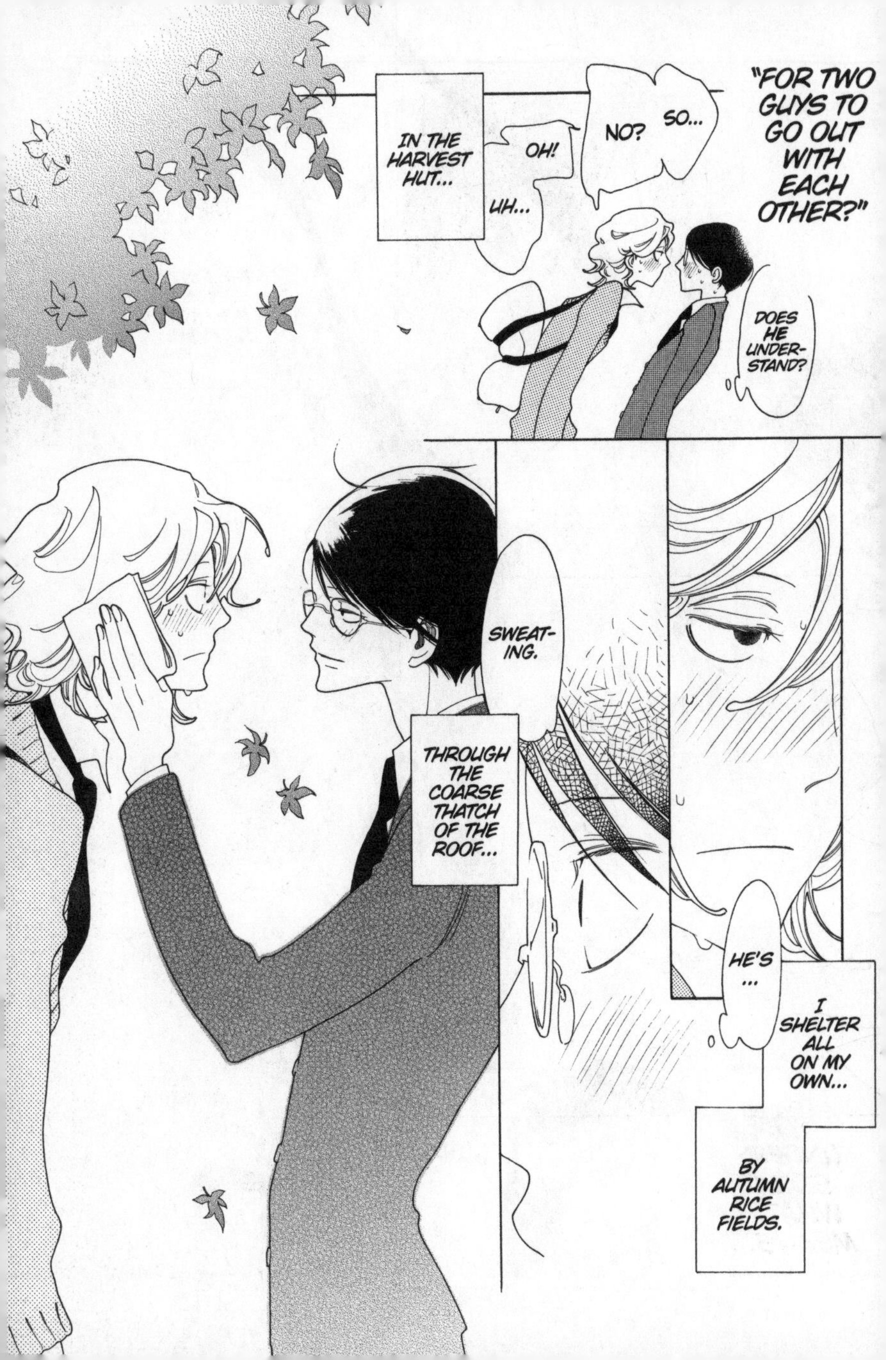
"FOR TWO GUYS TO GO OUT WITH EACH OTHER?"
SO... NO?
OH! UH...
IN THE HARVEST HUT...
DOES HE UNDERSTAND?
HE'S ...
I SHELTER ALL ON MY OWN...
BY AUTUMN RICE FIELDS.
SWEATING.
THROUGH THE COARSE THATCH OF THE ROOF...

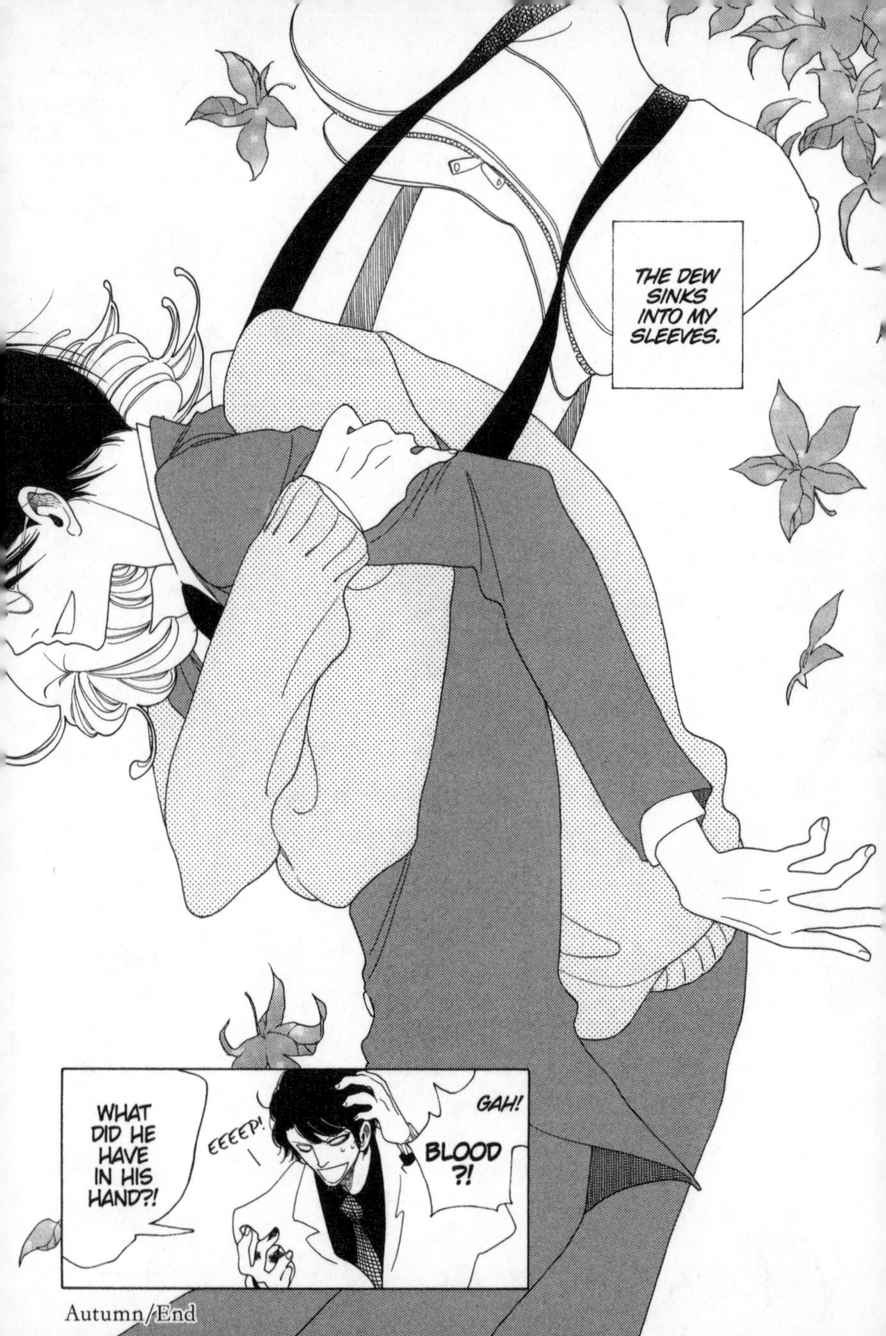
THE DEW SINKS INTO MY SLEEVES.
GAH!
BLOOD ?!
EEEEP!
WHAT DID HE HAVE IN HIS HAND?!

Autumn/End

Classmates

Intermission

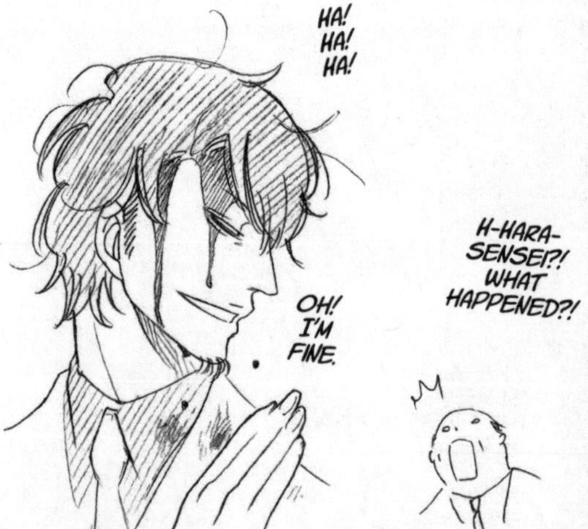
HA! HA! HA!
H-HARA-SENSEI?! WHAT HAPPENED?!
OH! I'M FINE.

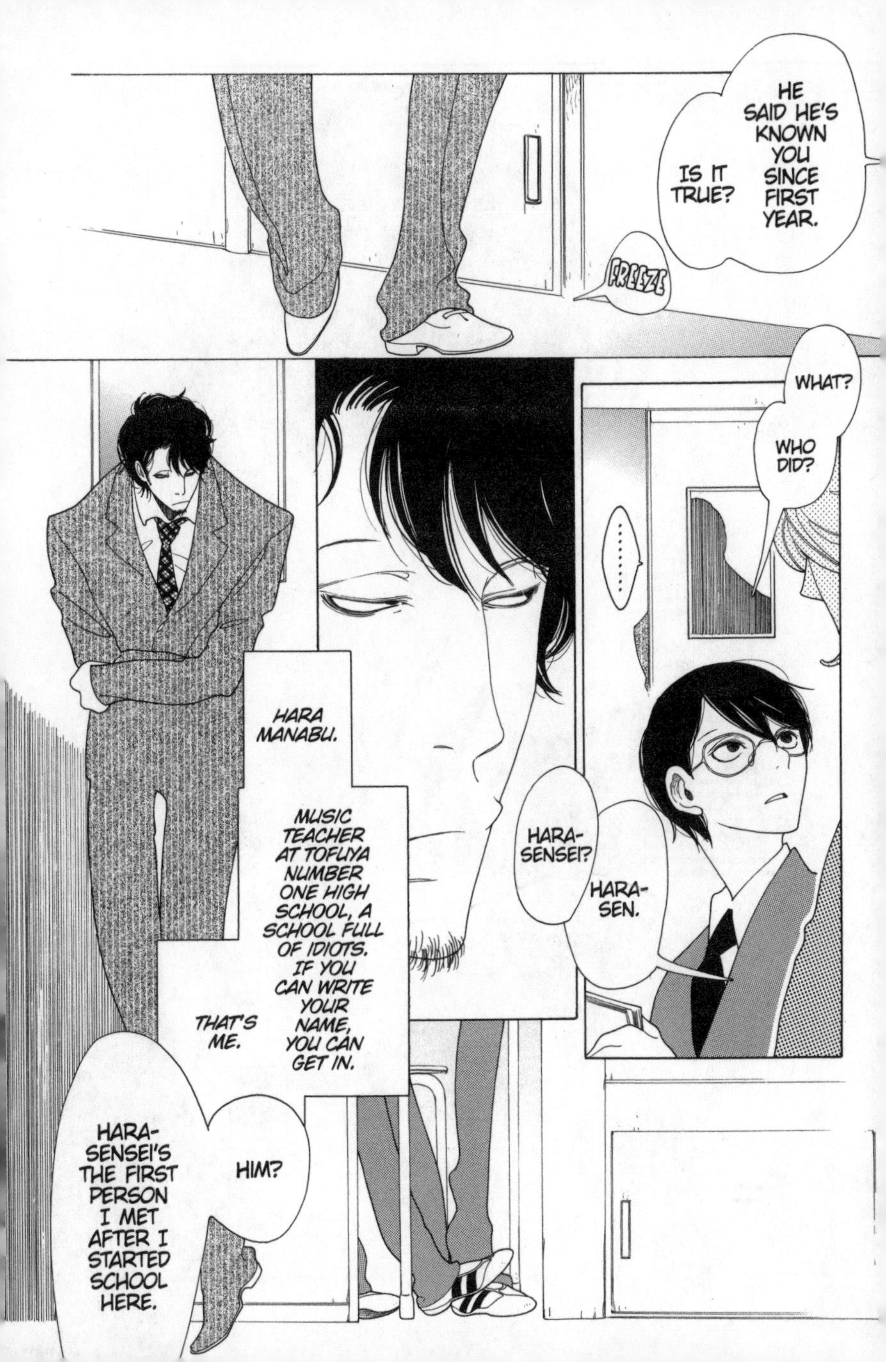
HE SAID HE'S KNOWN YOU SINCE FIRST YEAR.
IS IT TRUE?
FREEZE
WHAT?
WHO DID?
......
HARA-SENSEI?
HARA-SEN.
HARA MANABU.
MUSIC TEACHER AT TOFUYA NUMBER ONE HIGH SCHOOL, A SCHOOL FULL OF IDIOTS. IF YOU CAN WRITE YOUR NAME, YOU CAN GET IN.
THAT'S ME.
HIM?
HARA-SENSEI'S THE FIRST PERSON I MET AFTER I STARTED SCHOOL HERE.

[His First]

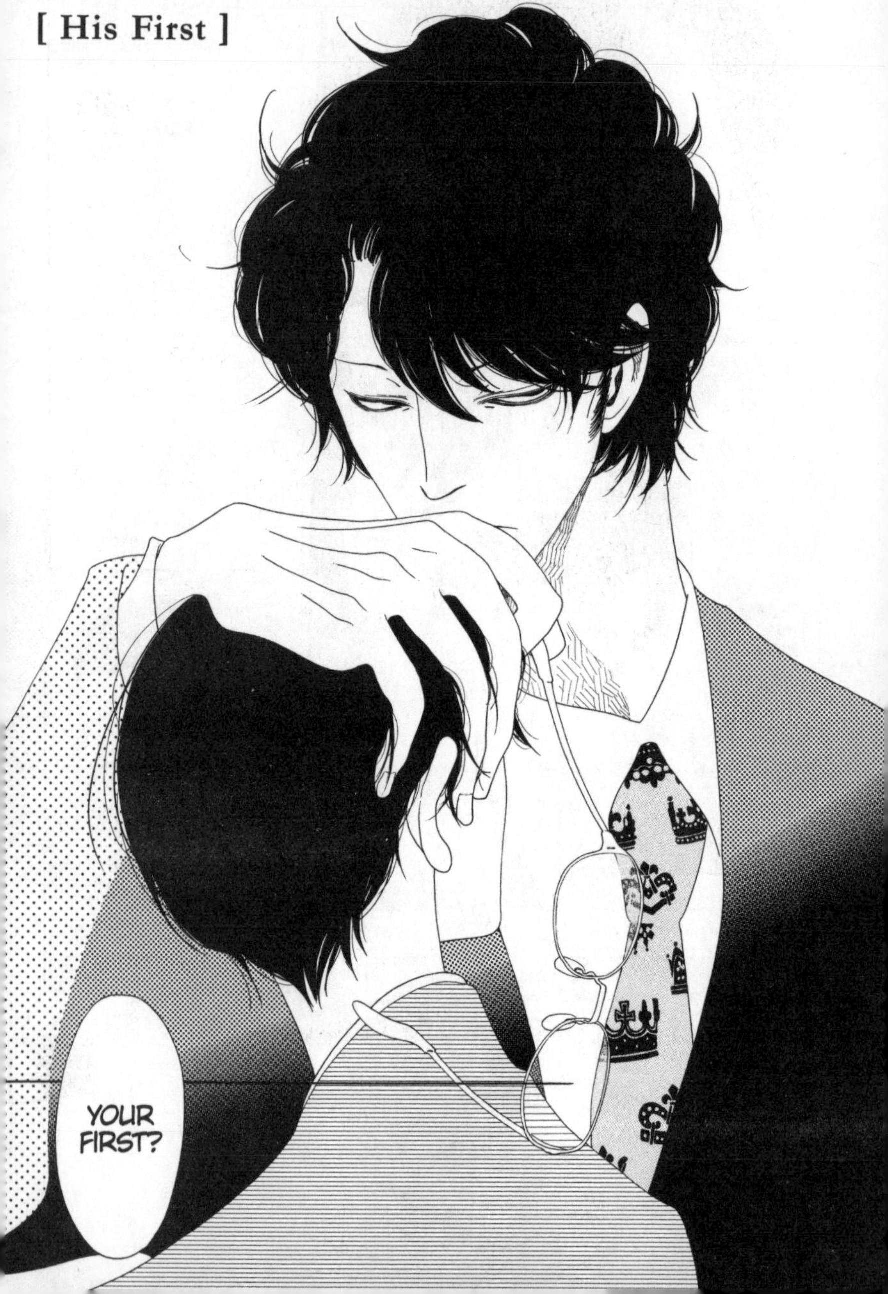
YOUR FIRST?

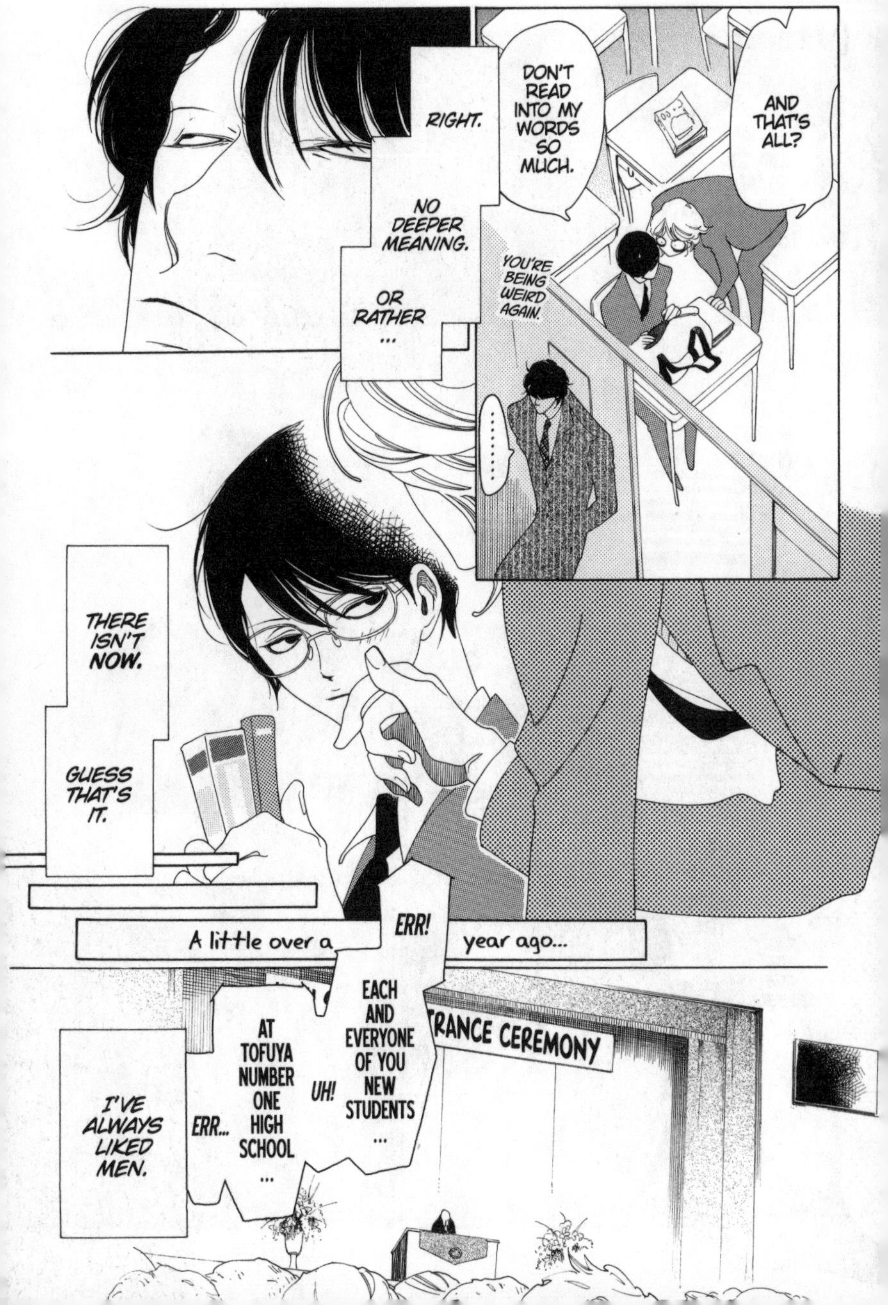
AND THAT'S ALL?
DON'T READ INTO MY WORDS SO MUCH.
YOU'RE BEING WEIRD AGAIN.
......
RIGHT.
NO DEEPER MEANING.
OR RATHER ...
THERE ISN'T NOW.
GUESS THAT'S IT.
A little over a year ago...
ERR!
TRANCE CEREMONY
EACH AND EVERYONE OF YOU NEW STUDENTS ...
UH!
AT TOFUYA NUMBER ONE HIGH SCHOOL ...
ERR...
I'VE ALWAYS LIKED MEN.

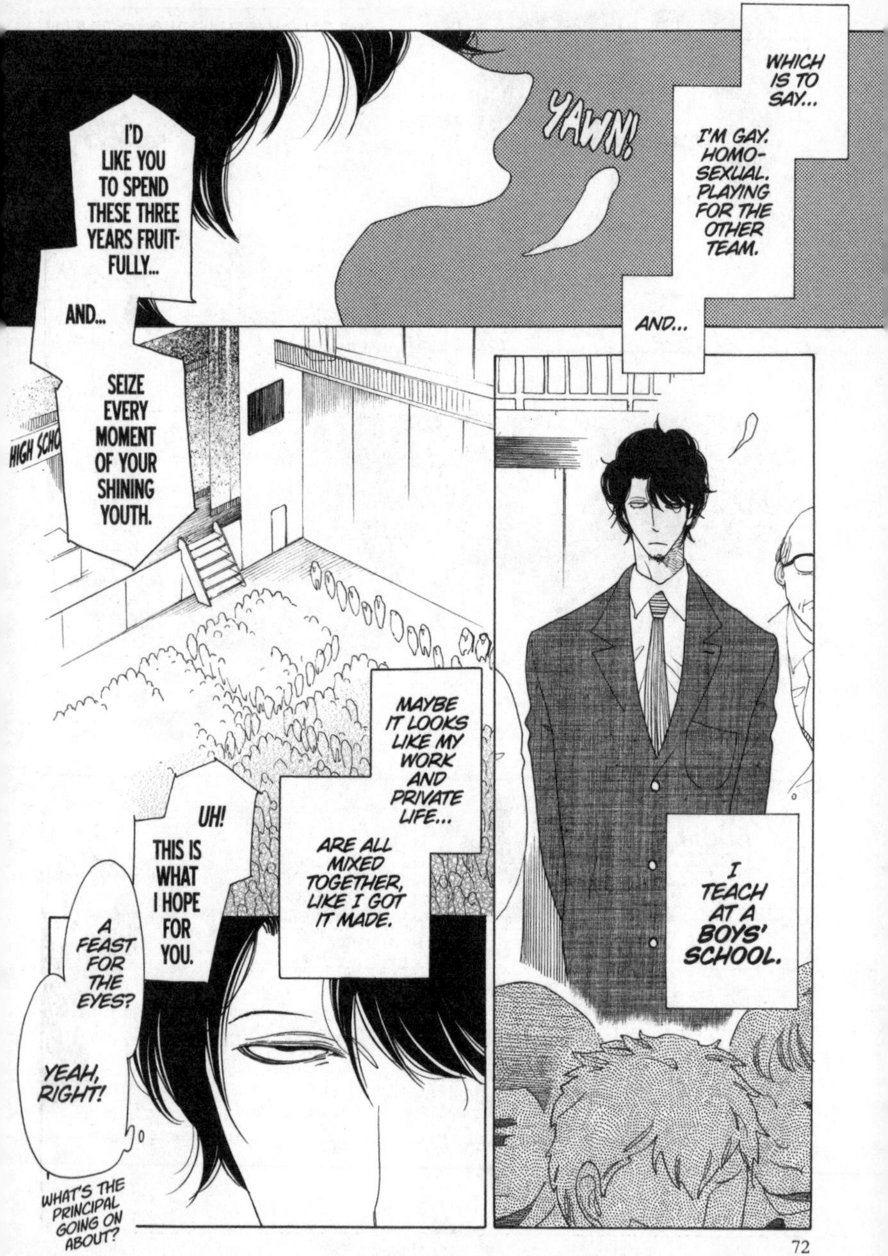
WHICH IS TO SAY...
I'M GAY. HOMO-SEXUAL. PLAYING FOR THE OTHER TEAM.
YAWN!
I'D LIKE YOU TO SPEND THESE THREE YEARS FRUIT-FULLY...
AND...
I TEACH AT A BOYS' SCHOOL.
AND...
SEIZE EVERY MOMENT OF YOUR SHINING YOUTH.
HIGH SCHO
MAYBE IT LOOKS LIKE MY WORK AND PRIVATE LIFE...
ARE ALL MIXED TOGETHER, LIKE I GOT IT MADE.
UH! THIS IS WHAT I HOPE FOR YOU.
A FEAST FOR THE EYES?
YEAH, RIGHT!
WHAT'S THE PRINCIPAL GOING ON ABOUT?

SPOT THE ERROR. (ANSWER AT THE END OF THE BOOK.)

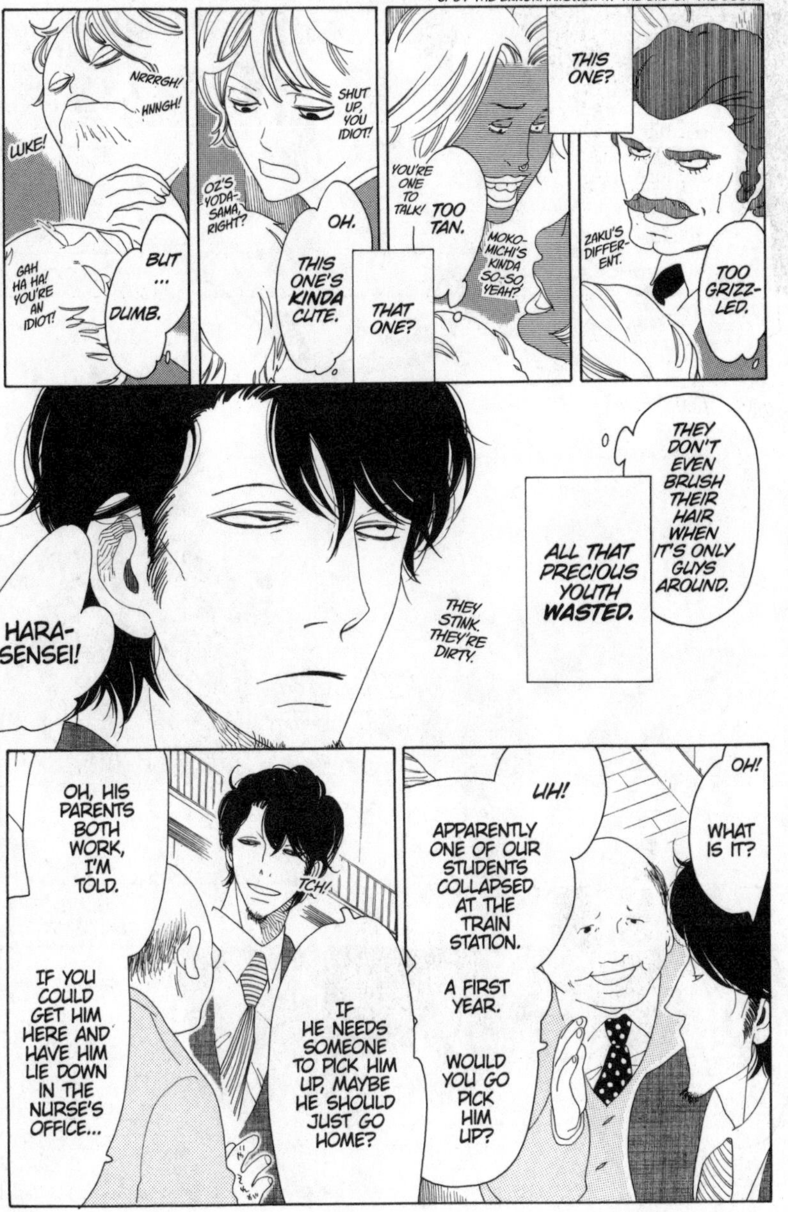
THIS ONE?
TOO GRIZZ-LED.
ZAKU'S DIFFER-ENT.
YOU'RE ONE TO TALK!
TOO TAN.
MOKO-MICHI'S KINDA SO-SO, YEAH?
THAT ONE?
SHUT UP, YOU IDIOT!
OZ'S YODA-SAMA, RIGHT?
OH.
THIS ONE'S KINDA CUTE.
NRRRGH!
HNNGH!
LUKE!
BUT ... DUMB.
GAH HA HA! YOU'RE AN IDIOT!
THEY DON'T EVEN BRUSH THEIR HAIR WHEN IT'S ONLY GUYS AROUND.
ALL THAT PRECIOUS YOUTH WASTED.
THEY STINK. THEY'RE DIRTY.
HARA-SENSEI!
OH!
WHAT IS IT?
UH!
APPARENTLY ONE OF OUR STUDENTS COLLAPSED AT THE TRAIN STATION.
A FIRST YEAR.
WOULD YOU GO PICK HIM UP?
OH, HIS PARENTS BOTH WORK, I'M TOLD.
TCH!
IF HE NEEDS SOMEONE TO PICK HIM UP, MAYBE HE SHOULD JUST GO HOME?
IF YOU COULD GET HIM HERE AND HAVE HIM LIE DOWN IN THE NURSE'S OFFICE...

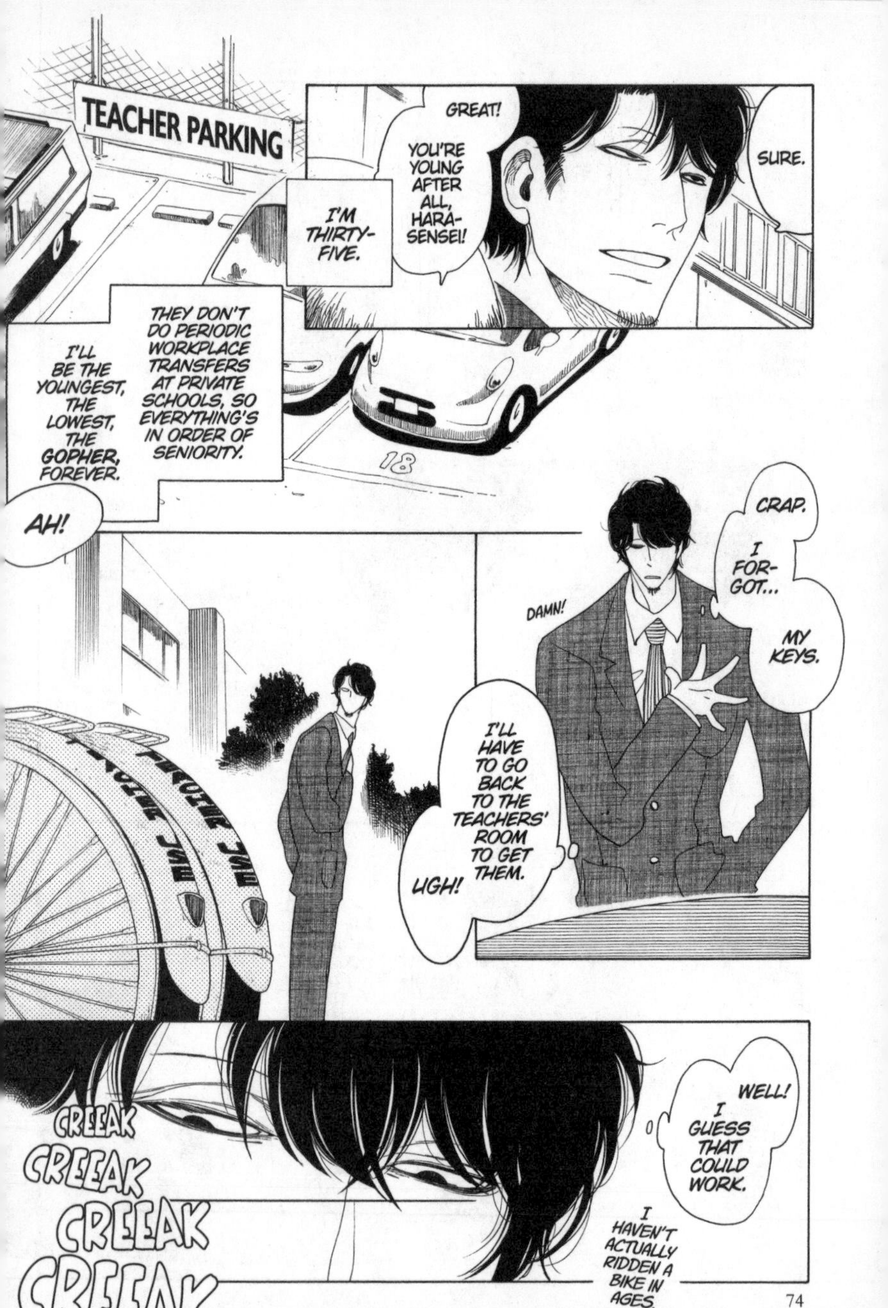
SURE.
GREAT!
YOU'RE YOUNG AFTER ALL, HARA-SENSEI!
I'M THIRTY-FIVE.
TEACHER PARKING
THEY DON'T DO PERIODIC WORKPLACE TRANSFERS AT PRIVATE SCHOOLS, SO EVERYTHING'S IN ORDER OF SENIORITY.
I'LL BE THE YOUNGEST, THE LOWEST, THE GOPHER, FOREVER.
18
AH!
CRAP.
I FORGOT...
MY KEYS.
DAMN!
I'LL HAVE TO GO BACK TO THE TEACHERS' ROOM TO GET THEM.
UGH!
WELL!
I GUESS THAT COULD WORK.
I HAVEN'T ACTUALLY RIDDEN A BIKE IN AGES.
CREEAK
CREEAK
CREEAK
CREEAK

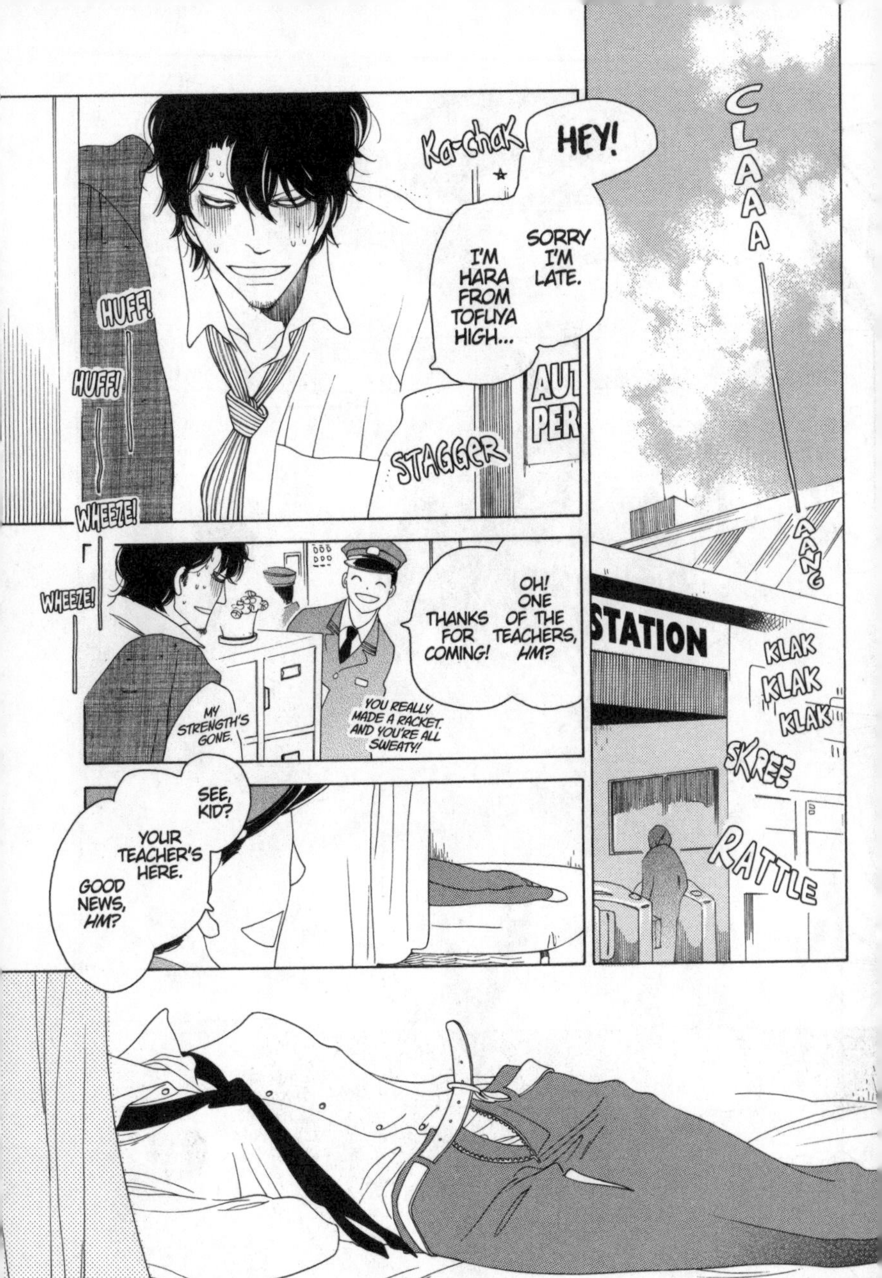
CLAAAAANG
STATION
KLAK KLAK KLAK
SKREE
RATTLE
Ka-chaK
HEY!
SORRY I'M LATE.
I'M HARA FROM TOFUYA HIGH...
STAGGER
HUFF!
HUFF!
WHEEZE!
WHEEZE!
OH! ONE OF THE TEACHERS, HM?
THANKS FOR COMING!
YOU REALLY MADE A RACKET. AND YOU'RE ALL SWEATY!
MY STRENGTH'S GONE.
SEE, KID?
YOUR TEACHER'S HERE.
GOOD NEWS, HM?

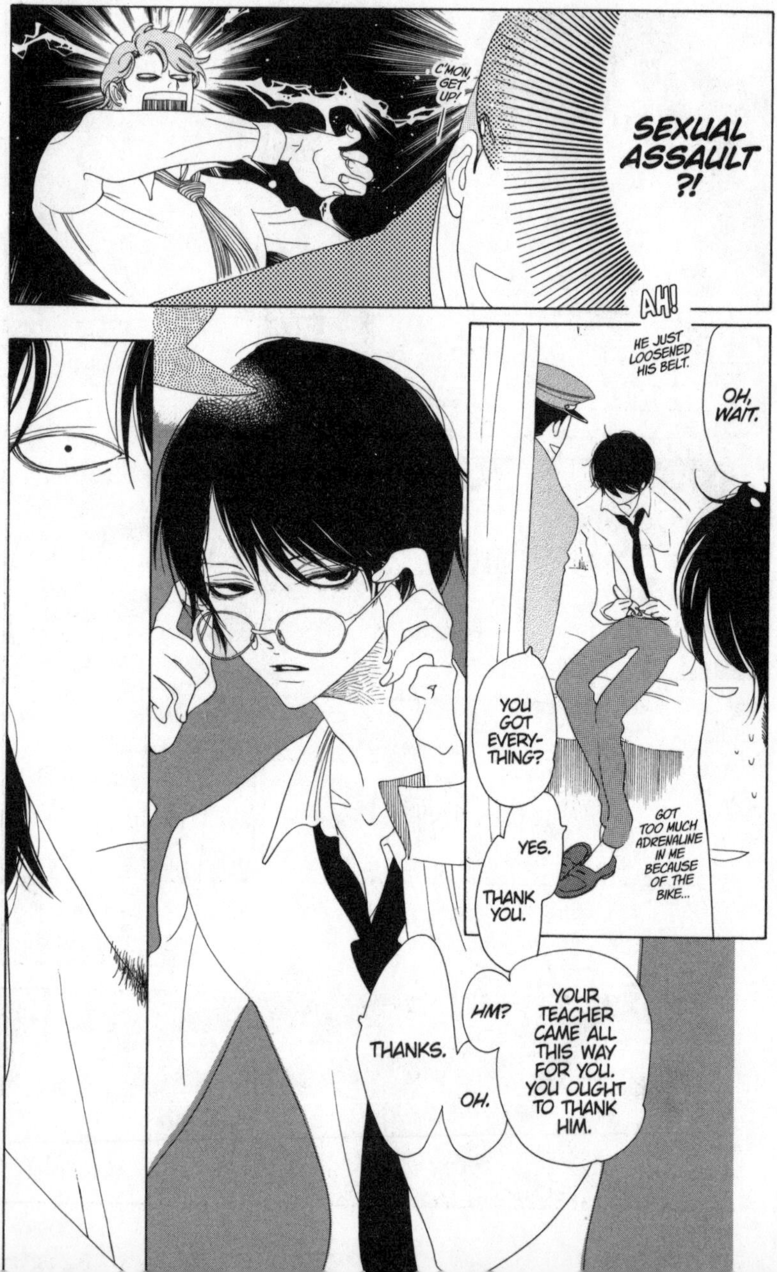
SEXUAL ASSAULT ?!
C'MON, GET UP!
AH!
OH, WAIT.
HE JUST LOOSENED HIS BELT.
GOT TOO MUCH ADRENALINE IN ME BECAUSE OF THE BIKE...
YOU GOT EVERYTHING?
YES.
THANK YOU.
YOUR TEACHER CAME ALL THIS WAY FOR YOU. YOU OUGHT TO THANK HIM.
HM?
OH.
THANKS.

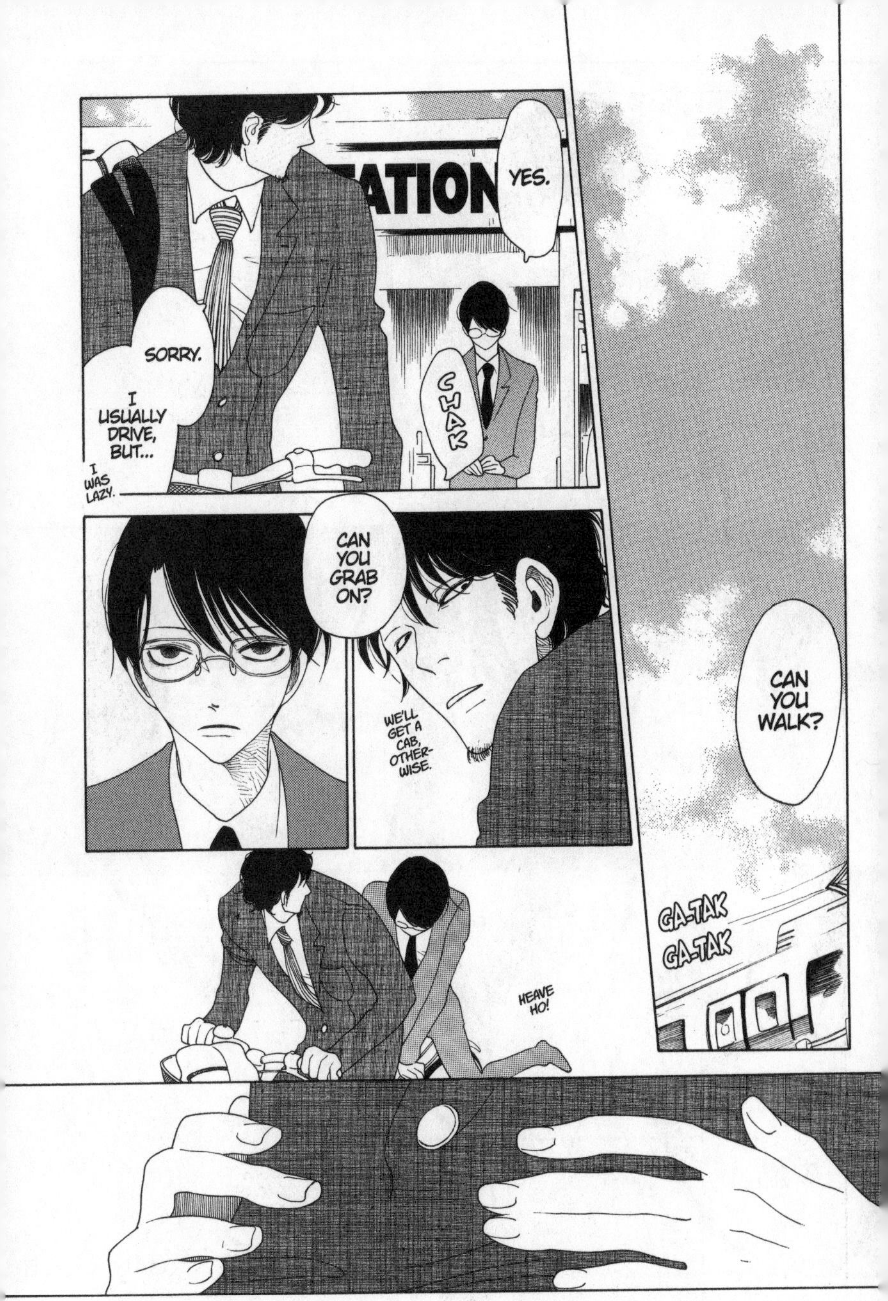
CAN YOU WALK?
GA-TAK GA-TAK
STATION
YES.
SORRY.
I USUALLY DRIVE, BUT...
I WAS LAZY.
CHAK
CAN YOU GRAB ON?
WE'LL GET A CAB, OTHERWISE.
HEAVE HO!

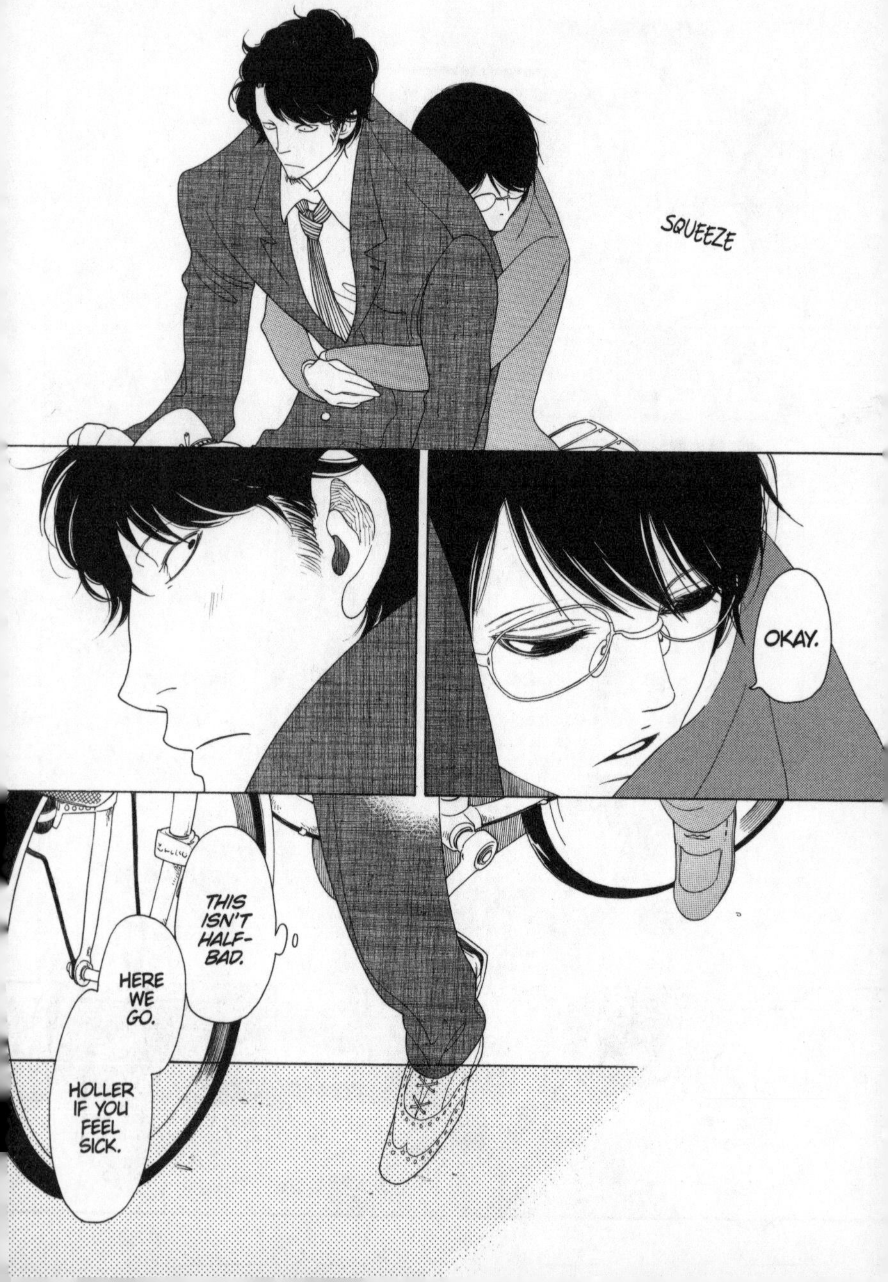
SQUEEZE
OKAY.
THIS ISN'T HALF-BAD.
HERE WE GO.
HOLLER IF YOU FEEL SICK.

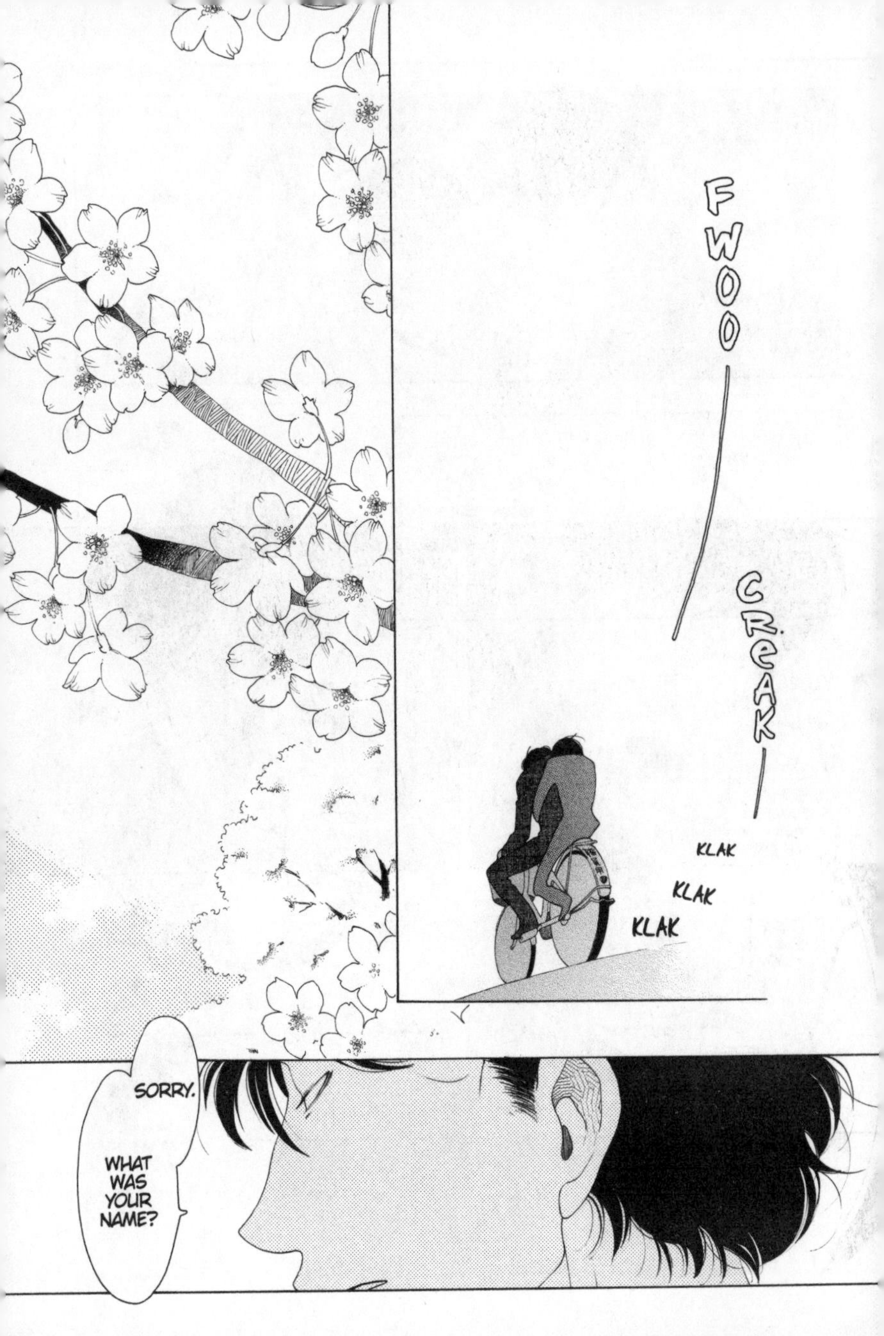
FWOO
CREAK
KLAK
KLAK
KLAK
SORRY.
WHAT WAS YOUR NAME?

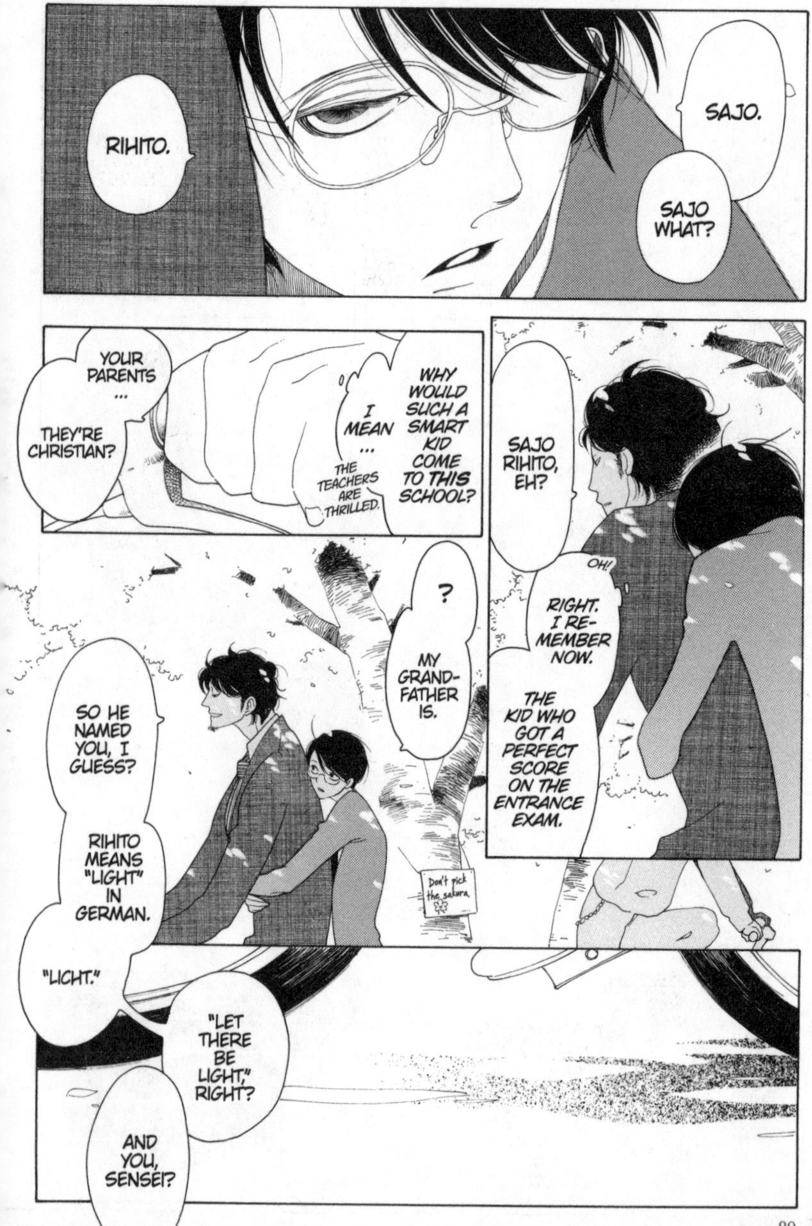
SAJO.
SAJO WHAT?
RIHITO.
SAJO RIHITO, EH?
OH!
RIGHT. I RE-MEMBER NOW.
THE KID WHO GOT A PERFECT SCORE ON THE ENTRANCE EXAM.
WHY WOULD SUCH A SMART KID COME TO THIS SCHOOL?
I MEAN ...
THE TEACHERS ARE THRILLED.
YOUR PARENTS ...
THEY'RE CHRISTIAN?
?
MY GRAND-FATHER IS.
SO HE NAMED YOU, I GUESS?
RIHITO MEANS "LIGHT" IN GERMAN.
Don't pick the sakura.
"LICHT."
"LET THERE BE LIGHT," RIGHT?
AND YOU, SENSEI?

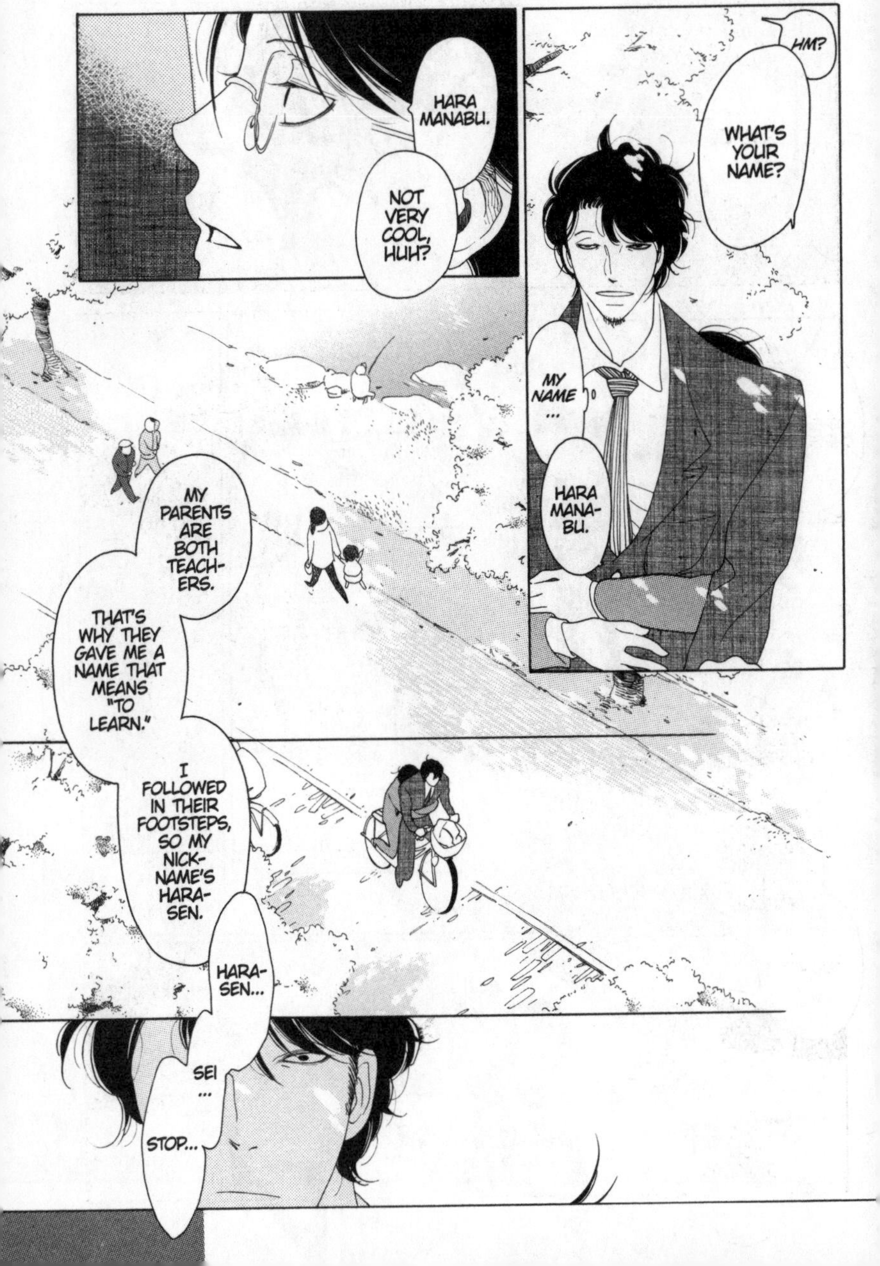
HM?
WHAT'S YOUR NAME?
MY NAME...
HARA MANABU.
HARA MANABU.
NOT VERY COOL, HUH?
MY PARENTS ARE BOTH TEACHERS.
THAT'S WHY THEY GAVE ME A NAME THAT MEANS "TO LEARN."
I FOLLOWED IN THEIR FOOTSTEPS, SO MY NICKNAME'S HARA-SEN.
HARA-SEN...
SEI...
STOP...

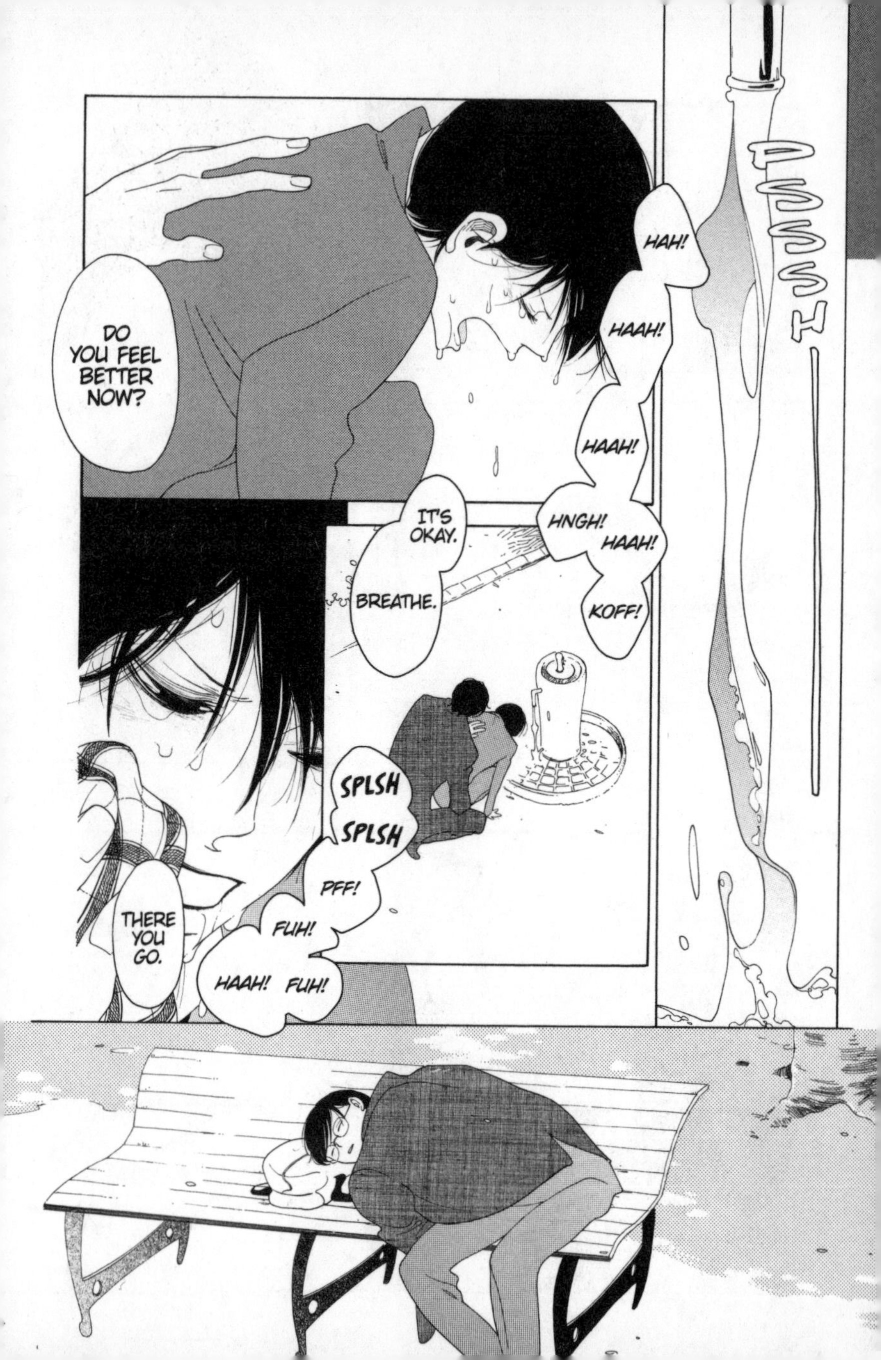
PSSSH—
HAH!
HAAH!
HAAH!
DO YOU FEEL BETTER NOW?
HNGH!
HAAH!
KOFF!
IT'S OKAY.
BREATHE.
SPLSH
SPLSH
PFF!
FUH!
FUH!
HAAH!
THERE YOU GO.

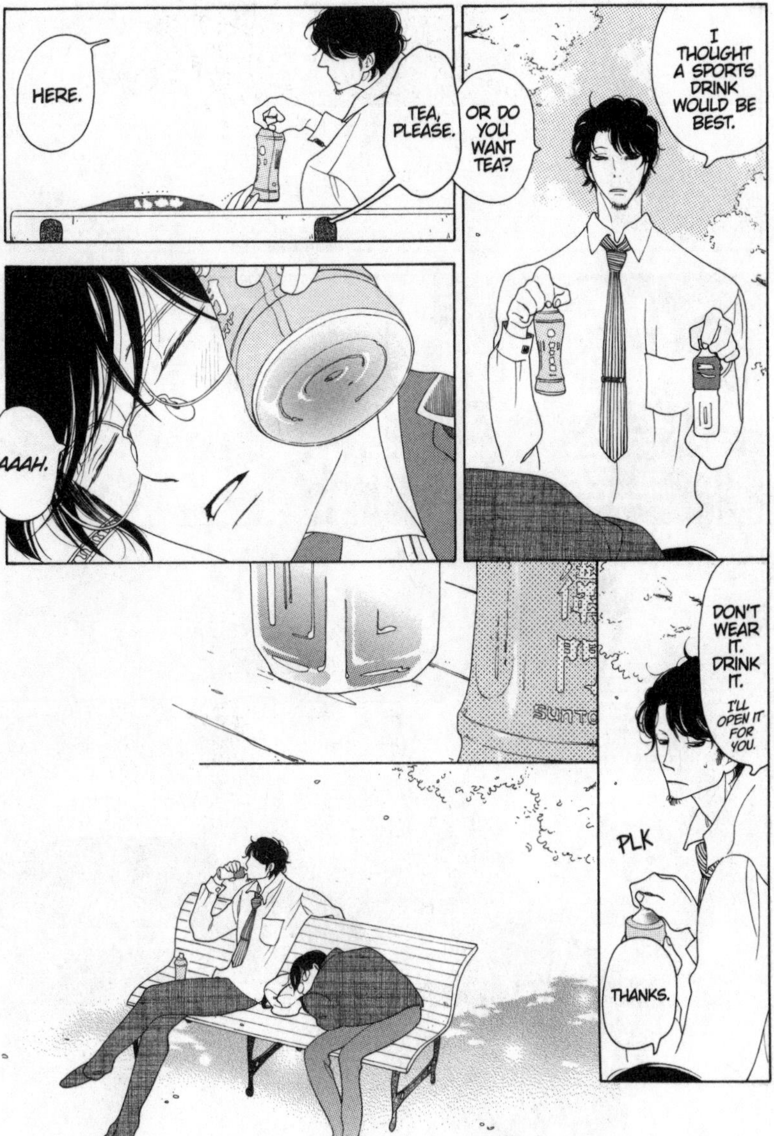
I THOUGHT A SPORTS DRINK WOULD BE BEST.
OR DO YOU WANT TEA?
TEA, PLEASE.
HERE.
AAAH.
DON'T WEAR IT. DRINK IT.
I'LL OPEN IT FOR YOU.
PLK
THANKS.

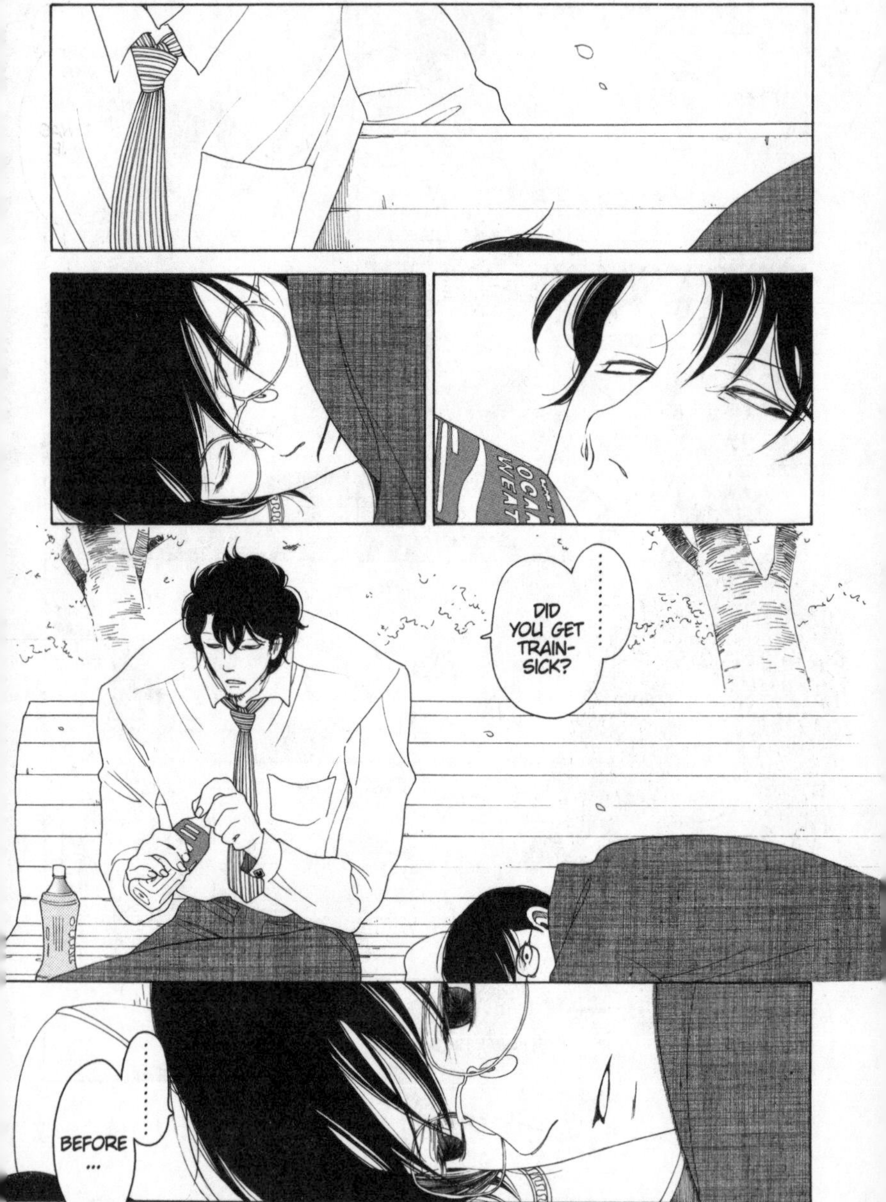
......
DID YOU GET TRAIN-SICK?
......
BEFORE ...

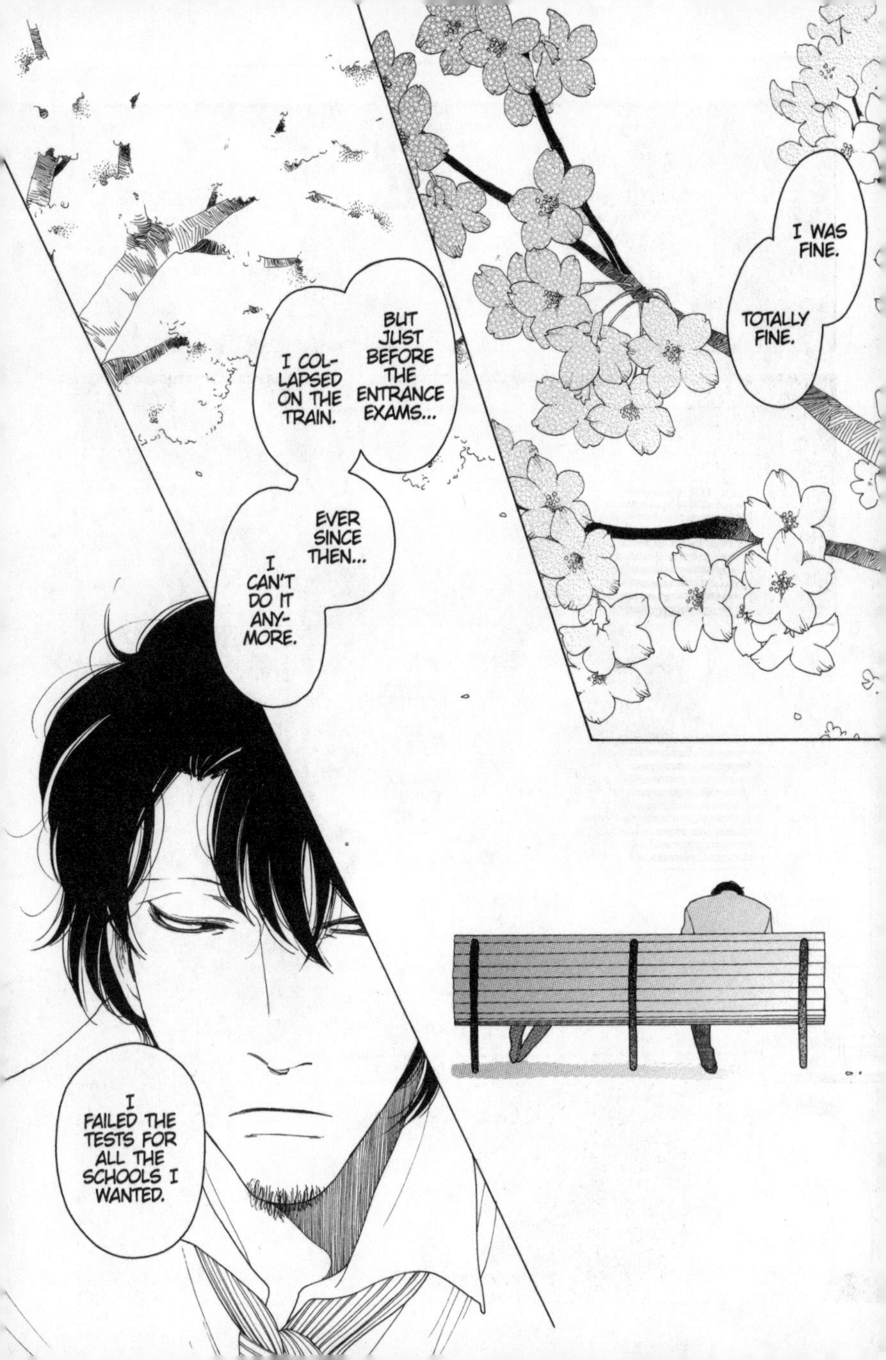
I WAS FINE.
TOTALLY FINE.
BUT JUST BEFORE THE ENTRANCE EXAMS...
I COLLAPSED ON THE TRAIN.
EVER SINCE THEN...
I CAN'T DO IT ANYMORE.
I FAILED THE TESTS FOR ALL THE SCHOOLS I WANTED.

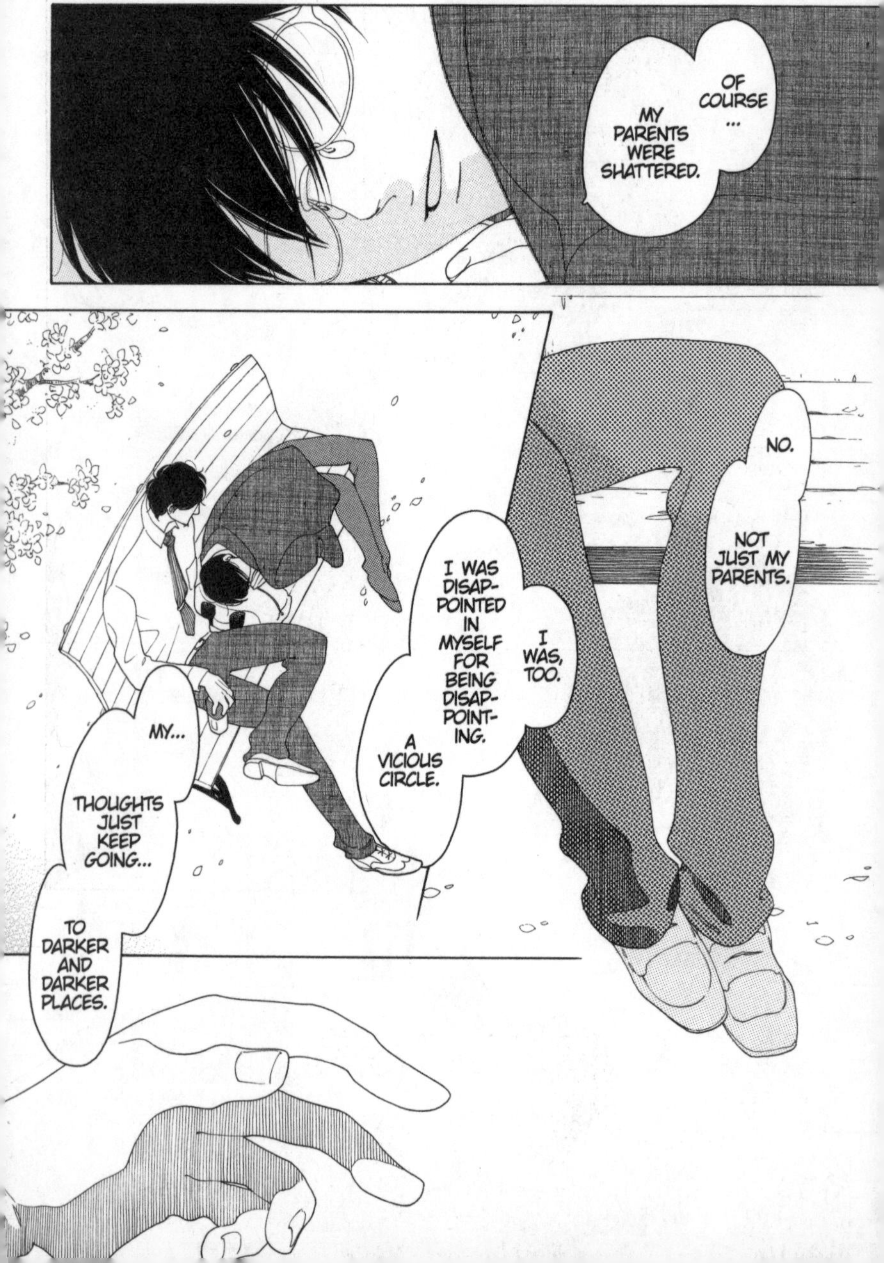
OF COURSE...
MY PARENTS WERE SHATTERED.
NO.
NOT JUST MY PARENTS.
I WAS, TOO.
I WAS DISAPPOINTED IN MYSELF FOR BEING DISAPPOINTING.
A VICIOUS CIRCLE.
MY...
THOUGHTS JUST KEEP GOING...
TO DARKER AND DARKER PLACES.

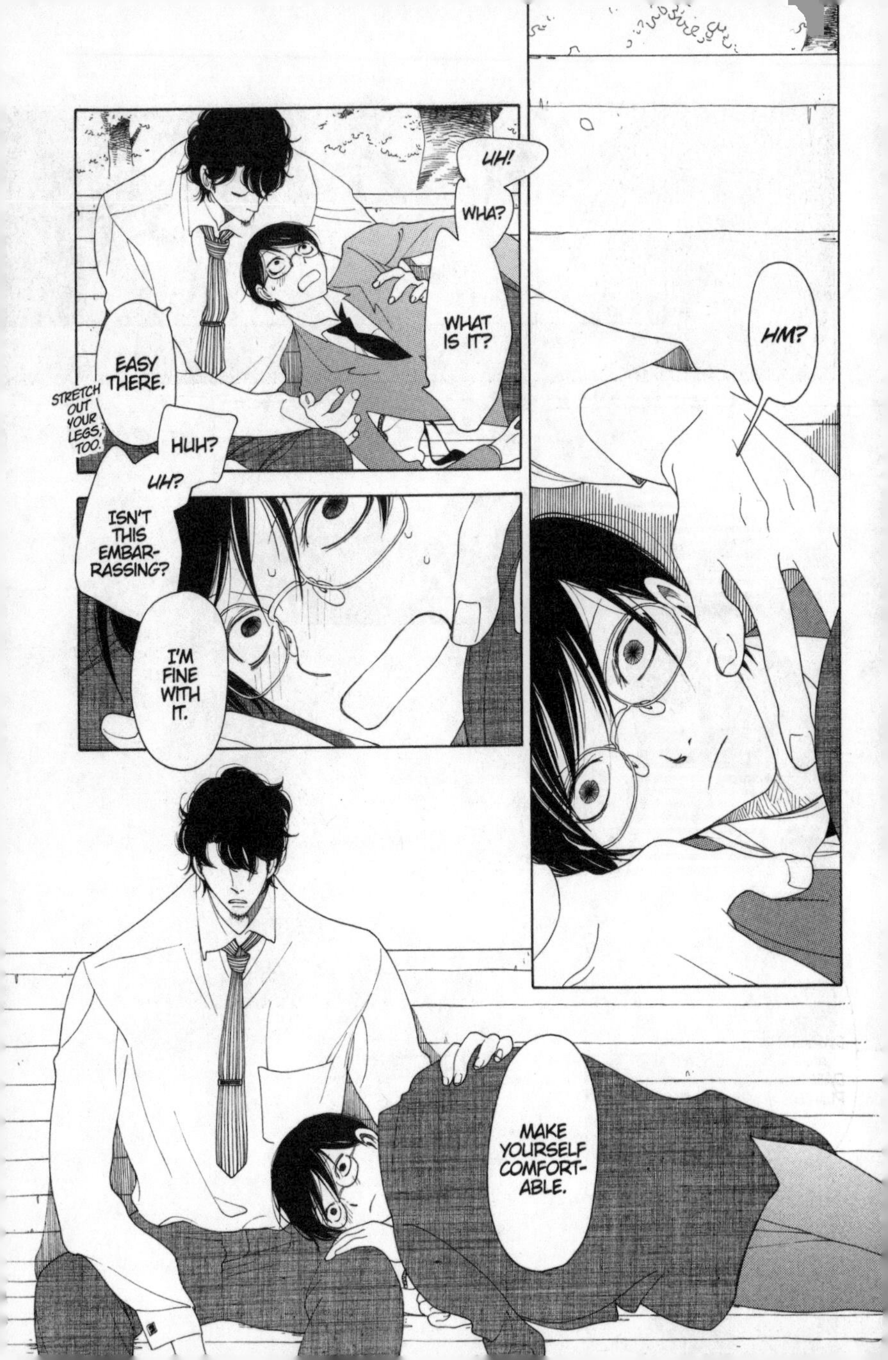
HM?
UH!
WHA?
WHAT IS IT?
EASY THERE.
STRETCH OUT YOUR LEGS, TOO.
HUH?
UH?
ISN'T THIS EMBARRASSING?
I'M FINE WITH IT.
MAKE YOURSELF COMFORTABLE.

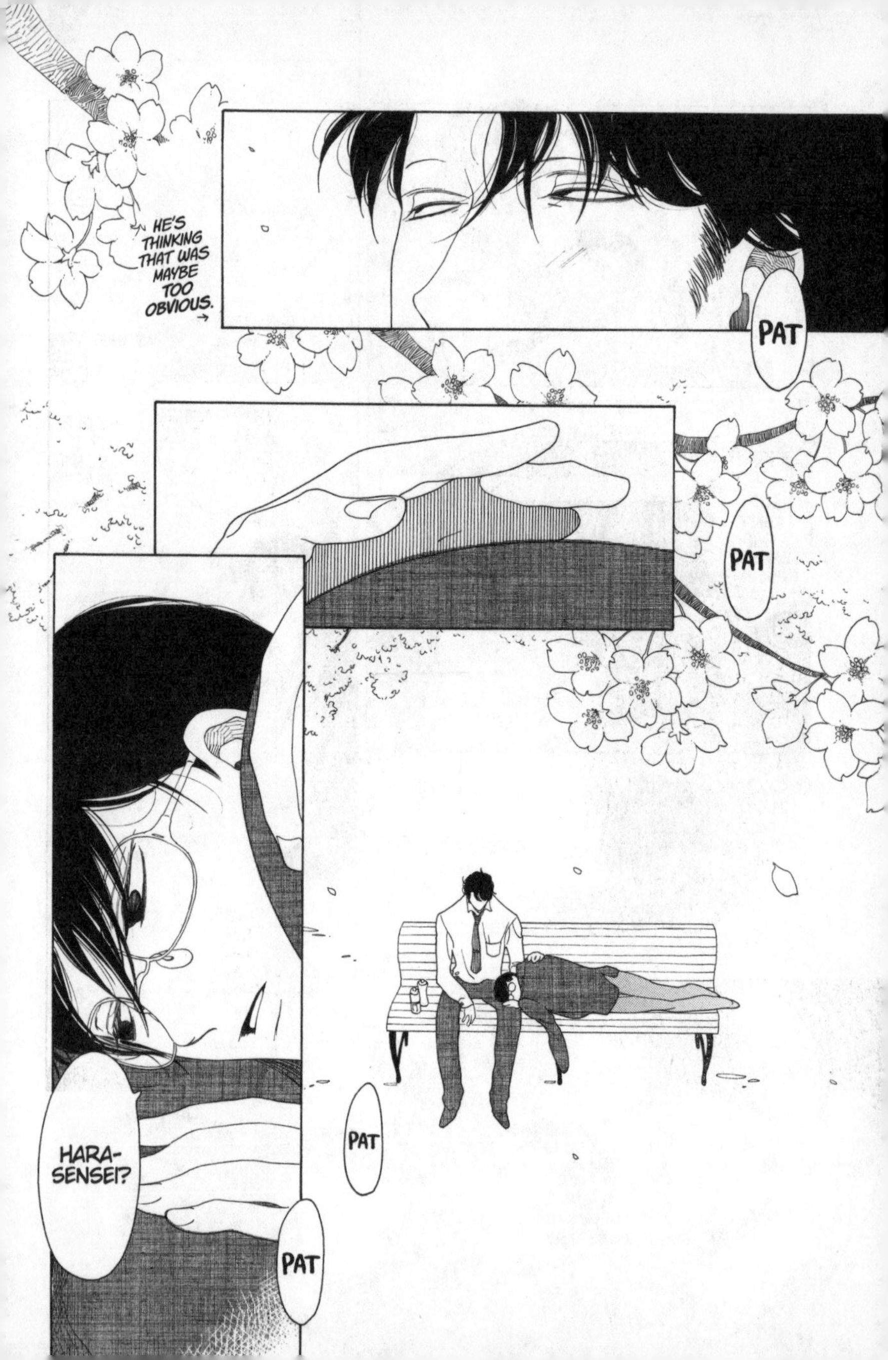

PAT
HE'S THINKING THAT WAS MAYBE TOO OBVIOUS.
PAT
PAT
HARA-SENSEI?
PAT

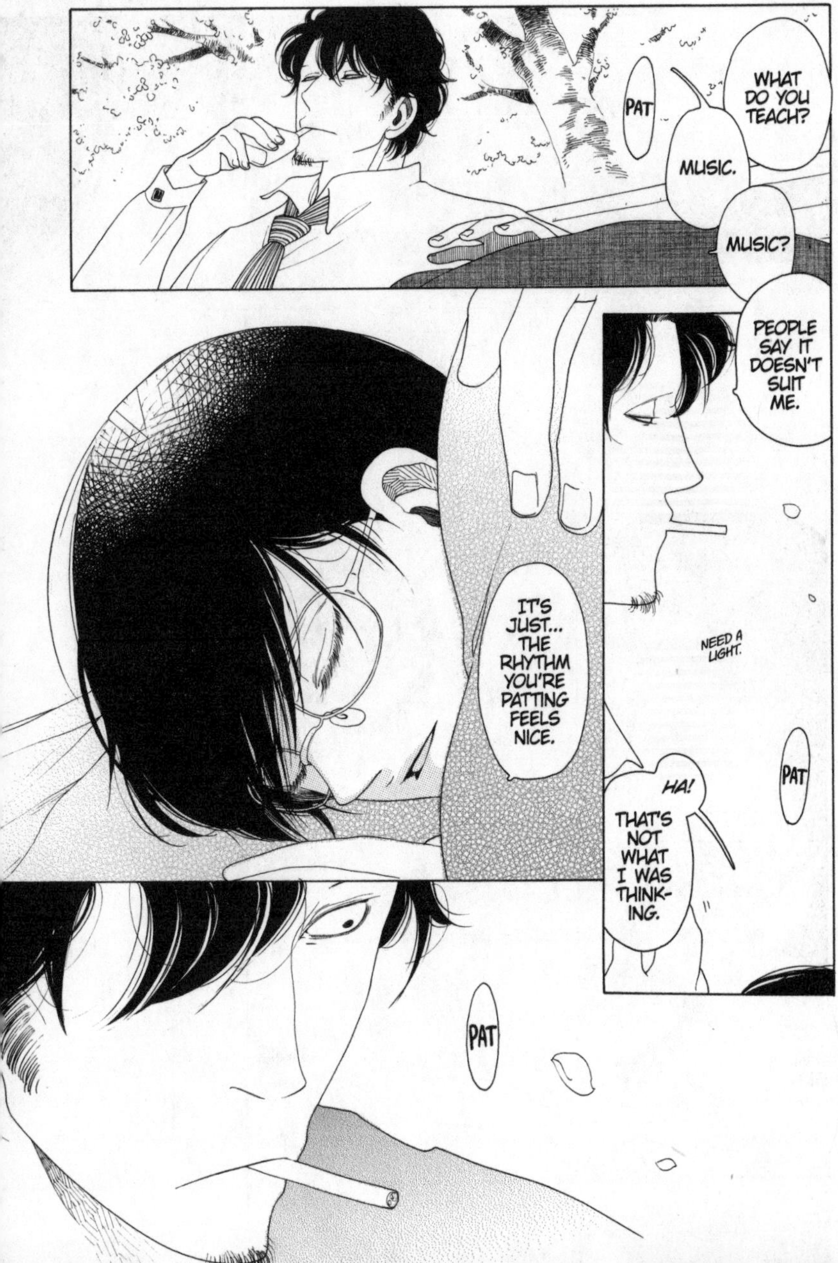
WHAT DO YOU TEACH?
PAT
MUSIC.
MUSIC?
PEOPLE SAY IT DOESN'T SUIT ME.
NEED A LIGHT.
PAT
HA! THAT'S NOT WHAT I WAS THINKING.
IT'S JUST... THE RHYTHM YOU'RE PATTING FEELS NICE.
PAT

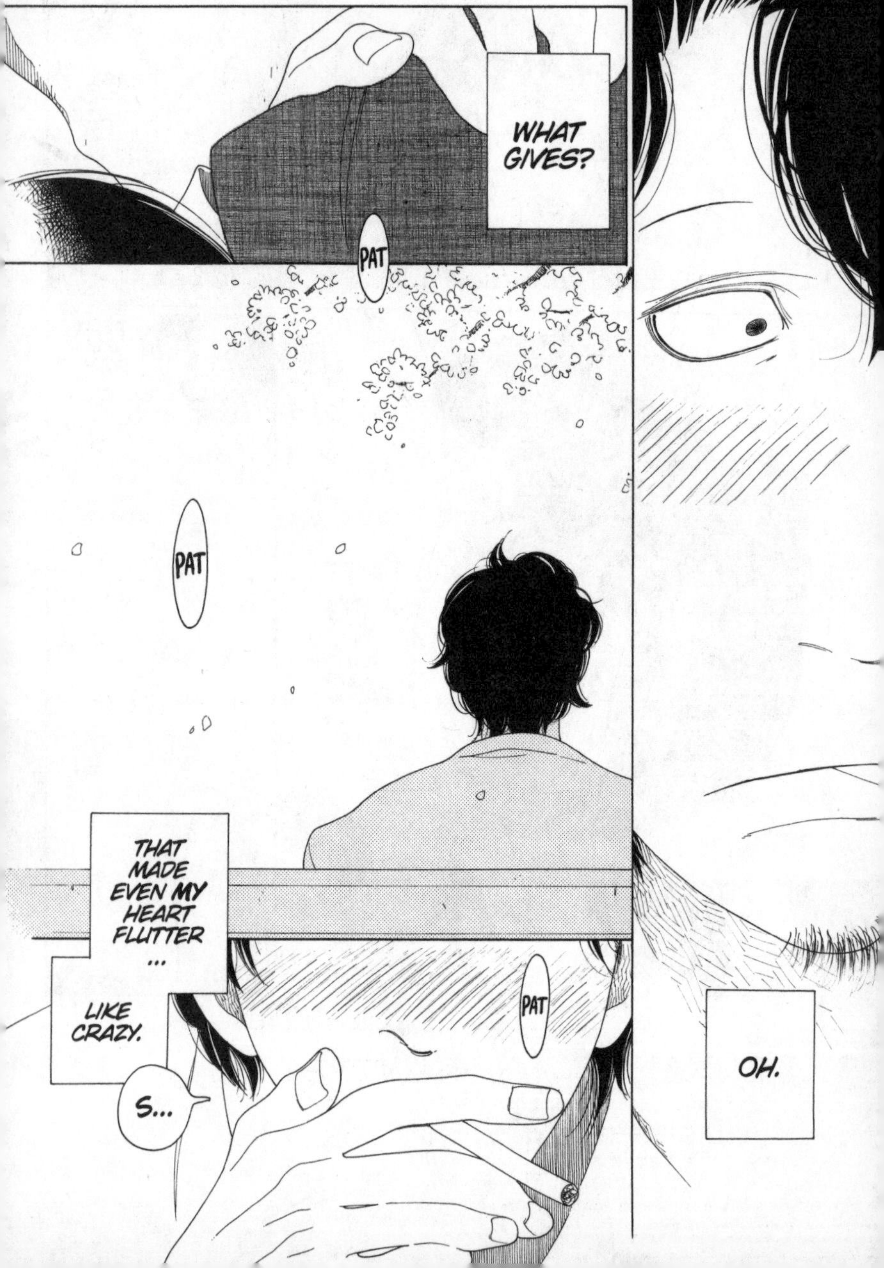
OH.
WHAT GIVES?
PAT
PAT
THAT MADE EVEN MY HEART FLUTTER...
LIKE CRAZY.
PAT
S...

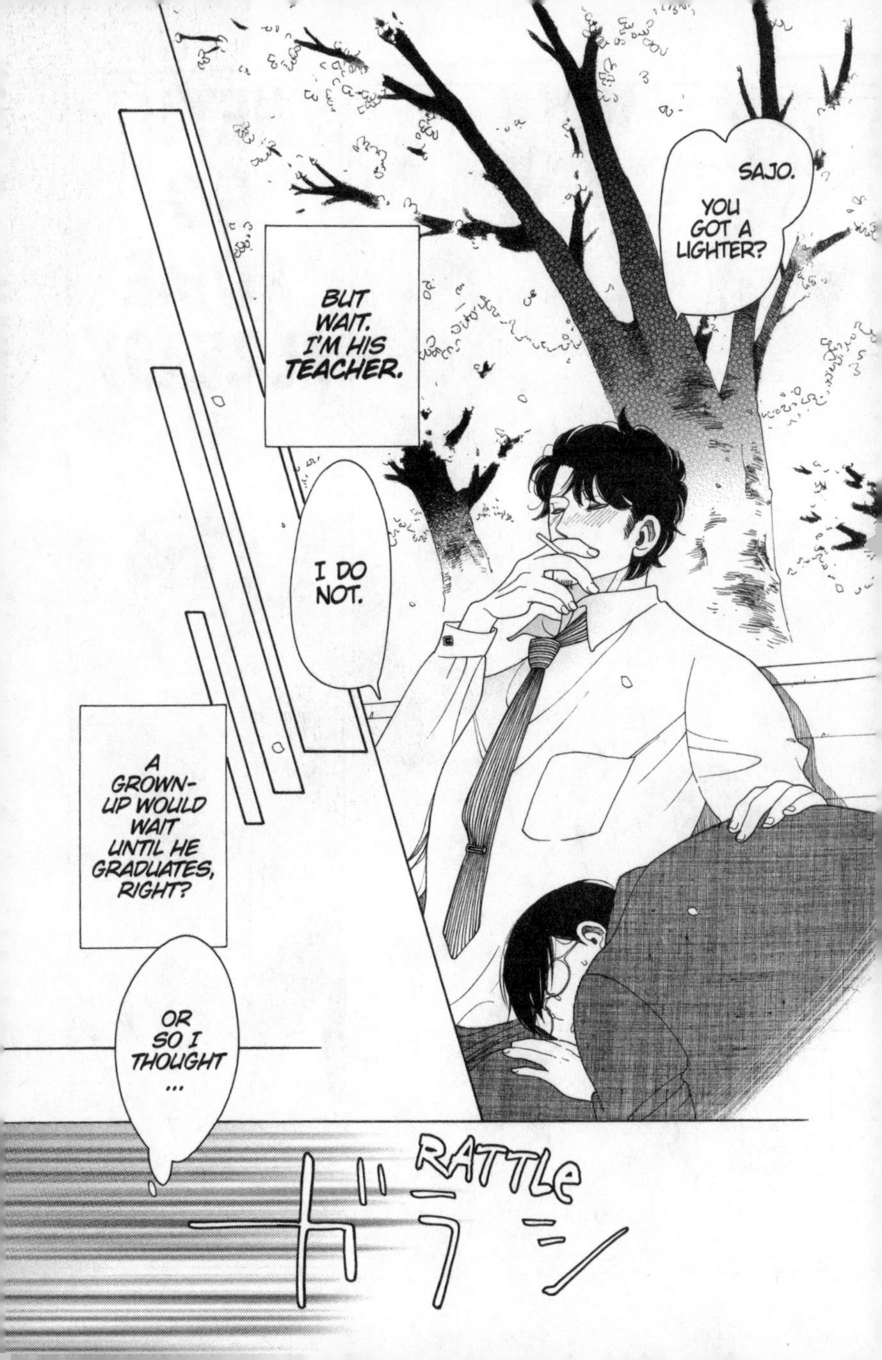
SAJO. YOU GOT A LIGHTER?
BUT WAIT. I'M HIS TEACHER.
I DO NOT.
A GROWN-UP WOULD WAIT UNTIL HE GRADUATES, RIGHT?
OR SO I THOUGHT ...
RATTLE

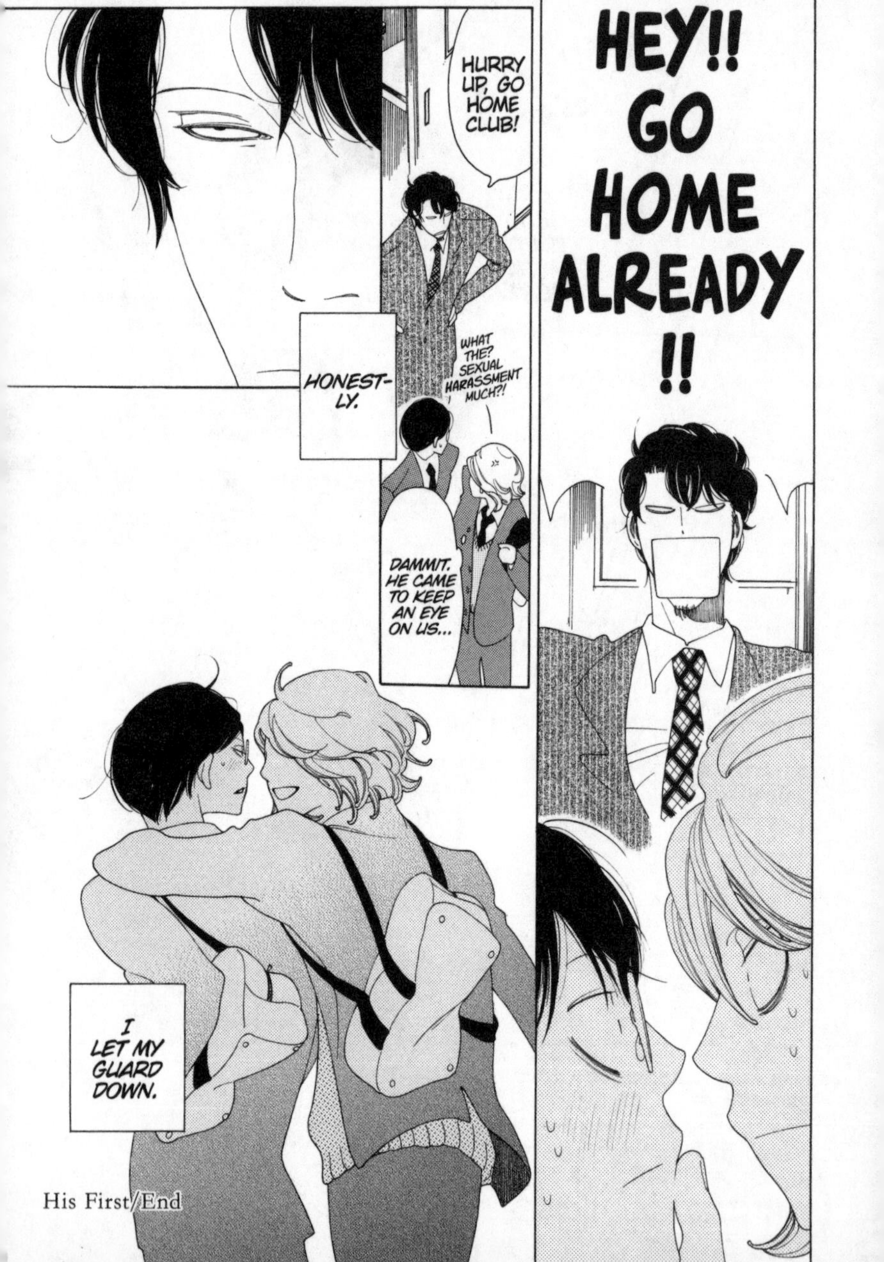
HEY!! GO HOME ALREADY !!
HURRY UP, GO HOME CLUB!
WHAT THE? SEXUAL HARASSMENT MUCH?!
DAMMIT. HE CAME TO KEEP AN EYE ON US...
HONEST-LY.
I LET MY GUARD DOWN.

His First/End

Classmates

Intermission

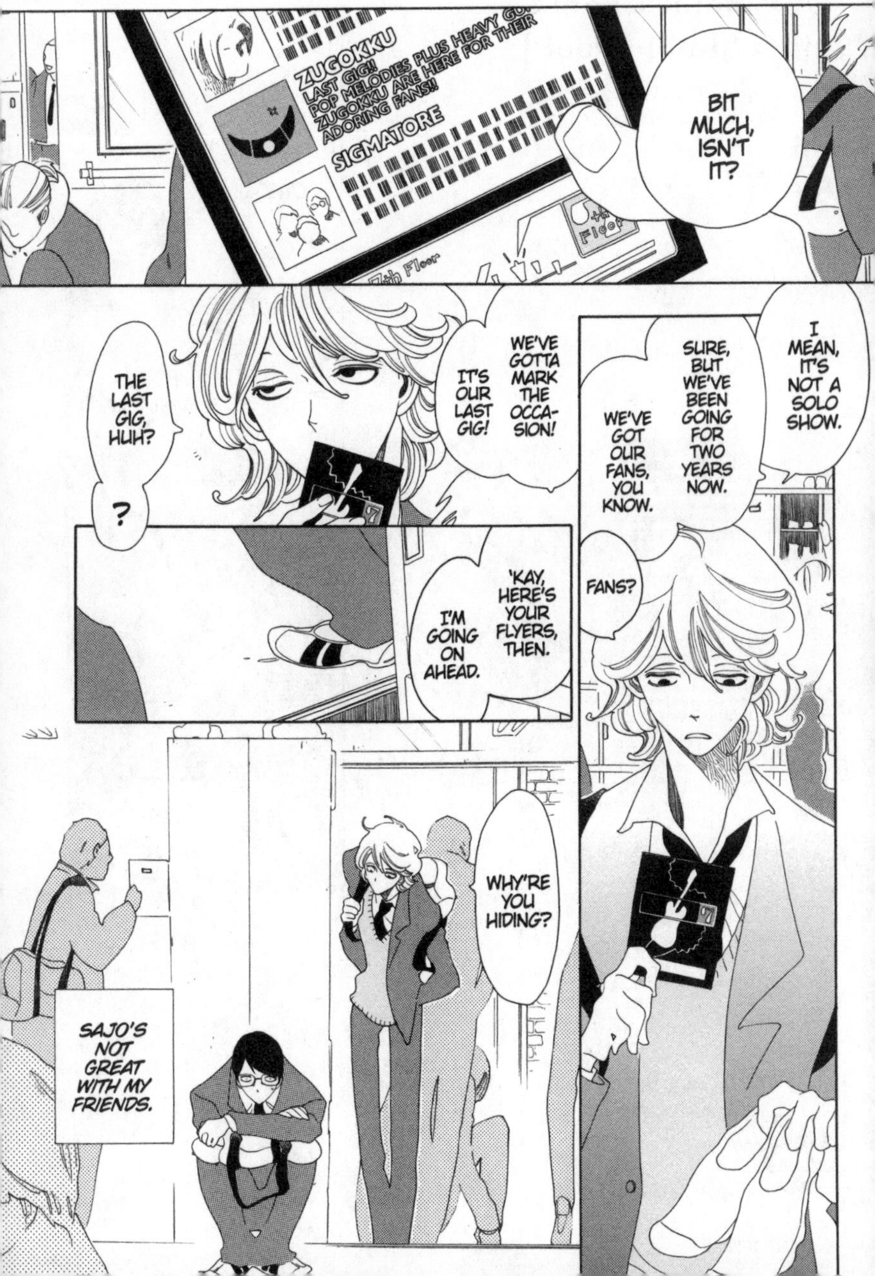
BIT MUCH, ISN'T IT?
ZUGOKKU
LAST GIG!!
POP MELODIES PLUS HEAVY GU
ZUGOKKU ARE HERE FOR THEIR ADORING FANS!!
SIGMATORE
7th Floor
I MEAN, IT'S NOT A SOLO SHOW.
SURE, BUT WE'VE BEEN GOING FOR TWO YEARS NOW.
WE'VE GOT OUR FANS, YOU KNOW.
FANS?
WE'VE GOTTA MARK THE OCCASION!
IT'S OUR LAST GIG!
THE LAST GIG, HUH?
?
'KAY, HERE'S YOUR FLYERS, THEN.
I'M GOING ON AHEAD.
WHY'RE YOU HIDING?
SAJO'S NOT GREAT WITH MY FRIENDS.

[A Complex Fool and a Simple Fool]

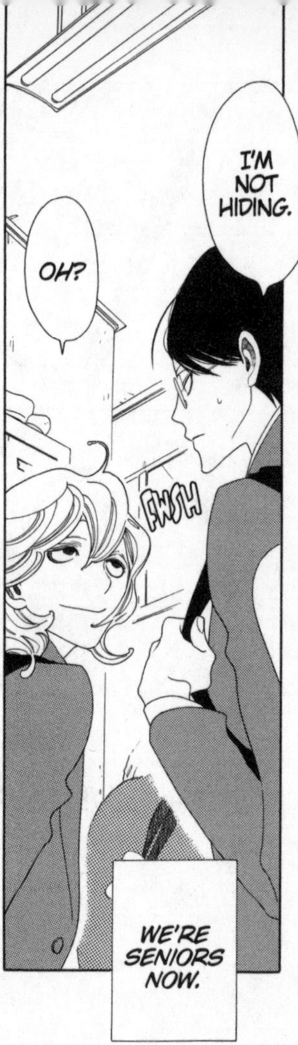
I'M NOT HIDING.
OH?
FWSH
WE'RE SENIORS NOW.

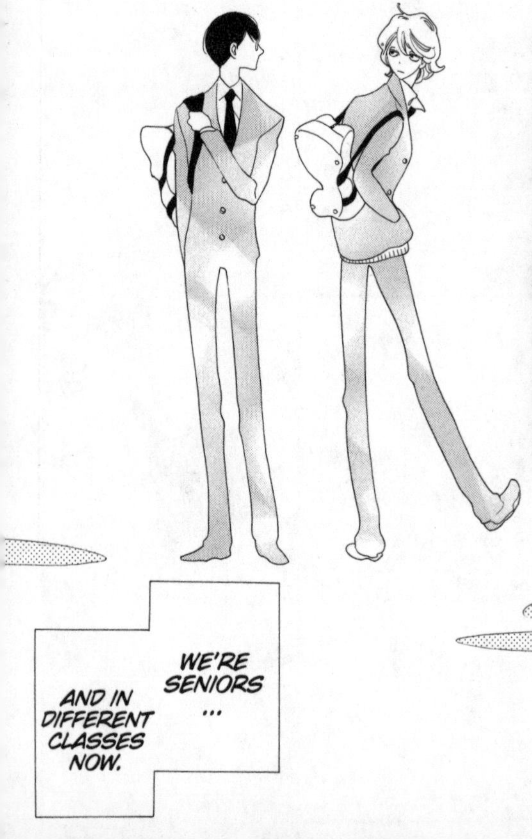
WE'RE SENIORS ...
AND IN DIFFERENT CLASSES NOW.

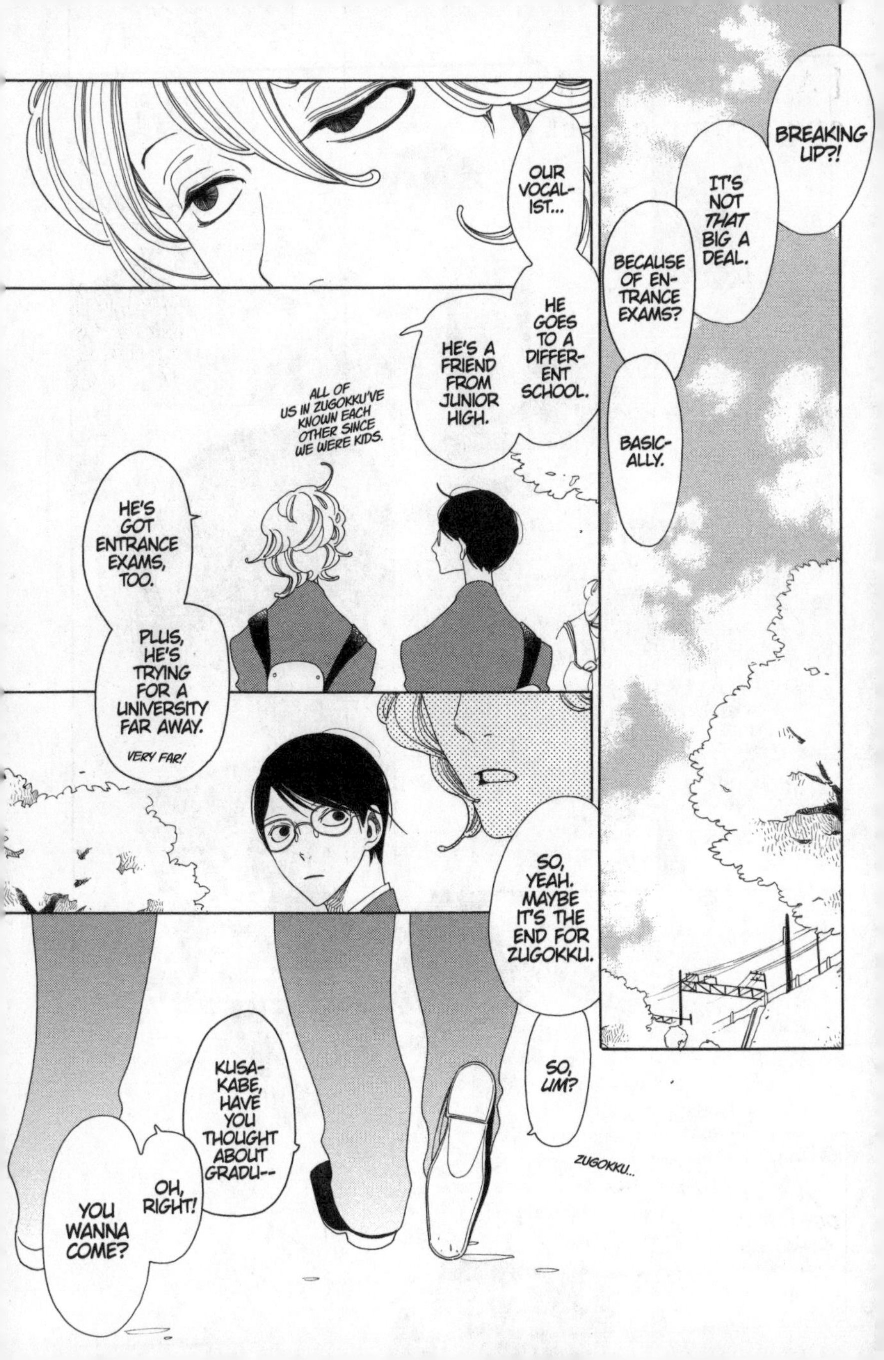
BREAKING UP?!
IT'S NOT *THAT* BIG A DEAL.
BECAUSE OF ENTRANCE EXAMS?
BASICALLY.
OUR VOCALIST...
HE GOES TO A DIFFERENT SCHOOL.
HE'S A FRIEND FROM JUNIOR HIGH.
ALL OF US IN ZUGOKKU'VE KNOWN EACH OTHER SINCE WE WERE KIDS.
HE'S GOT ENTRANCE EXAMS, TOO.
PLUS, HE'S TRYING FOR A UNIVERSITY FAR AWAY.
VERY FAR!
SO, YEAH. MAYBE IT'S THE END FOR ZUGOKKU.
SO, UM?
ZUGOKKU...
KUSAKABE, HAVE YOU THOUGHT ABOUT GRADU--
OH, RIGHT!
YOU WANNA COME?

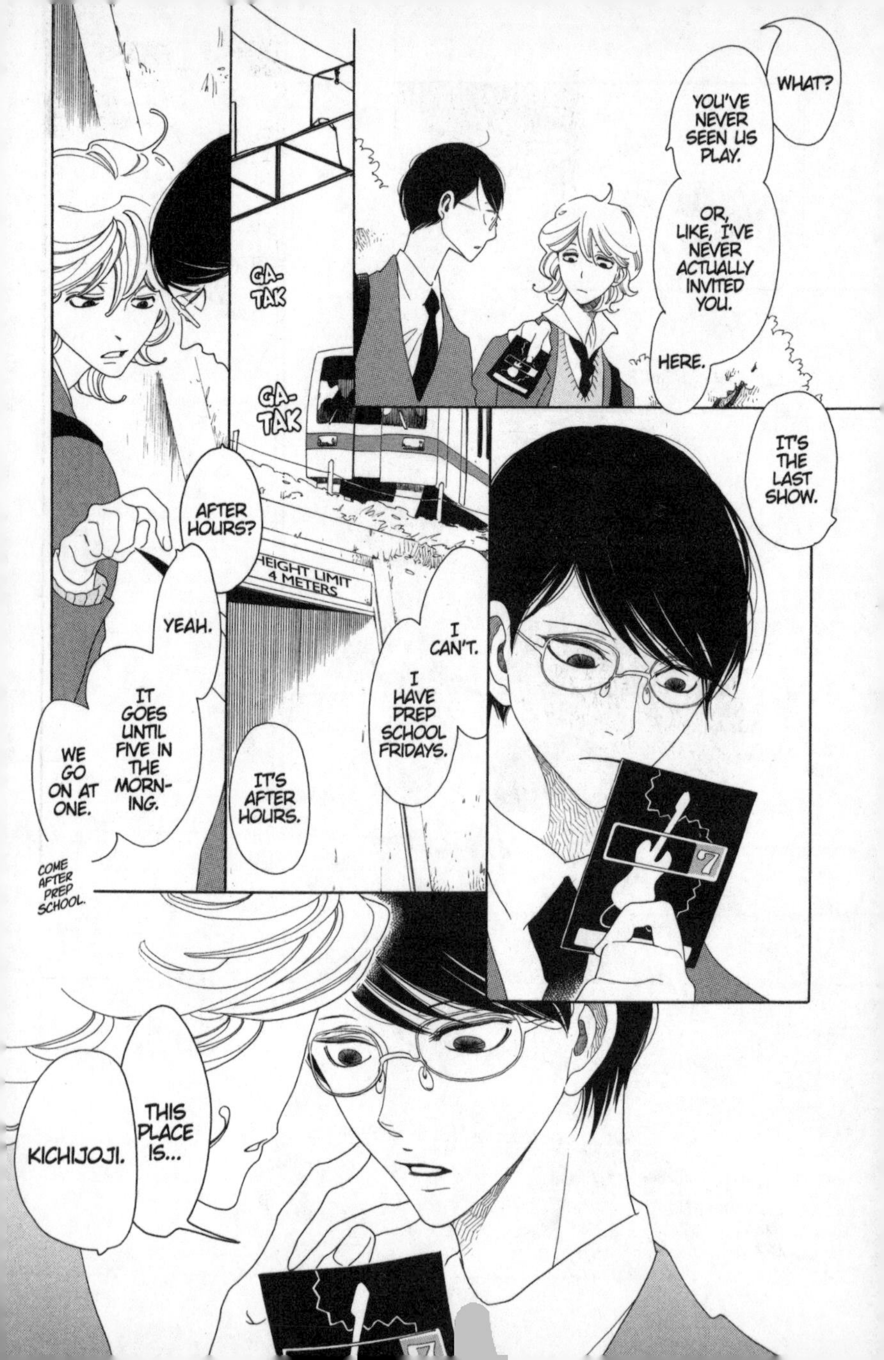
WHAT?
YOU'VE NEVER SEEN US PLAY.
OR, LIKE, I'VE NEVER ACTUALLY INVITED YOU.
HERE.
IT'S THE LAST SHOW.
GA-TAK
GA-TAK
HEIGHT LIMIT 4 METERS
I CAN'T.
I HAVE PREP SCHOOL FRIDAYS.
IT'S AFTER HOURS.
AFTER HOURS?
YEAH.
IT GOES UNTIL FIVE IN THE MORNING.
WE GO ON AT ONE.
COME AFTER PREP SCHOOL.
THIS PLACE IS...
KICHIJOJI.

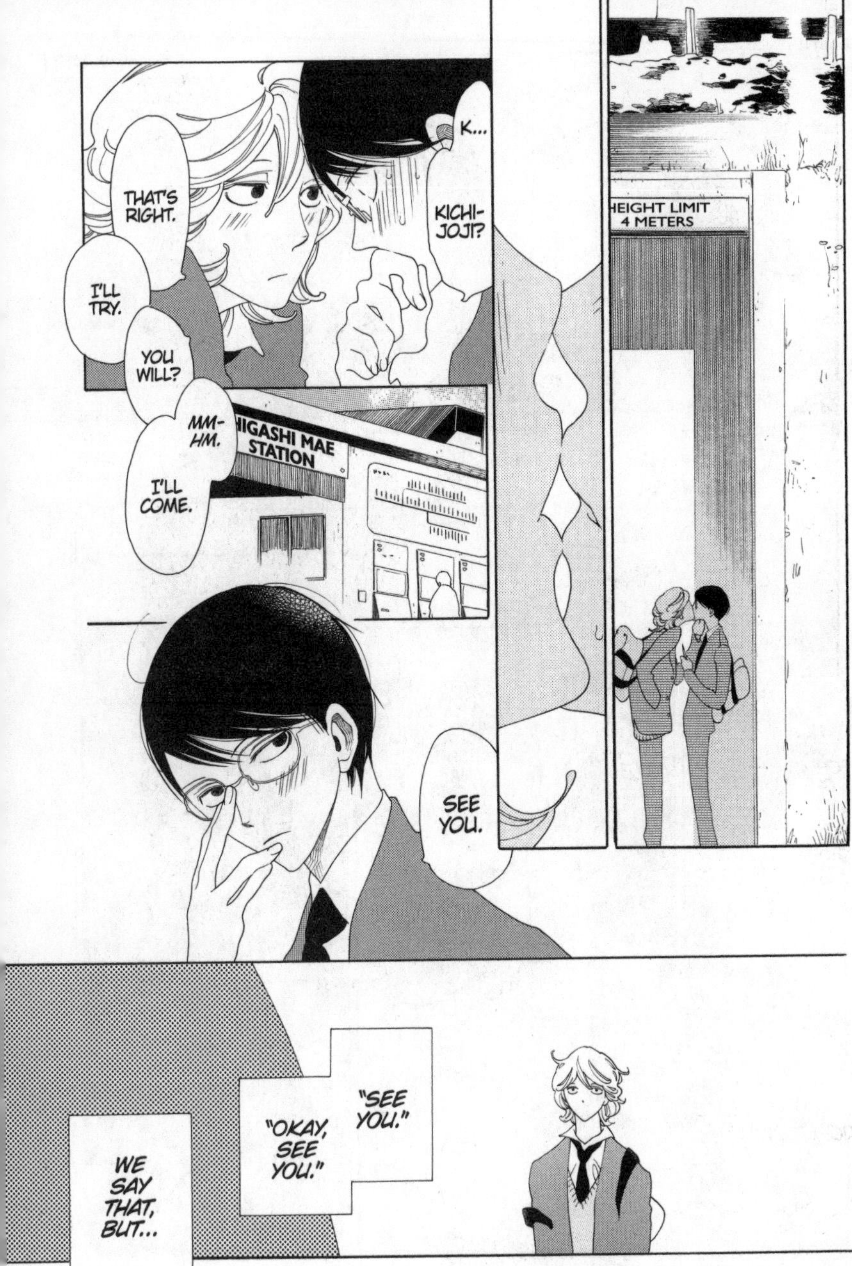
HEIGHT LIMIT
4 METERS
K...
KICHI-JOJI?
THAT'S RIGHT.
I'LL TRY.
YOU WILL?
HIGASHI MAE STATION
MM-HM.
I'LL COME.
SEE YOU.
"SEE YOU."
"OKAY, SEE YOU."
WE SAY THAT, BUT...

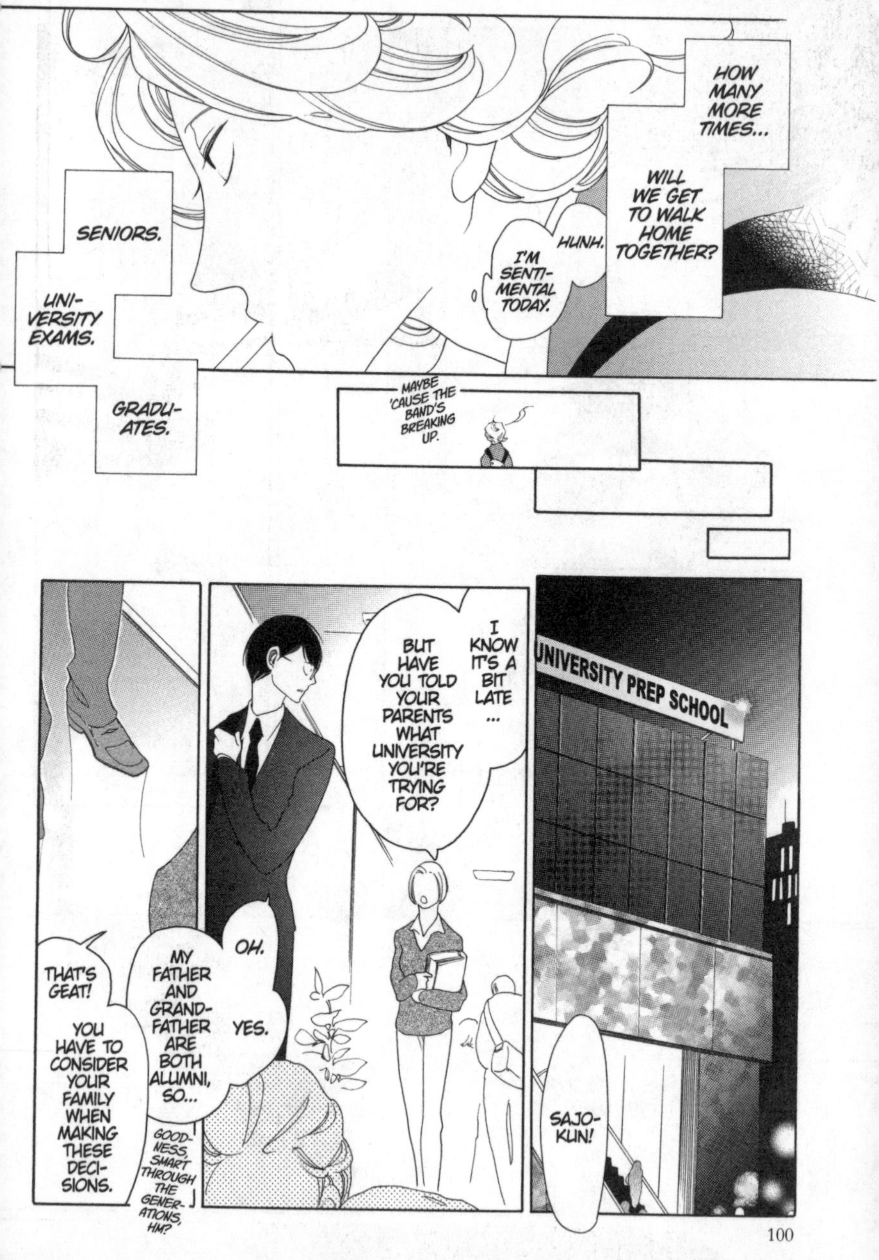
HOW MANY MORE TIMES...
WILL WE GET TO WALK HOME TOGETHER?
HUNH.
I'M SENTI-MENTAL TODAY.
SENIORS.
UNI-VERSITY EXAMS.
GRADU-ATES.
MAYBE 'CAUSE THE BAND'S BREAKING UP.
UNIVERSITY PREP SCHOOL
SAJO-KUN!
I KNOW IT'S A BIT LATE...
BUT HAVE YOU TOLD YOUR PARENTS WHAT UNIVERSITY YOU'RE TRYING FOR?
OH.
YES.
MY FATHER AND GRAND-FATHER ARE BOTH ALUMNI, SO...
THAT'S GEAT!
YOU HAVE TO CONSIDER YOUR FAMILY WHEN MAKING THESE DECI-SIONS.
GOOD-NESS, SMART THROUGH THE GENER-ATIONS, HM?

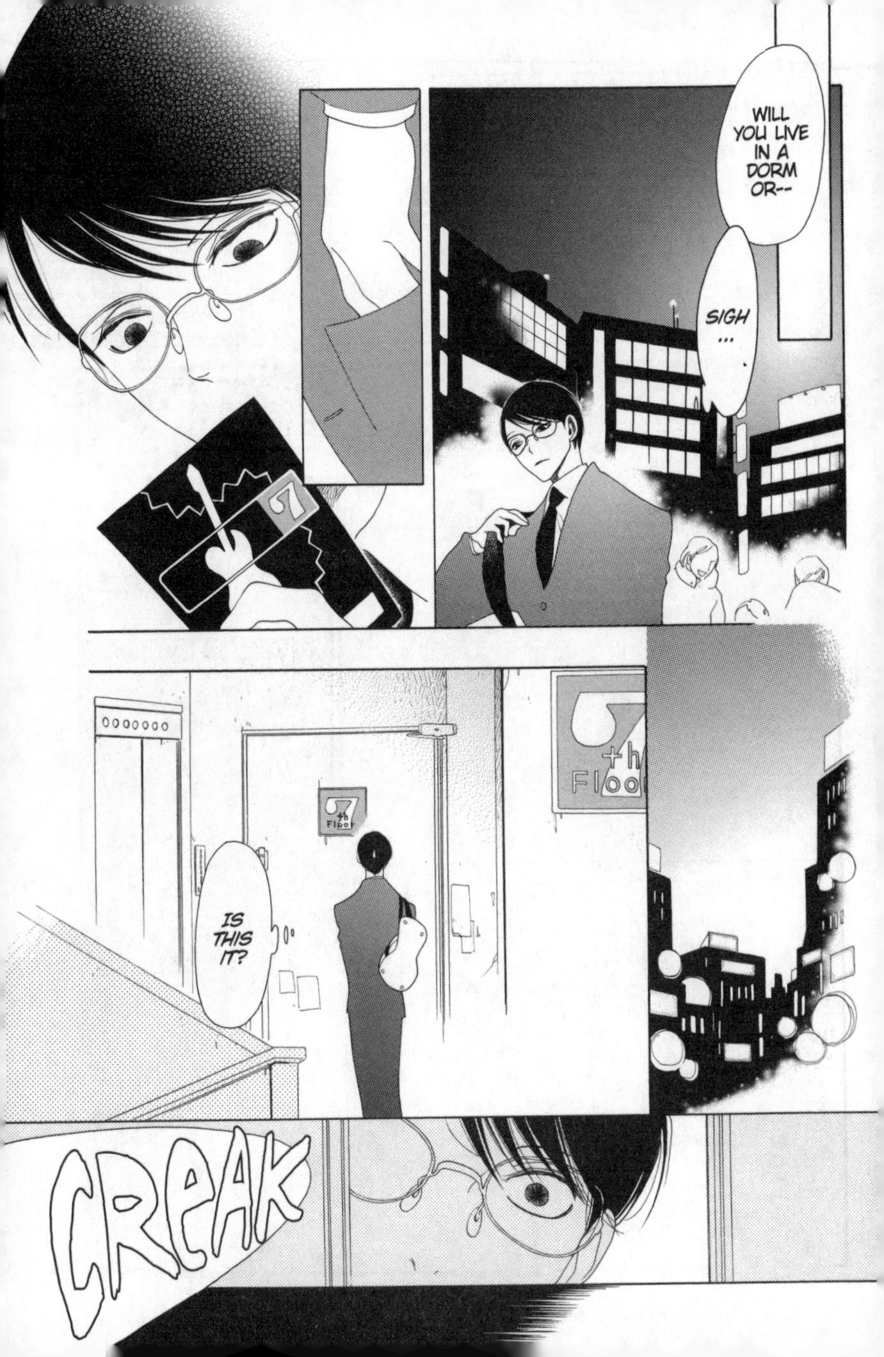
WILL YOU LIVE IN A DORM OR--
SIGH ...
IS THIS IT?
CREAK

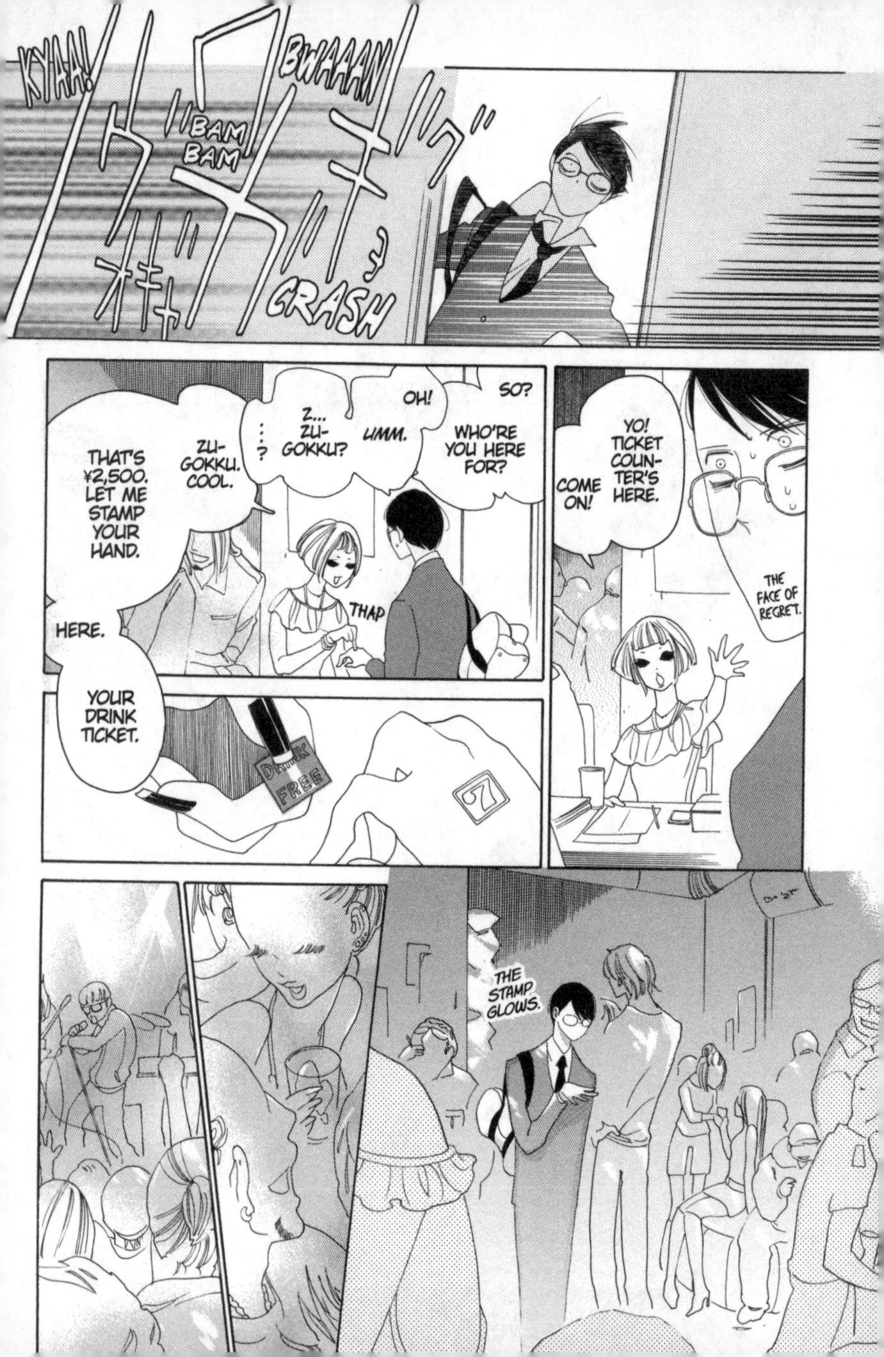
BWAAAN!
BAM BAM
CRASH
KYAA!
YO! TICKET COUNTER'S HERE.
COME ON!
THE FACE OF REGRET.
SO?
WHO'RE YOU HERE FOR?
OH!
UMM.
Z... ZU-GOKKU?
...?
ZU-GOKKU. COOL.
THAT'S ¥2,500. LET ME STAMP YOUR HAND.
THAP
HERE.
YOUR DRINK TICKET.
FREE
THE STAMP GLOWS.

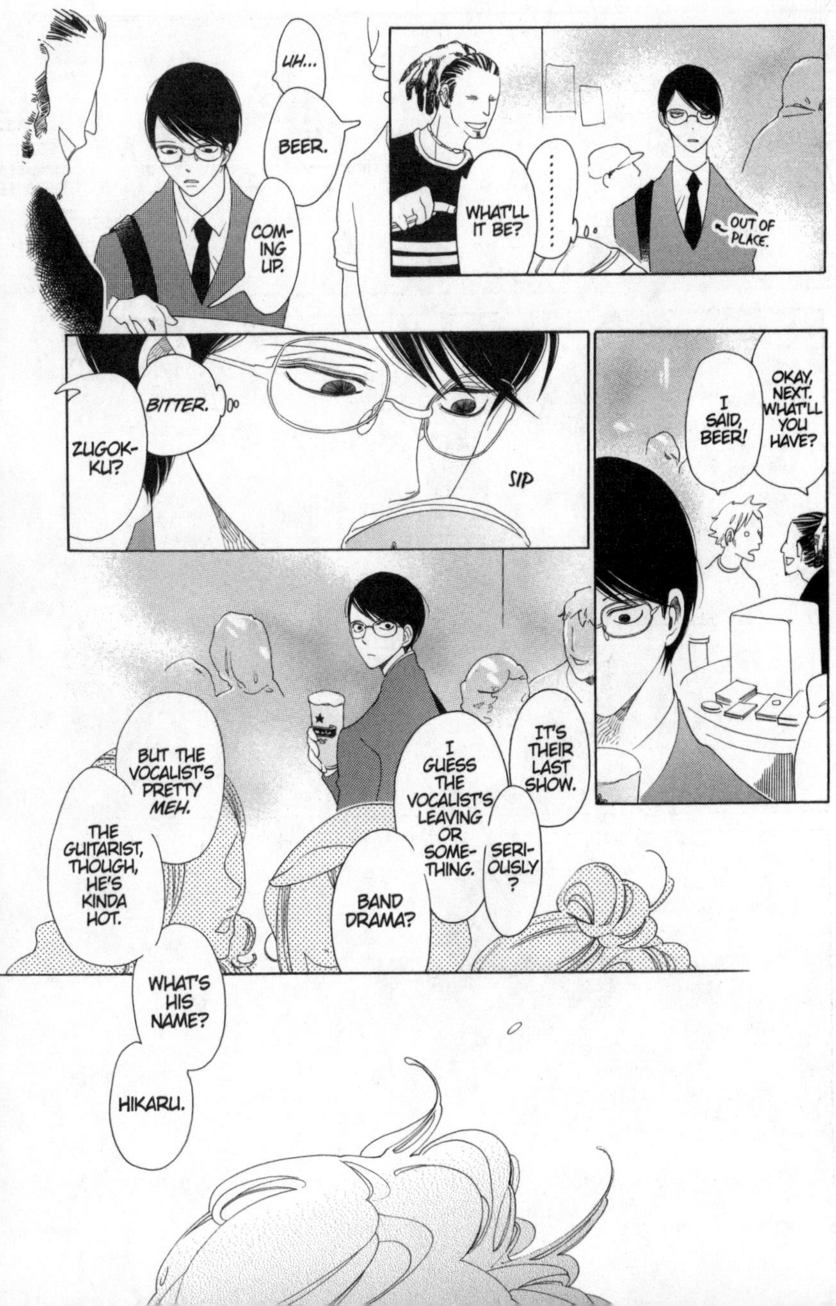

WHAT'LL IT BE?
......
OUT OF PLACE.
UH...
BEER.
COMING UP.
OKAY, NEXT. WHAT'LL YOU HAVE?
I SAID, BEER!
SIP
BITTER.
ZUGOKKU?
IT'S THEIR LAST SHOW.
I GUESS THE VOCALIST'S LEAVING OR SOMETHING.
SERIOUSLY?
BAND DRAMA?
BUT THE VOCALIST'S PRETTY *MEH.*
THE GUITARIST, THOUGH, HE'S KINDA HOT.
WHAT'S HIS NAME?
HIKARU.

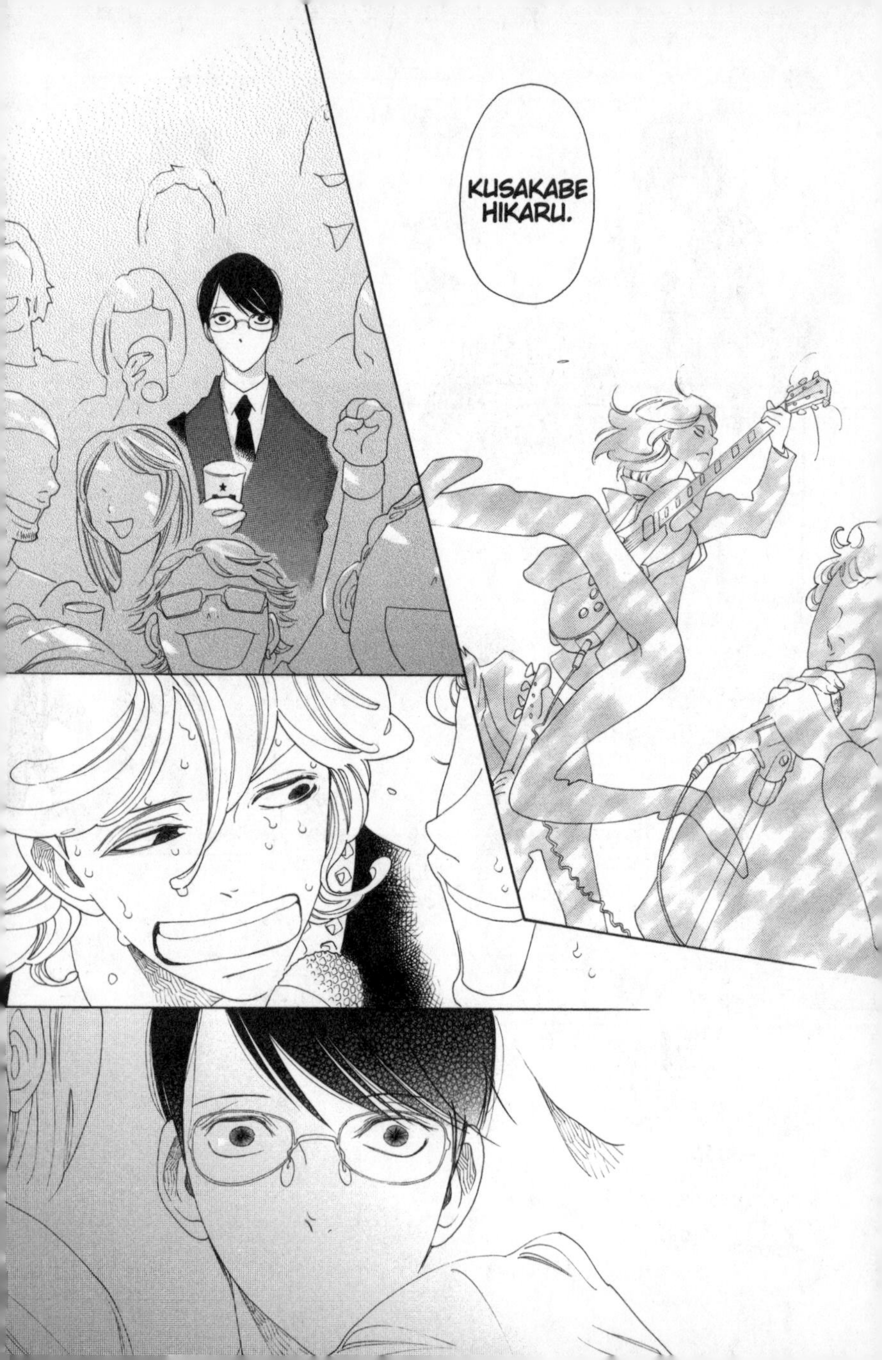
KUSAKABE HIKARU.

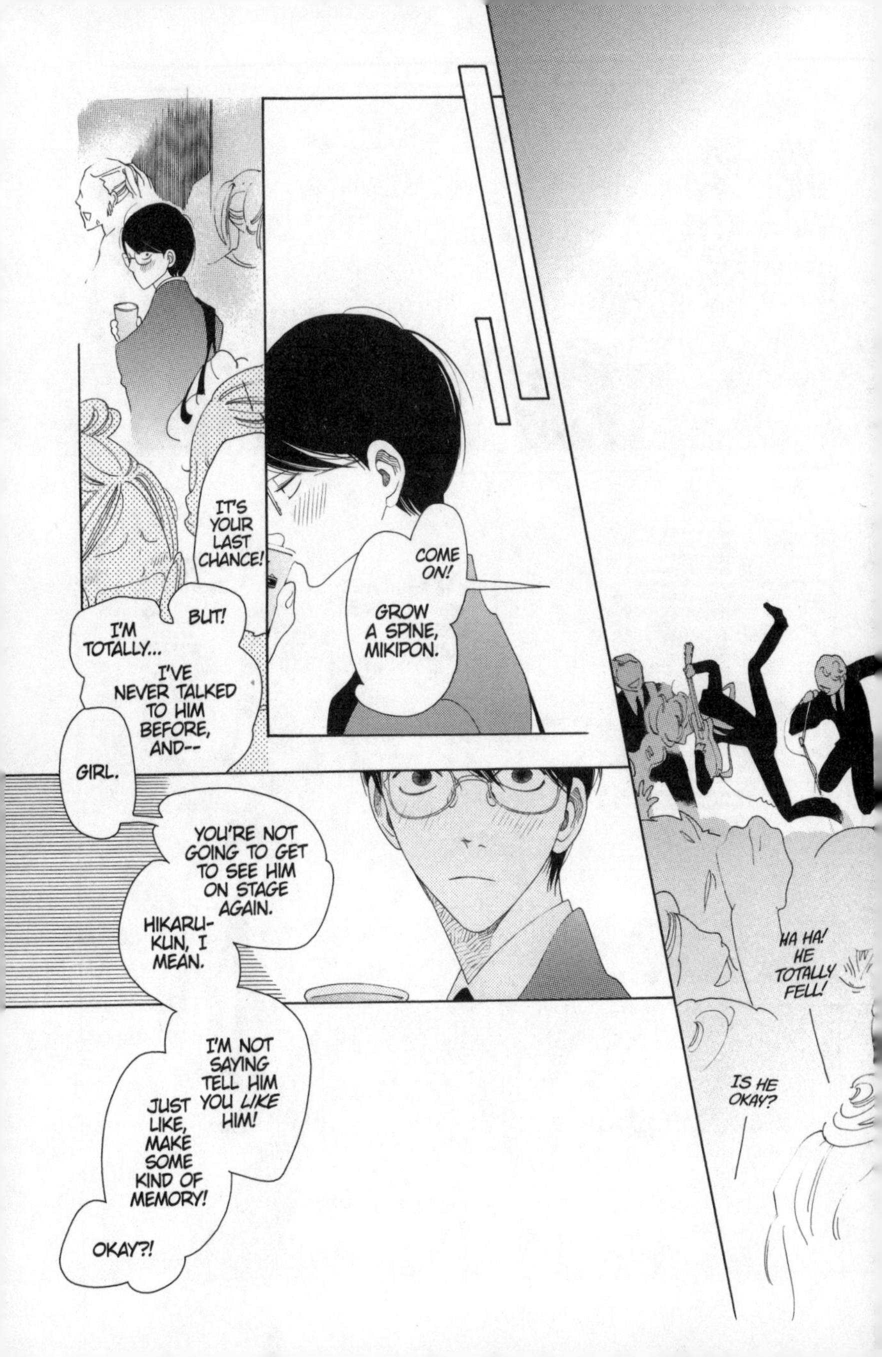
HA HA! HE TOTALLY FELL!
IS HE OKAY?
COME ON!
GROW A SPINE, MIKIPON.
IT'S YOUR LAST CHANCE!
BUT!
I'M TOTALLY...
I'VE NEVER TALKED TO HIM BEFORE, AND--
GIRL.
YOU'RE NOT GOING TO GET TO SEE HIM ON STAGE AGAIN.
HIKARU-KUN, I MEAN.
I'M NOT SAYING TELL HIM YOU *LIKE* HIM!
JUST LIKE, MAKE SOME KIND OF MEMORY!
OKAY?!

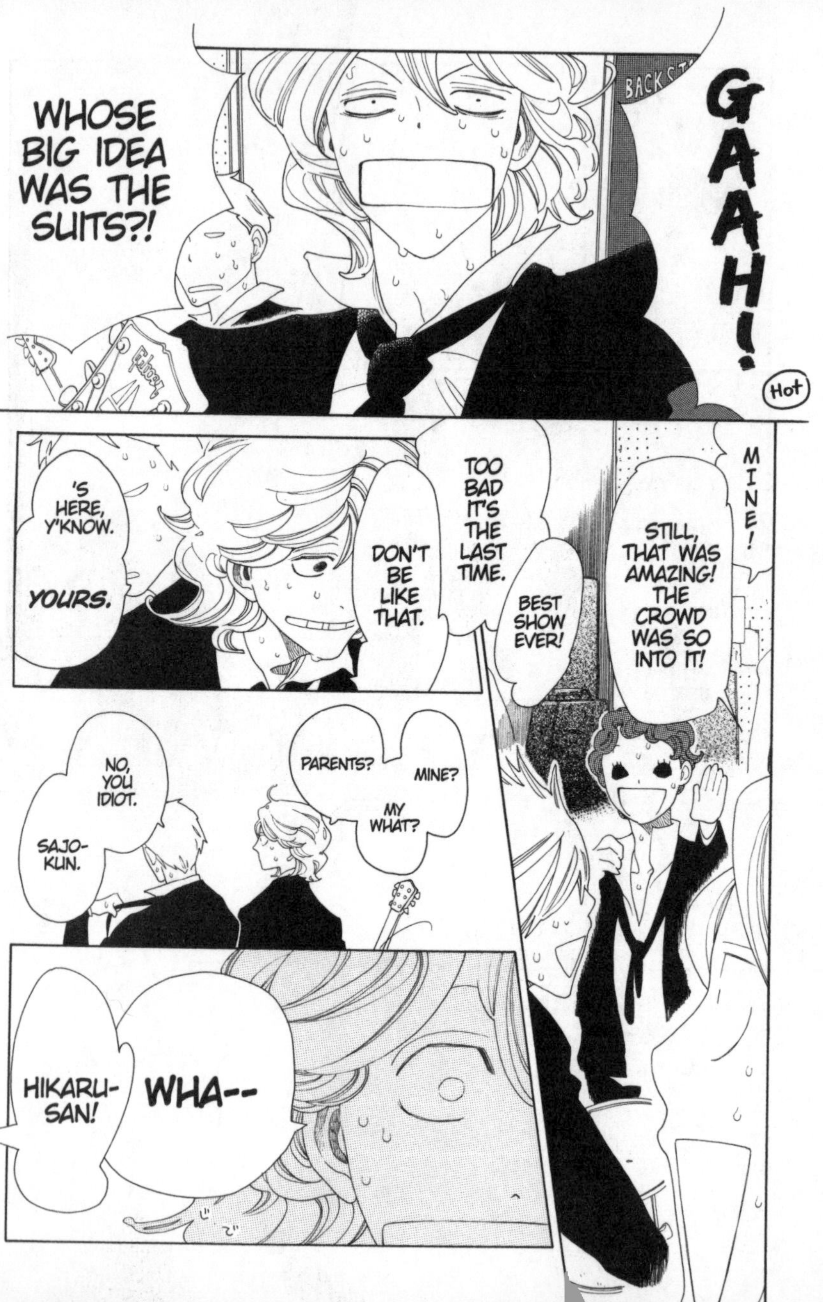
GAAH!
Hot
WHOSE BIG IDEA WAS THE SUITS?!
MINE!
STILL, THAT WAS AMAZING! THE CROWD WAS SO INTO IT!
BEST SHOW EVER!
TOO BAD IT'S THE LAST TIME.
DON'T BE LIKE THAT.
YOURS.
'S HERE, Y'KNOW.
PARENTS? MINE?
MY WHAT?
NO, YOU IDIOT.
SAJO-KUN.
WHA--
HIKARU-SAN!

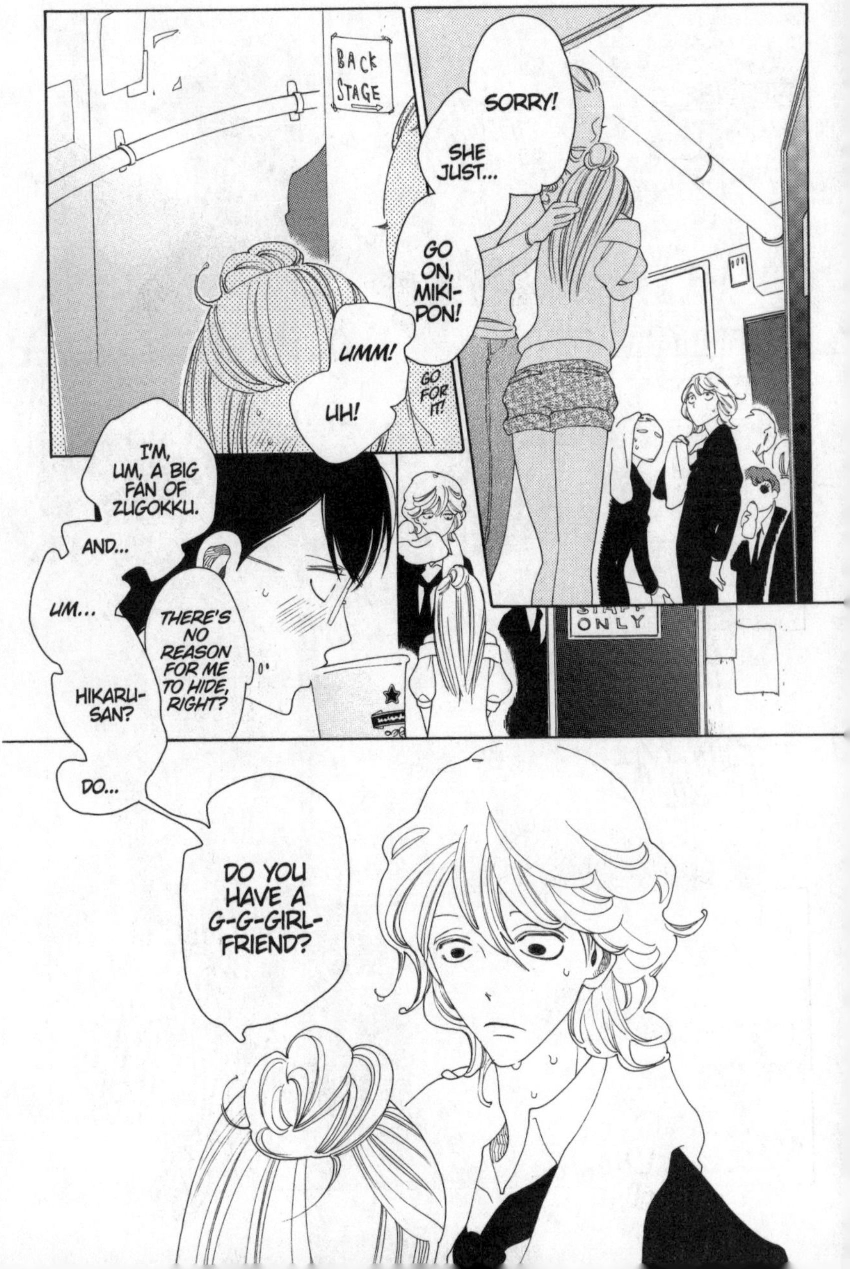
BACK STAGE
SORRY!
SHE JUST...
GO ON, MIKI-PON!
GO FOR IT!
UMM!
UH!
STAFF ONLY
THERE'S NO REASON FOR ME TO HIDE, RIGHT?
I'M, UM, A BIG FAN OF ZUGOKKU.
AND...
UM...
HIKARU-SAN?
DO...
DO YOU HAVE A G-G-GIRL-FRIEND?

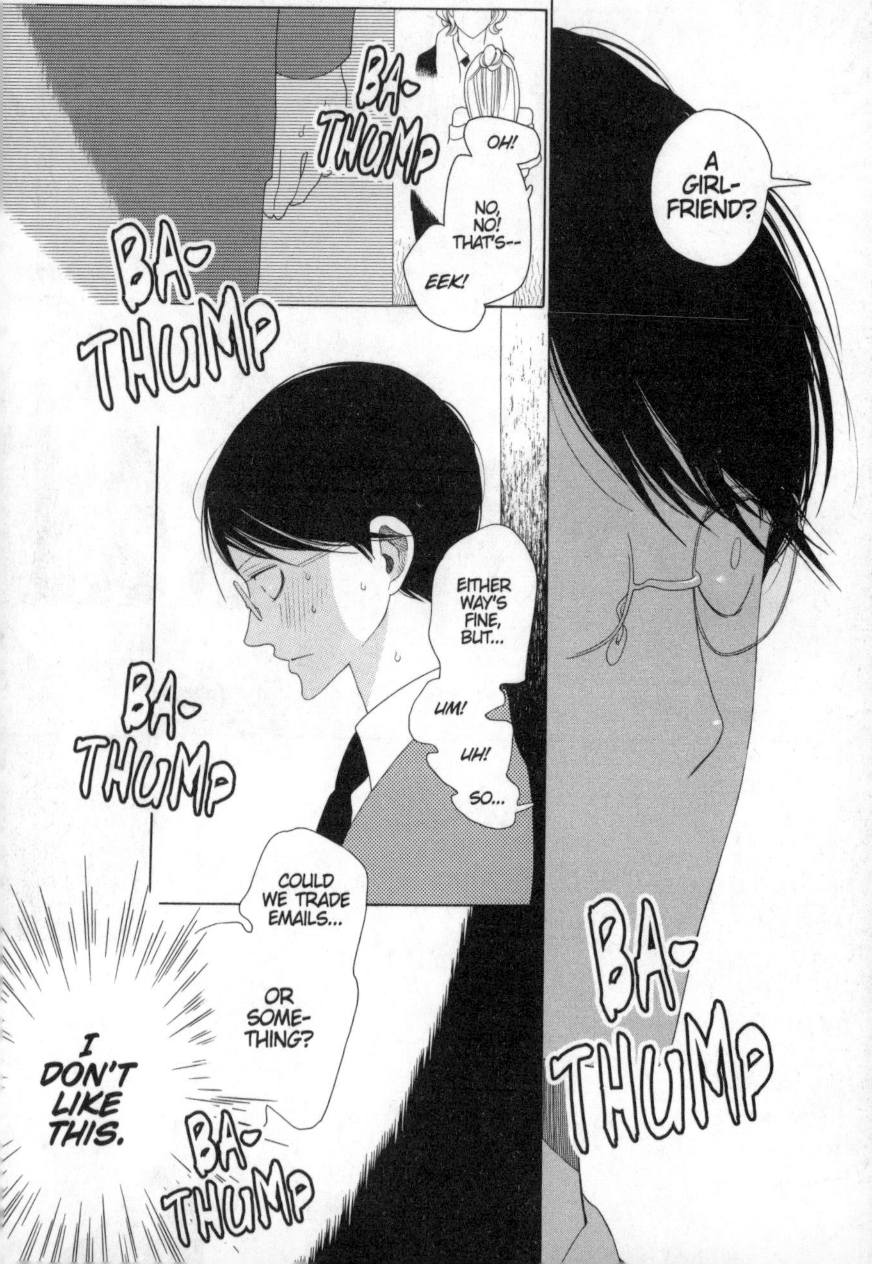
A GIRL-FRIEND?
BA-THUMP
BA-THUMP
OH!
NO, NO! THAT'S--
EEK!
BA-THUMP
EITHER WAY'S FINE, BUT...
UM!
UH!
SO...
BA-THUMP
COULD WE TRADE EMAILS...
OR SOME-THING?
I DON'T LIKE THIS.
BA-THUMP

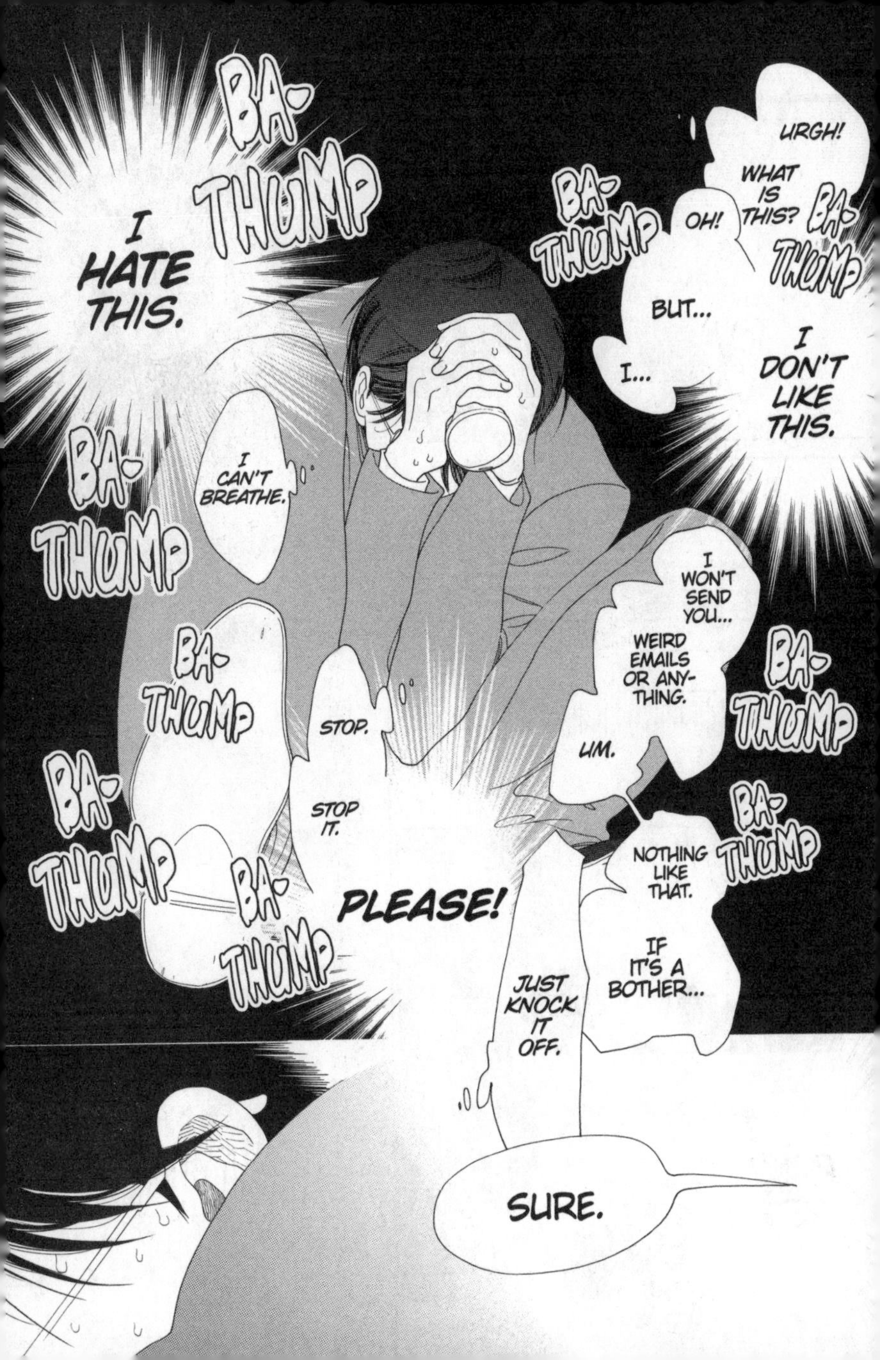
URGH!
WHAT IS THIS?
BA-THUMP
OH!
BA-THUMP
BUT...
I DON'T LIKE THIS.
I...
BA-THUMP
I HATE THIS.
BA-THUMP
I CAN'T BREATHE.
I WON'T SEND YOU...
WEIRD EMAILS OR ANY-THING.
BA-THUMP
UM.
BA-THUMP
STOP.
BA-THUMP
STOP IT.
NOTHING LIKE THAT.
BA-THUMP
BA-THUMP
IF IT'S A BOTHER...
PLEASE!
JUST KNOCK IT OFF.
SURE.

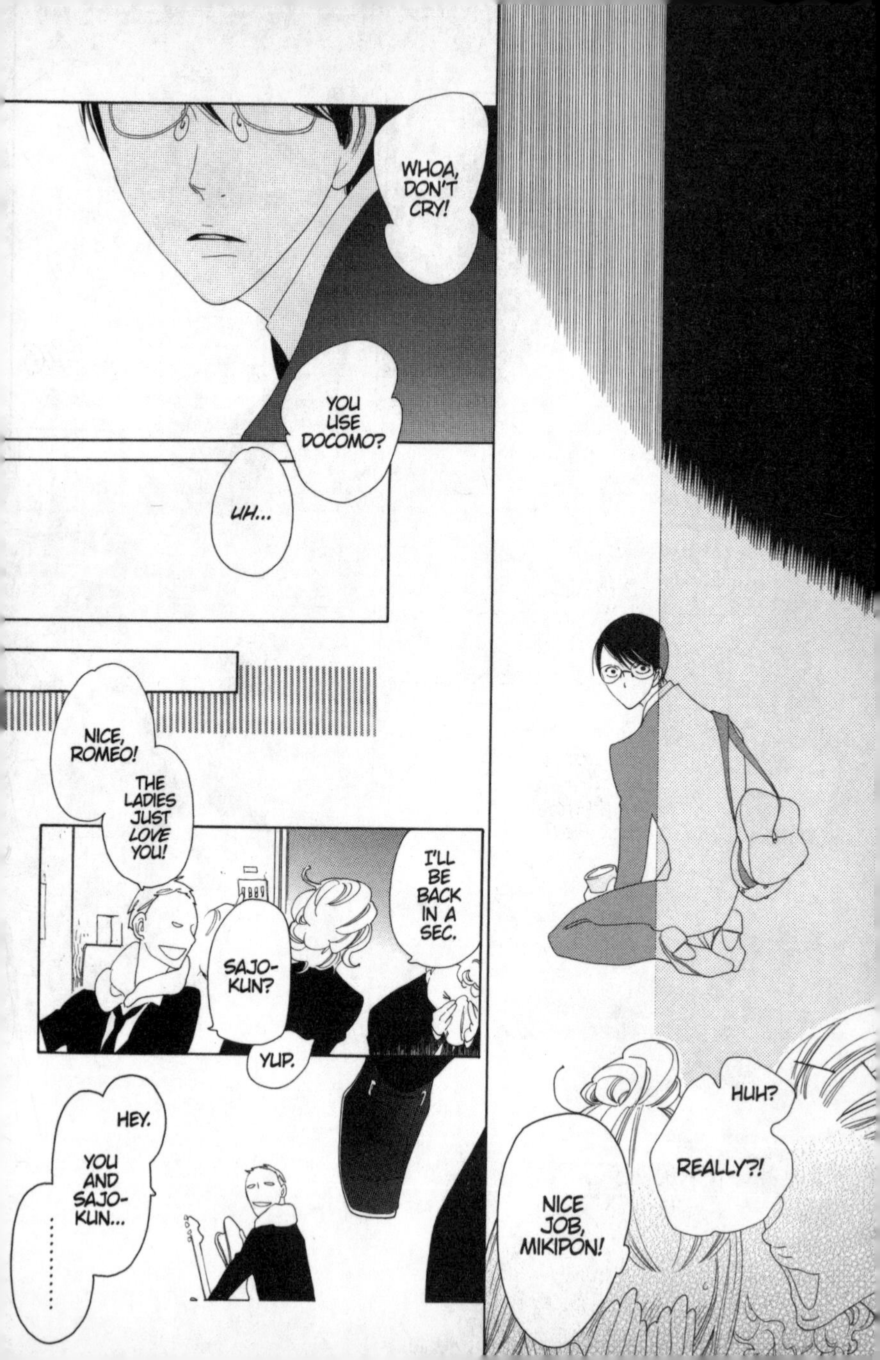
HUH?
REALLY?!
NICE JOB, MIKIPON!
WHOA, DON'T CRY!
YOU USE DOCOMO?
UH...
NICE, ROMEO! THE LADIES JUST LOVE YOU!
I'LL BE BACK IN A SEC.
SAJO-KUN?
YUP.
HEY.
YOU AND SAJO-KUN...
......

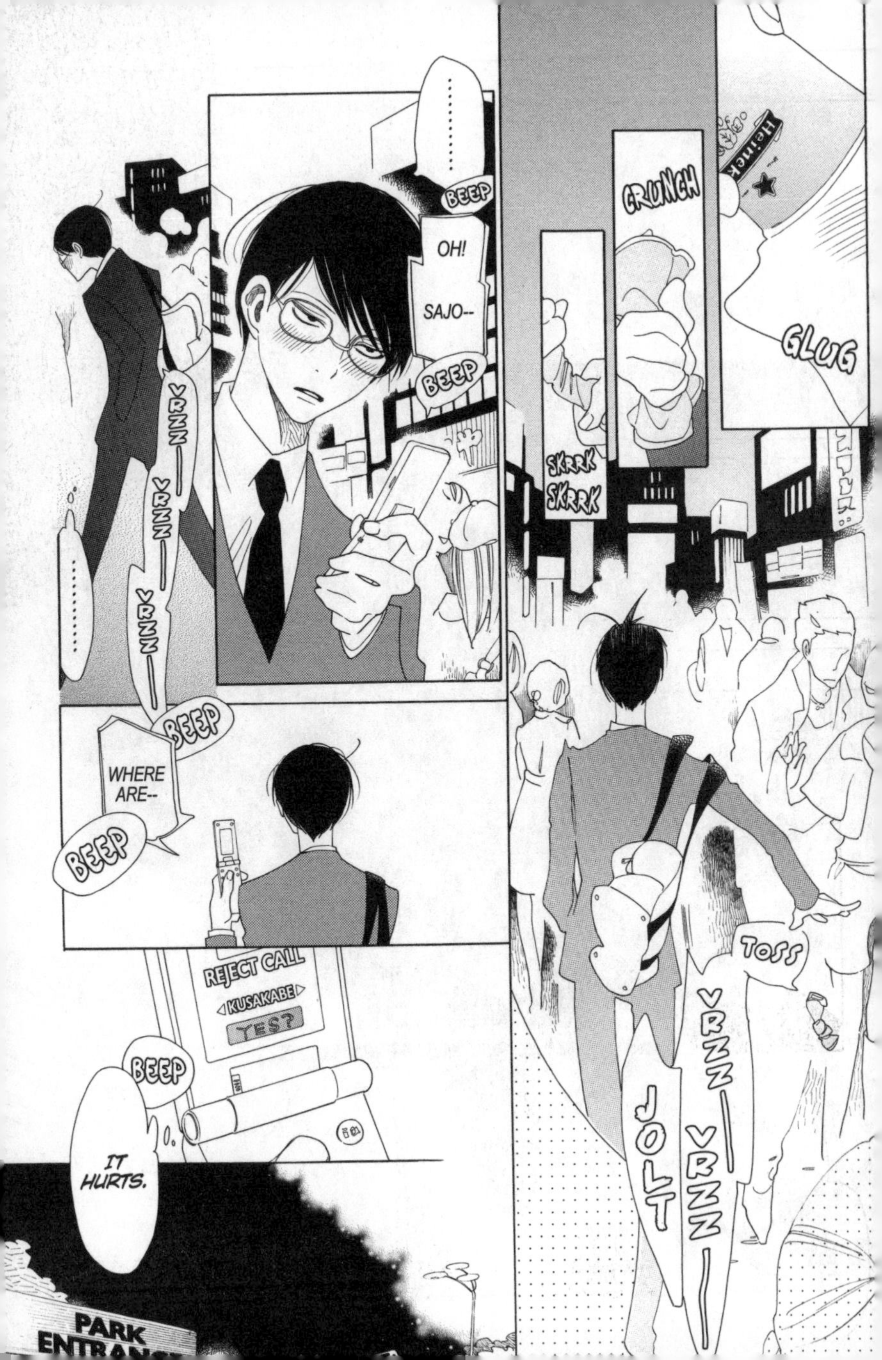
GLUG
CRUNCH
SKRRK SKRRK
TOSS
VRZZ— VRZZ—
JOLT
......
BEEP
OH!
SAJO--
BEEP
VRZZ— VRZZ— VRZZ—
......
BEEP
WHERE ARE--
BEEP
REJECT CALL
KUSAKABE
YES?
BEEP
IT HURTS.
PARK

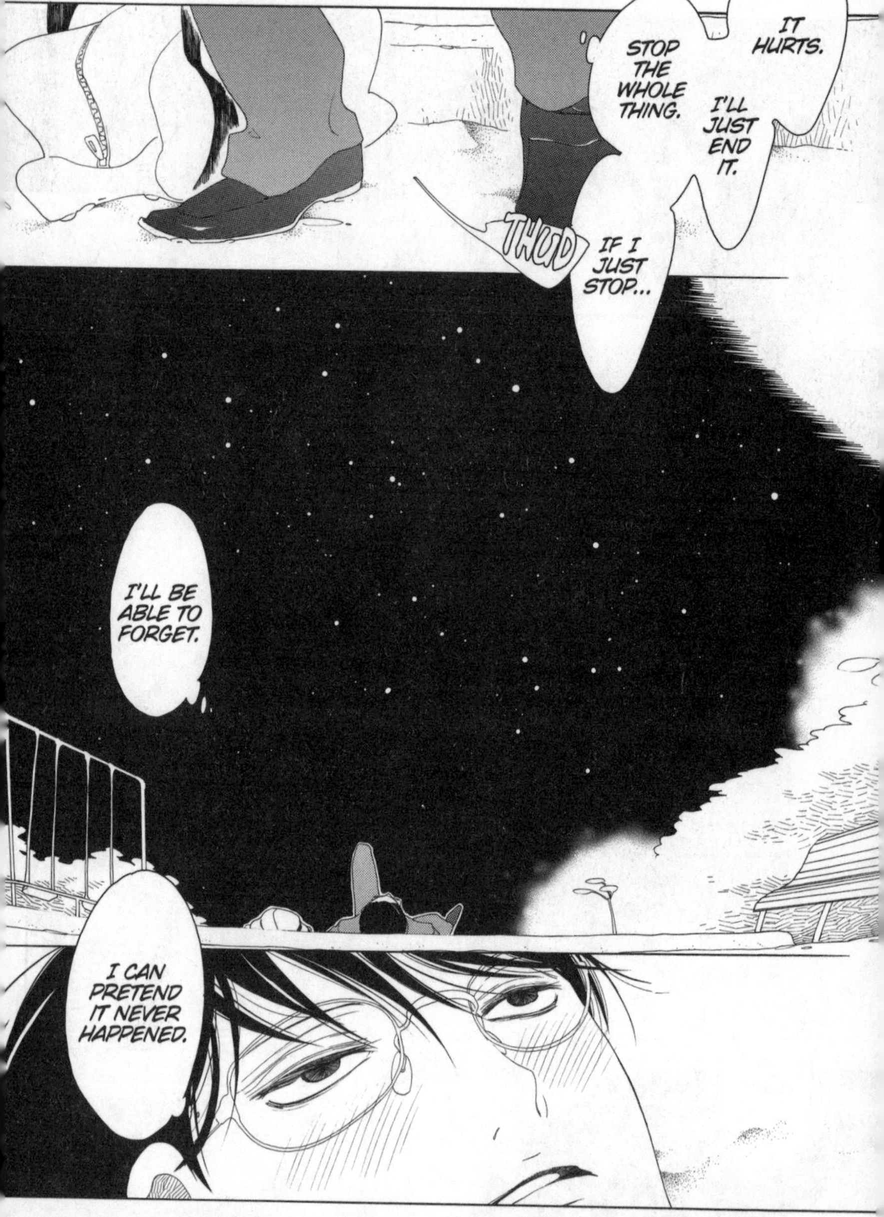
IT HURTS.
I'LL JUST END IT.
STOP THE WHOLE THING.
THUD
IF I JUST STOP...
I'LL BE ABLE TO FORGET.
I CAN PRETEND IT NEVER HAPPENED.

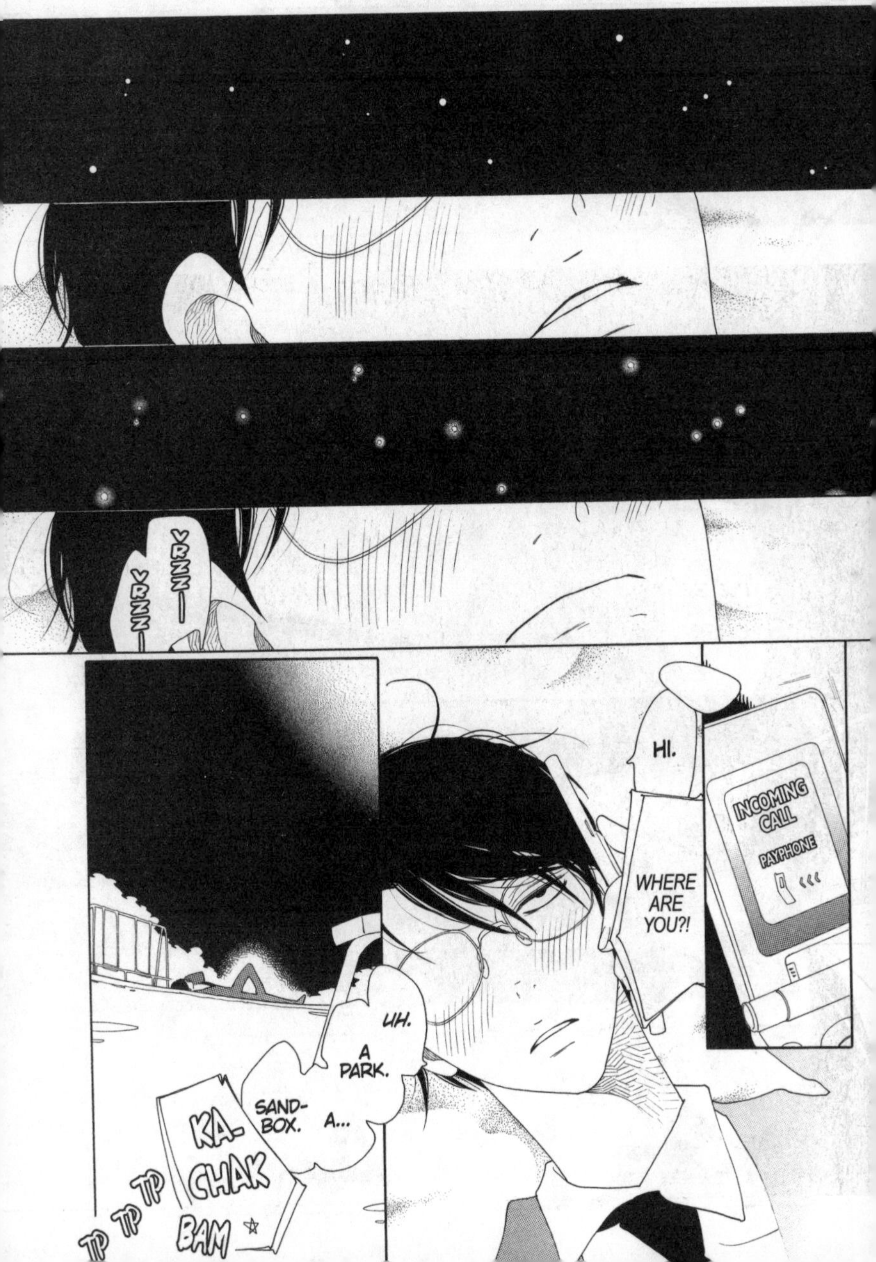
VRZZ—
VRZZ—
INCOMING CALL
PAYPHONE
HI.
WHERE ARE YOU?!
UH.
A PARK.
A...
SAND-BOX.
KA-CHAK
BAM
TP TP TP

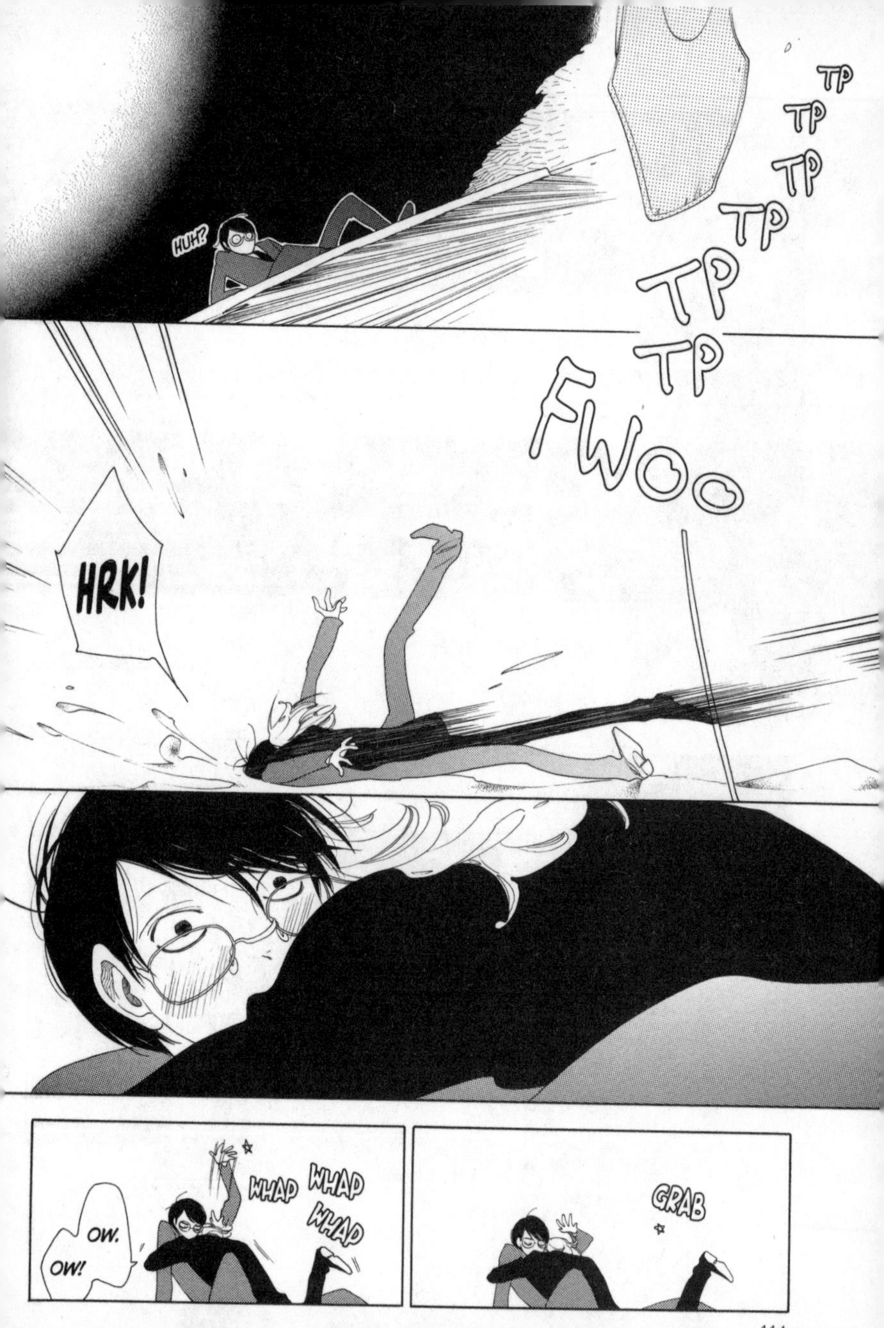
TP
TP
TP
TP
TP
HUH?
TP
FWOO
HRK!
GRAB
WHAP
WHAP
WHAP
OW.
OW!

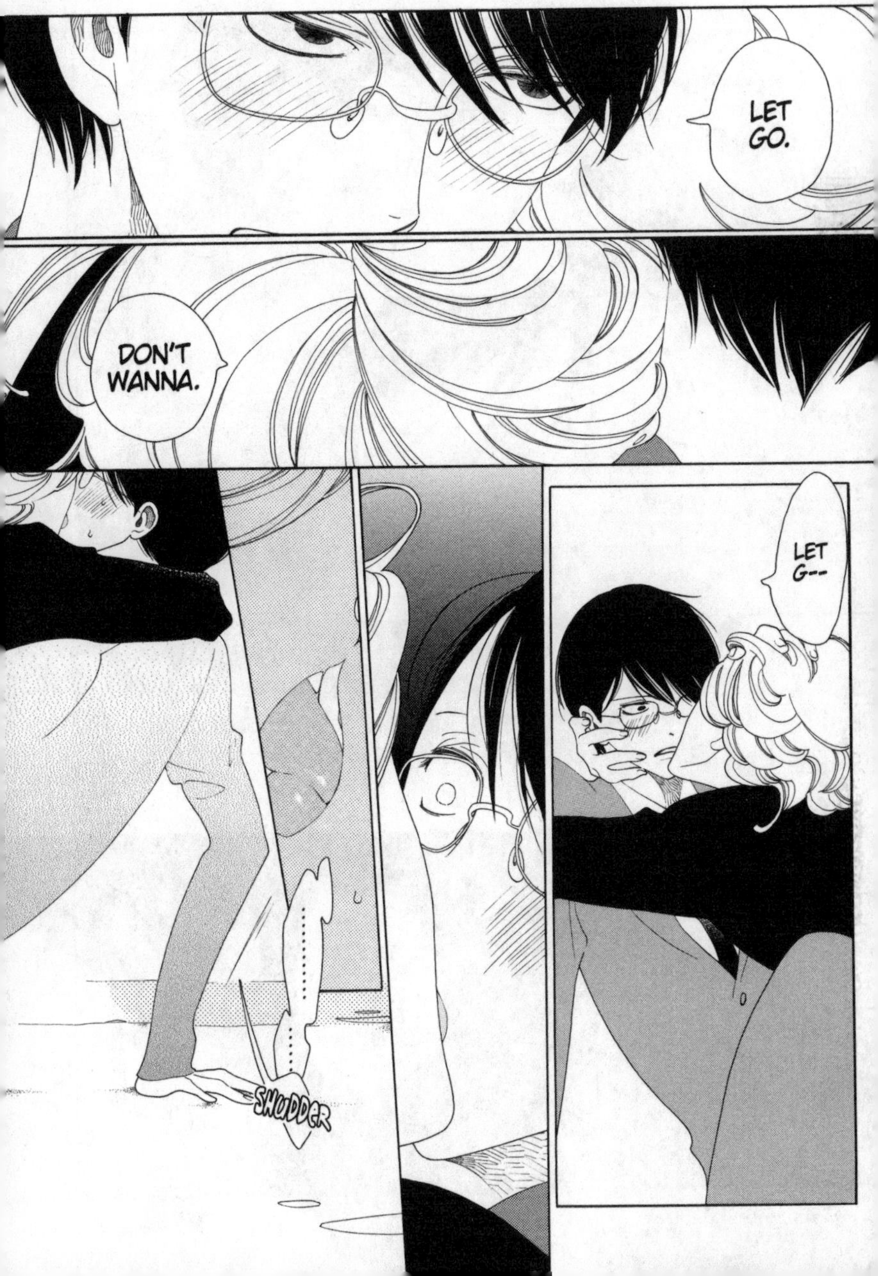
LET GO.
DON'T WANNA.
LET G--
SHUDDER

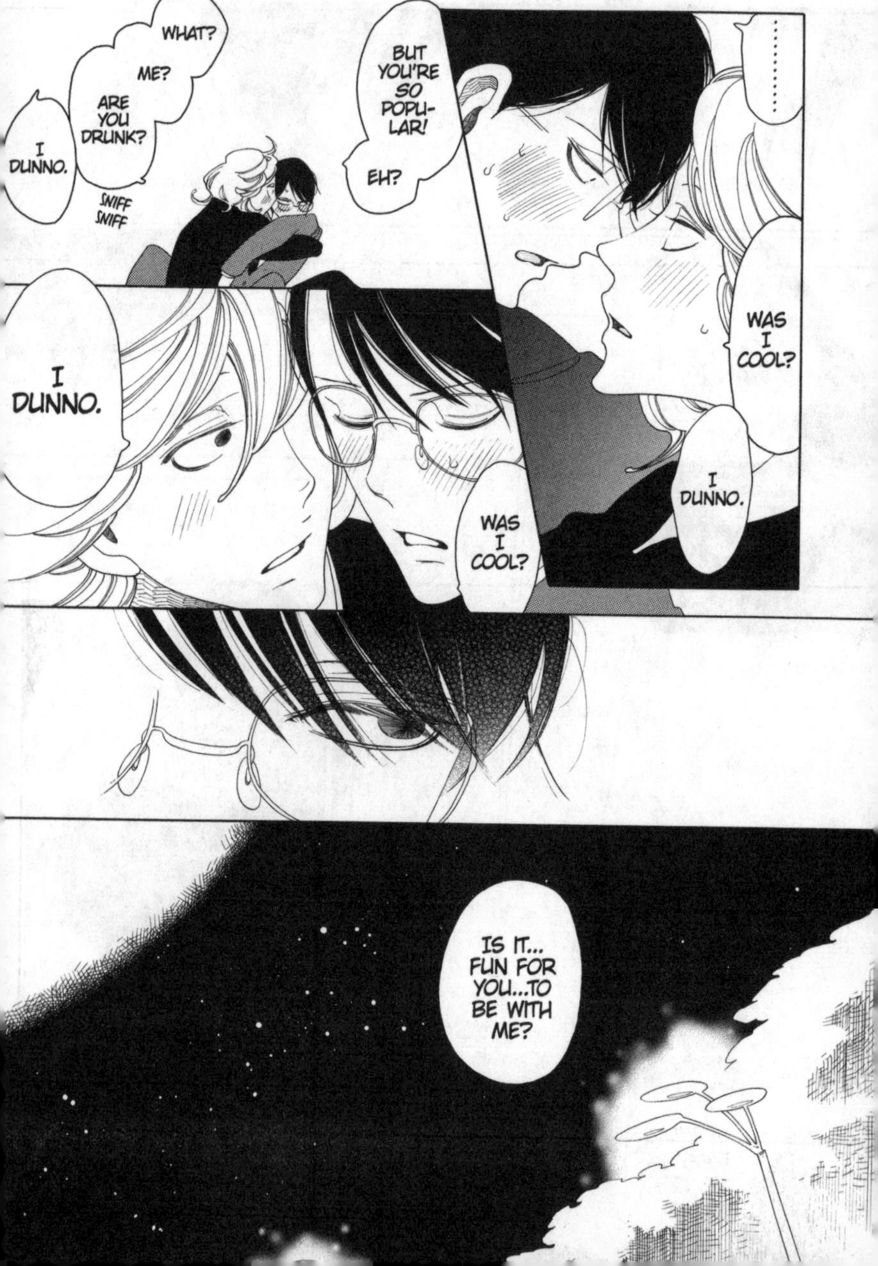
......
WAS I COOL?
I DUNNO.
BUT YOU'RE SO POPULAR!
EH?
WHAT?
ME?
ARE YOU DRUNK?
I DUNNO.
SNIFF SNIFF
WAS I COOL?
I DUNNO.
IS IT... FUN FOR YOU...TO BE WITH ME?

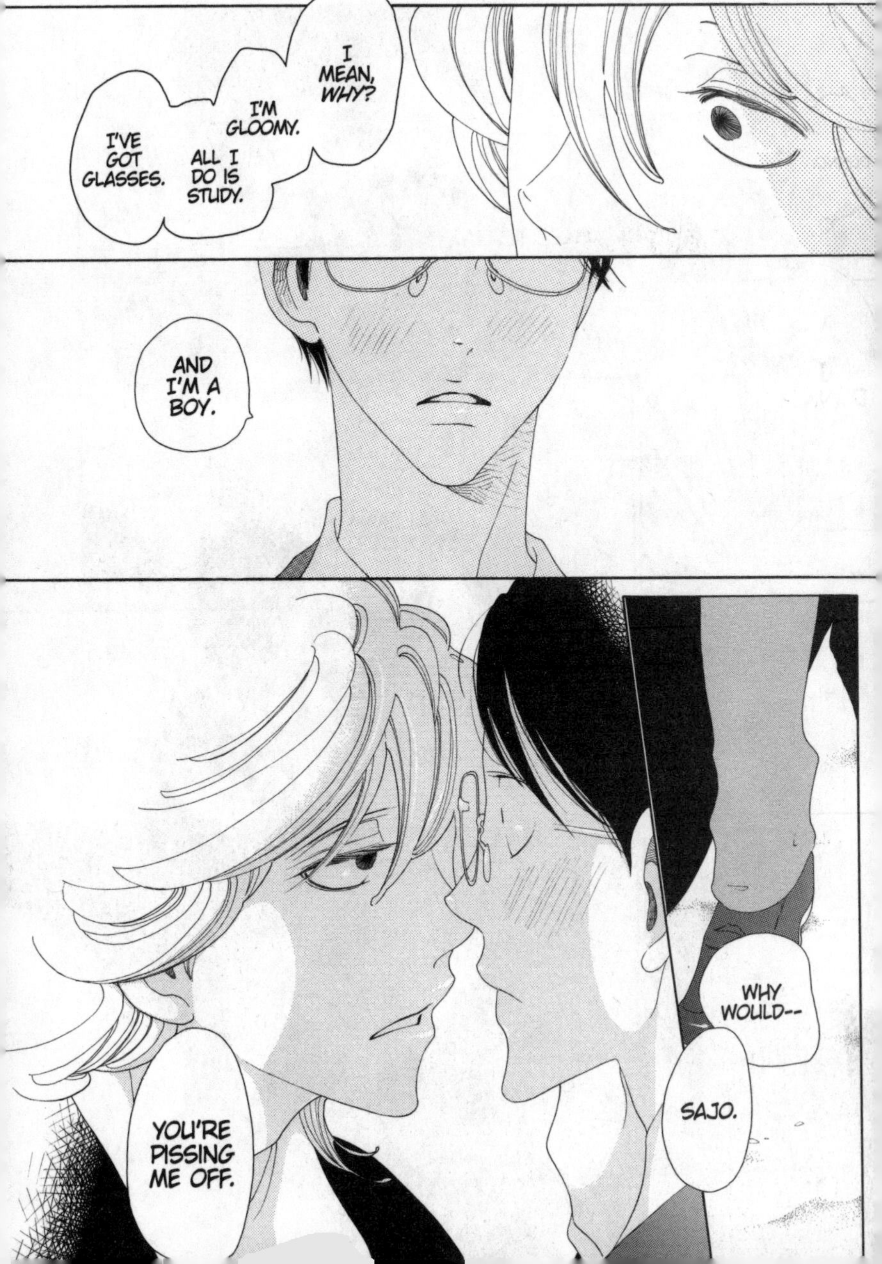
I MEAN, WHY?
I'M GLOOMY.
ALL I DO IS STUDY.
I'VE GOT GLASSES.
AND I'M A BOY.
WHY WOULD--
SAJO.
YOU'RE PISSING ME OFF.

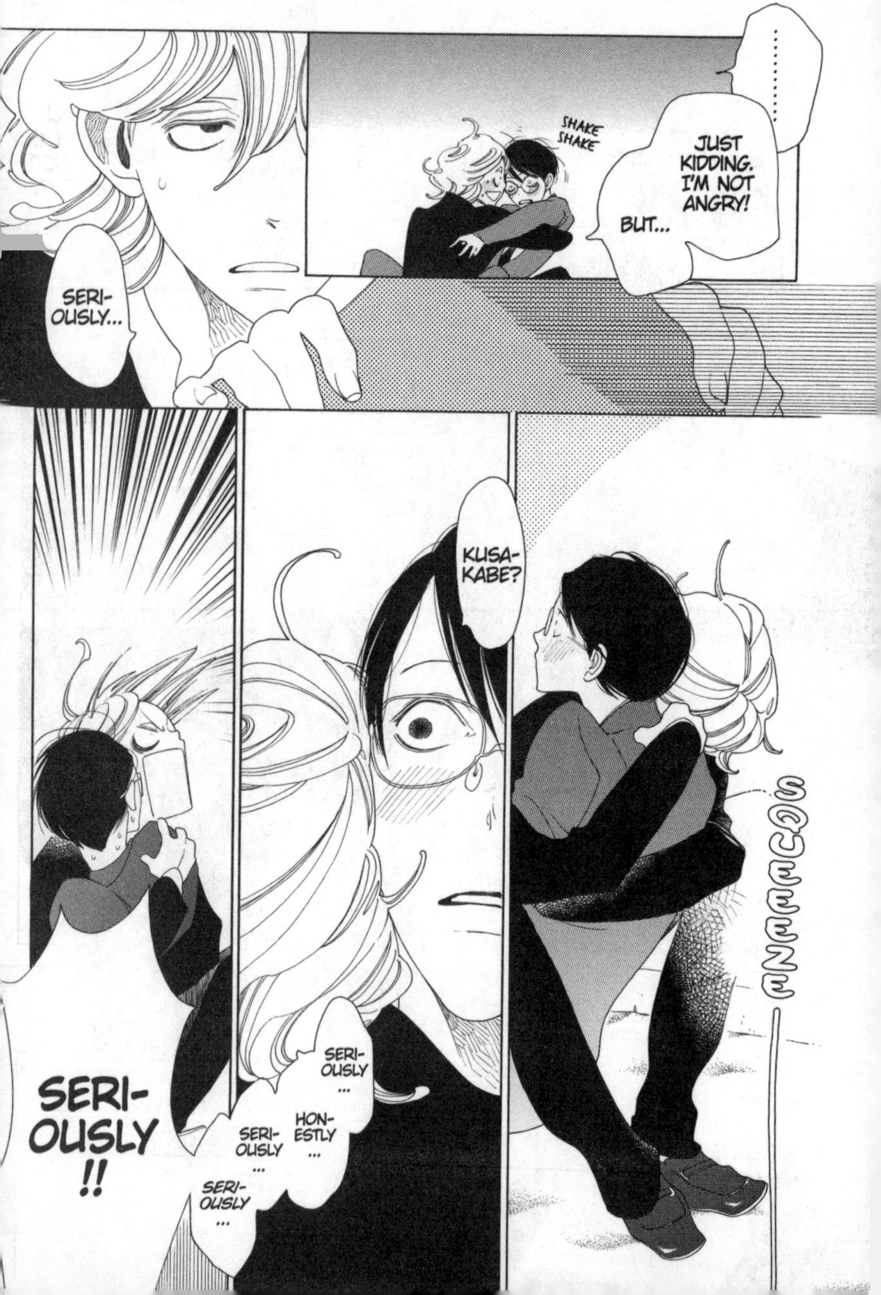
......
JUST KIDDING. I'M NOT ANGRY!
BUT...
SHAKE SHAKE
SERI-OUSLY...
KUSA-KABE?
SQUEEEEZE
SERI-OUSLY ...
HON-ESTLY ...
SERI-OUSLY ...
SERI-OUSLY ...
SERI-OUSLY !!

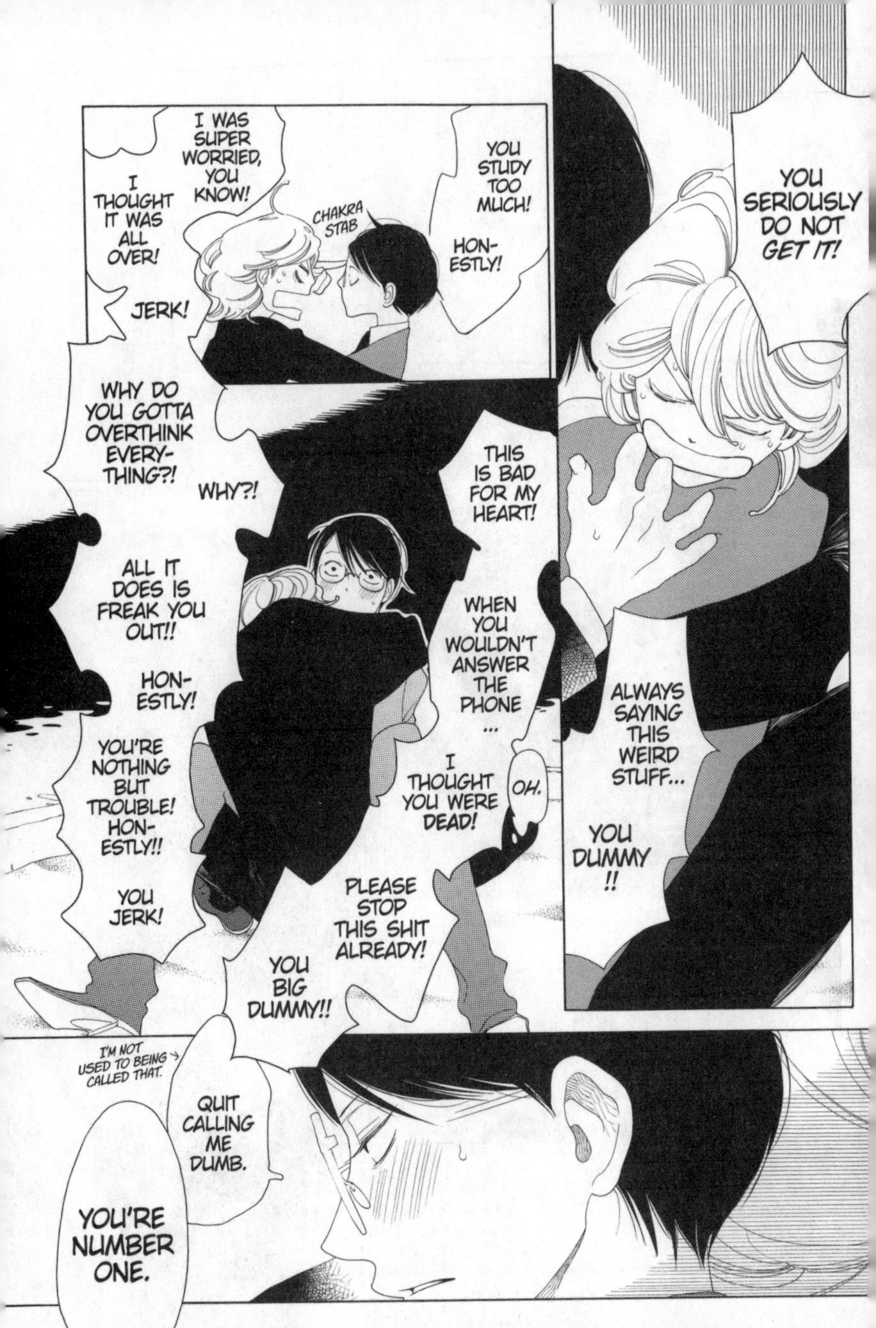
YOU SERIOUSLY DO NOT GET IT!
ALWAYS SAYING THIS WEIRD STUFF...
YOU DUMMY!!
YOU STUDY TOO MUCH!
HON-ESTLY!
CHAKRA STAB
I WAS SUPER WORRIED, YOU KNOW!
I THOUGHT IT WAS ALL OVER!
JERK!
THIS IS BAD FOR MY HEART!
WHEN YOU WOULDN'T ANSWER THE PHONE ...
I THOUGHT YOU WERE DEAD!
OH.
PLEASE STOP THIS SHIT ALREADY!
YOU BIG DUMMY!!
WHY DO YOU GOTTA OVERTHINK EVERY-THING?!
WHY?!
ALL IT DOES IS FREAK YOU OUT!!
HON-ESTLY!
YOU'RE NOTHING BUT TROUBLE! HON-ESTLY!!
YOU JERK!
QUIT CALLING ME DUMB.
I'M NOT USED TO BEING CALLED THAT.
YOU'RE NUMBER ONE.

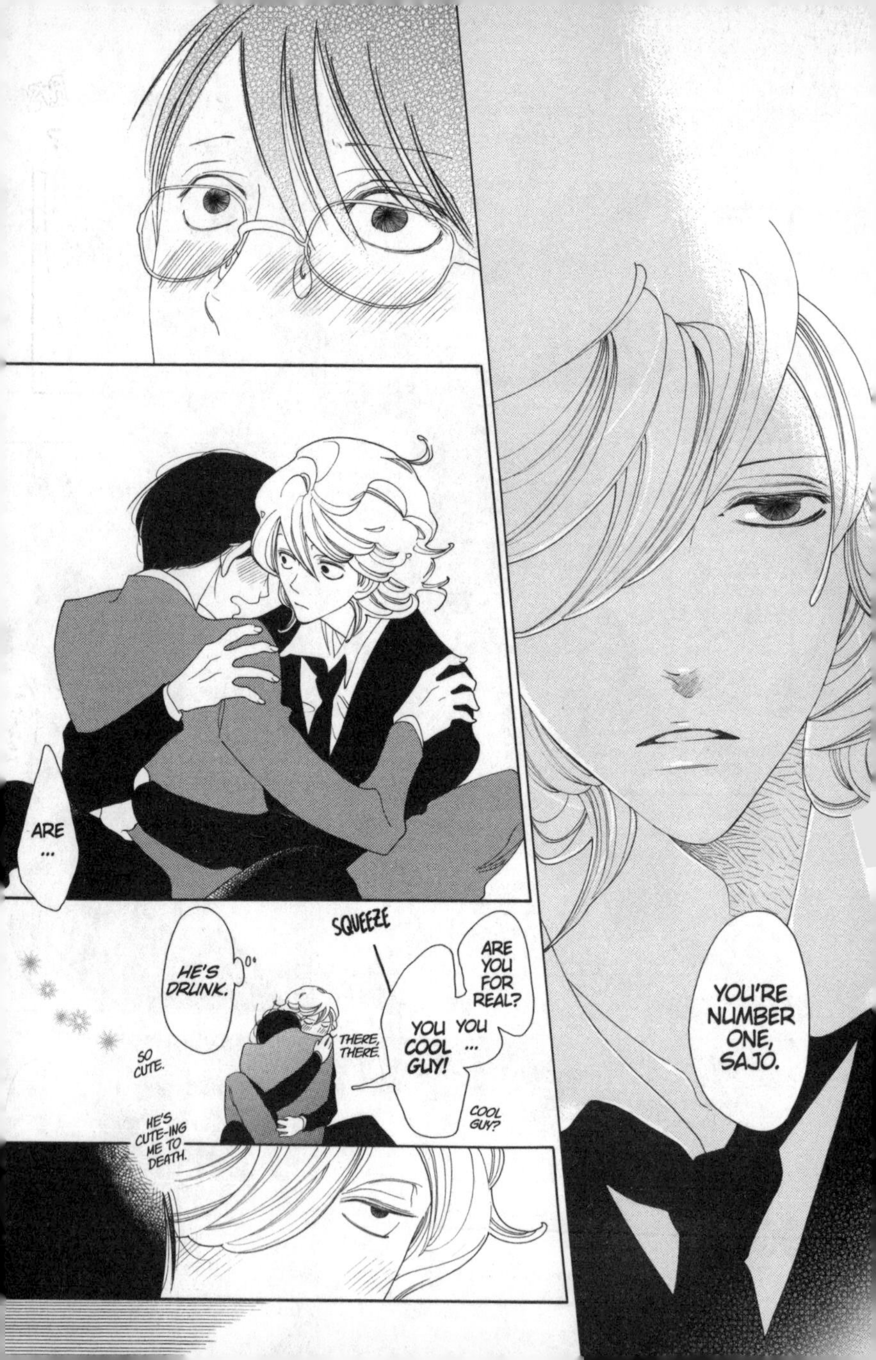
YOU'RE NUMBER ONE, SAJO.
ARE ...
SQUEEZE
ARE YOU FOR REAL?
YOU ...
YOU COOL GUY!
COOL GUY?
THERE, THERE.
HE'S DRUNK.
SO CUTE.
HE'S CUTE-ING ME TO DEATH.

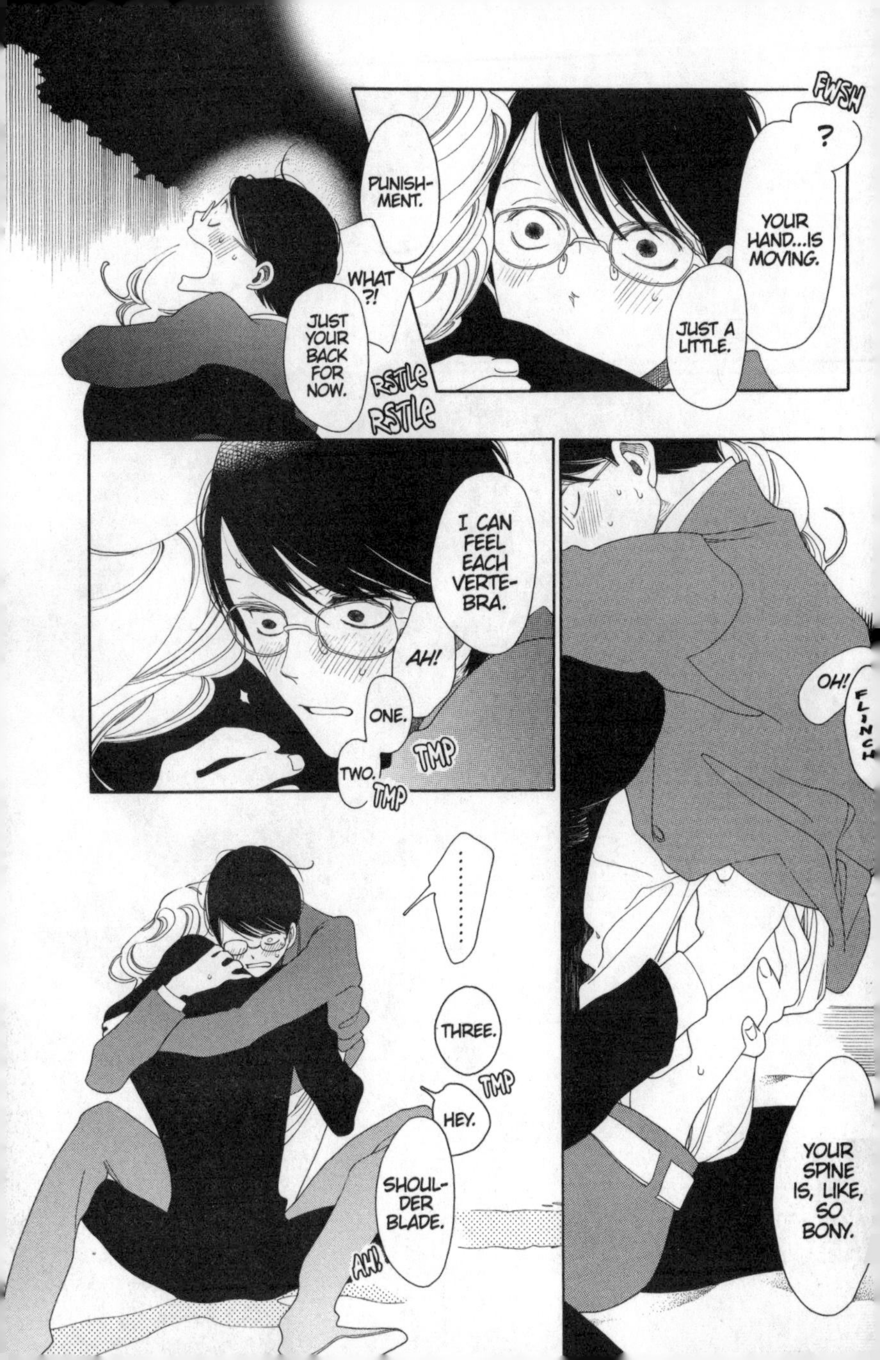
FWSH
?
YOUR HAND...IS MOVING.
JUST A LITTLE.
PUNISHMENT.
WHAT?!
JUST YOUR BACK FOR NOW.
RSTLE
RSTLE
OH!
FLINCH
YOUR SPINE IS, LIKE, SO BONY.
I CAN FEEL EACH VERTEBRA.
AH!
ONE.
TMP
TWO.
TMP
......
THREE.
TMP
HEY.
SHOULDER BLADE.
AH!

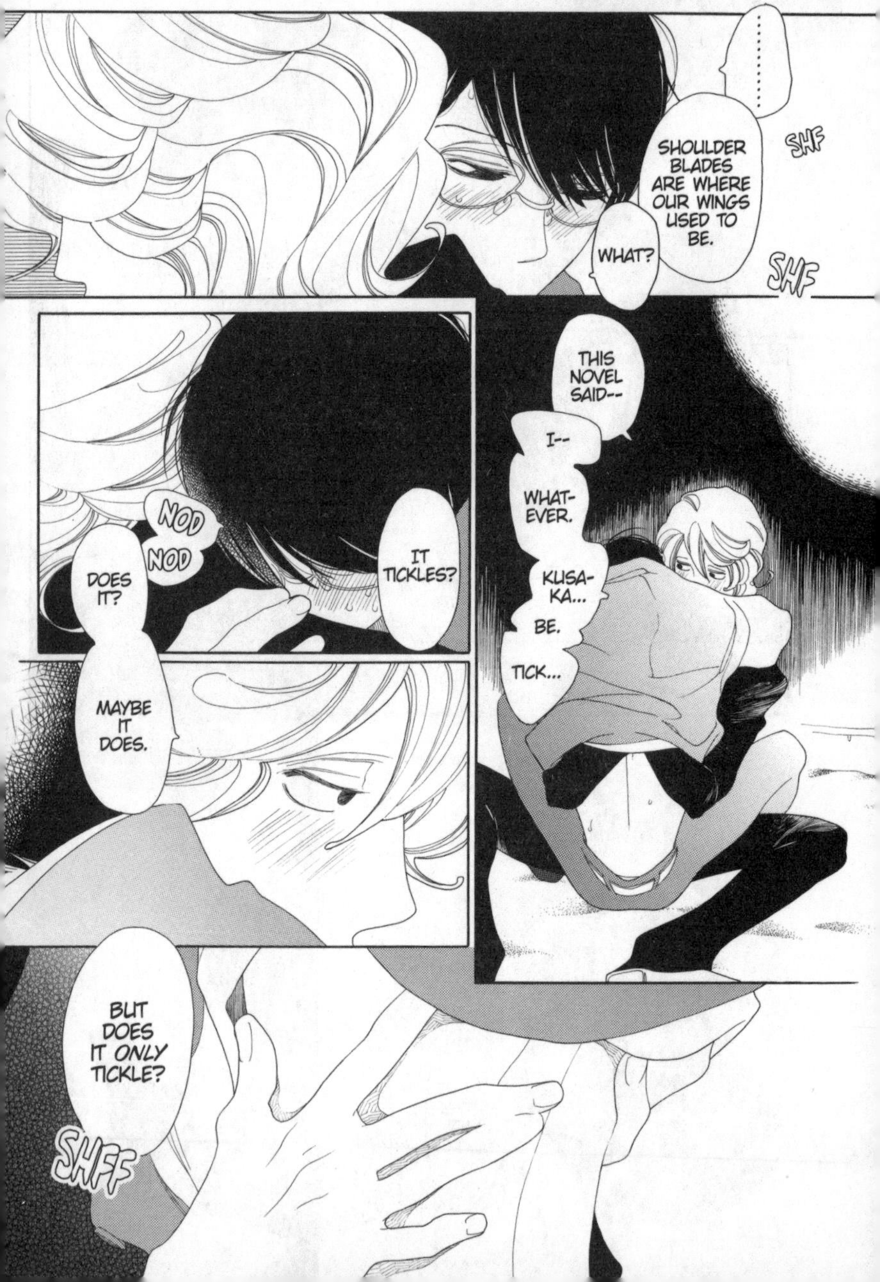
......
SHF
SHOULDER BLADES ARE WHERE OUR WINGS USED TO BE.
WHAT?
SHF
THIS NOVEL SAID--
I--
WHAT-EVER.
KUSA-KA...
BE.
TICK...
IT TICKLES?
NOD
NOD
DOES IT?
MAYBE IT DOES.
BUT DOES IT *ONLY* TICKLE?
SHFF

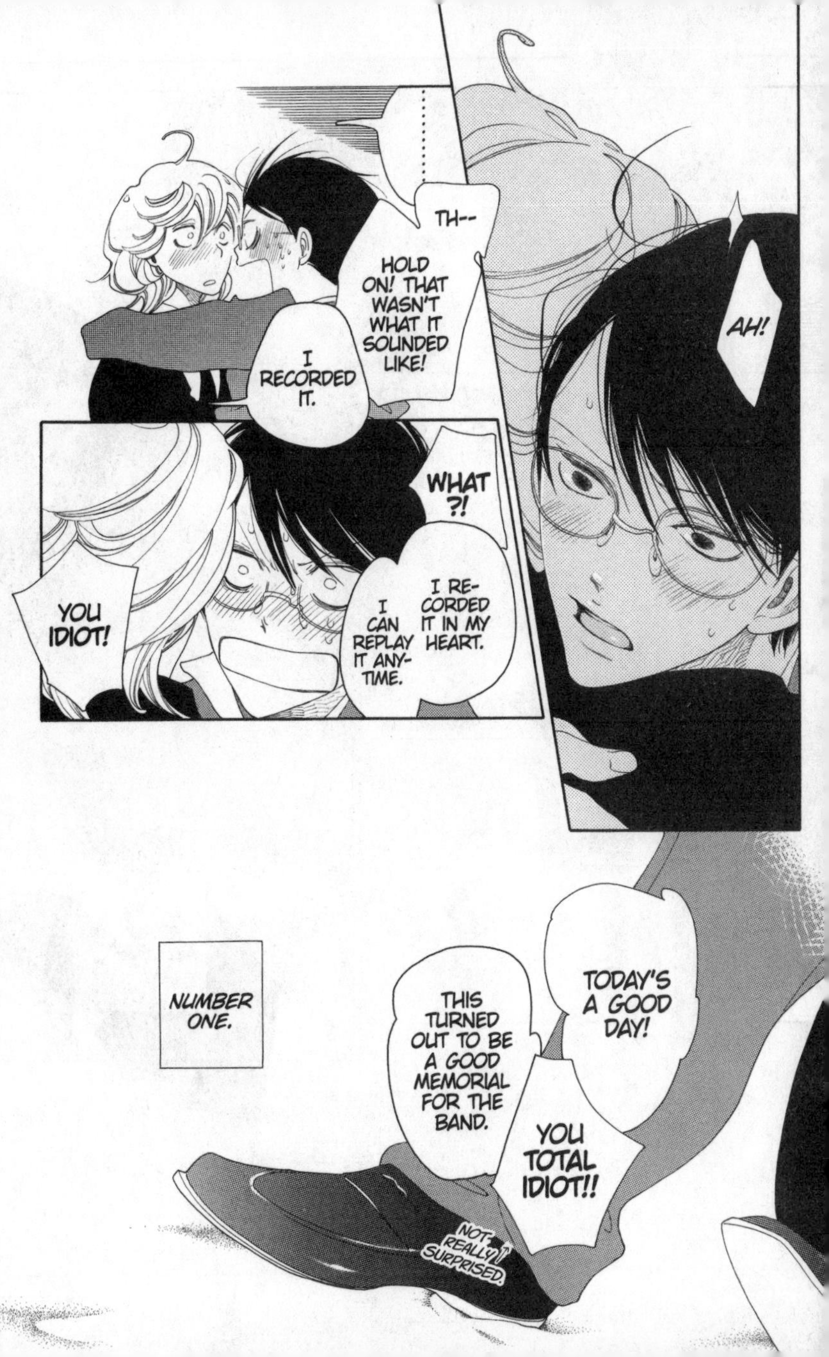
AH!
TH--
HOLD ON! THAT WASN'T WHAT IT SOUNDED LIKE!
I RECORDED IT.
WHAT?!
I RE-CORDED IT IN MY HEART.
I CAN REPLAY IT ANY-TIME.
YOU IDIOT!
TODAY'S A GOOD DAY!
THIS TURNED OUT TO BE A GOOD MEMORIAL FOR THE BAND.
YOU TOTAL IDIOT!!
NOT REALLY SURPRISED.
NUMBER ONE.

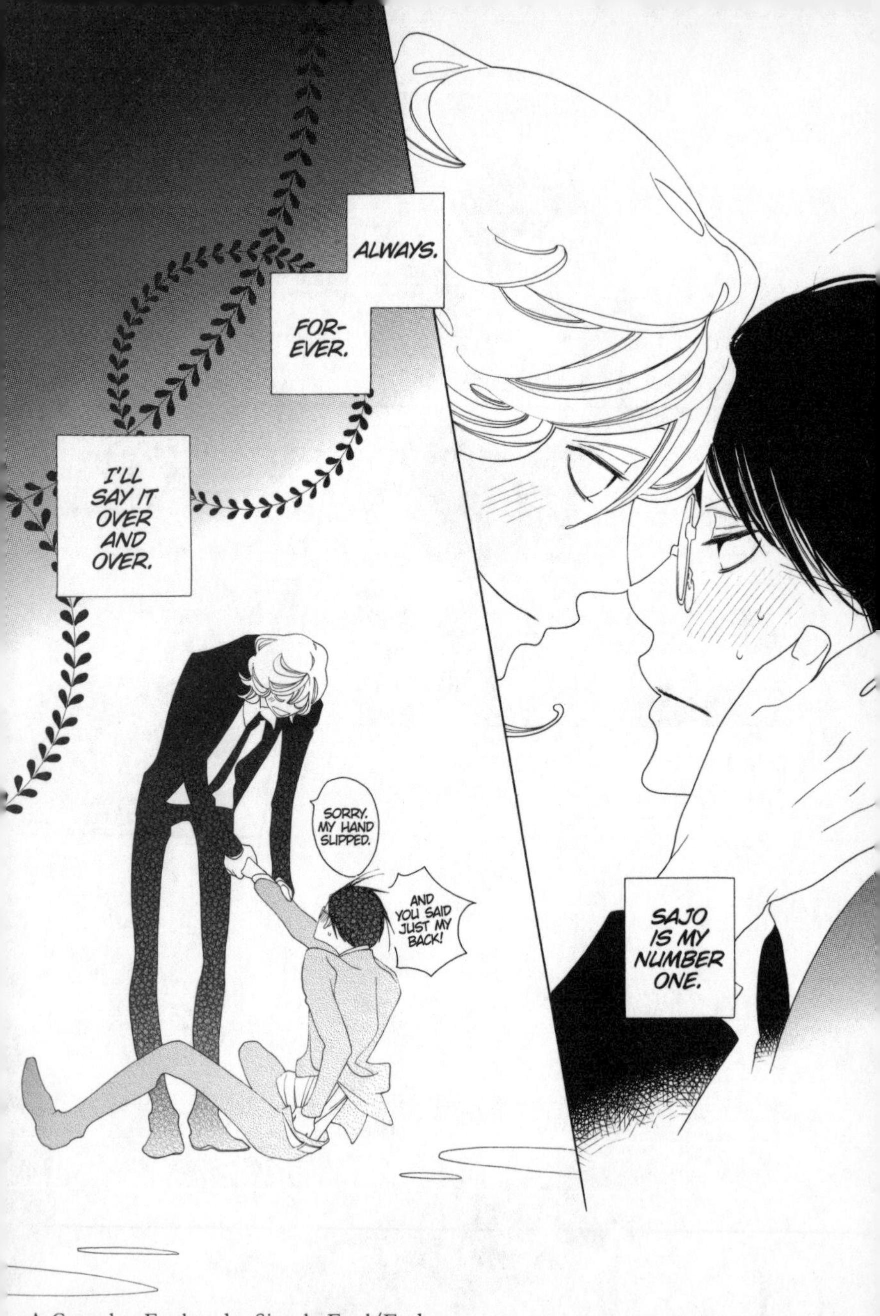
SAJO IS MY NUMBER ONE.
ALWAYS.
FOR-EVER.
I'LL SAY IT OVER AND OVER.
SORRY. MY HAND SLIPPED.
AND YOU SAID JUST MY BACK!

A Complex Fool and a Simple Fool/End

Classmates

Intermission

[The Second Summer]

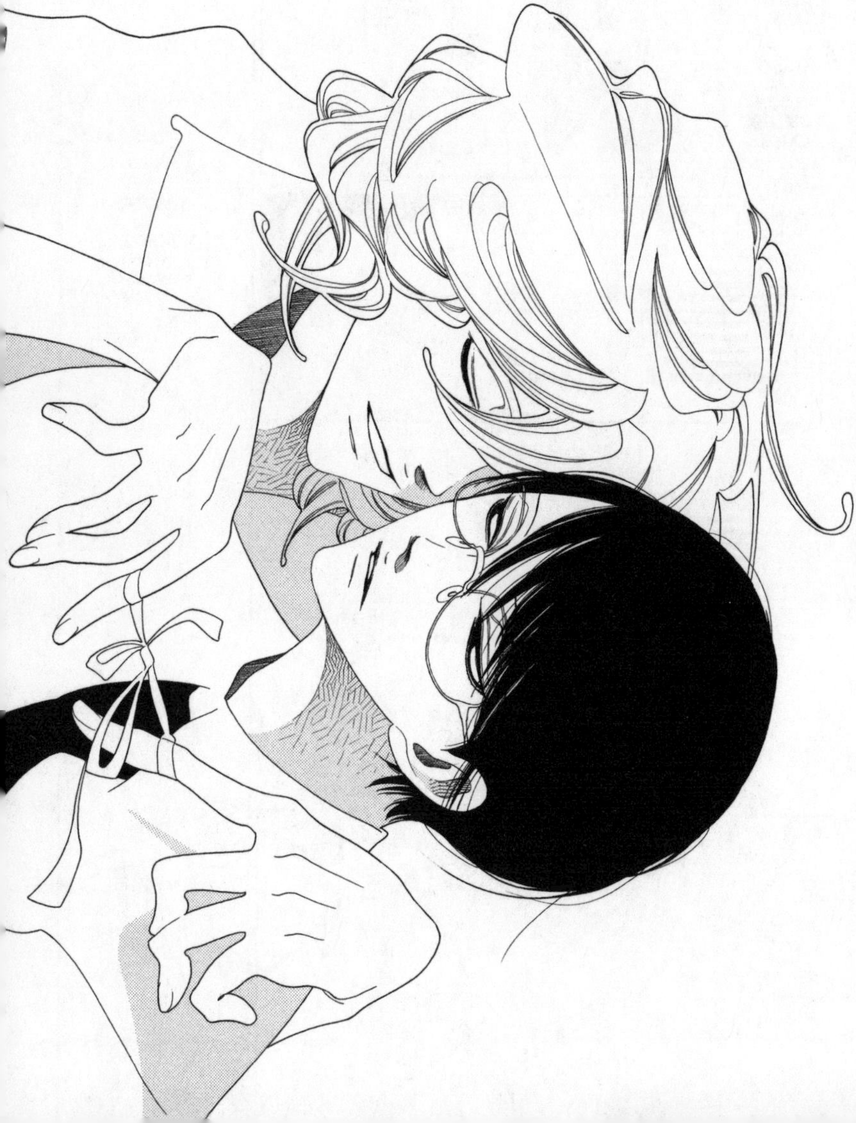

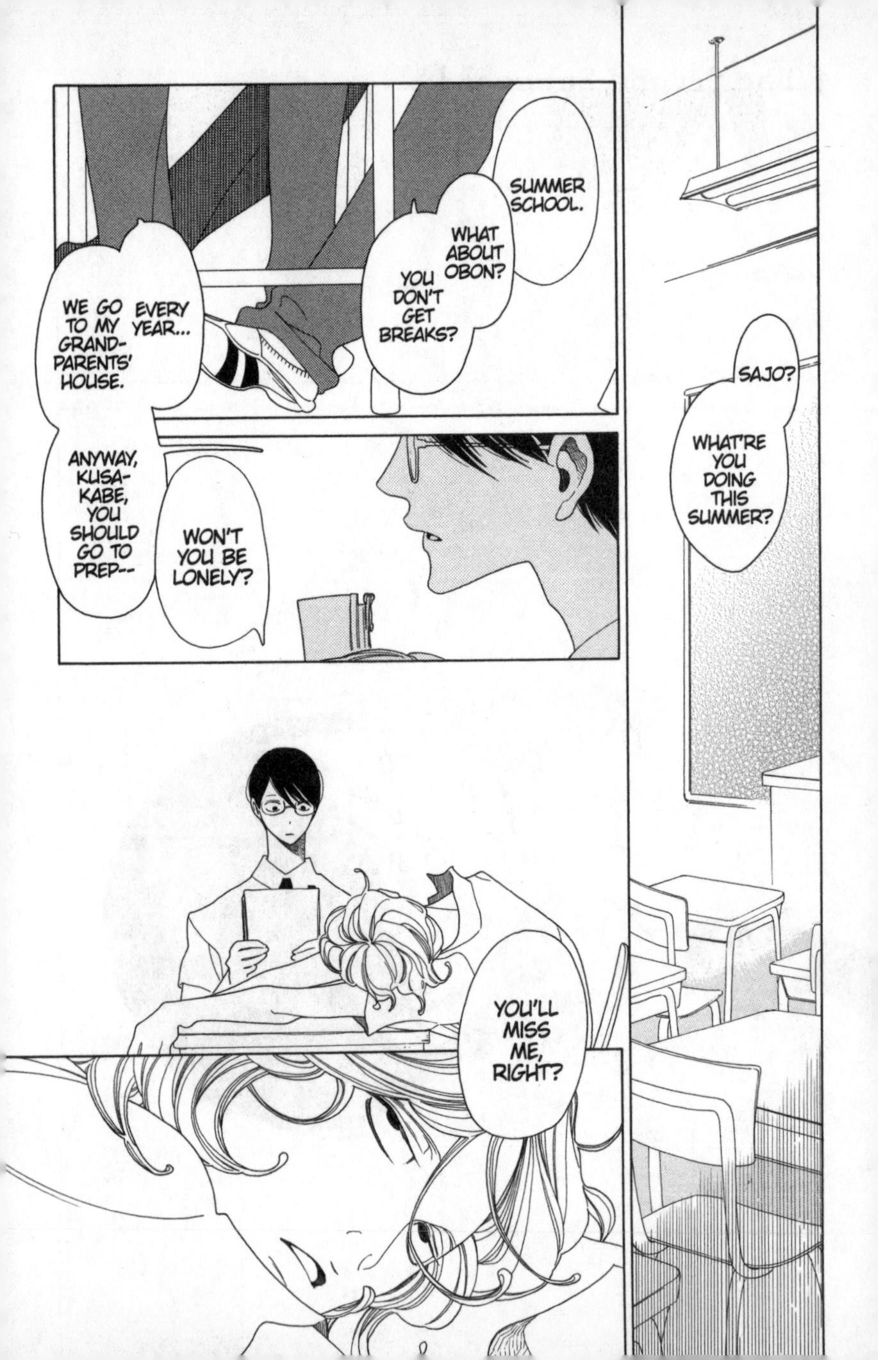
SAJO?
WHAT'RE YOU DOING THIS SUMMER?
SUMMER SCHOOL.
WHAT ABOUT OBON?
YOU DON'T GET BREAKS?
WE GO TO MY GRAND-PARENTS' HOUSE.
EVERY YEAR...
WON'T YOU BE LONELY?
ANYWAY, KUSA-KABE, YOU SHOULD GO TO PREP--
YOU'LL MISS ME, RIGHT?

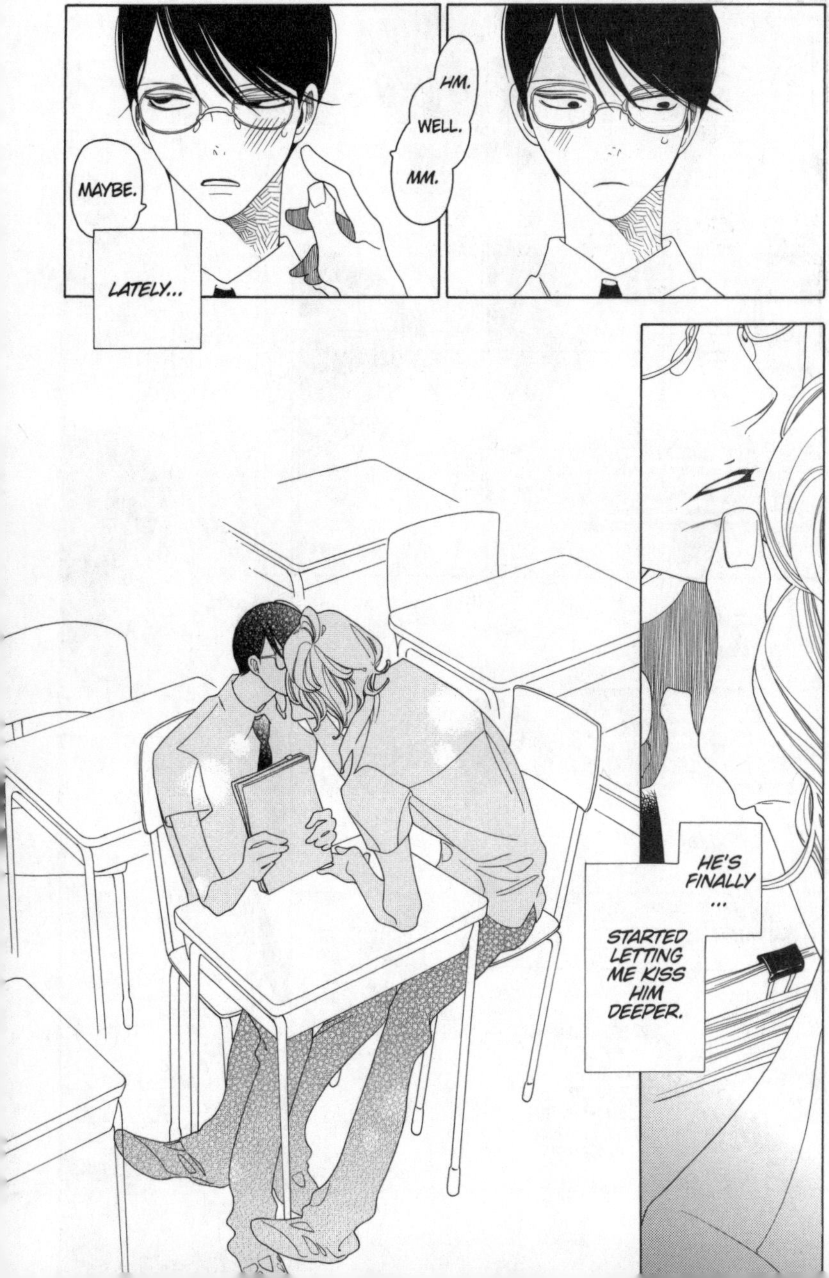
HM.
WELL.
MM.
MAYBE.
LATELY...
HE'S FINALLY ...
STARTED LETTING ME KISS HIM DEEPER.

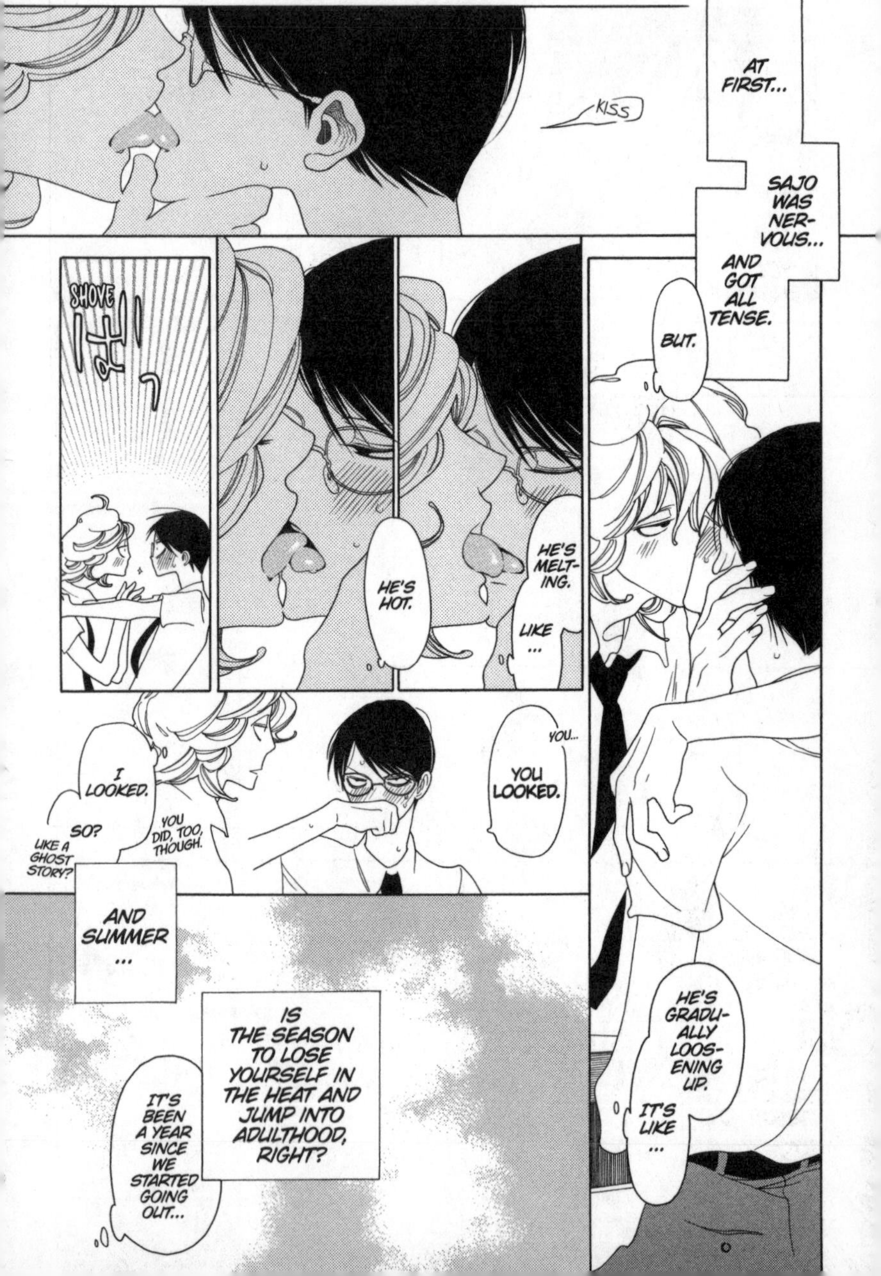
AT FIRST...
SAJO WAS NERVOUS...
AND GOT ALL TENSE.
KISS
BUT.
HE'S GRADUALLY LOOSENING UP.
IT'S LIKE ...
HE'S MELTING.
LIKE ...
HE'S HOT.
SHOVE
はっ
YOU...
YOU LOOKED.
I LOOKED.
YOU DID, TOO, THOUGH.
SO?
LIKE A GHOST STORY?
AND SUMMER ...
IS THE SEASON TO LOSE YOURSELF IN THE HEAT AND JUMP INTO ADULTHOOD, RIGHT?
IT'S BEEN A YEAR SINCE WE STARTED GOING OUT...

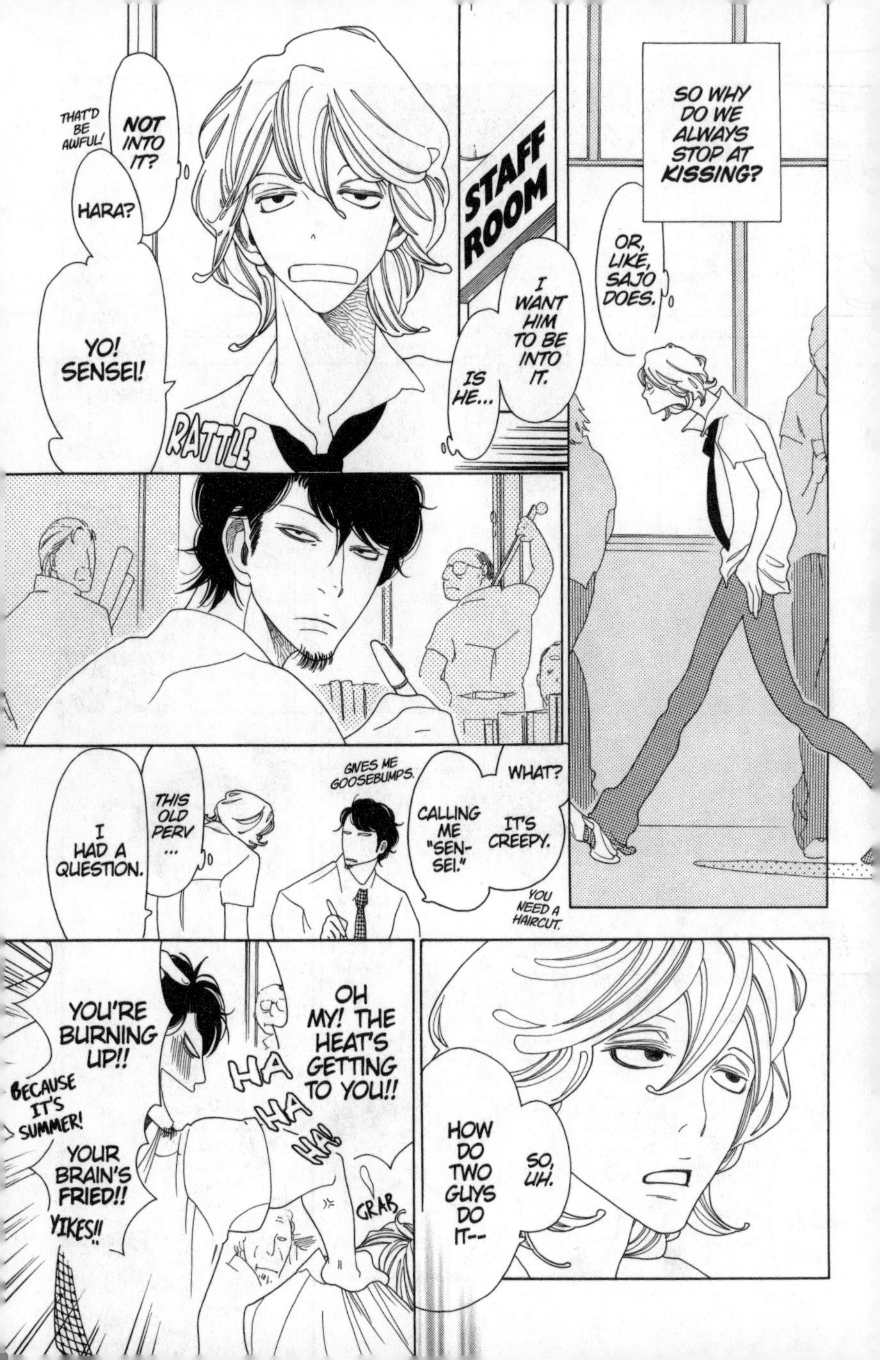
SO WHY DO WE ALWAYS STOP AT KISSING?
OR, LIKE, SAJO DOES.
I WANT HIM TO BE INTO IT.
IS HE...
STAFF ROOM
NOT INTO IT?
THAT'D BE AWFUL!
HARA?
YO! SENSEI!
RATTLE
WHAT?
GIVES ME GOOSEBUMPS.
IT'S CREEPY.
CALLING ME "SEN-SEI."
YOU NEED A HAIRCUT.
THIS OLD PERV...
I HAD A QUESTION.
SO, UH.
HOW DO TWO GUYS DO IT--
OH MY! THE HEAT'S GETTING TO YOU!!
HA HA HA
YOU'RE BURNING UP!!
BECAUSE IT'S SUMMER!
YOUR BRAIN'S FRIED!!
GRAB
YIKES!!

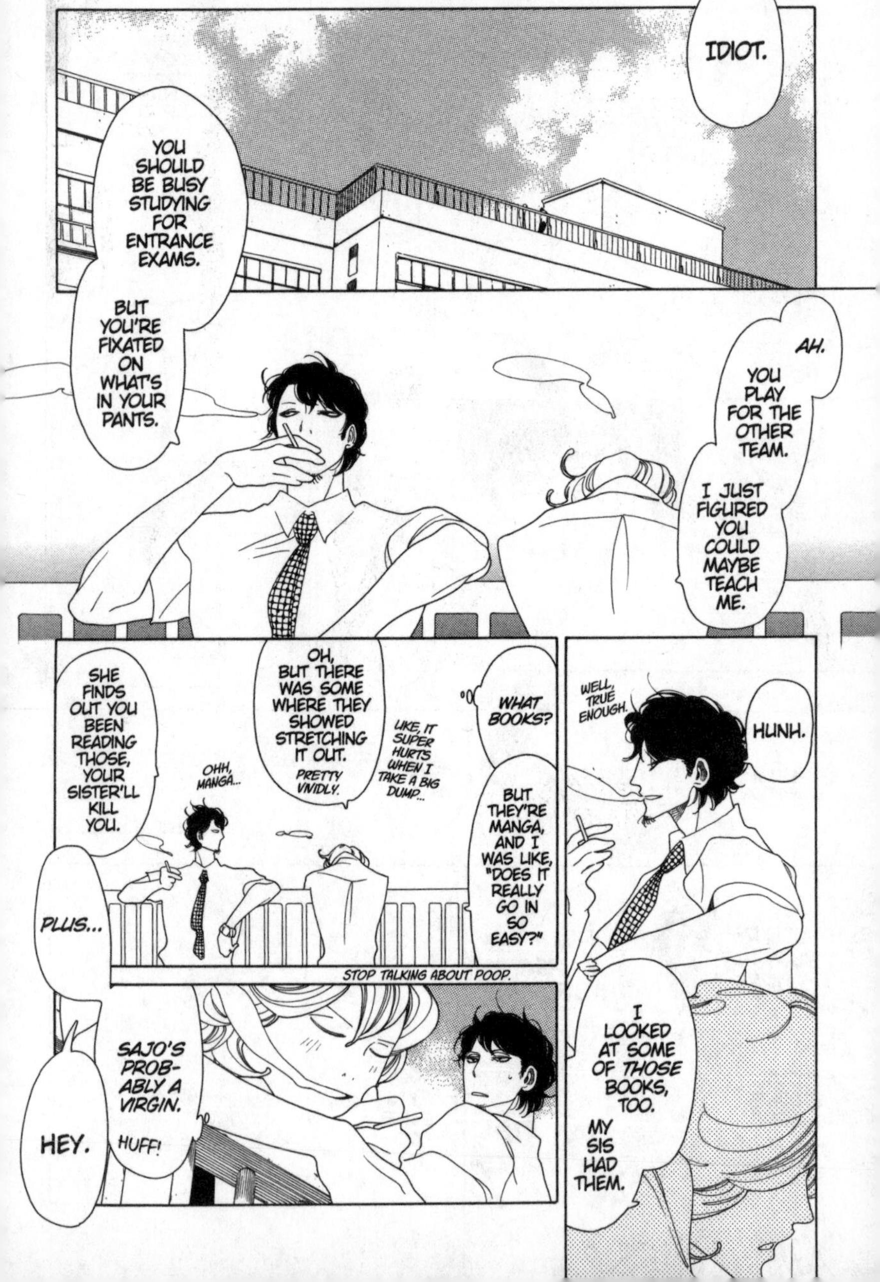
IDIOT.
YOU SHOULD BE BUSY STUDYING FOR ENTRANCE EXAMS.
AH.
YOU PLAY FOR THE OTHER TEAM.
I JUST FIGURED YOU COULD MAYBE TEACH ME.
BUT YOU'RE FIXATED ON WHAT'S IN YOUR PANTS.
HUNH.
WELL, TRUE ENOUGH.
I LOOKED AT SOME OF THOSE BOOKS, TOO.
MY SIS HAD THEM.
WHAT BOOKS?
BUT THEY'RE MANGA, AND I WAS LIKE, "DOES IT REALLY GO IN SO EASY?"
LIKE, IT SUPER HURTS WHEN I TAKE A BIG DUMP...
OH, BUT THERE WAS SOME WHERE THEY SHOWED STRETCHING IT OUT.
PRETTY VIVIDLY.
OHH, MANGA...
SHE FINDS OUT YOU BEEN READING THOSE, YOUR SISTER'LL KILL YOU.
PLUS...
STOP TALKING ABOUT POOP.
SAJO'S PROB-ABLY A VIRGIN.
HUFF!
HEY.

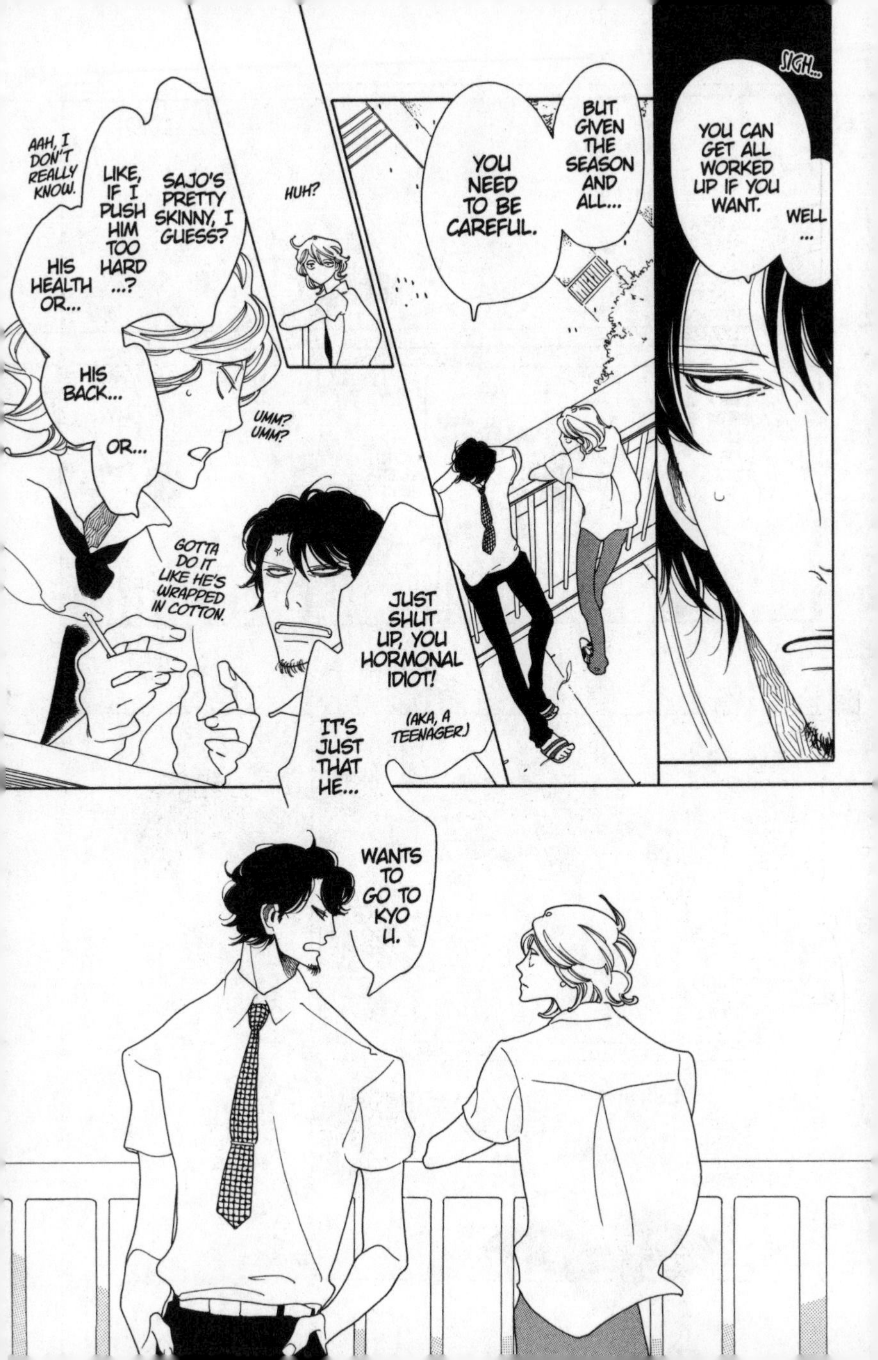
SIGH...
YOU CAN GET ALL WORKED UP IF YOU WANT.
WELL...
BUT GIVEN THE SEASON AND ALL...
YOU NEED TO BE CAREFUL.
HUH?
SAJO'S PRETTY SKINNY, I GUESS?
LIKE, IF I PUSH HIM TOO HARD ...?
AAH, I DON'T REALLY KNOW.
HIS HEALTH OR...
HIS BACK...
OR...
UMM? UMM?
GOTTA DO IT LIKE HE'S WRAPPED IN COTTON.
JUST SHUT UP, YOU HORMONAL IDIOT!
(AKA, A TEENAGER)
IT'S JUST THAT HE...
WANTS TO GO TO KYO U.

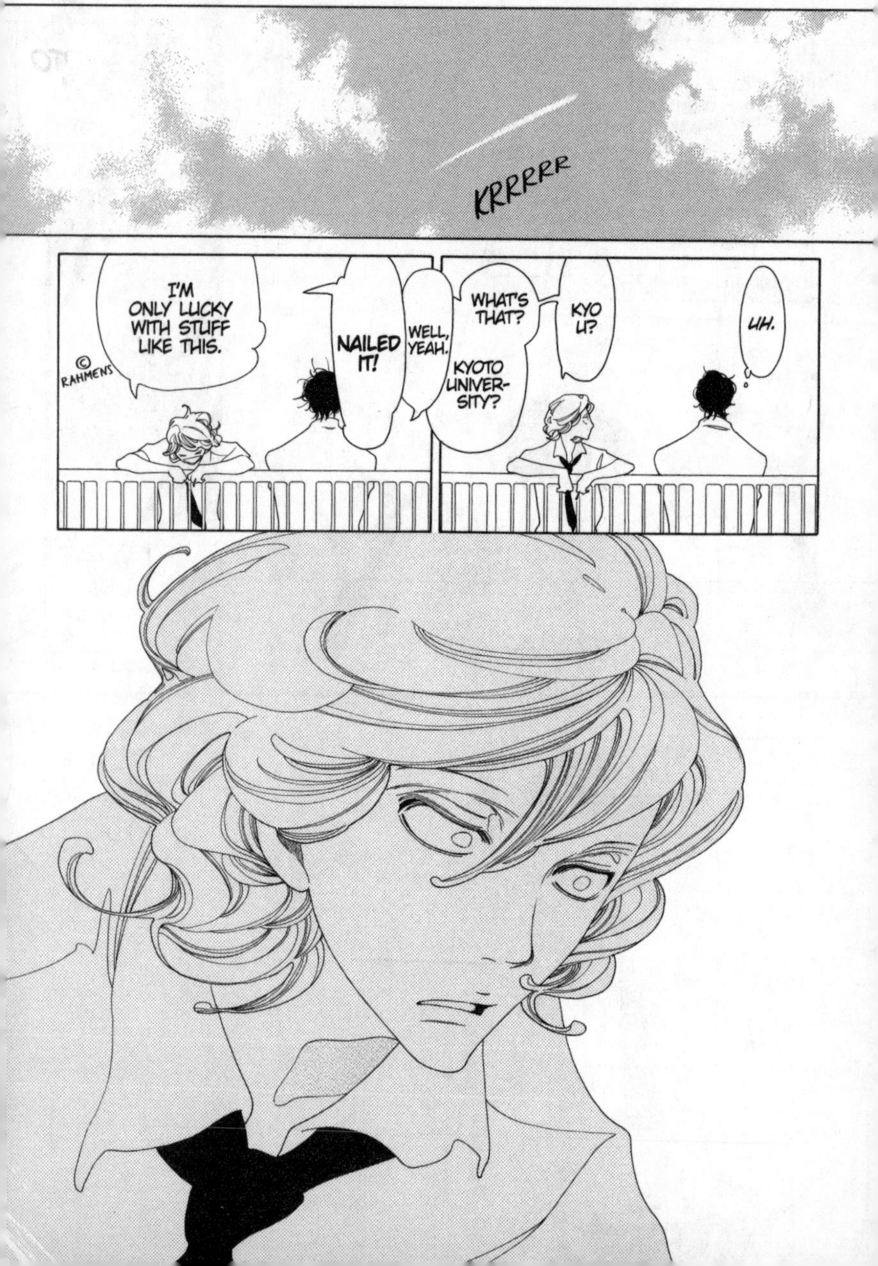
KRRRRR
UH.
KYO U?
WHAT'S THAT?
KYOTO UNIVERSITY?
WELL, YEAH.
NAILED IT!
I'M ONLY LUCKY WITH STUFF LIKE THIS.
© RAHMENS

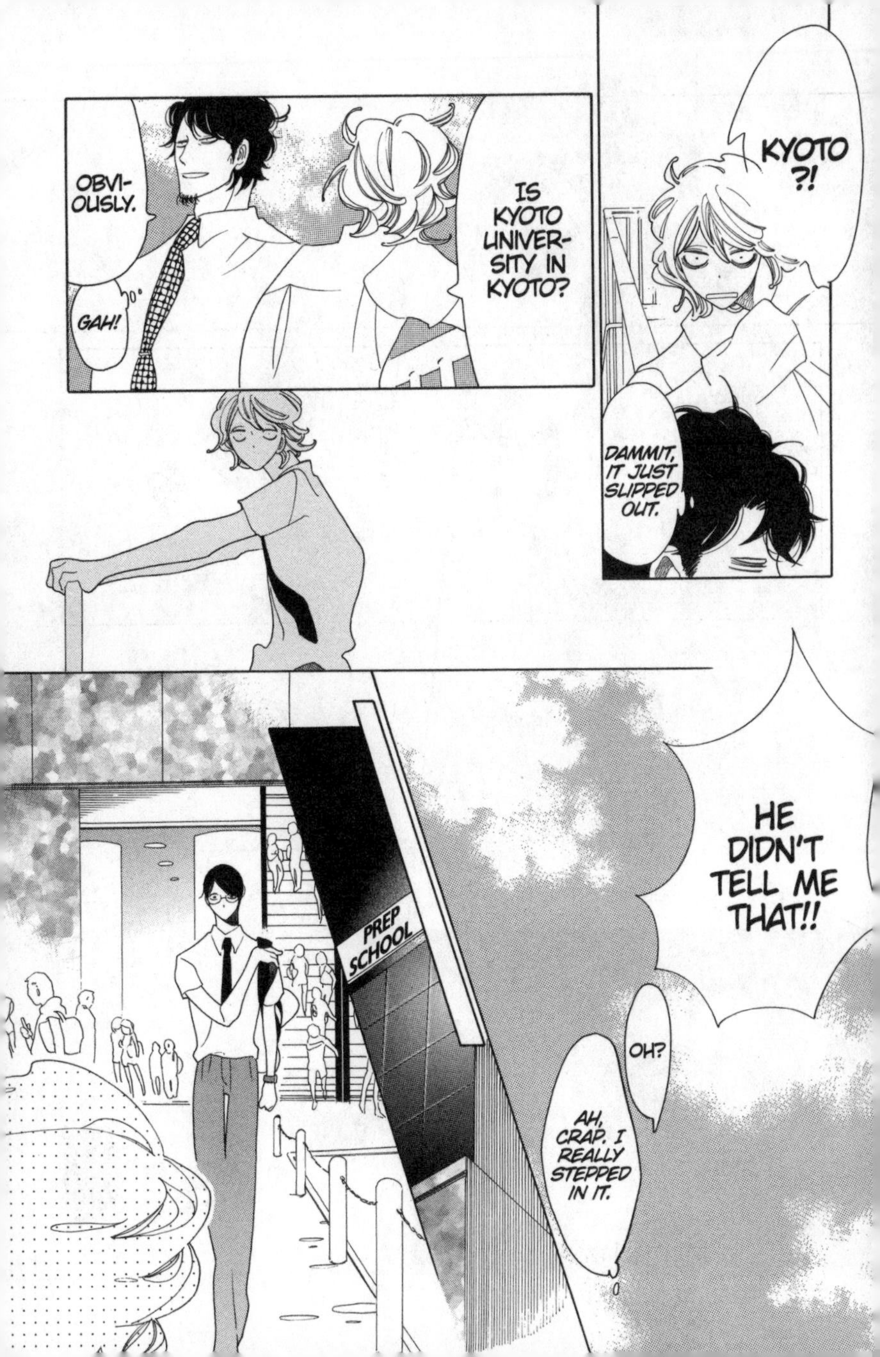
KYOTO ?!
DAMMIT, IT JUST SLIPPED OUT.
IS KYOTO UNIVERSITY IN KYOTO?
OBVIOUSLY.
GAH!
HE DIDN'T TELL ME THAT!!
OH?
AH, CRAP. I REALLY STEPPED IN IT.
PREP SCHOOL

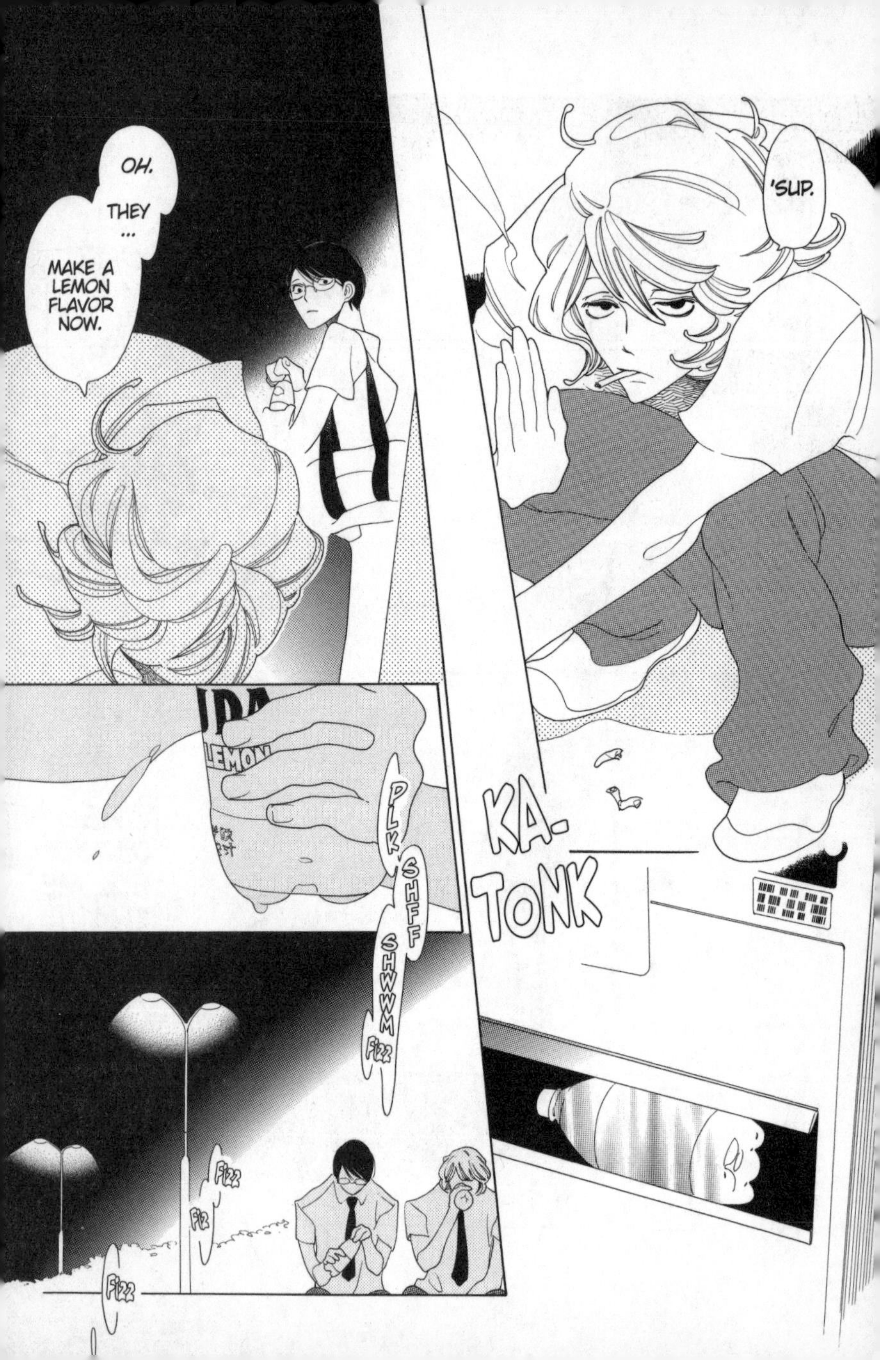
'SUP.
KA-TONK
OH.
THEY ...
MAKE A LEMON FLAVOR NOW.
LEMON
PLK
SHFF
SHWWM
FIZZ
FIZZ
FIZ
FIZZ

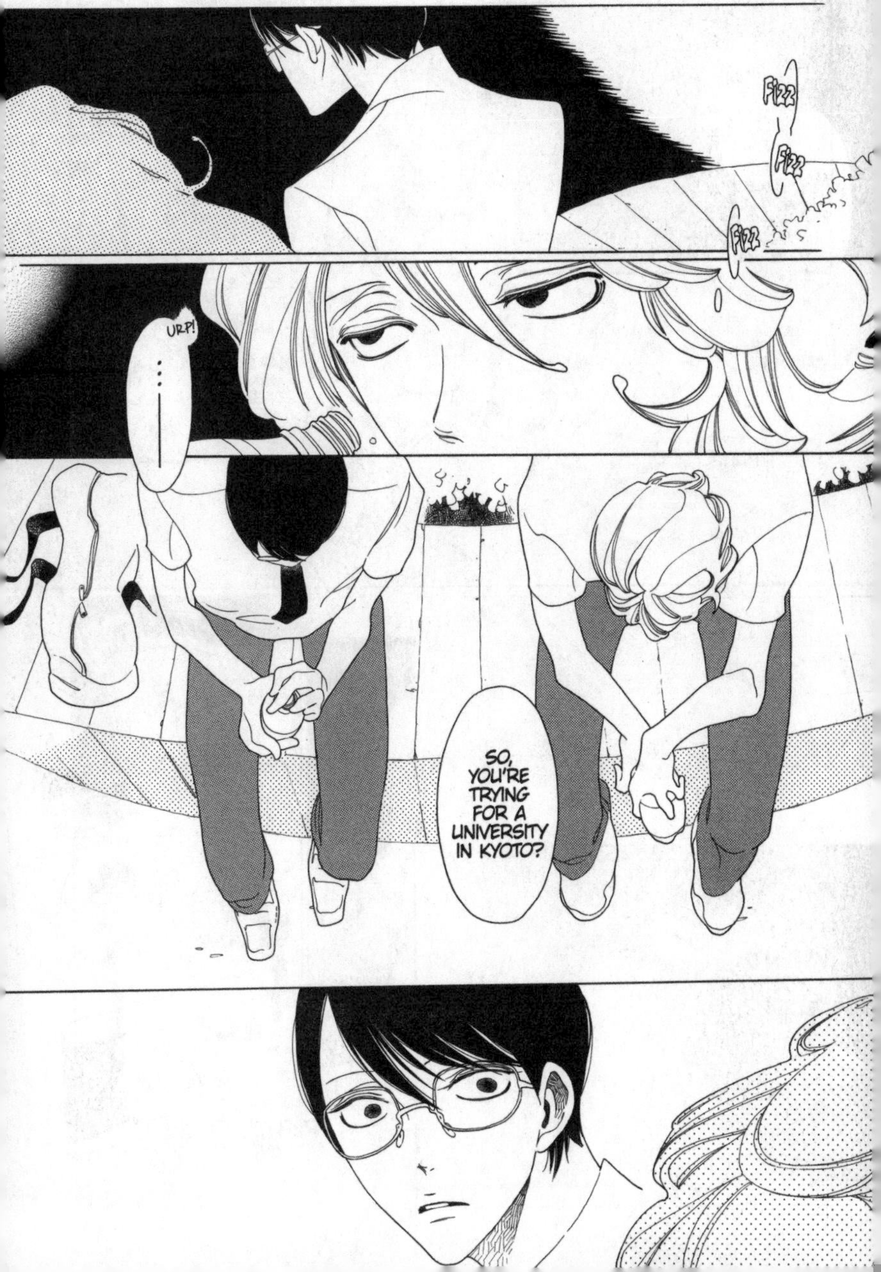
FIZZ
FIZZ
FIZZ
URP!
...!
SO, YOU'RE TRYING FOR A UNIVERSITY IN KYOTO?

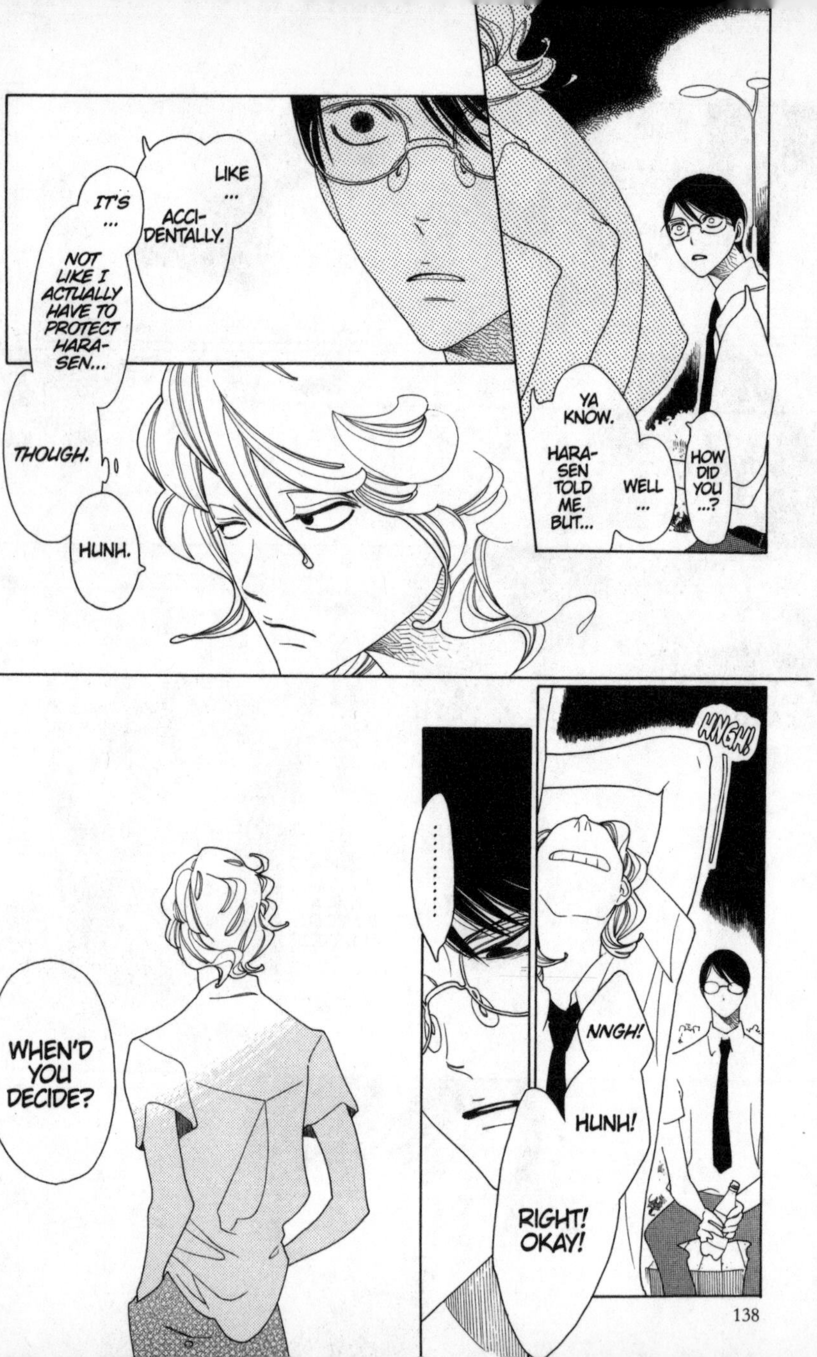
HOW DID YOU ...?
WELL ...
YA KNOW.
HARA-SEN TOLD ME. BUT...
LIKE ... ACCI-DENTALLY.
IT'S ... NOT LIKE I ACTUALLY HAVE TO PROTECT HARA-SEN...
THOUGH.
HUNH.
HNGH!
NNGH!
HUNH!
RIGHT! OKAY!
......
WHEN'D YOU DECIDE?

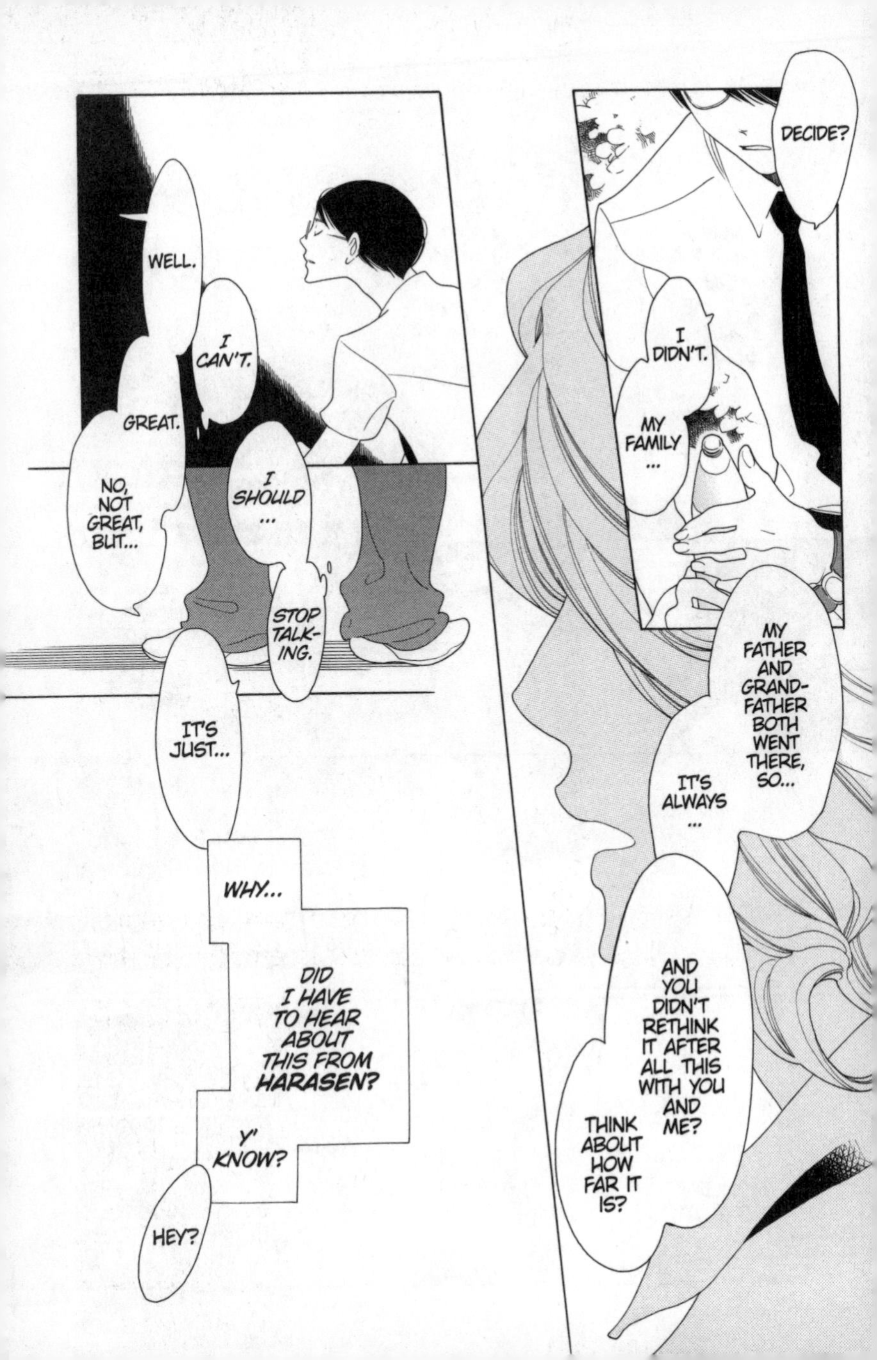
DECIDE?
I DIDN'T.
MY FAMILY ...
MY FATHER AND GRANDFATHER BOTH WENT THERE, SO...
IT'S ALWAYS ...
AND YOU DIDN'T RETHINK IT AFTER ALL THIS WITH YOU AND ME?
THINK ABOUT HOW FAR IT IS?
WELL.
I CAN'T.
GREAT.
NO, NOT GREAT, BUT...
I SHOULD ...
STOP TALKING.
IT'S JUST...
WHY...
DID I HAVE TO HEAR ABOUT THIS FROM HARASEN?
Y' KNOW?
HEY?

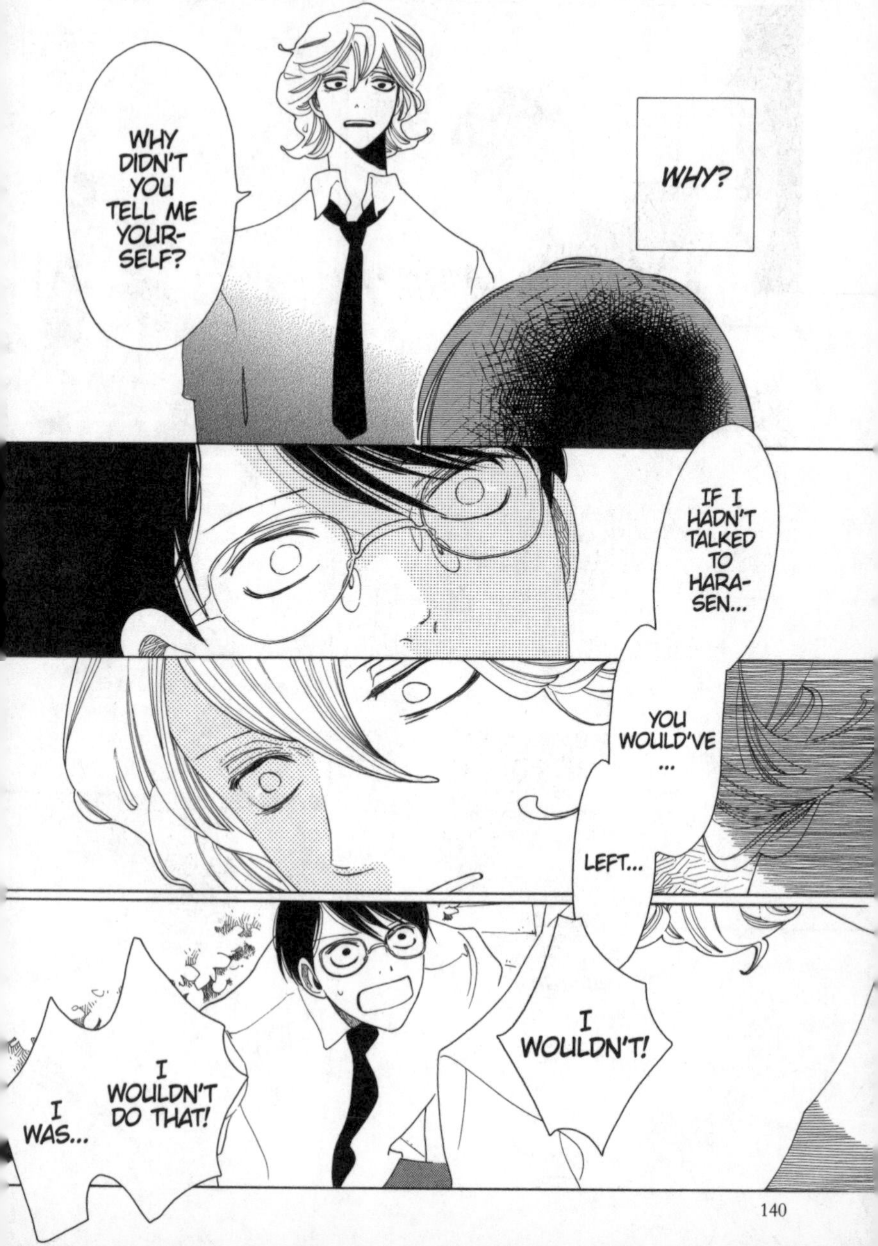
WHY?
WHY DIDN'T YOU TELL ME YOURSELF?
IF I HADN'T TALKED TO HARA-SEN...
YOU WOULD'VE ...
LEFT...
I WOULDN'T!
I WOULDN'T DO THAT!
I WAS...

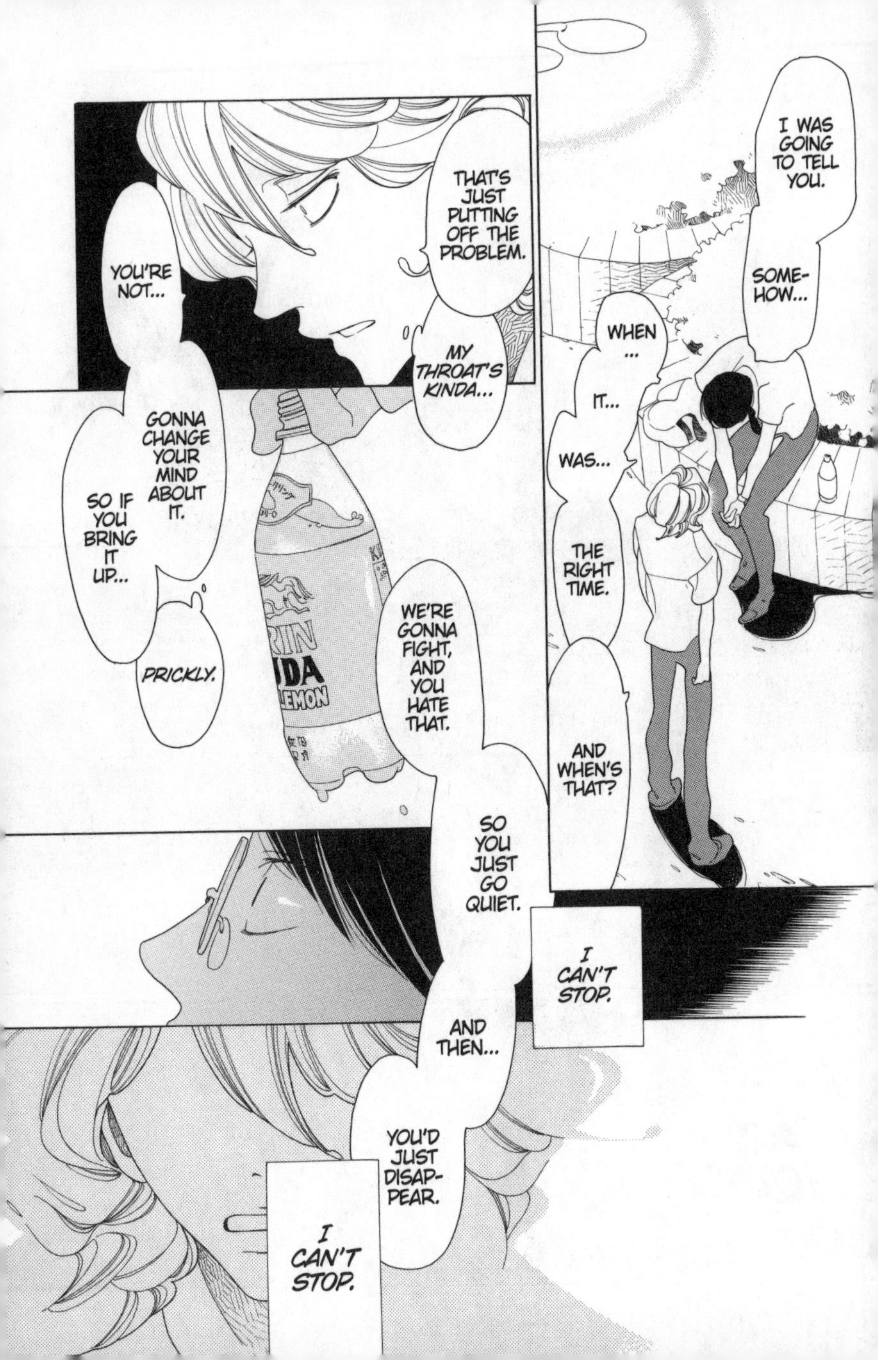
I WAS GOING TO TELL YOU.
SOME-HOW...
WHEN...
IT...
WAS...
THE RIGHT TIME.
AND WHEN'S THAT?
THAT'S JUST PUTTING OFF THE PROBLEM.
YOU'RE NOT...
MY THROAT'S KINDA...
GONNA CHANGE YOUR MIND ABOUT IT.
SO IF YOU BRING IT UP...
PRICKLY.
WE'RE GONNA FIGHT, AND YOU HATE THAT.
SO YOU JUST GO QUIET.
I CAN'T STOP.
AND THEN...
YOU'D JUST DISAPPEAR.
I CAN'T STOP.

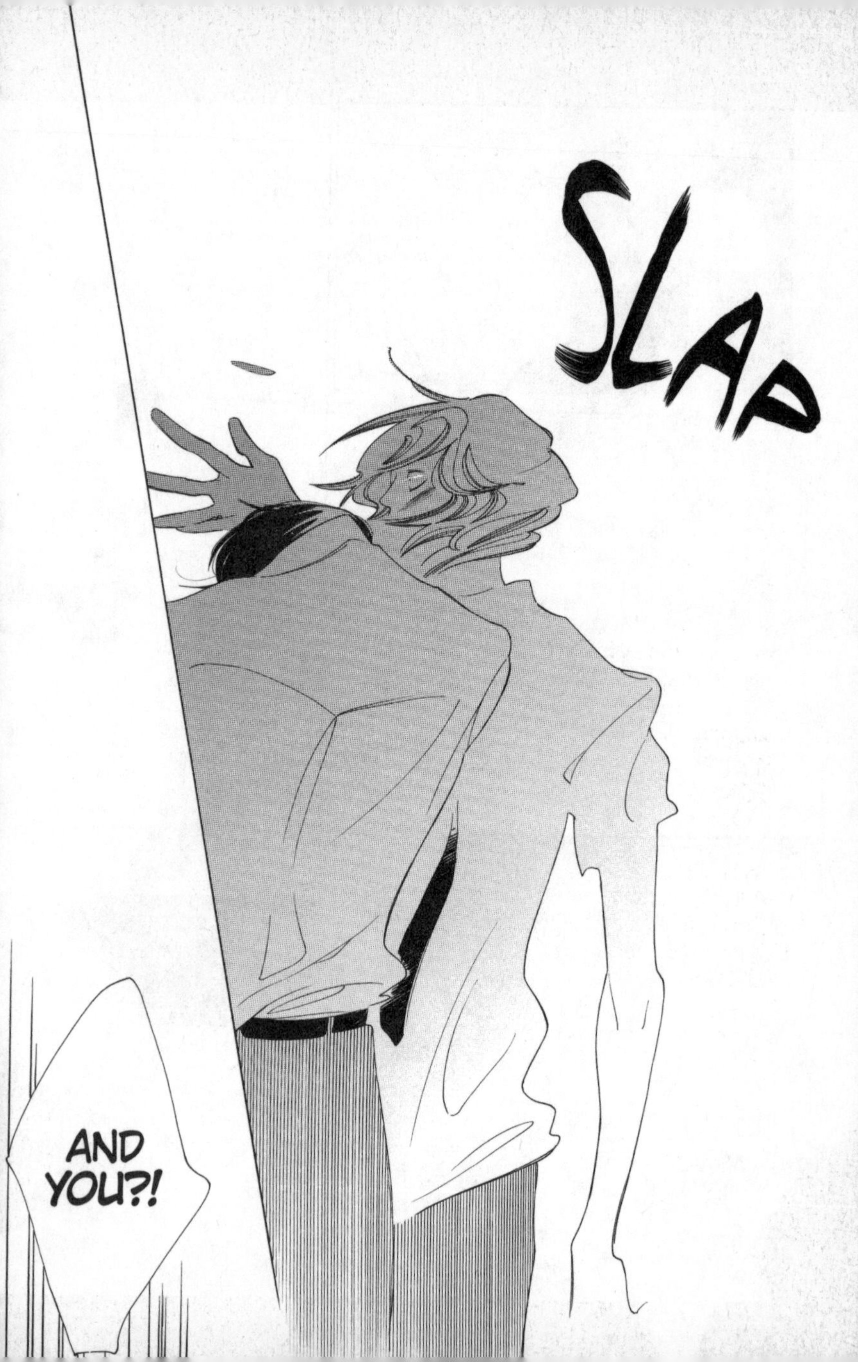
SLAP
AND YOU?!

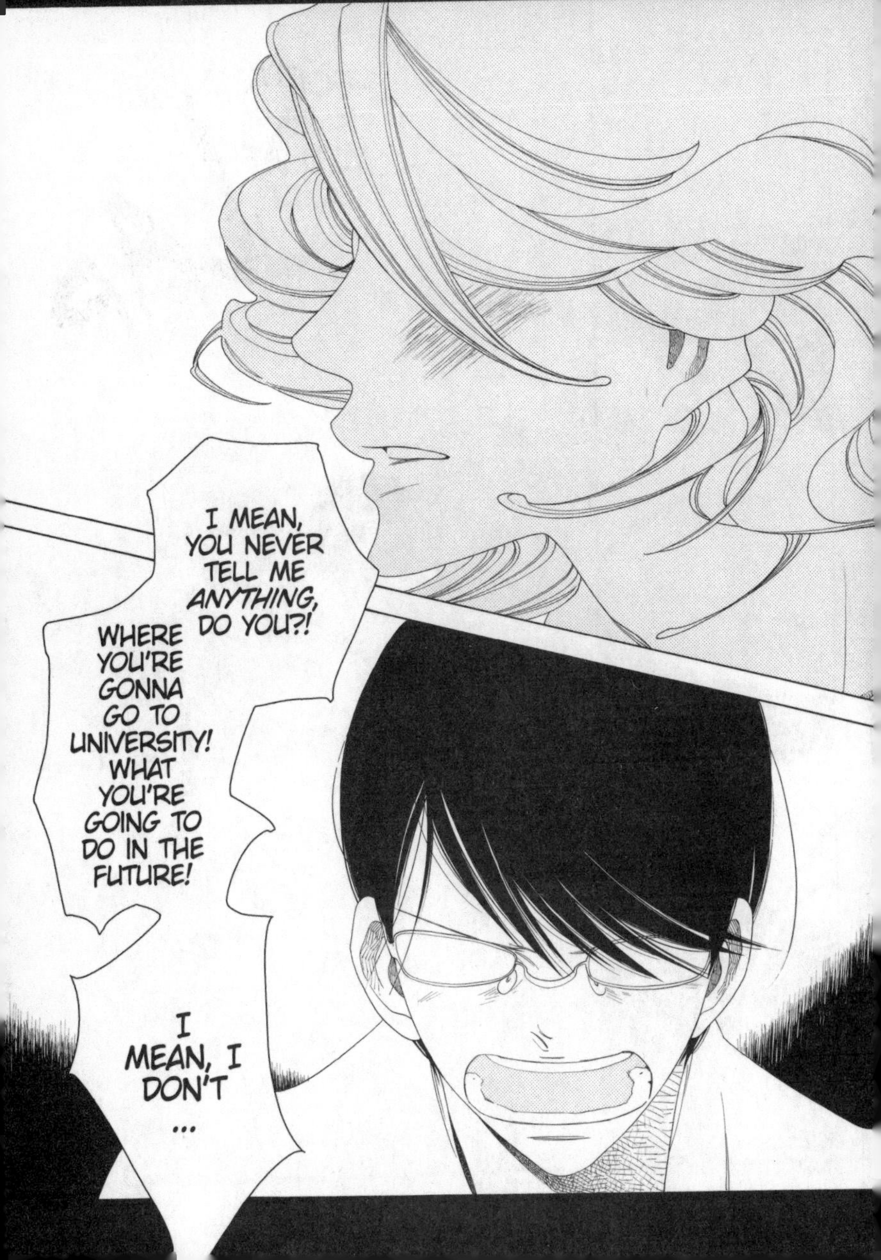
I MEAN, YOU NEVER TELL ME ANYTHING, DO YOU?!
WHERE YOU'RE GONNA GO TO UNIVERSITY! WHAT YOU'RE GOING TO DO IN THE FUTURE!
I MEAN, I DON'T ...

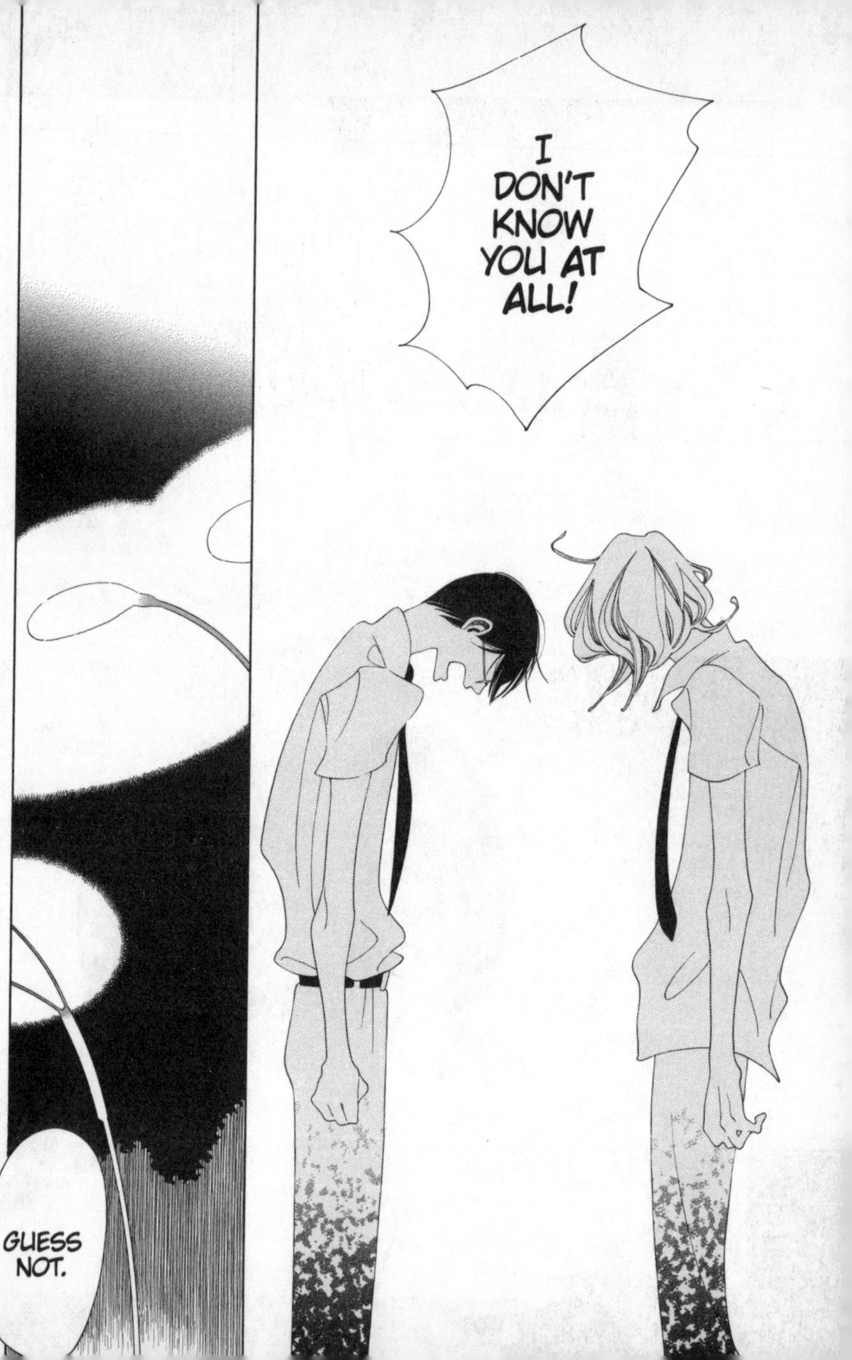
I DON'T KNOW YOU AT ALL!
GUESS NOT.

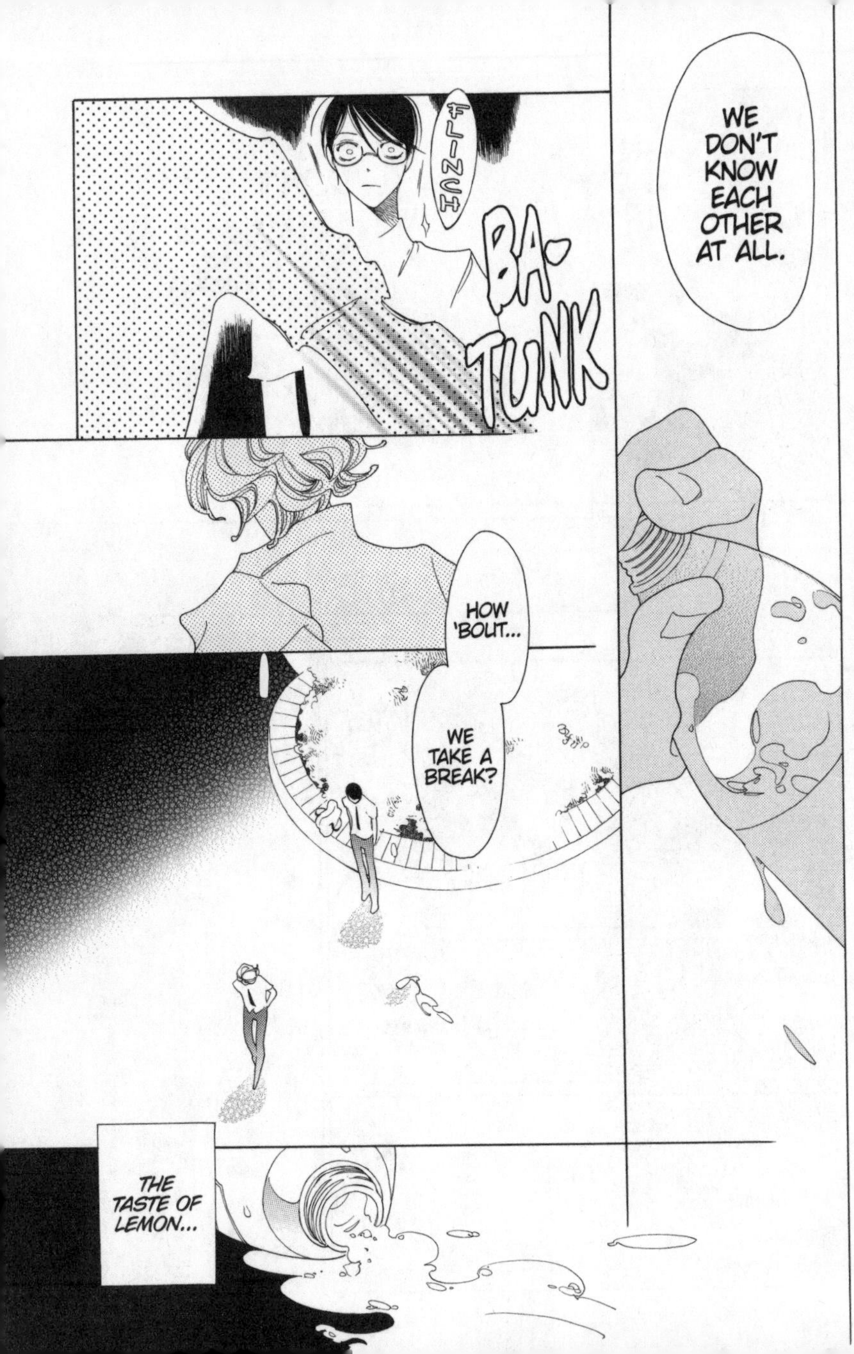
WE DON'T KNOW EACH OTHER AT ALL.
FLINCH
BA-TUNK
HOW 'BOUT...
WE TAKE A BREAK?
THE TASTE OF LEMON...

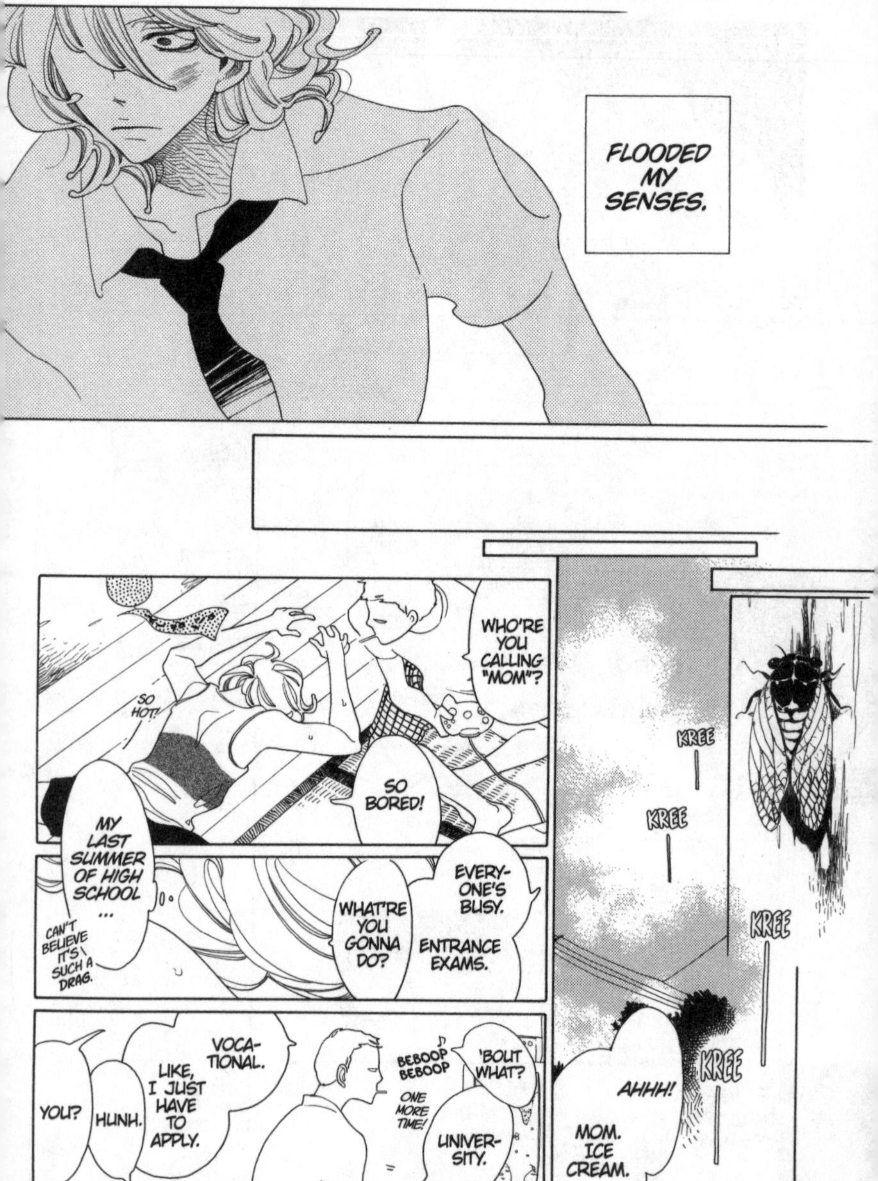
FLOODED MY SENSES.
KREE
KREE
KREE
KREE
AHHH!
MOM. ICE CREAM.
WHO'RE YOU CALLING "MOM"?
SO HOT!
SO BORED!
EVERY-ONE'S BUSY.
ENTRANCE EXAMS.
WHAT'RE YOU GONNA DO?
MY LAST SUMMER OF HIGH SCHOOL ...
CAN'T BELIEVE IT'S SUCH A DRAG.
'BOUT WHAT?
BEBOOP BEBOOP
UNIVER-SITY.
ONE MORE TIME!
VOCA-TIONAL.
LIKE, I JUST HAVE TO APPLY.
HUNH.
YOU?

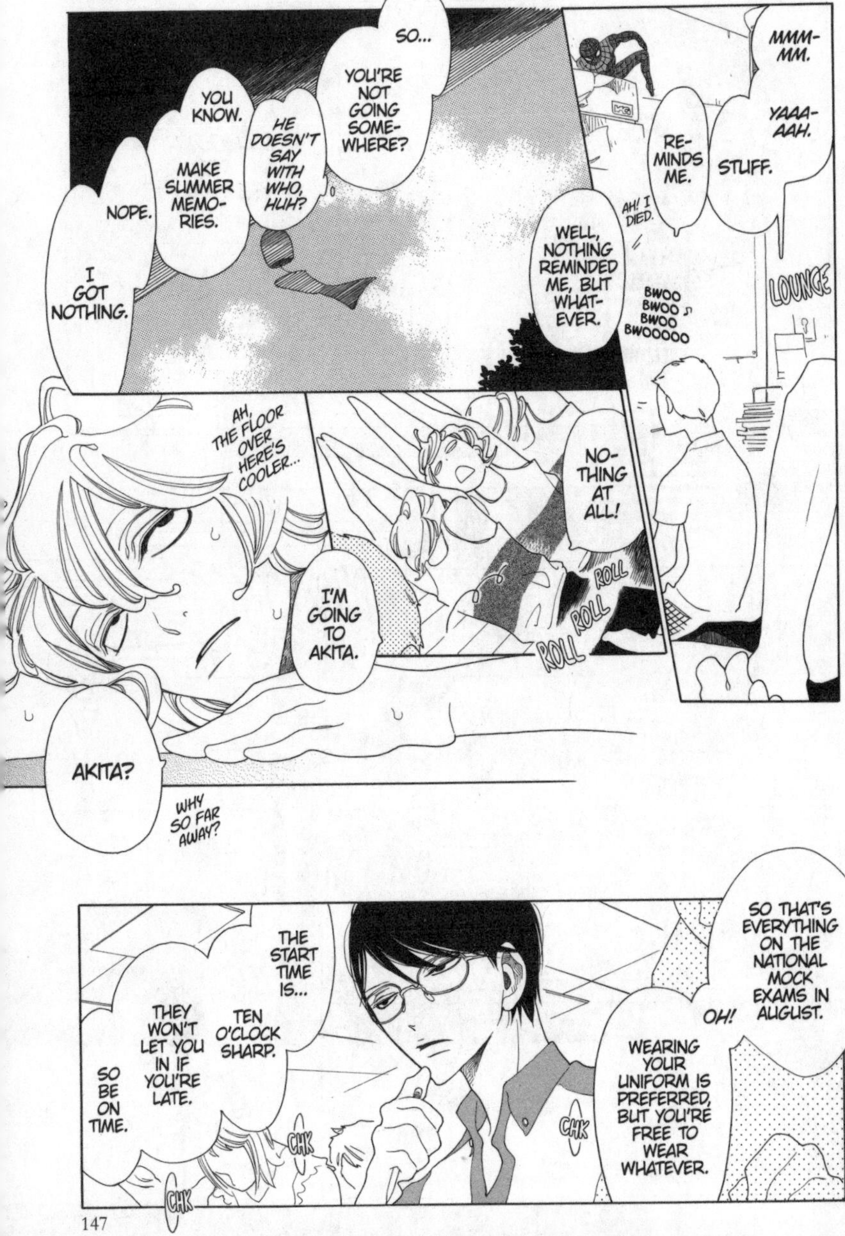
MMM-MM.
YAAAA-AAH.
STUFF.
RE-MINDS ME.
AH! I DIED.
WELL, NOTHING REMINDED ME, BUT WHAT-EVER.
LOUNGE
BWOO BWOO ♪ BWOO BWOOOOO
SO...
YOU'RE NOT GOING SOME-WHERE?
HE DOESN'T SAY WITH WHO, HUH?
YOU KNOW.
MAKE SUMMER MEMO-RIES.
NOPE.
I GOT NOTHING.
NO-THING AT ALL!
ROLL ROLL ROLL
I'M GOING TO AKITA.
AH, THE FLOOR OVER HERE'S COOLER...
AKITA?
WHY SO FAR AWAY?
SO THAT'S EVERYTHING ON THE NATIONAL MOCK EXAMS IN AUGUST.
OH!
WEARING YOUR UNIFORM IS PREFERRED, BUT YOU'RE FREE TO WEAR WHATEVER.
CHK
THE START TIME IS...
TEN O'CLOCK SHARP.
THEY WON'T LET YOU IN IF YOU'RE LATE.
SO BE ON TIME.
CHK
CHK

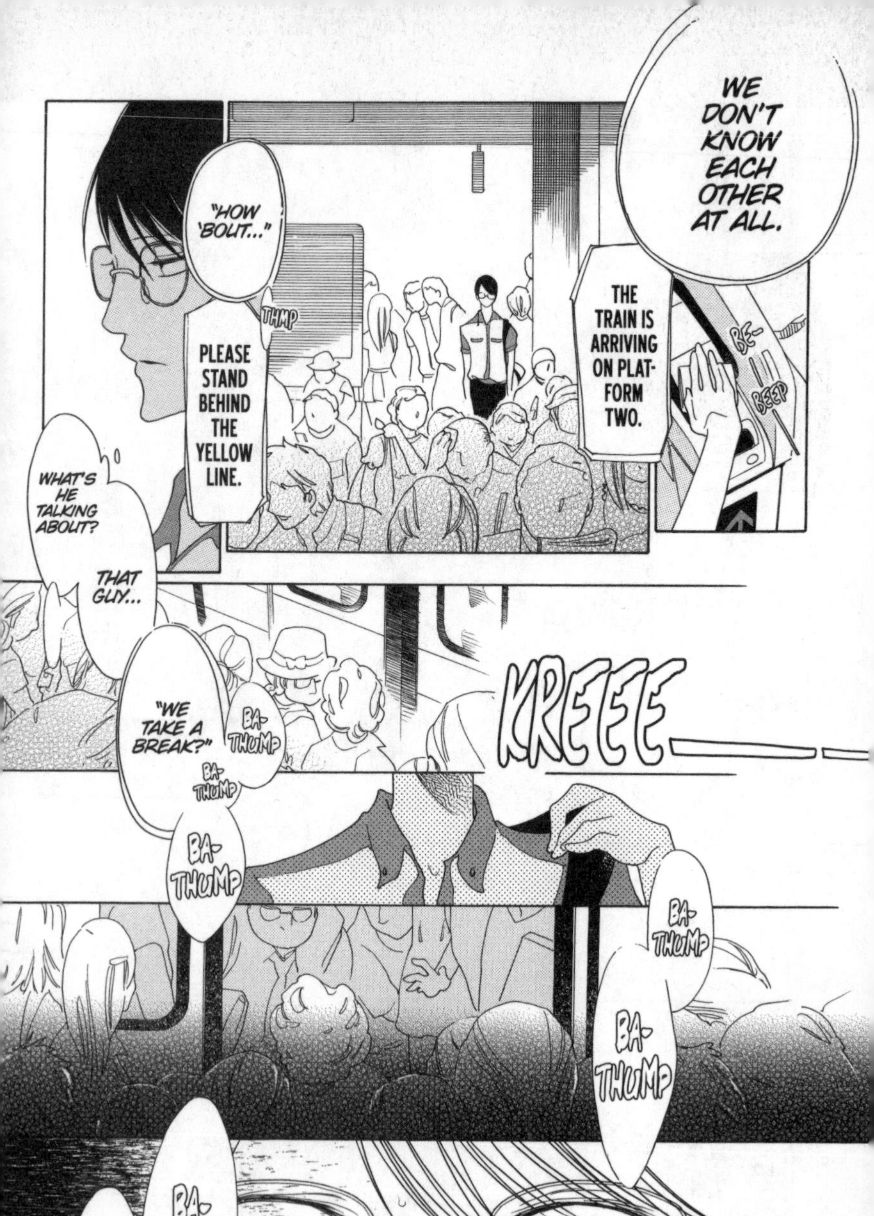
WE DON'T KNOW EACH OTHER AT ALL.
THE TRAIN IS ARRIVING ON PLAT-FORM TWO.
BE-BEEP
"HOW 'BOUT..."
THMP
PLEASE STAND BEHIND THE YELLOW LINE.
WHAT'S HE TALKING ABOUT?
THAT GUY...
KREEE
"WE TAKE A BREAK?"
BA-THUMP
BA-THUMP
BA-THUMP
BA-THUMP
BA-THUMP
BA-THUMP
BA-

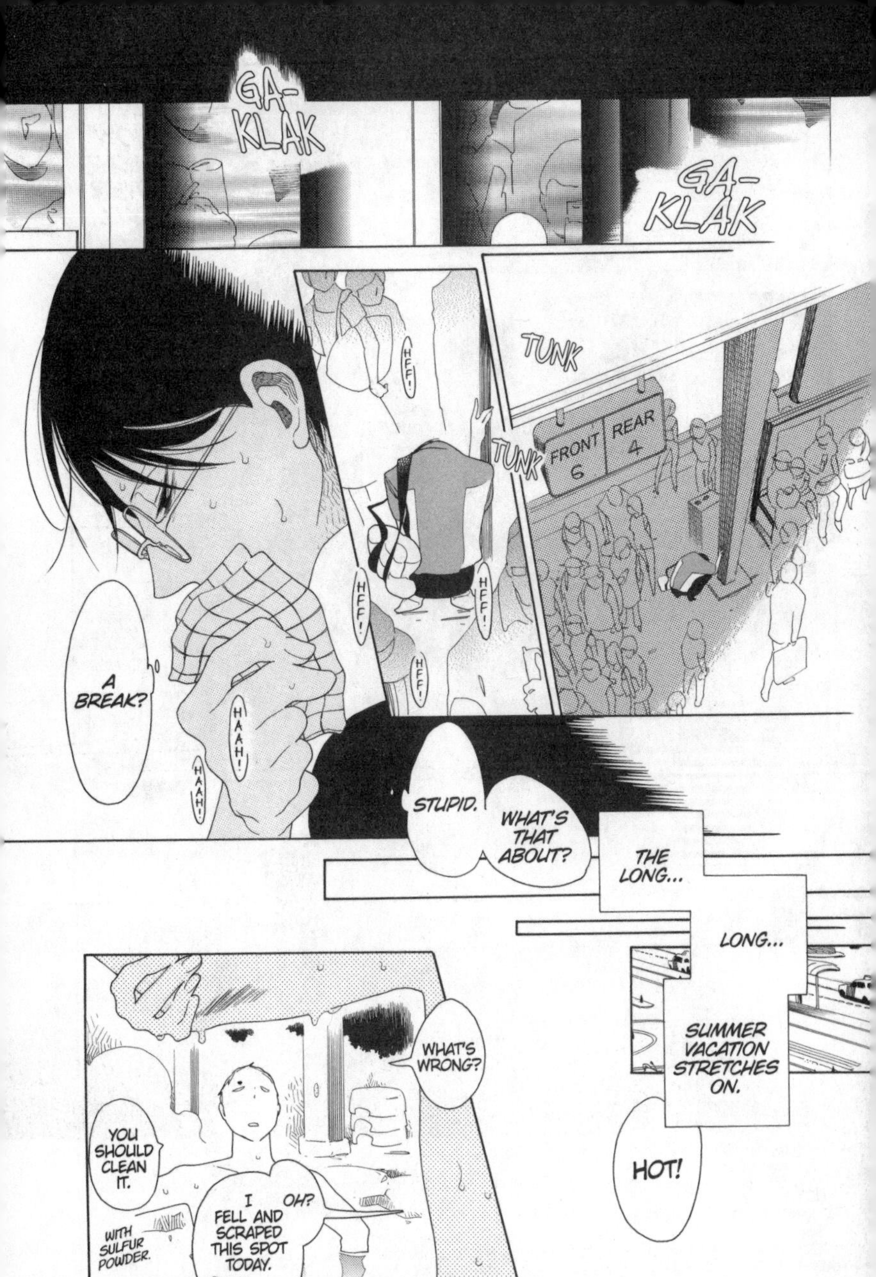
GA-KLAK
GA-KLAK
TUNK
FRONT 6
REAR 4
TUNK
HFF!
HFF!
HFF!
HFF!
A BREAK?
HAAAH!
HAAAH!
STUPID.
WHAT'S THAT ABOUT?
THE LONG...
LONG...
SUMMER VACATION STRETCHES ON.
HOT!
WHAT'S WRONG?
I FELL AND SCRAPED THIS SPOT TODAY.
OH?
YOU SHOULD CLEAN IT.
WITH SULFUR POWDER.
OUCH!

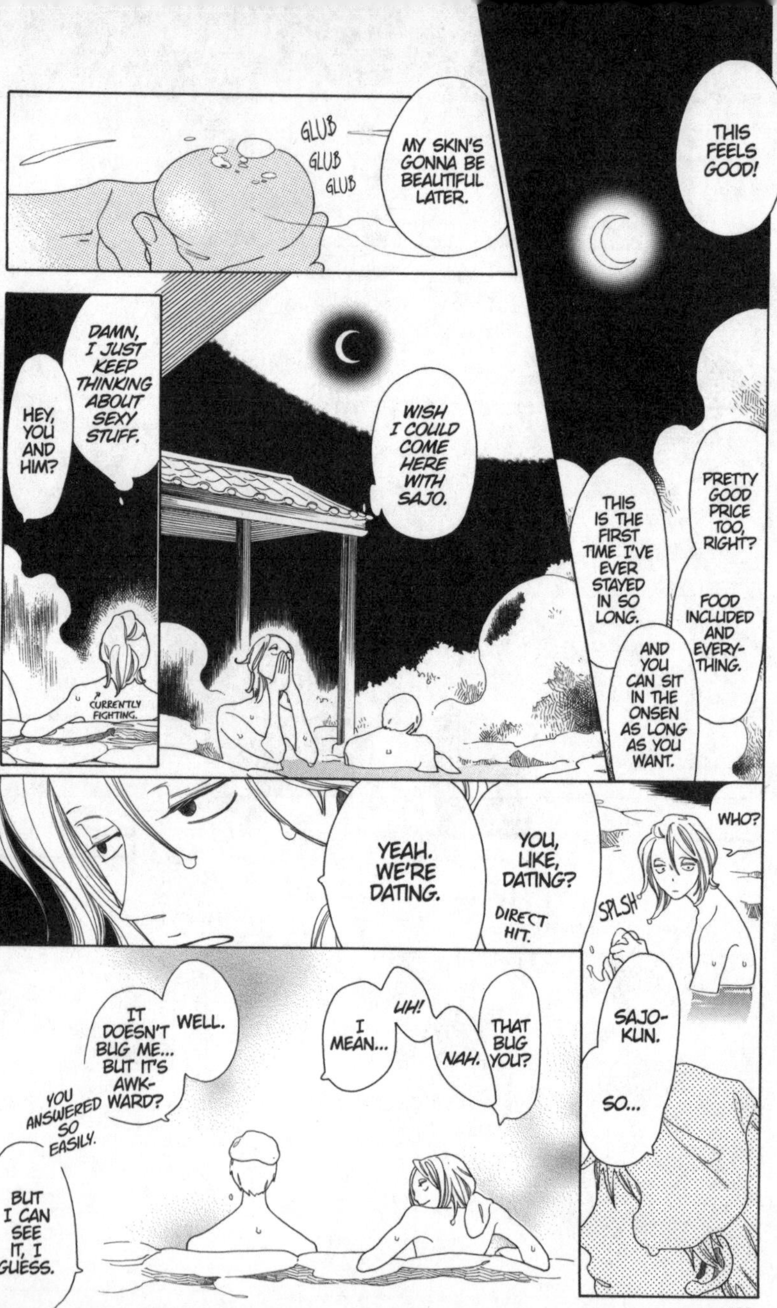
THIS FEELS GOOD!
PRETTY GOOD PRICE TOO, RIGHT?
FOOD INCLUDED AND EVERYTHING.
THIS IS THE FIRST TIME I'VE EVER STAYED IN SO LONG.
AND YOU CAN SIT IN THE ONSEN AS LONG AS YOU WANT.
GLUB
GLUB
GLUB
MY SKIN'S GONNA BE BEAUTIFUL LATER.
WISH I COULD COME HERE WITH SAJO.
DAMN, I JUST KEEP THINKING ABOUT SEXY STUFF.
HEY, YOU AND HIM?
CURRENTLY FIGHTING.
WHO?
SPLSH
YOU, LIKE, DATING?
DIRECT HIT.
YEAH. WE'RE DATING.
SAJO-KUN.
SO...
THAT BUG YOU?
NAH.
UH!
I MEAN...
WELL.
IT DOESN'T BUG ME... BUT IT'S AWKWARD?
YOU ANSWERED SO EASILY.
BUT I CAN SEE IT, I GUESS.

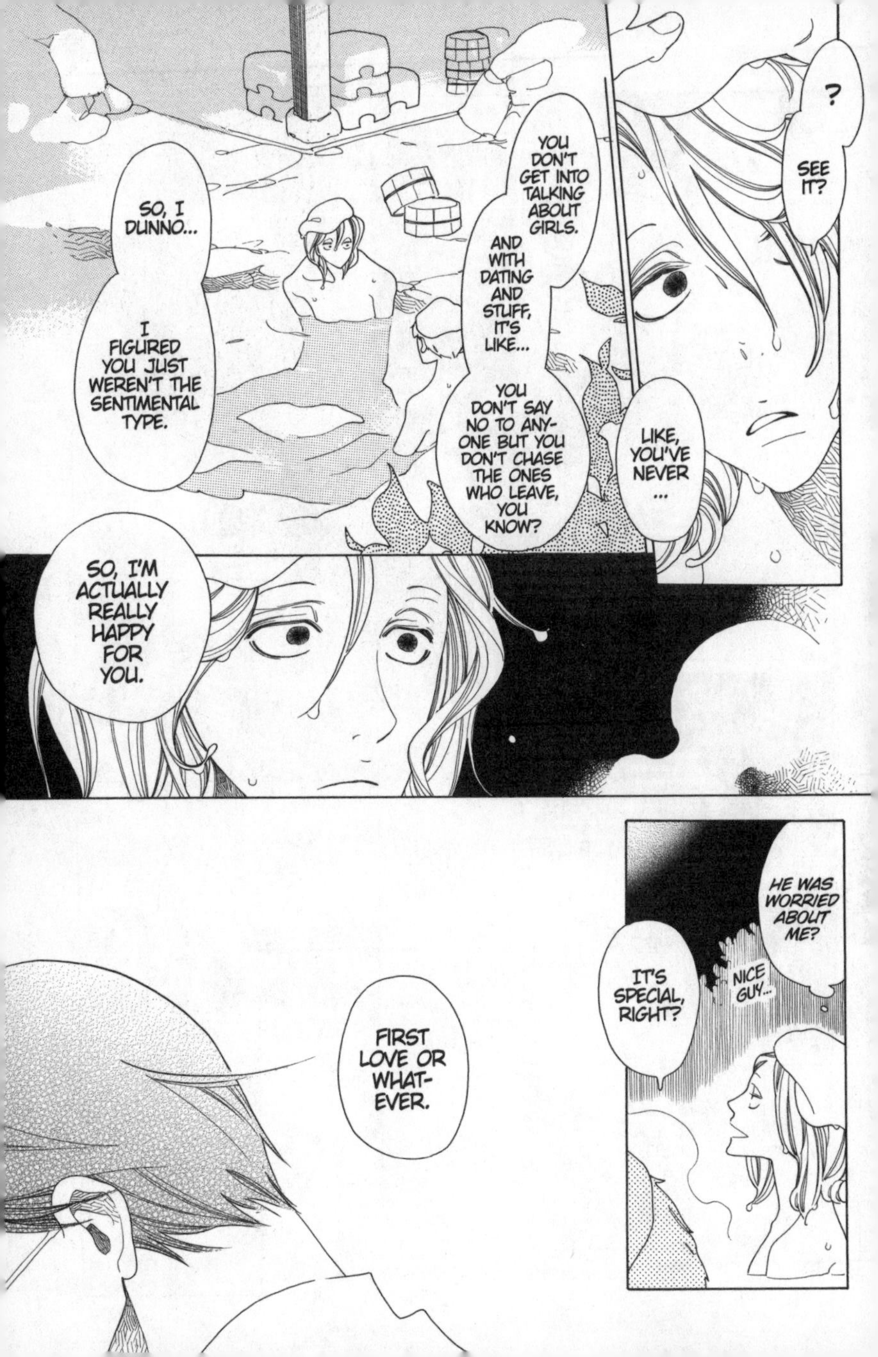
?
SEE IT?
LIKE, YOU'VE NEVER ...
YOU DON'T GET INTO TALKING ABOUT GIRLS.
AND WITH DATING AND STUFF, IT'S LIKE...
YOU DON'T SAY NO TO ANY-ONE BUT YOU DON'T CHASE THE ONES WHO LEAVE, YOU KNOW?
SO, I DUNNO...
I FIGURED YOU JUST WEREN'T THE SENTIMENTAL TYPE.
SO, I'M ACTUALLY REALLY HAPPY FOR YOU.
HE WAS WORRIED ABOUT ME?
NICE GUY...
IT'S SPECIAL, RIGHT?
FIRST LOVE OR WHAT-EVER.

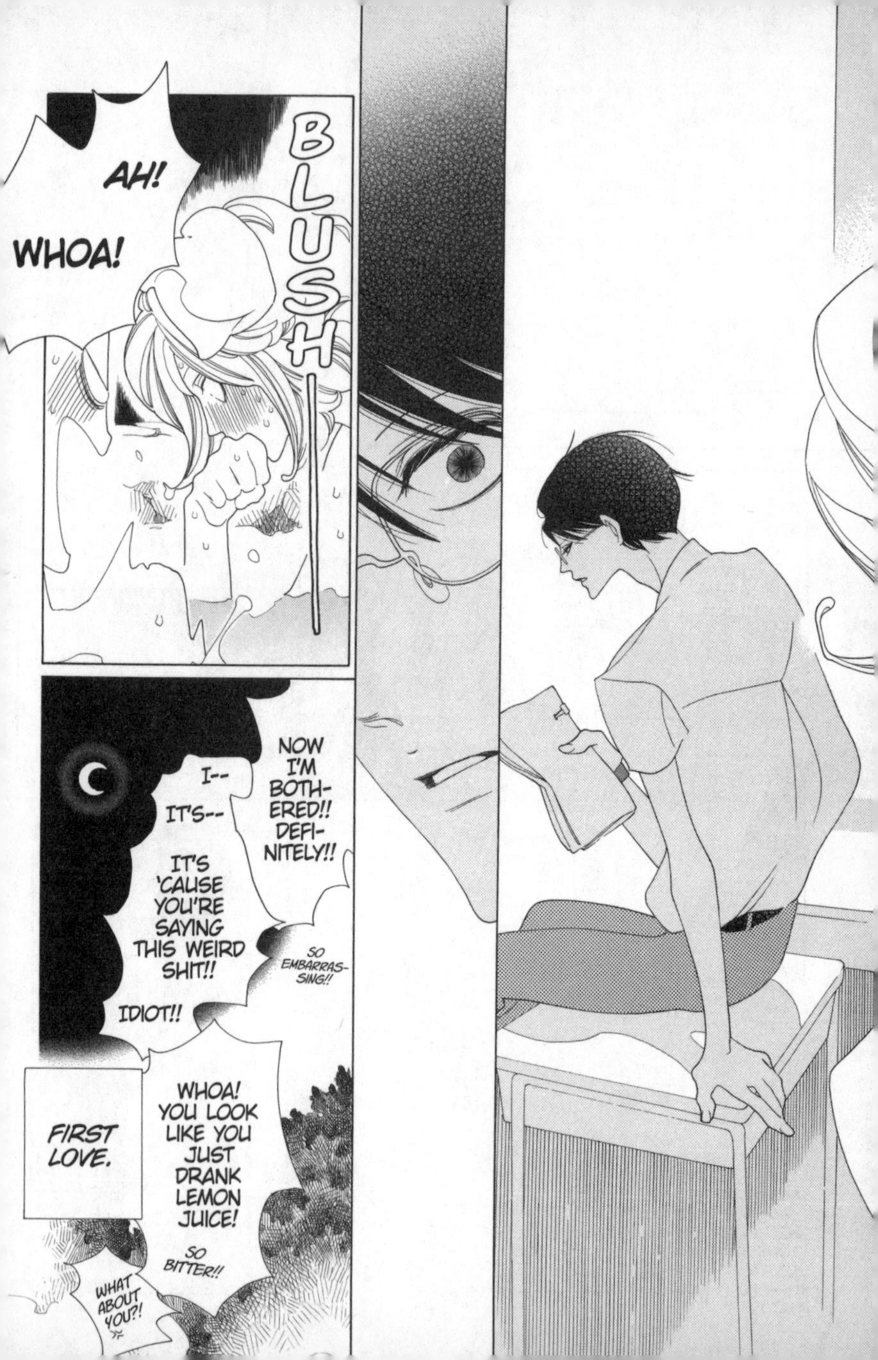
BLUSH
AH!
WHOA!
NOW I'M BOTHERED!! DEFINITELY!!
I--
IT'S--
IT'S 'CAUSE YOU'RE SAYING THIS WEIRD SHIT!!
SO EMBARRASSING!!
IDIOT!!
WHOA! YOU LOOK LIKE YOU JUST DRANK LEMON JUICE!
FIRST LOVE.
SO BITTER!!
WHAT ABOUT YOU?!

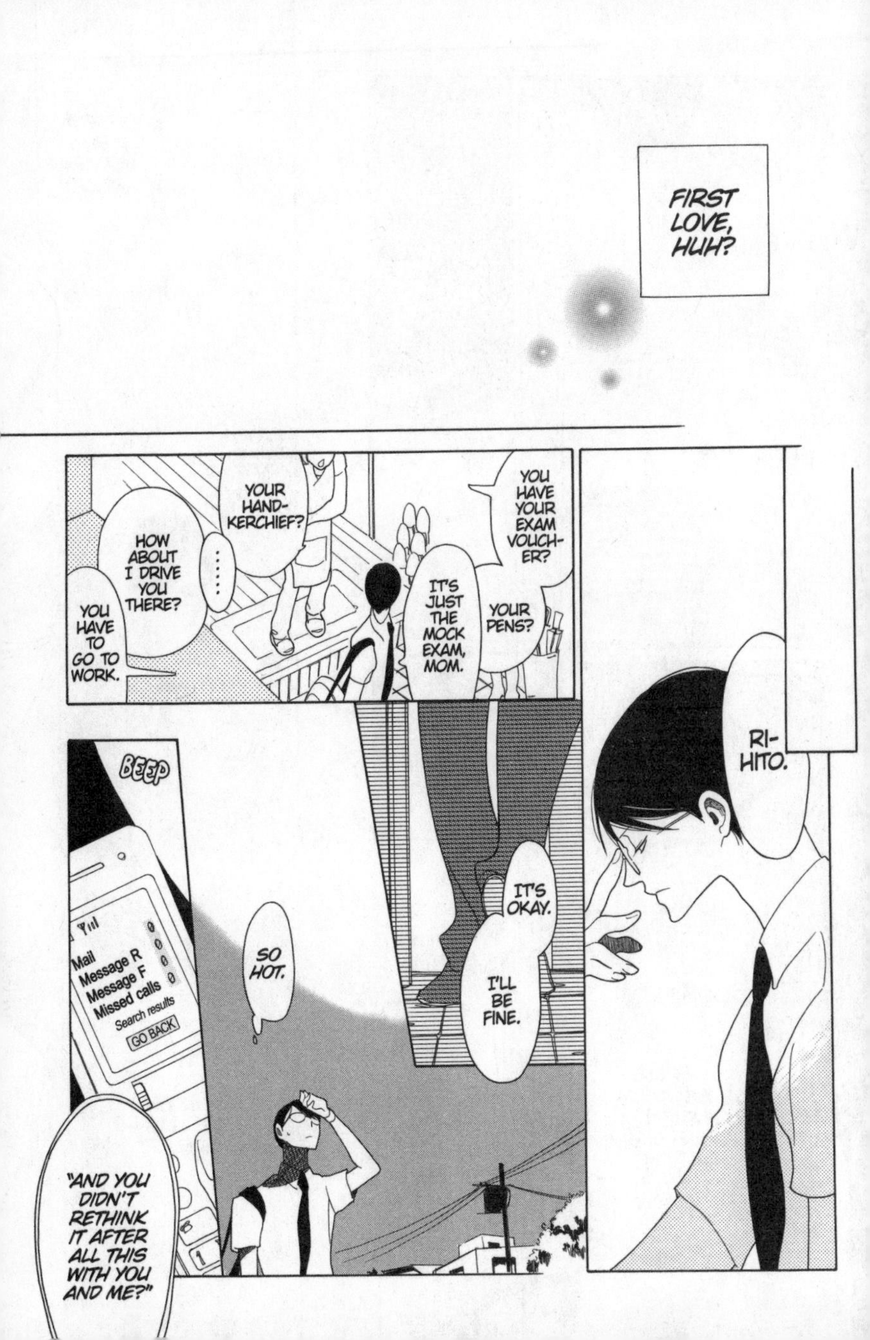
FIRST LOVE, HUH?
RI-HITO.
YOU HAVE YOUR EXAM VOUCHER?
YOUR PENS?
IT'S JUST THE MOCK EXAM, MOM.
YOUR HAND-KERCHIEF?
......
HOW ABOUT I DRIVE YOU THERE?
YOU HAVE TO GO TO WORK.
IT'S OKAY.
I'LL BE FINE.
BEEP
Mail
Message R
Message F
Missed calls
Search results
GO BACK
SO HOT.
"AND YOU DIDN'T RETHINK IT AFTER ALL THIS WITH YOU AND ME?"

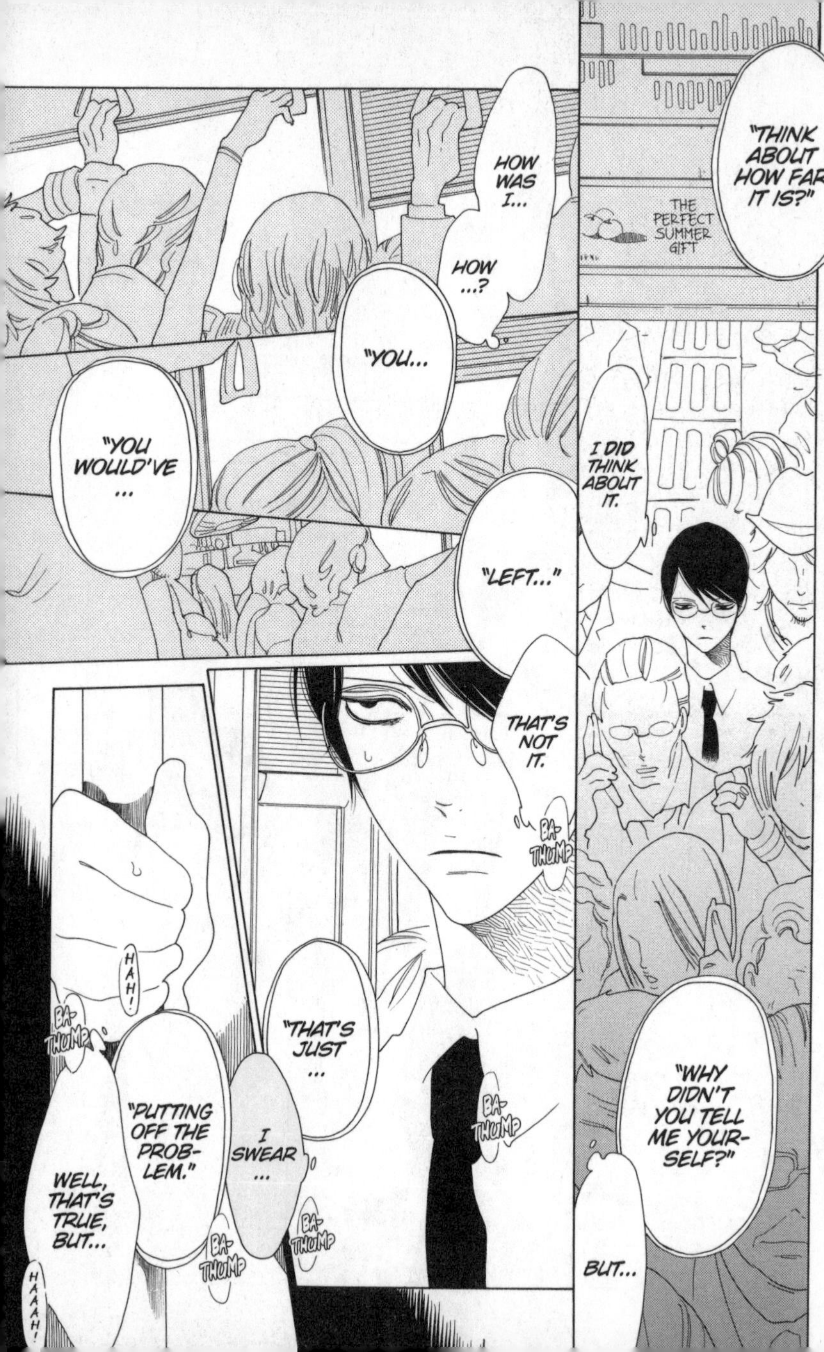
"THINK ABOUT HOW FAR IT IS?"
THE PERFECT SUMMER GIFT
I DID THINK ABOUT IT.
"WHY DIDN'T YOU TELL ME YOURSELF?"
BUT...
HOW WAS I...
HOW ...?
"YOU...
"YOU WOULD'VE ...
"LEFT..."
THAT'S NOT IT.
BA-THUMP
"THAT'S JUST ...
BA-THUMP
"PUTTING OFF THE PROB-LEM."
I SWEAR ...
BA-THUMP
BA-THUMP
HAH!
BA-THUMP
WELL, THAT'S TRUE, BUT...
HAAAH!

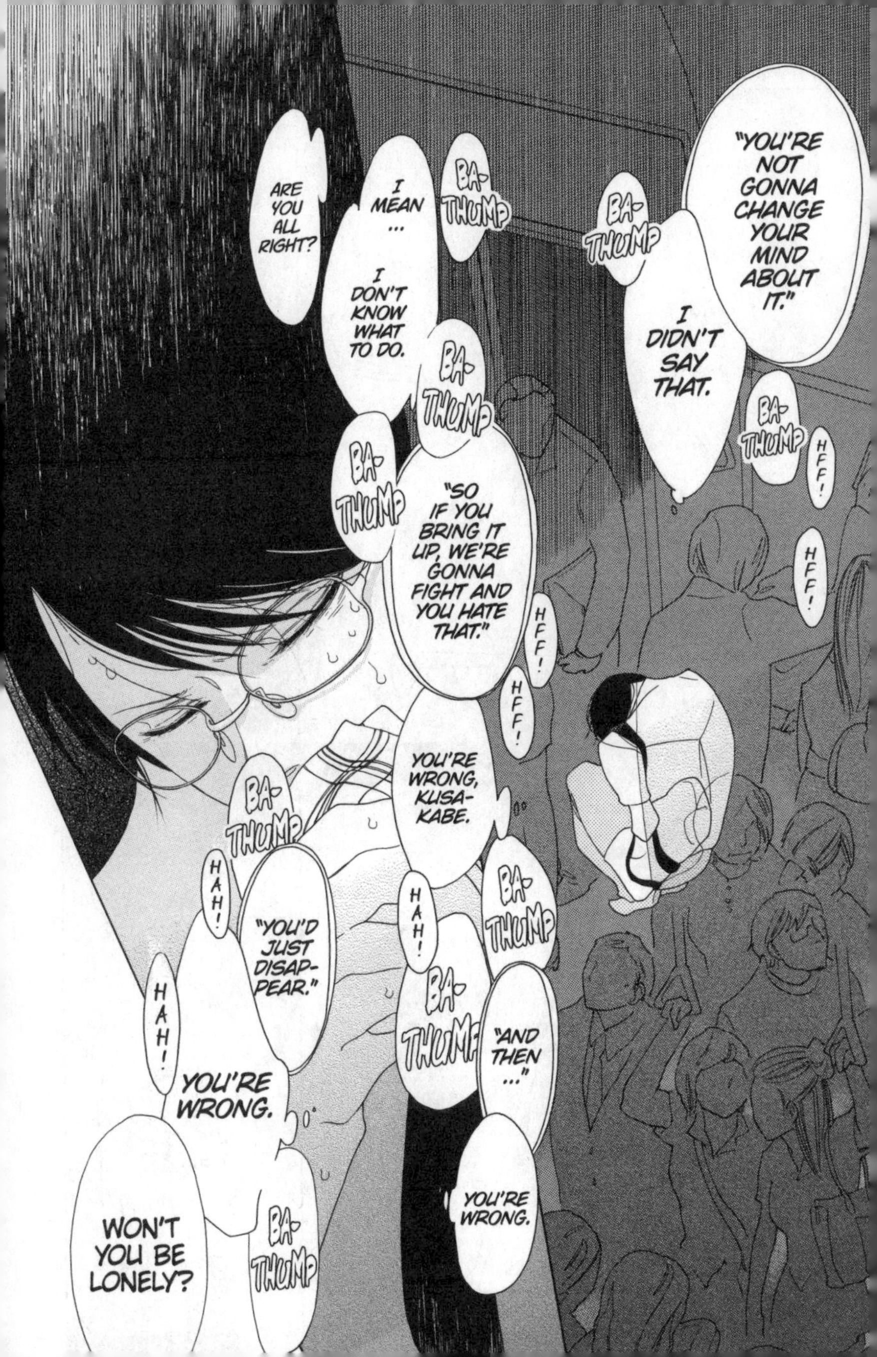
"YOU'RE NOT GONNA CHANGE YOUR MIND ABOUT IT."
BA-THUMP
I DIDN'T SAY THAT.
BA-THUMP
HFF!
HFF!
BA-THUMP
I MEAN ...
I DON'T KNOW WHAT TO DO.
ARE YOU ALL RIGHT?
BA-THUMP
BA-THUMP
"SO IF YOU BRING IT UP, WE'RE GONNA FIGHT AND YOU HATE THAT."
HFF!
HFF!
YOU'RE WRONG, KUSA-KABE.
BA-THUMP
HAH!
"AND THEN ..."
BA-THUMP
YOU'RE WRONG.
"YOU'D JUST DISAP-PEAR."
HAH!
BA-THUMP
HAH!
YOU'RE WRONG.
BA-THUMP
WON'T YOU BE LONELY?

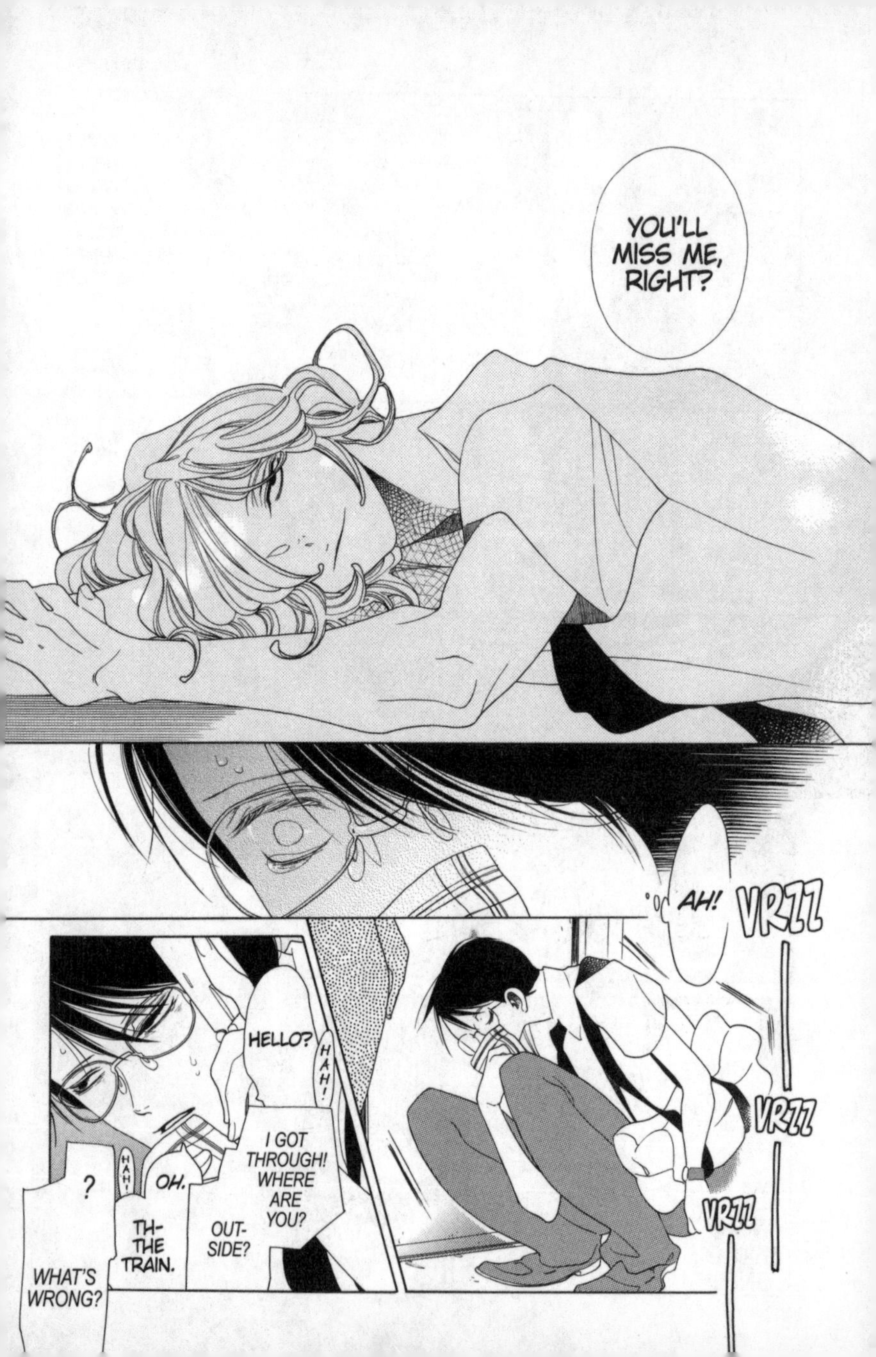
YOU'LL MISS ME, RIGHT?
AH!
VRZZ
VRZZ
VRZZ
HELLO?
HAH! HAH!
I GOT THROUGH! WHERE ARE YOU?
OUT-SIDE?
HAH!
OH.
TH-THE TRAIN.
?
WHAT'S WRONG?

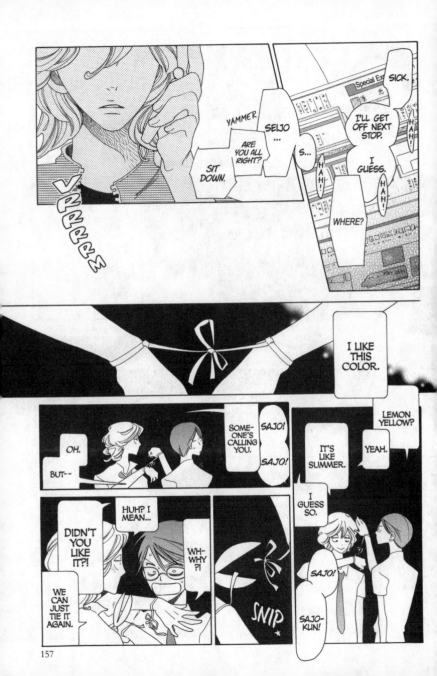

SICK.

I'LL GET OFF NEXT STOP.

I GUESS.

HAH!
HAH!
HAH!

WHERE?

YAMMER

SEIJO...

S...

ARE YOU ALL RIGHT?

SIT DOWN.

VRRRRM

I LIKE THIS COLOR.

LEMON YELLOW?

YEAH.

IT'S LIKE SUMMER.

SOMEONE'S CALLING YOU.

SAJO!

SAJO!

OH.

BUT--

I GUESS SO.

SAJO!

SAJO-KUN!

DIDN'T YOU LIKE IT?!

WE CAN JUST TIE IT AGAIN.

HUH? I MEAN...

WH-WHY ?!

SNIP

157

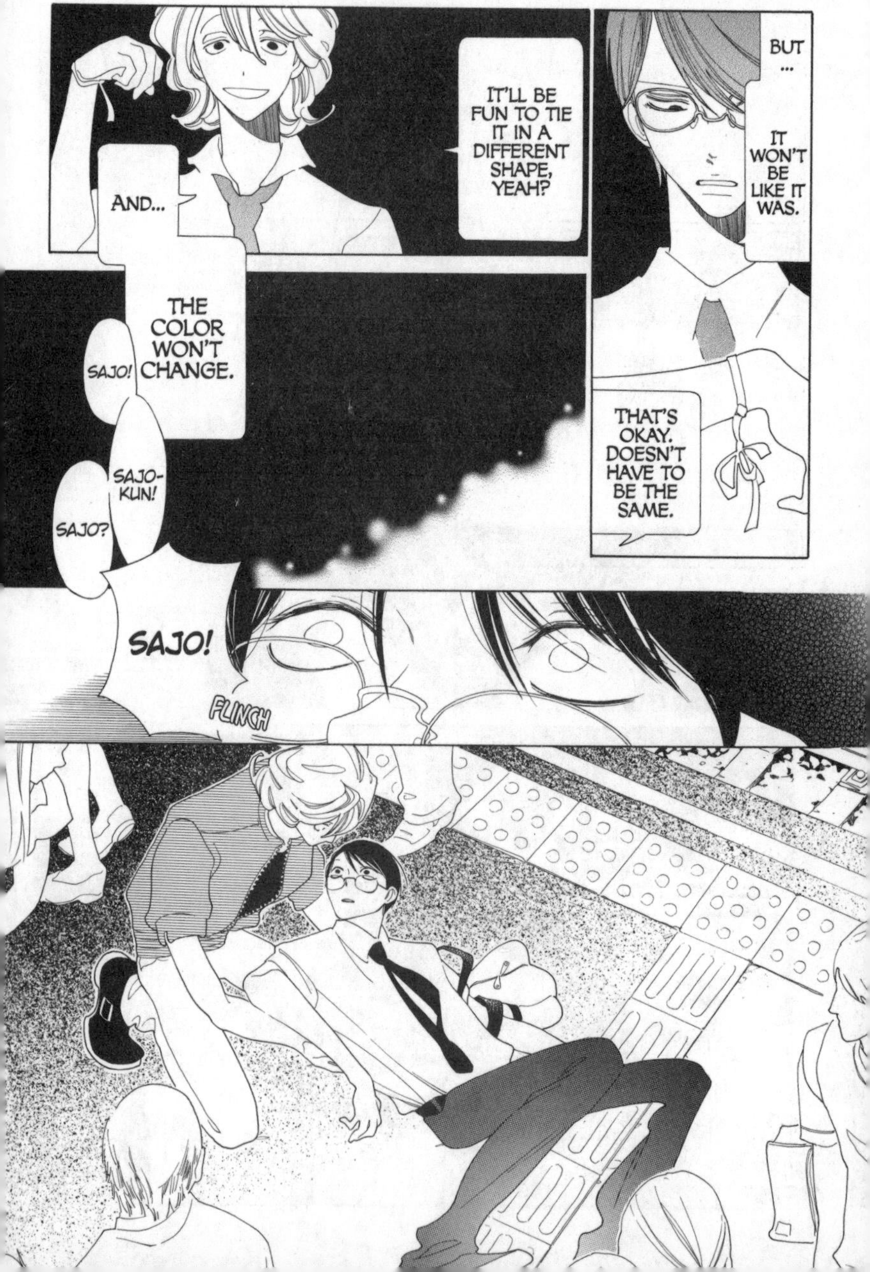
BUT ...
IT WON'T BE LIKE IT WAS.
THAT'S OKAY. DOESN'T HAVE TO BE THE SAME.
IT'LL BE FUN TO TIE IT IN A DIFFERENT SHAPE, YEAH?
AND...
THE COLOR WON'T CHANGE.
SAJO!
SAJO-KUN!
SAJO?
SAJO!
FLINCH

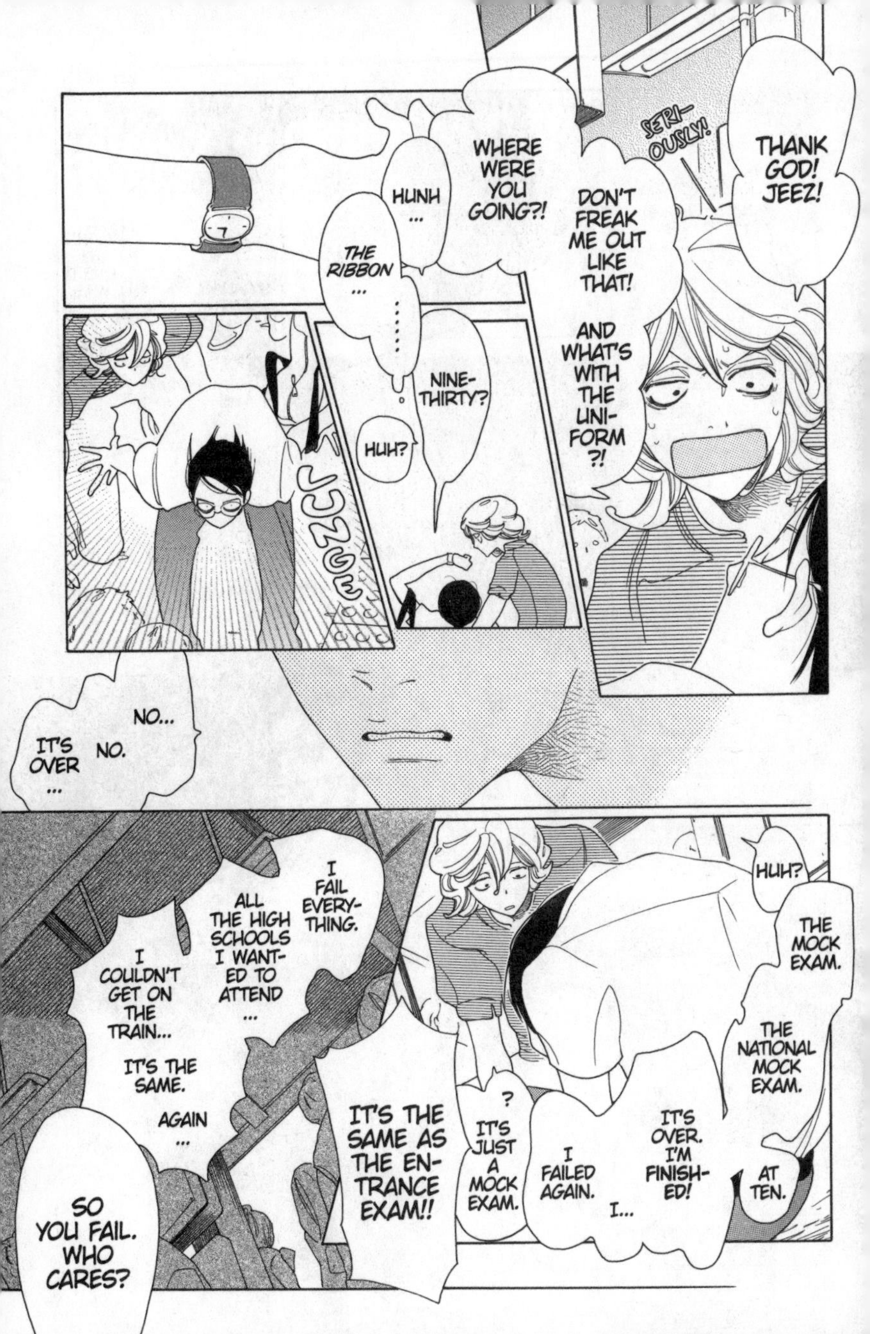
THANK GOD! JEEZ!
SERI-OUSLY!
DON'T FREAK ME OUT LIKE THAT!
WHERE WERE YOU GOING?!
HUNH ...
THE RIBBON ...
AND WHAT'S WITH THE UNI-FORM ?!
......
NINE-THIRTY?
HUH?
NO...
NO.
IT'S OVER ...
HUH?
THE MOCK EXAM.
THE NATIONAL MOCK EXAM.
AT TEN.
IT'S OVER. I'M FINISH-ED!
I...
I FAILED AGAIN.
?
IT'S JUST A MOCK EXAM.
IT'S THE SAME AS THE EN-TRANCE EXAM!!
I FAIL EVERY-THING.
ALL THE HIGH SCHOOLS I WANT-ED TO ATTEND ...
I COULDN'T GET ON THE TRAIN...
IT'S THE SAME.
AGAIN ...
SO YOU FAIL. WHO CARES?

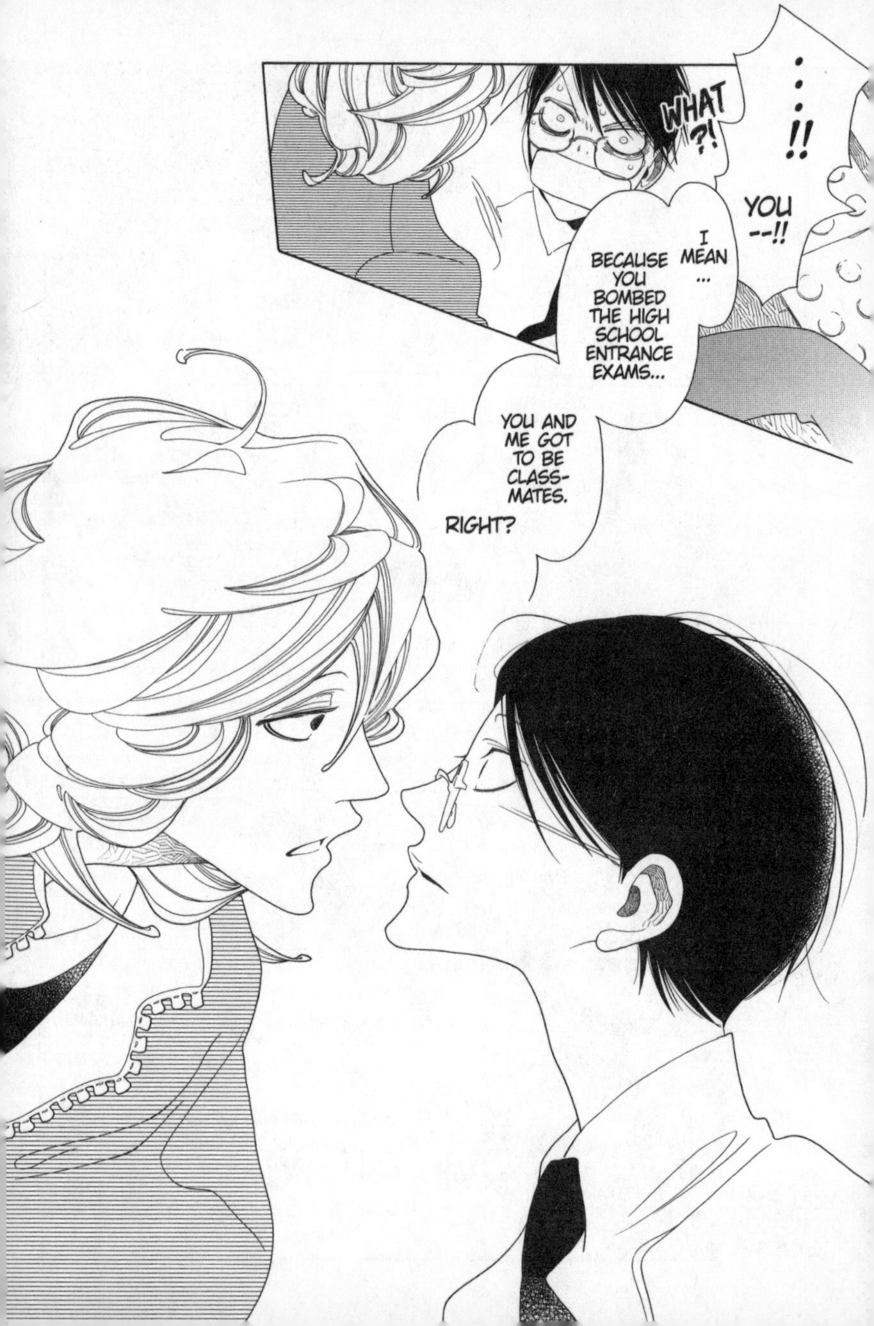
...!!
YOU --!!
WHAT ?!
I MEAN ... BECAUSE YOU BOMBED THE HIGH SCHOOL ENTRANCE EXAMS...
YOU AND ME GOT TO BE CLASS-MATES.
RIGHT?

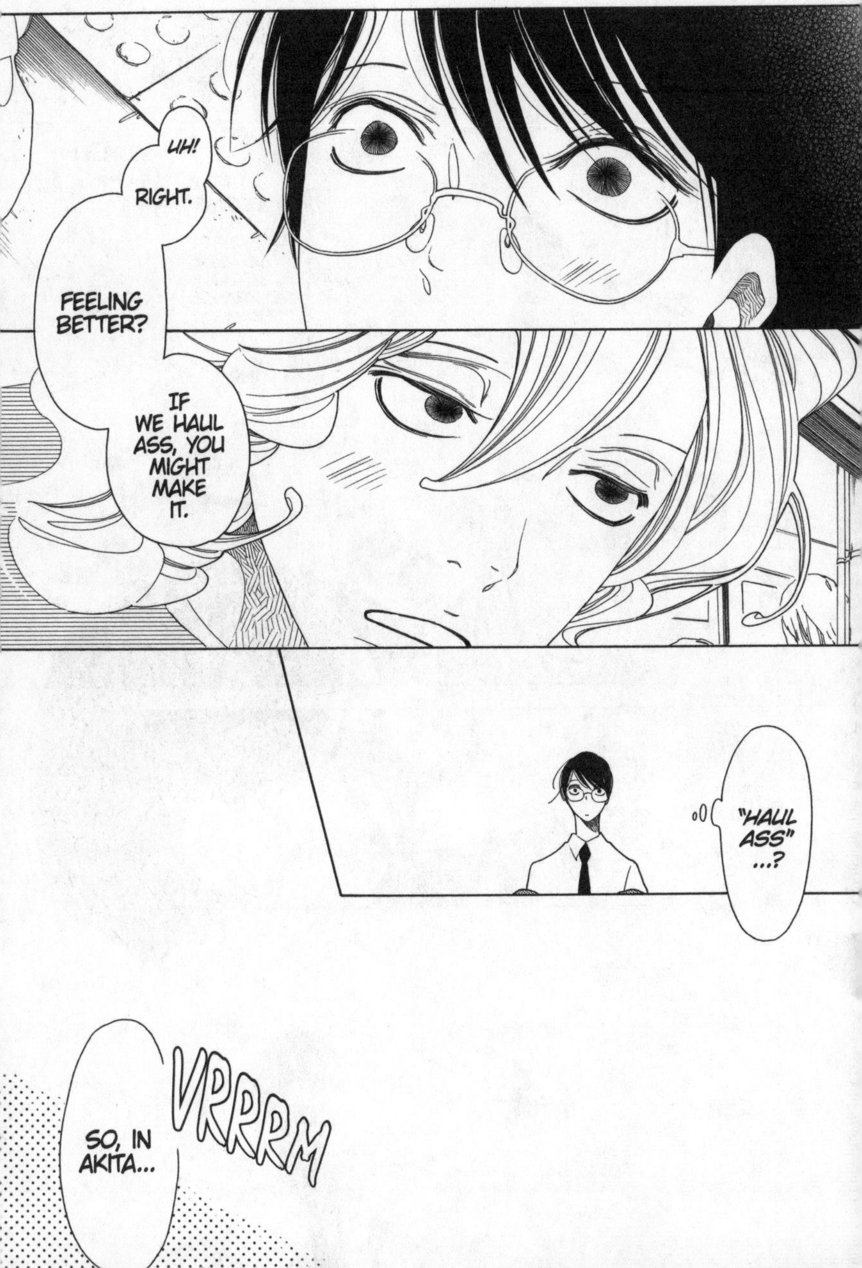
UH!
RIGHT.
FEELING BETTER?
IF WE HAUL ASS, YOU MIGHT MAKE IT.
"HAUL ASS" ...?
VRRRM
SO, IN AKITA...

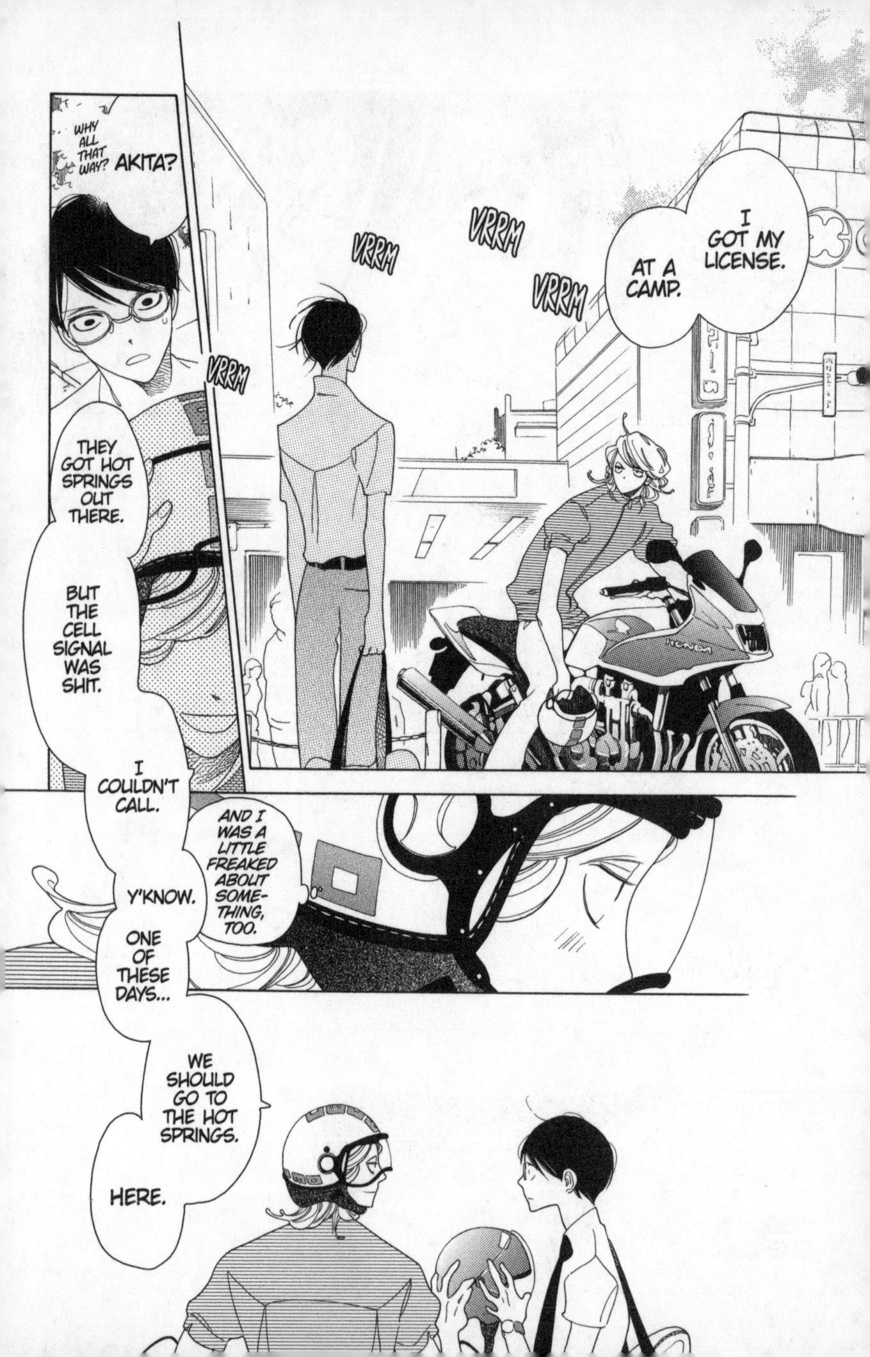
VRRM
VRRM
VRRM
VRRM
I GOT MY LICENSE.
AT A CAMP.
AKITA?
WHY ALL THAT WAY?
THEY GOT HOT SPRINGS OUT THERE.
BUT THE CELL SIGNAL WAS SHIT.
I COULDN'T CALL.
AND I WAS A LITTLE FREAKED ABOUT SOMETHING, TOO.
Y'KNOW.
ONE OF THESE DAYS...
WE SHOULD GO TO THE HOT SPRINGS.
HERE.

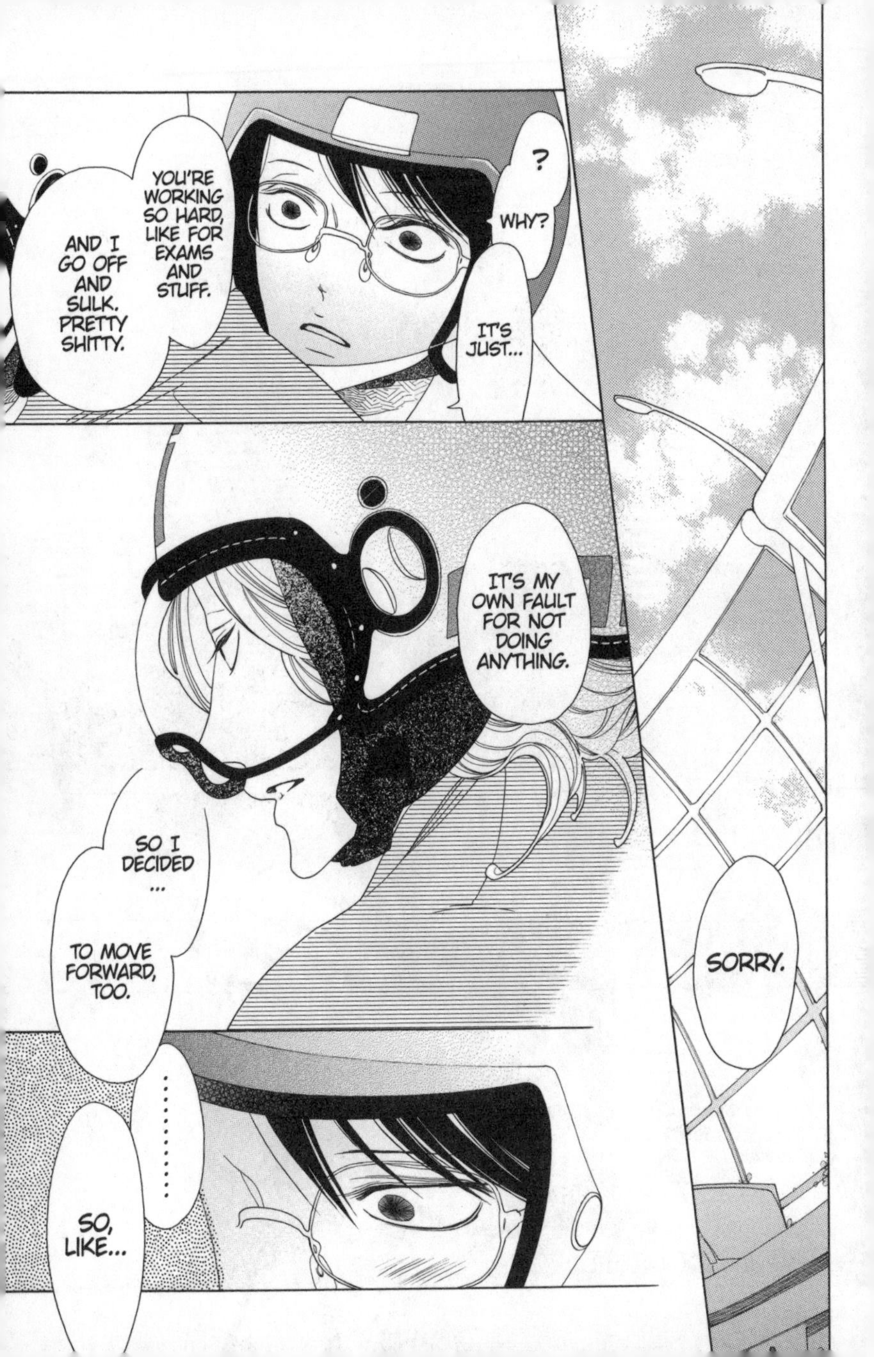
SORRY.
?
WHY?
IT'S JUST...
YOU'RE WORKING SO HARD, LIKE FOR EXAMS AND STUFF.
AND I GO OFF AND SULK. PRETTY SHITTY.
IT'S MY OWN FAULT FOR NOT DOING ANYTHING.
SO I DECIDED ...
TO MOVE FORWARD, TOO.
......
SO, LIKE...

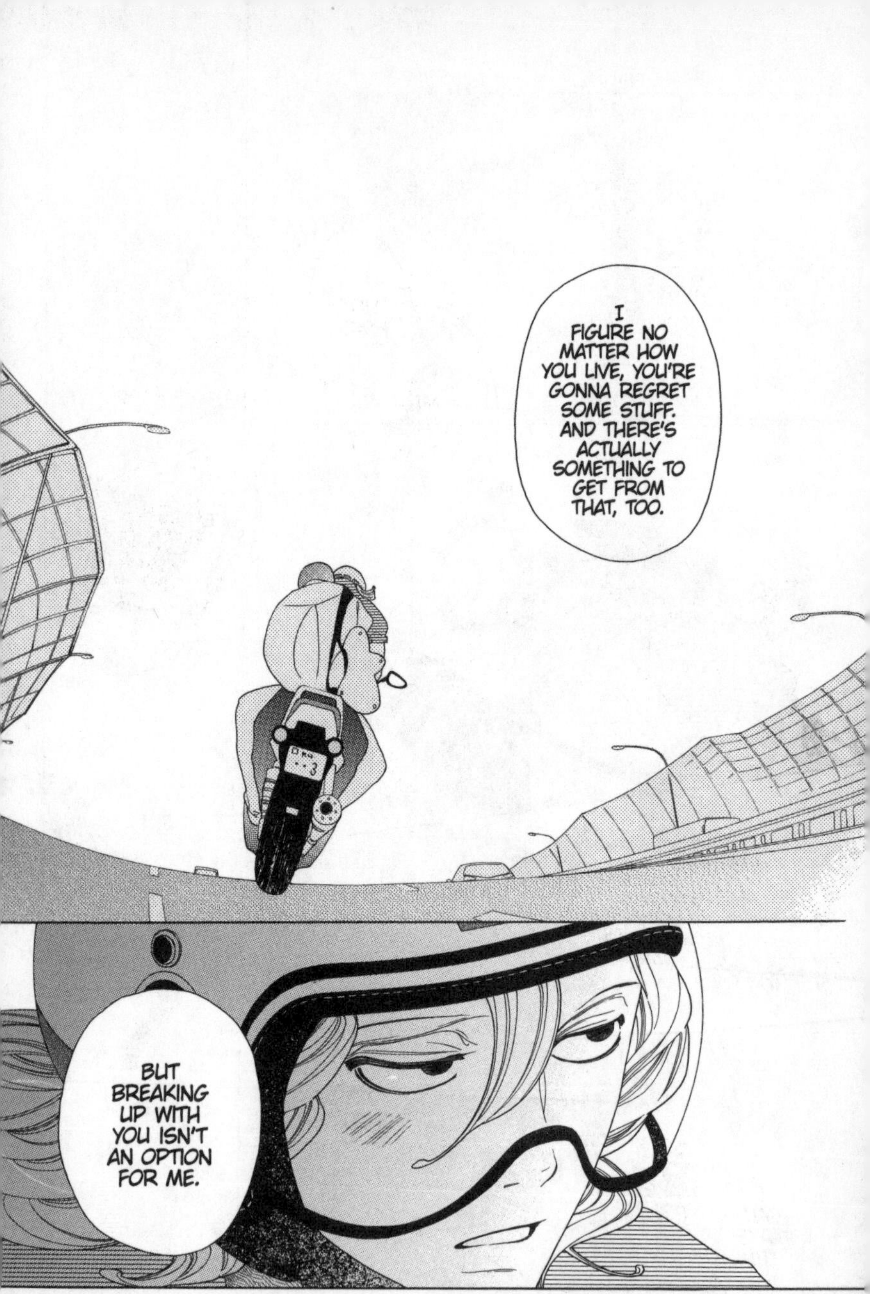
I FIGURE NO MATTER HOW YOU LIVE, YOU'RE GONNA REGRET SOME STUFF. AND THERE'S ACTUALLY SOMETHING TO GET FROM THAT, TOO.
BUT BREAKING UP WITH YOU ISN'T AN OPTION FOR ME.

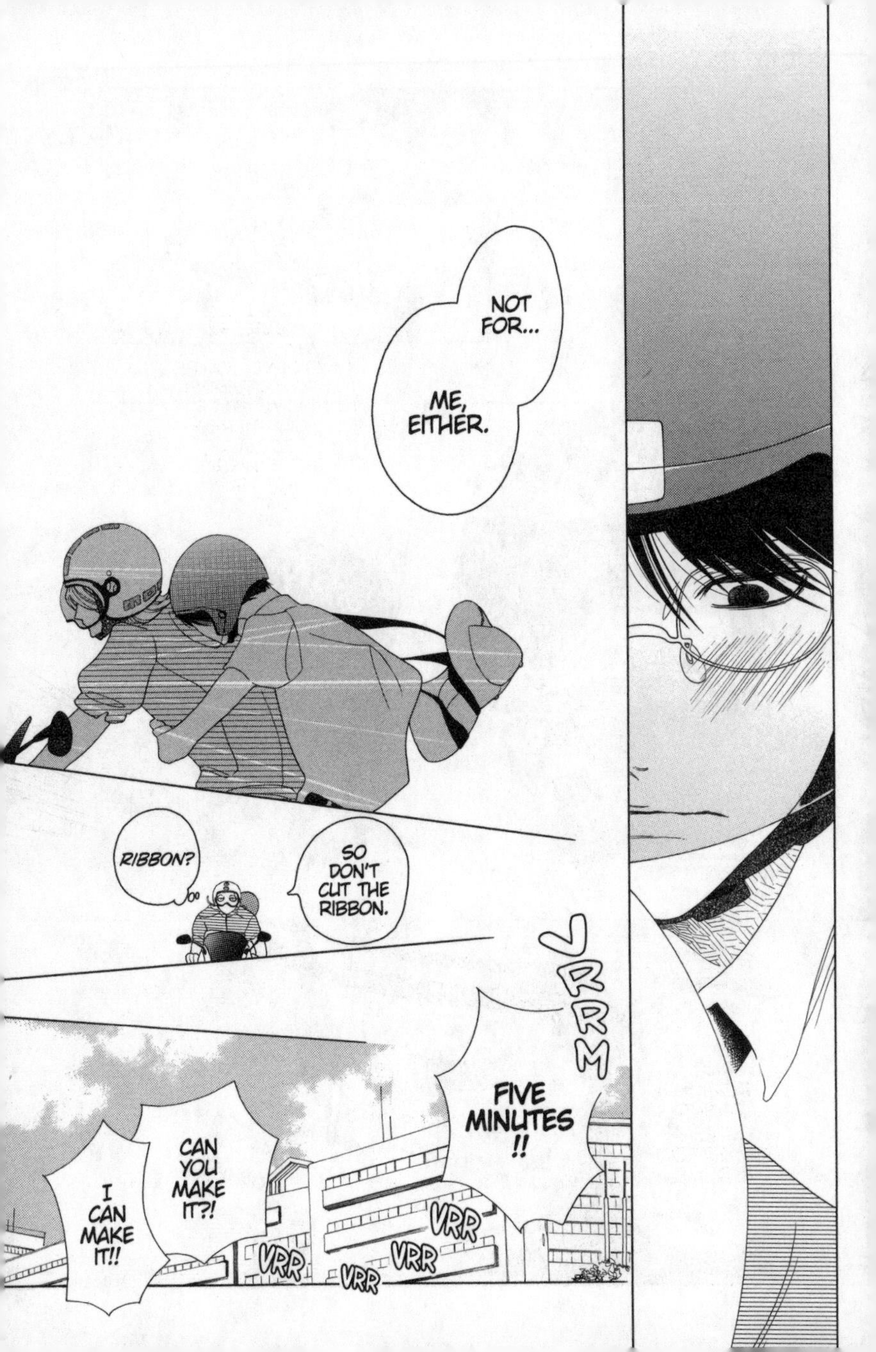
NOT FOR...
ME, EITHER.
SO DON'T CUT THE RIBBON.
RIBBON?
VRRM
FIVE MINUTES!!
CAN YOU MAKE IT?!
I CAN MAKE IT!!
VRR
VRR
VRR
VRR

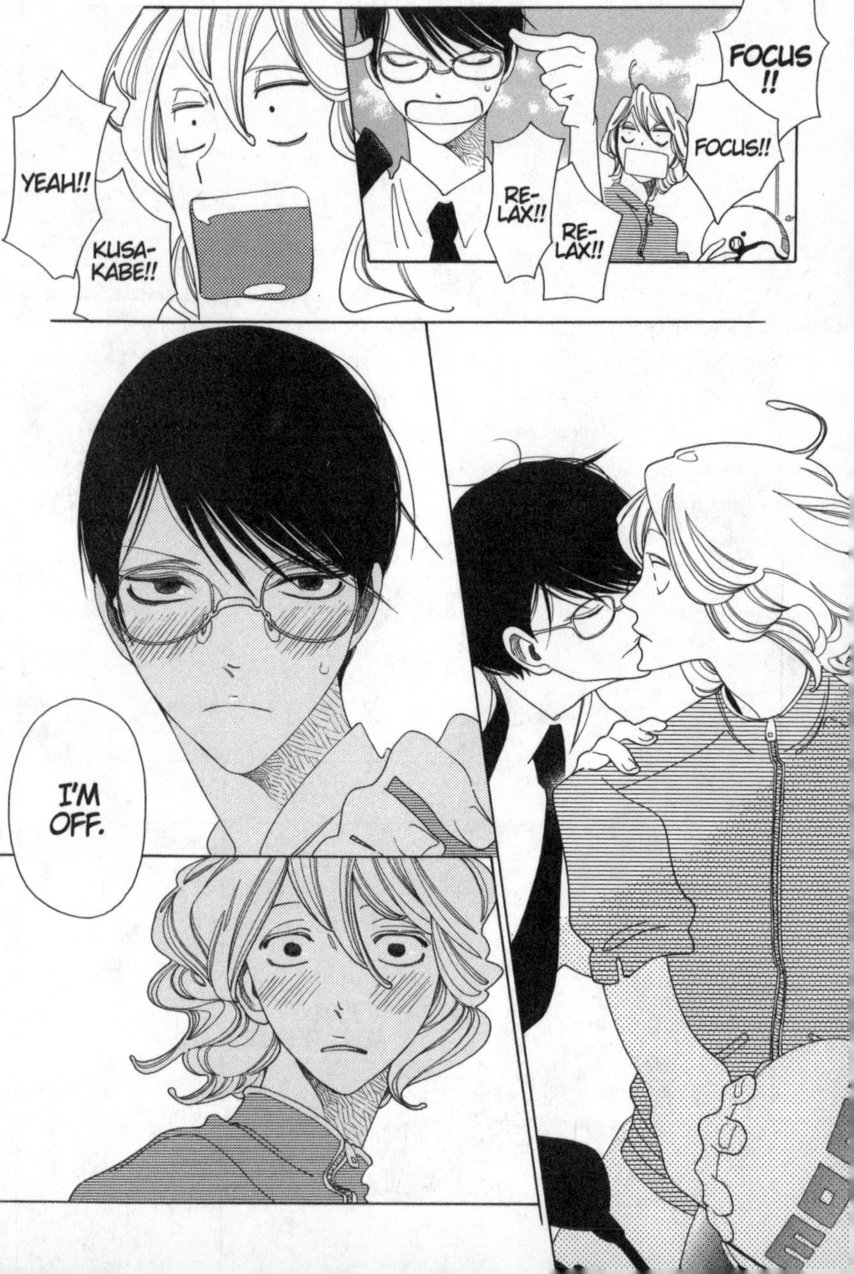
FOCUS!!
FOCUS!!
RE-LAX!!
RE-LAX!!
KUSA-KABE!!
YEAH!!
I'M OFF.

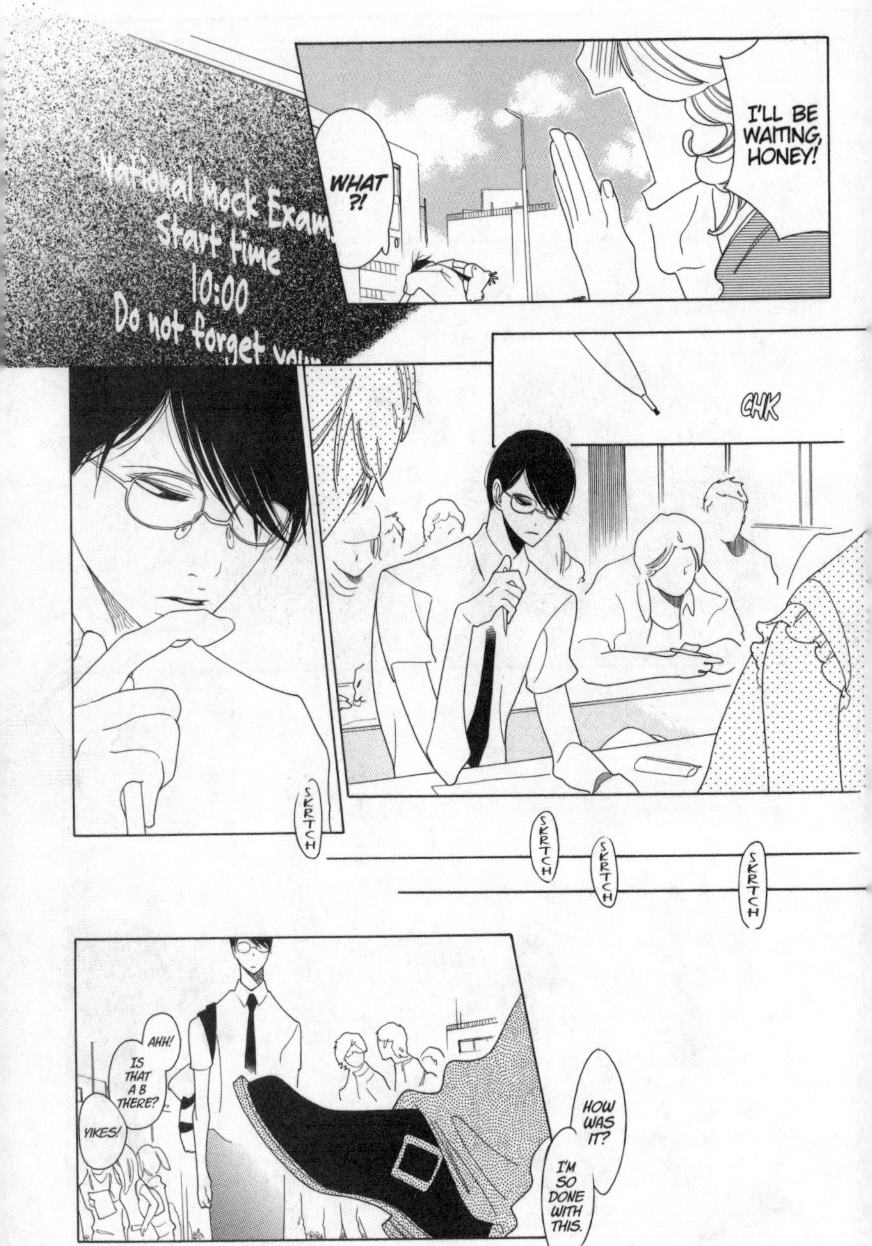
I'LL BE WAITING, HONEY!
WHAT ?!
National Mock Exam
Start time
10:00
Do not forget
CHK
SKRTCH
SKRTCH
SKRTCH
SKRTCH
HOW WAS IT?
I'M SO DONE WITH THIS.
AHH! IS THAT A B THERE?
YIKES!

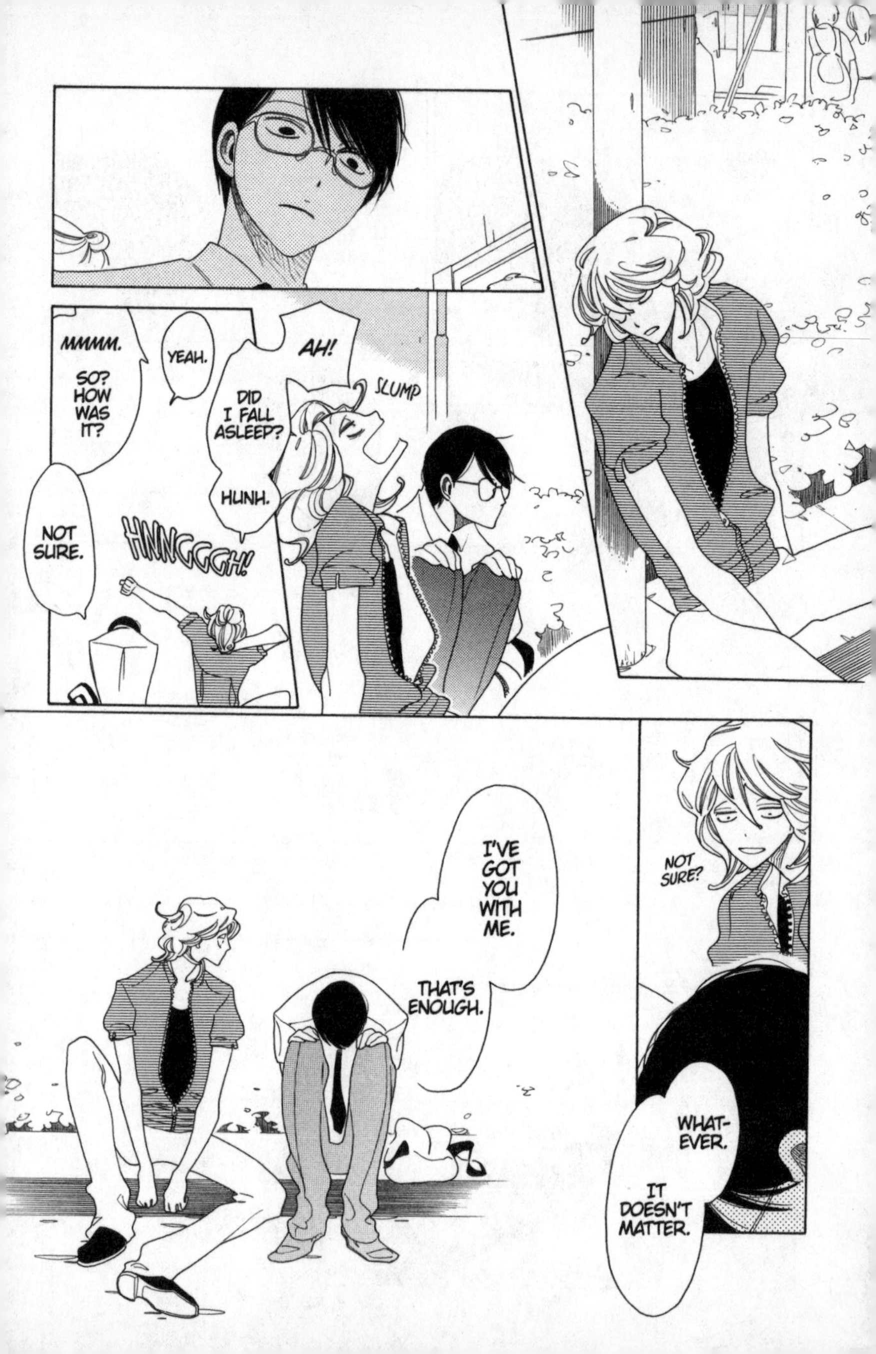
SLUMP
AH!
DID I FALL ASLEEP?
YEAH.
HUNH.
MMMM.
SO? HOW WAS IT?
HNNGGGH!
NOT SURE.
NOT SURE?
WHAT-EVER.
IT DOESN'T MATTER.
I'VE GOT YOU WITH ME.
THAT'S ENOUGH.

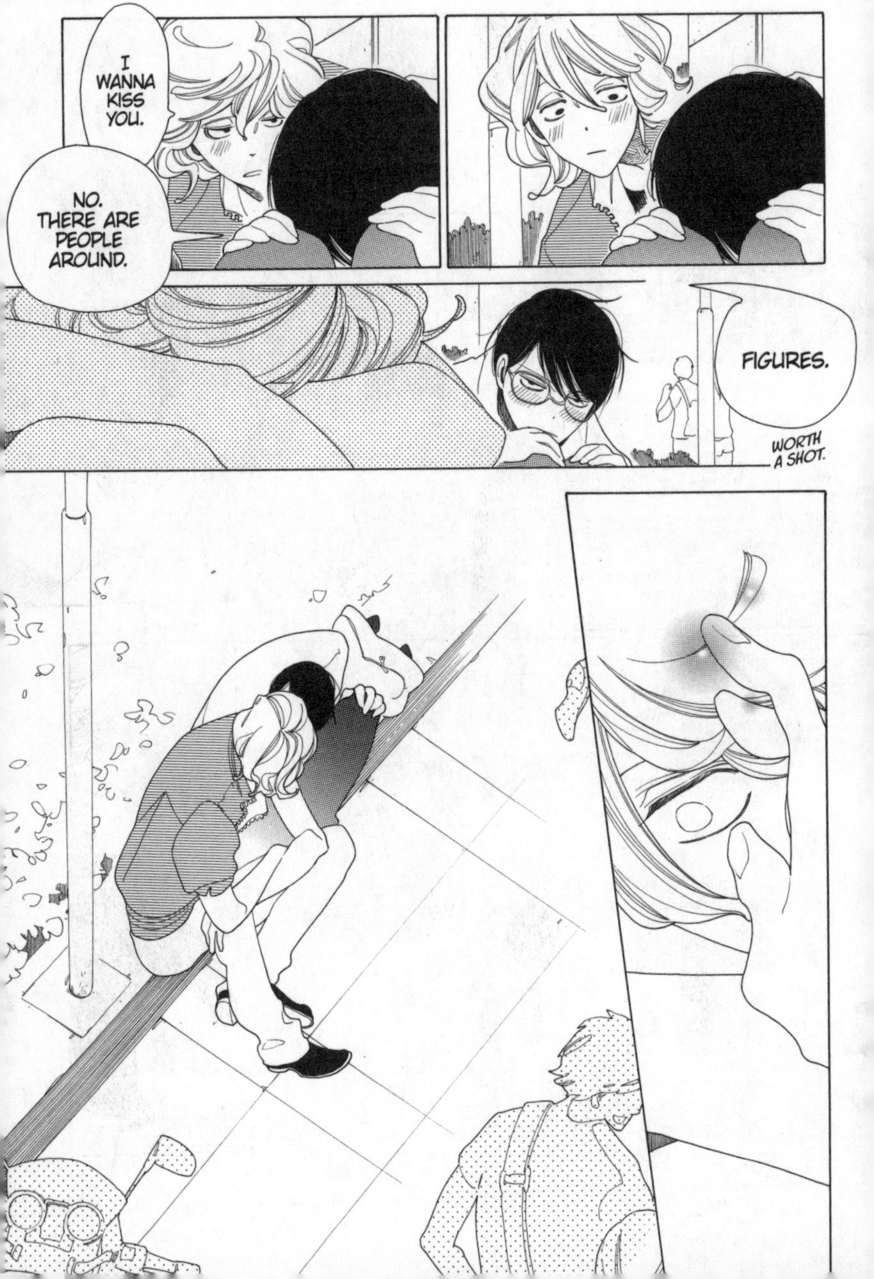
I WANNA KISS YOU.
NO. THERE ARE PEOPLE AROUND.
FIGURES.
WORTH A SHOT.

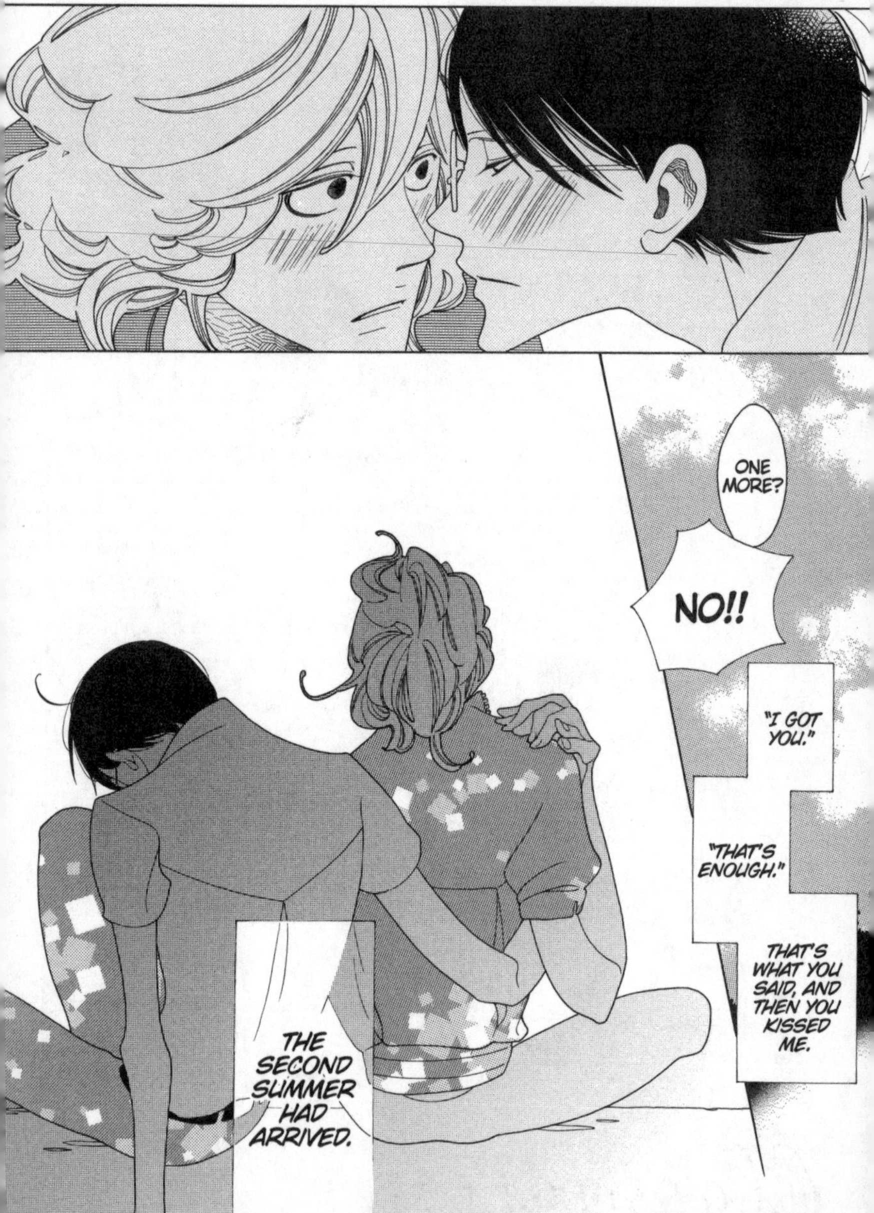
ONE MORE?
NO!!
"I GOT YOU."
"THAT'S ENOUGH."
THAT'S WHAT YOU SAID, AND THEN YOU KISSED ME.
THE SECOND SUMMER HAD ARRIVED.

The Second Summer/End

Classmates

Intermission

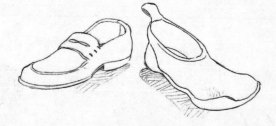

[Sabotage]

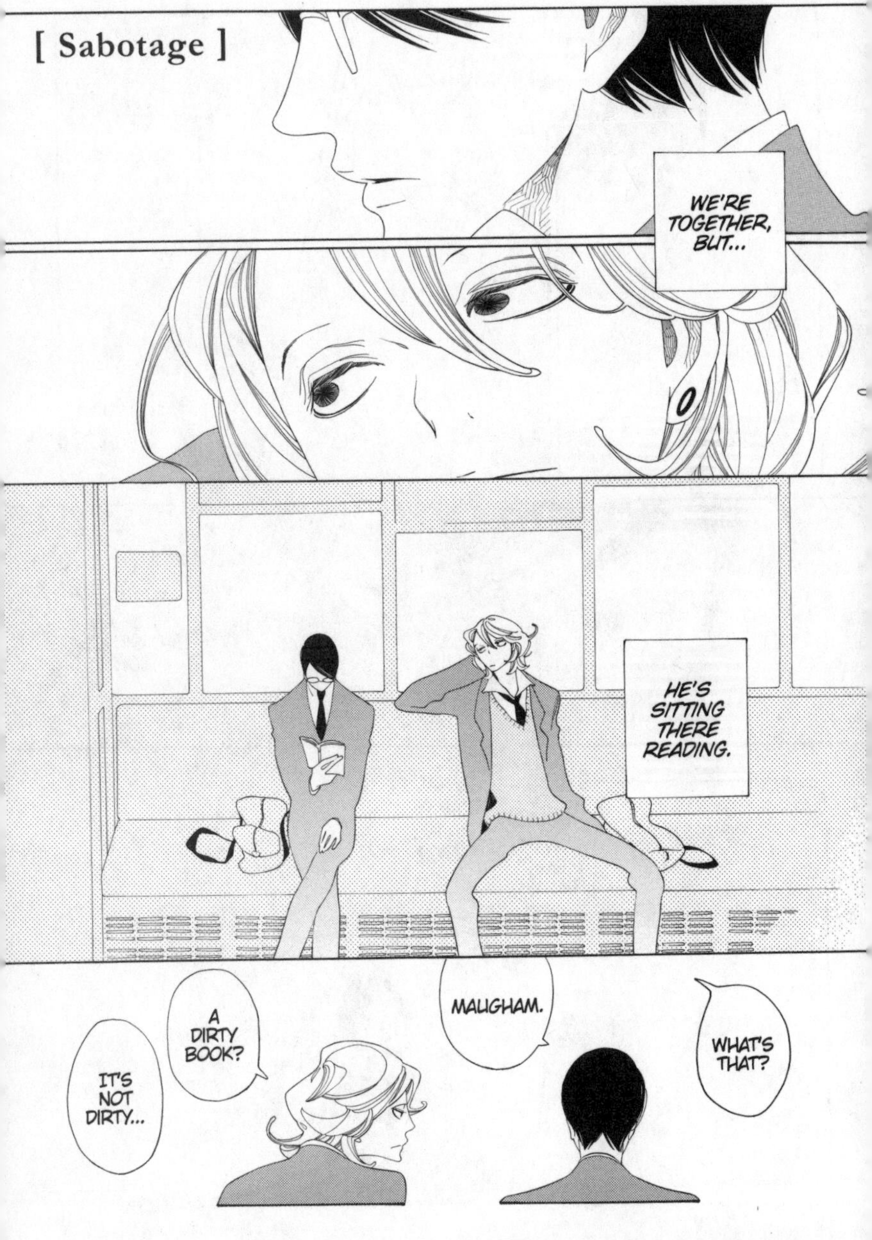
WE'RE TOGETHER, BUT...
HE'S SITTING THERE READING.
WHAT'S THAT?
MAUGHAM.
A DIRTY BOOK?
IT'S NOT DIRTY...

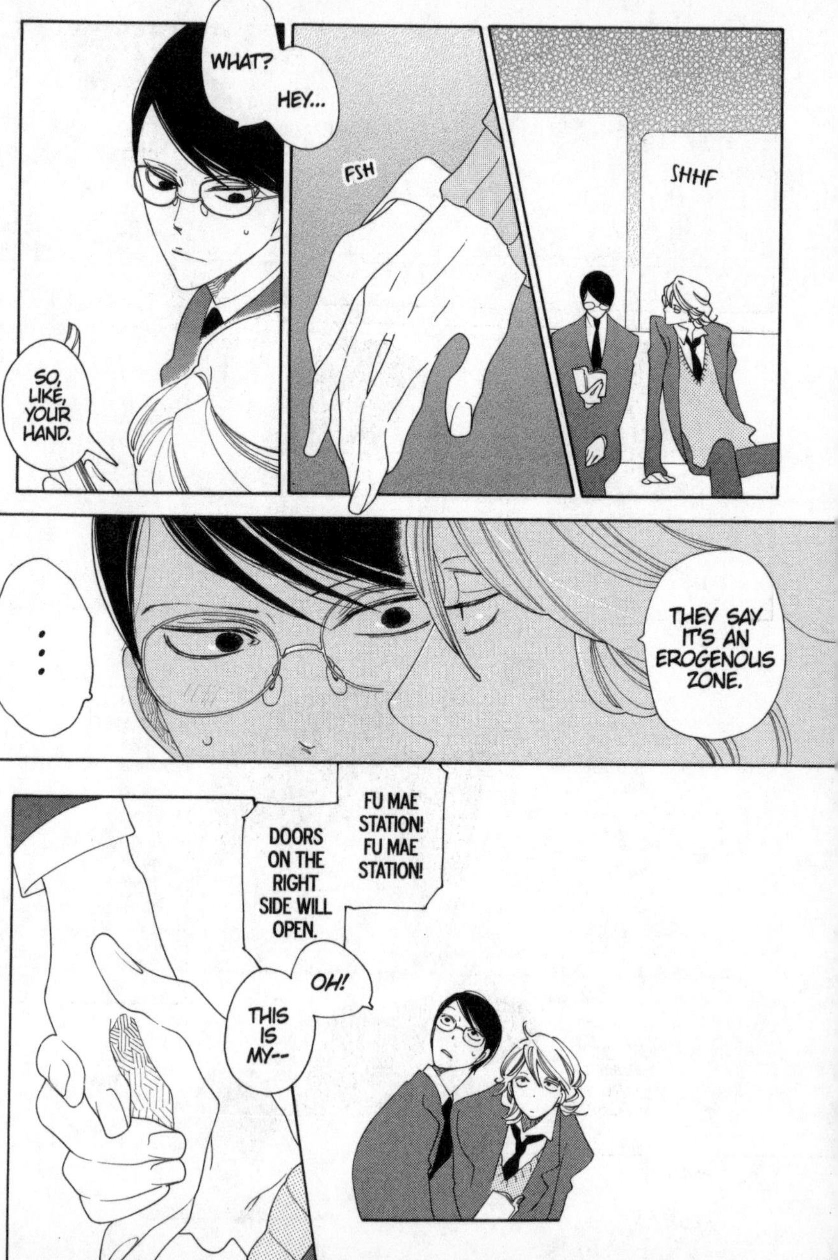
SHHF
FSH
WHAT? HEY...
SO, LIKE, YOUR HAND.
THEY SAY IT'S AN EROGENOUS ZONE.
...
FU MAE STATION! FU MAE STATION!
DOORS ON THE RIGHT SIDE WILL OPEN.
OH! THIS IS MY--

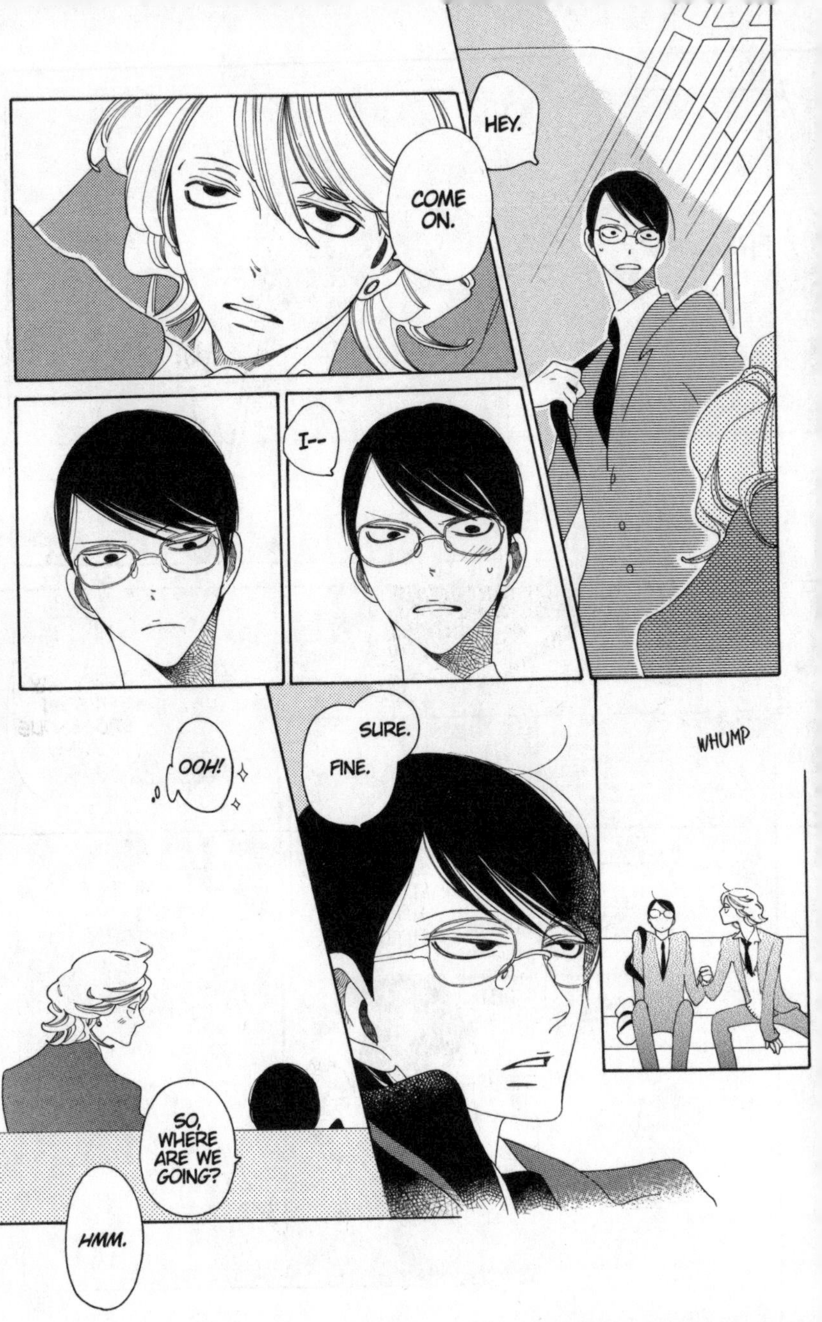
HEY.
COME ON.
I--
WHUMP
SURE.
FINE.
OOH!
SO, WHERE ARE WE GOING?
HMM.

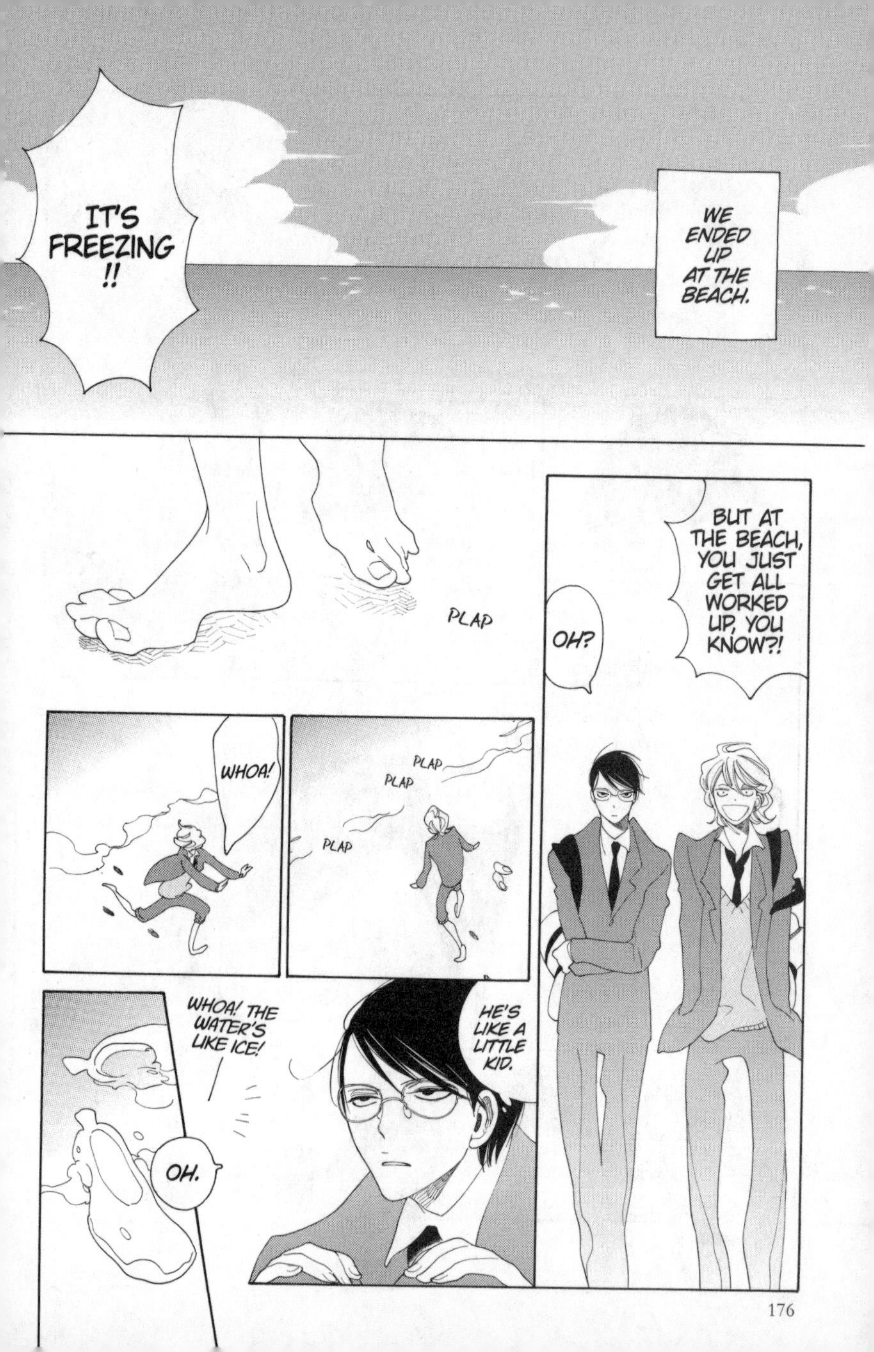
WE ENDED UP AT THE BEACH.
IT'S FREEZING!!
BUT AT THE BEACH, YOU JUST GET ALL WORKED UP, YOU KNOW?!
OH?
PLAP
PLAP
PLAP
PLAP
WHOA!
HE'S LIKE A LITTLE KID.
WHOA! THE WATER'S LIKE ICE!
OH.

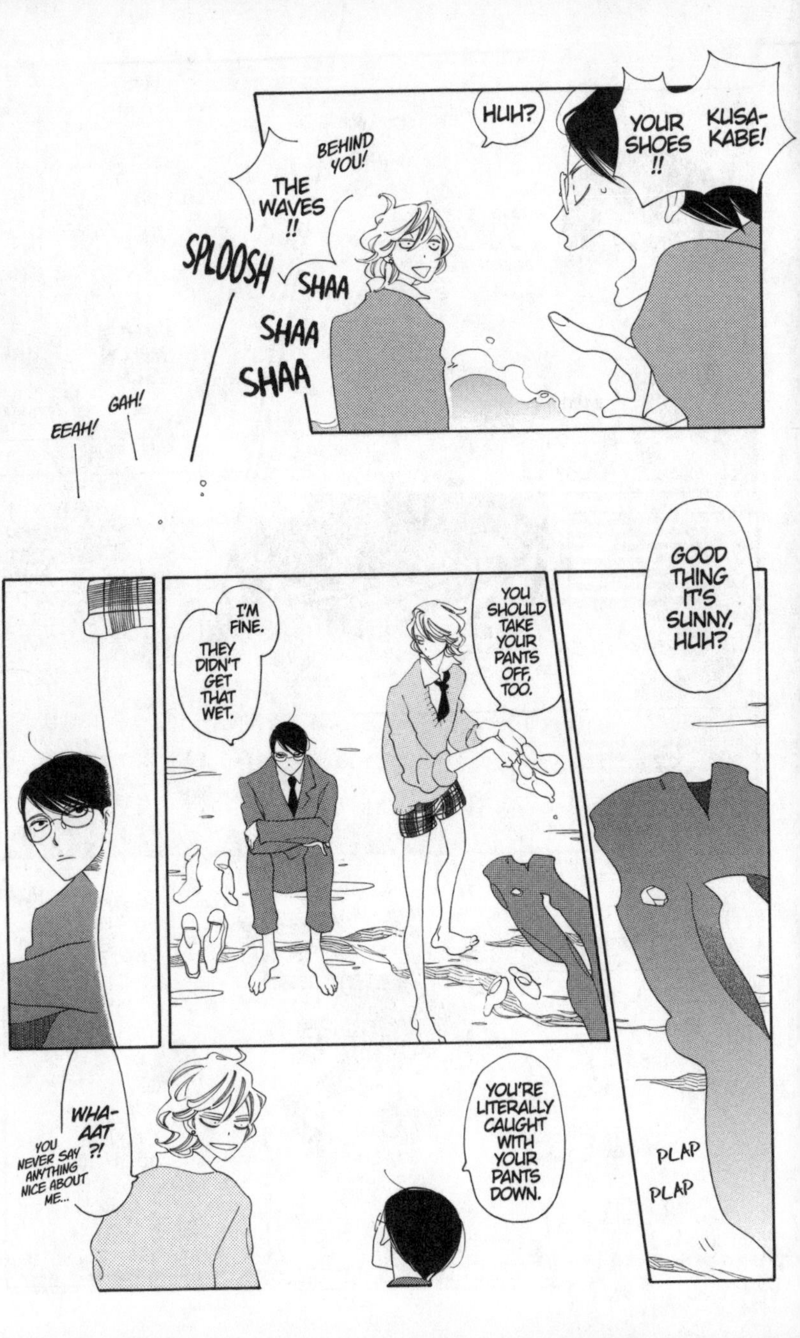
KUSA-KABE!
YOUR SHOES !!
HUH?
BEHIND YOU!
THE WAVES !!
SHAA
SHAA
SHAA
SPLOOSH
GAH!
EEAH!
GOOD THING IT'S SUNNY, HUH?
PLAP
PLAP
YOU SHOULD TAKE YOUR PANTS OFF, TOO.
I'M FINE. THEY DIDN'T GET THAT WET.
YOU'RE LITERALLY CAUGHT WITH YOUR PANTS DOWN.
WHA-AAT ?!
YOU NEVER SAY ANYTHING NICE ABOUT ME...

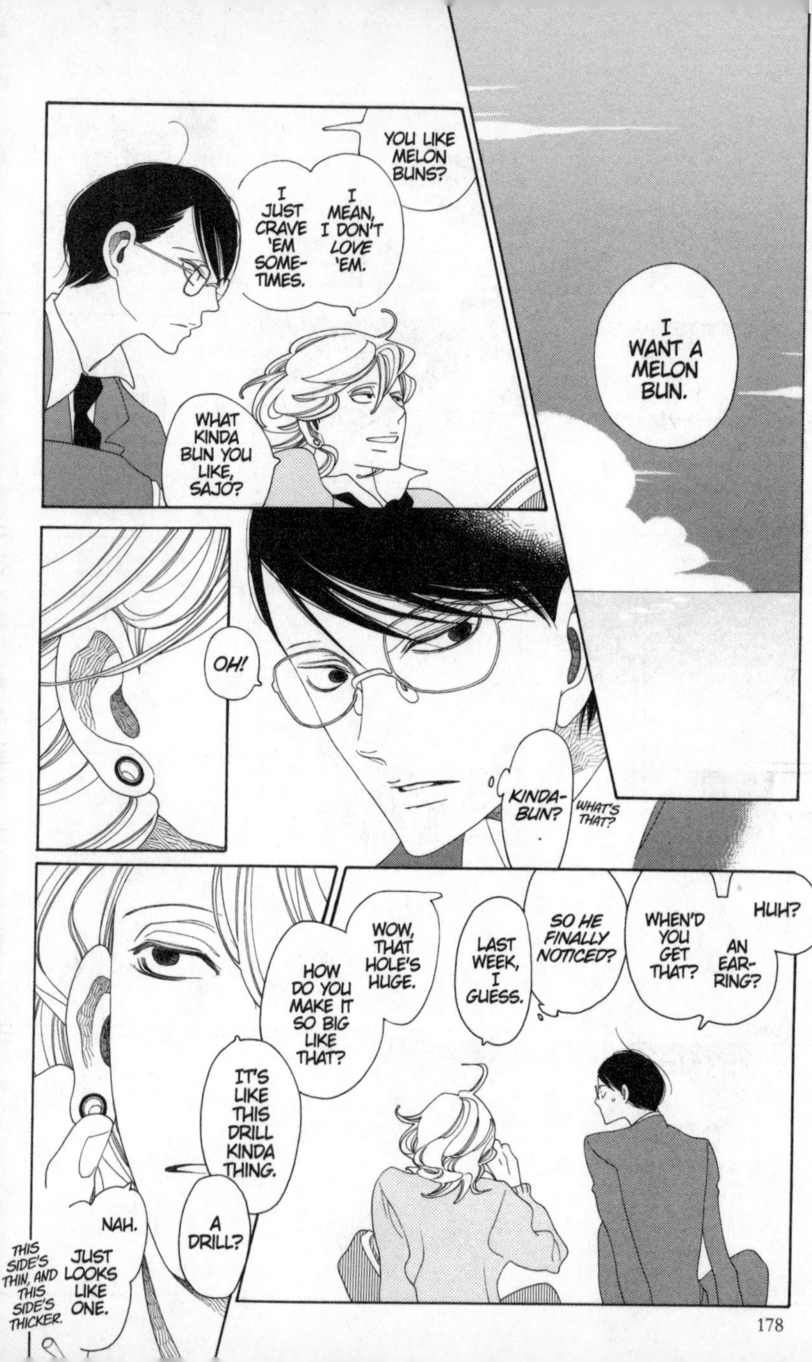
I WANT A MELON BUN.
YOU LIKE MELON BUNS?
I MEAN, I DON'T LOVE 'EM.
I JUST CRAVE 'EM SOME-TIMES.
WHAT KINDA BUN YOU LIKE, SAJO?
KINDA-BUN?
WHAT'S THAT?
OH!
HUH?
AN EAR-RING?
WHEN'D YOU GET THAT?
SO HE FINALLY NOTICED?
LAST WEEK, I GUESS.
WOW, THAT HOLE'S HUGE.
HOW DO YOU MAKE IT SO BIG LIKE THAT?
IT'S LIKE THIS DRILL KINDA THING.
A DRILL?
NAH.
JUST LOOKS LIKE ONE.
THIS SIDE'S THIN, AND THIS SIDE'S THICKER.

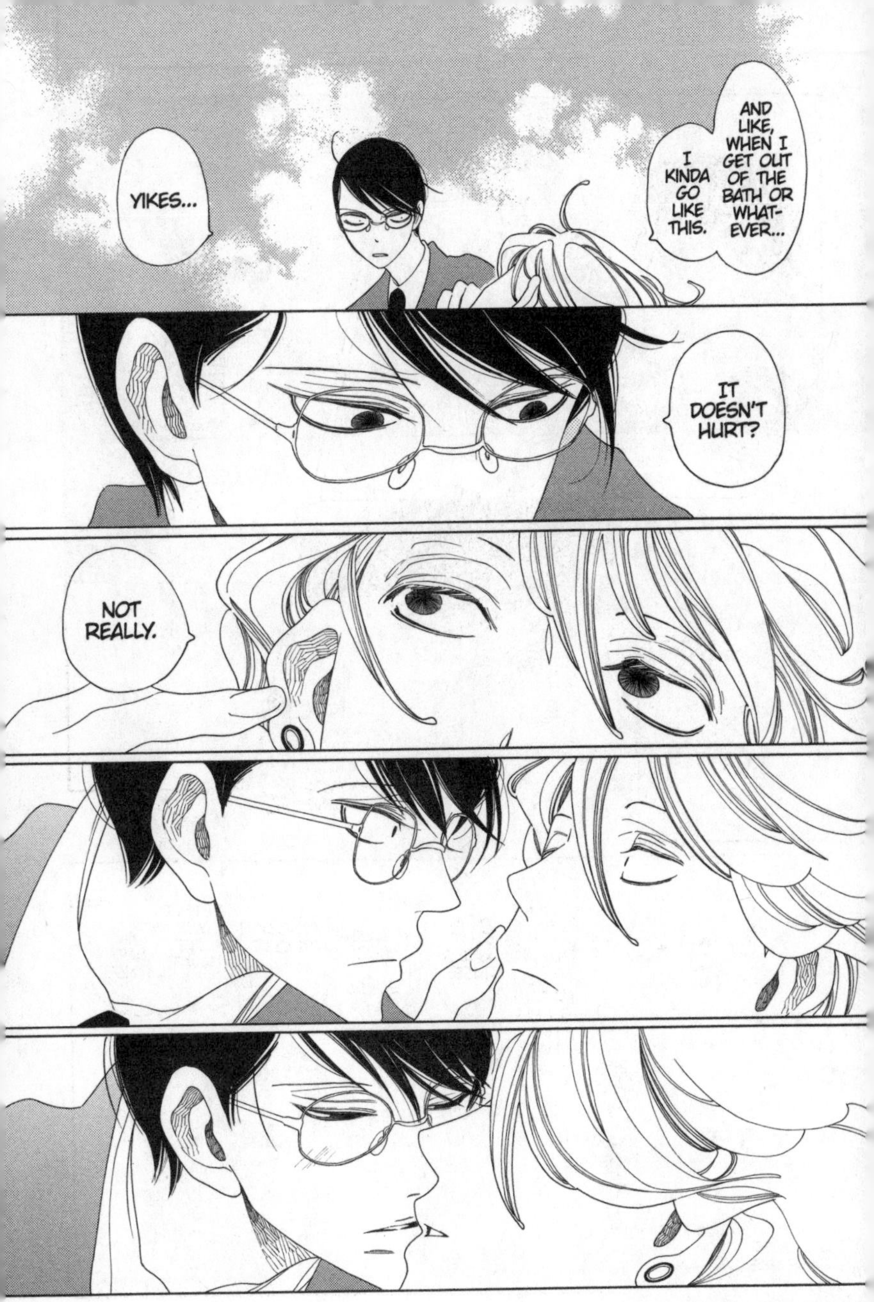
AND LIKE, WHEN I GET OUT OF THE BATH OR WHAT-EVER...
I KINDA GO LIKE THIS.
YIKES...
IT DOESN'T HURT?
NOT REALLY.

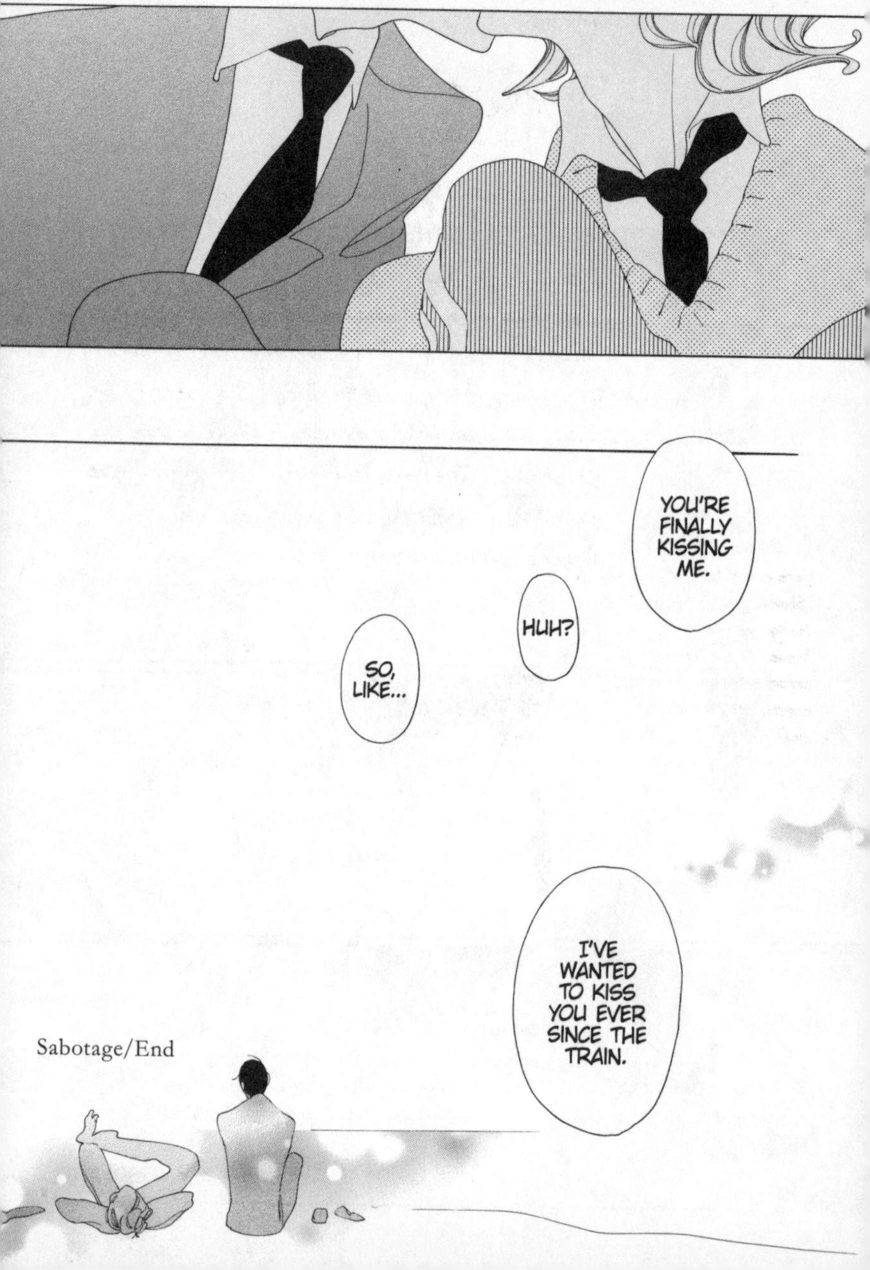
YOU'RE FINALLY KISSING ME.
HUH?
SO, LIKE...
I'VE WANTED TO KISS YOU EVER SINCE THE TRAIN.
Sabotage/End

"A slow, serious love."

That was the theme I decided on when I started to write Classmates. It was the first job I got from a BL magazine, so I wanted to go with something cliché, almost hackneyed. The idea was to make it the "f" of fundamentals, the "b" of basics, something naïve, reckless, impatient. I'll be happy if I managed to give you a taste of the bittersweet freshness of youth, the sort to give you an itchy feeling in your sides, to make your fingers shake and pop.

More correctly: "Shoulder blades are a vestige of angel wings." Answer to the "spot the error" on page 93: The captain does not have a cleft chin.

ゆりはめもと. 2007.
Asumiko Nakamura

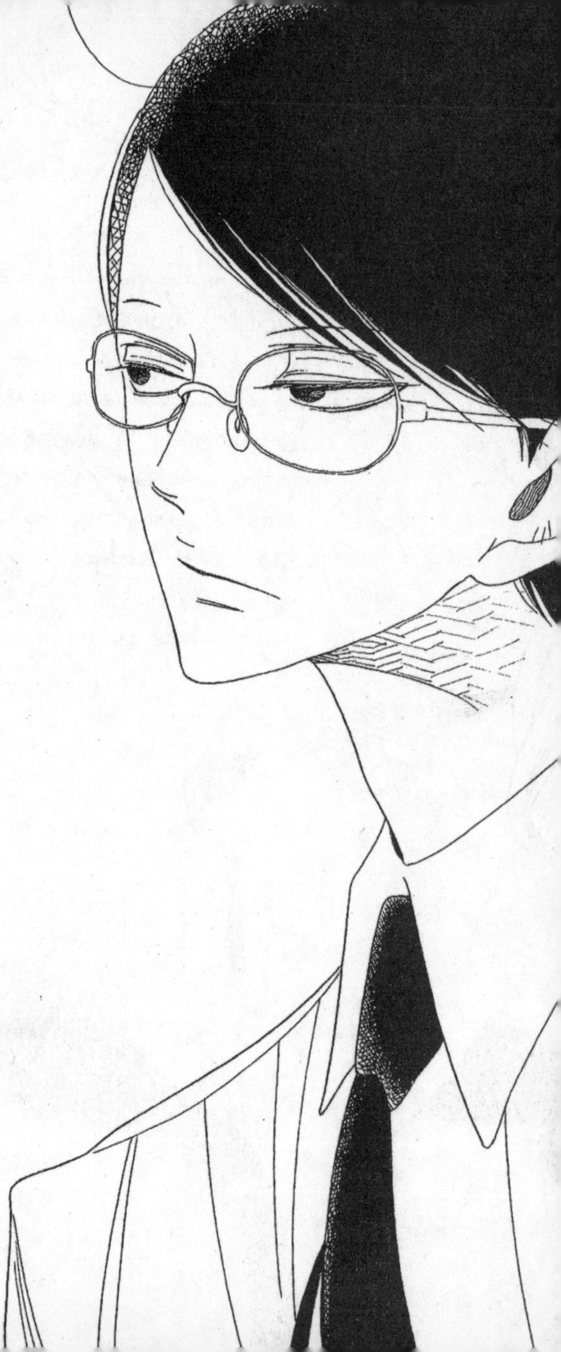

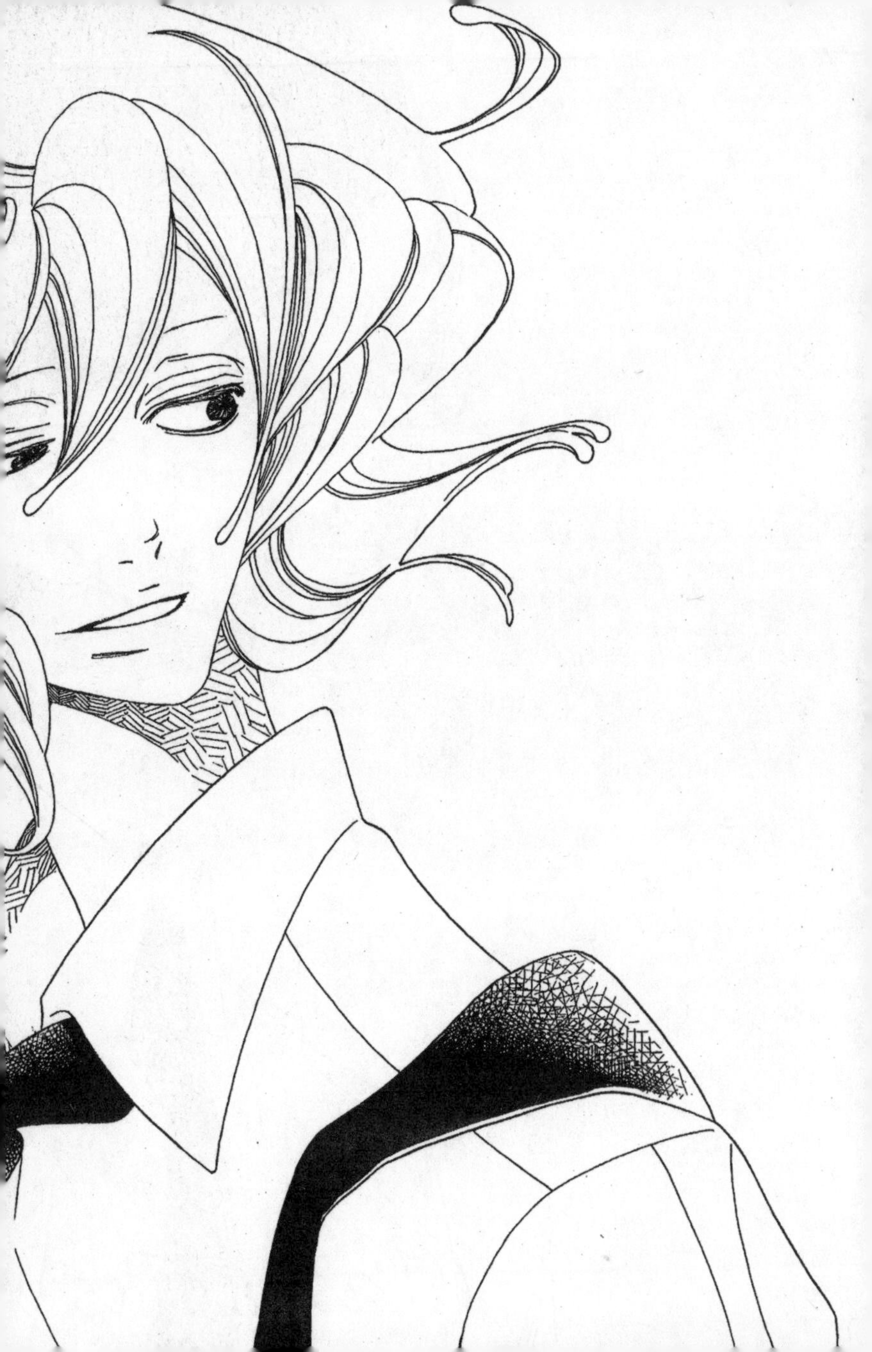

Classmates

SEVEN SEAS ENTERTAINMENT PRESENTS

Classmates

story and art by ASUMIKO NAKAMURA

VOL. 1 Dou kyu sei

TRANSLATION
Jocelyne Allen

ADAPTATION
Lillian Diaz-Przybyl

LETTERING AND RETOUCH
Ray Steeves

COVER DESIGN
KC Fabellon

PROOFREADER
Stephanie Cohen
Shanti Whitesides

EDITOR
Shannon Fay

PRODUCTION MANAGER
Lissa Pattillo

MANAGING EDITOR
Julie Davis

EDITOR-IN-CHIEF
Adam Arnold

PUBLISHER
Jason DeAngelis

DOU KYU SEI
© Asumiko Nakamura 2008
Originally published in Japan in 2008 by AKANESHINSHA, Tokyo.
English translation rights arranged with COMIC HOUSE, Tokyo,
through TOHAN CORPORATION, Tokyo.

Seven Seas press and purchase enquiries can be sent to Marketing Manager
Lianne Sentar at press@gomanga.com. Information regarding the distribution
and purchase of digital editions is available from Digital Manager CK Russell
at digital@gomanga.com.

Seven Seas and the Seven Seas logo are trademarks of
Seven Seas Entertainment. All rights reserved.

ISBN: 978-1-642750-66-9

Printed in Canada

First Printing: June 2019

10 9 8 7 6 5 4 3 2 1

FOLLOW US ONLINE: *www.sevenseasentertainment.com*

READING DIRECTIONS

This book reads from *right to left*, Japanese style.
If this is your first time reading manga, you start
reading from the top right panel on each page and
take it from there. If you get lost, just follow the
numbered diagram here. It may seem backwards at
first, but you'll get the hang of it! Have fun!!

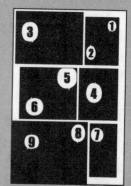